Philip

Philip Davies

Vivienne Westwood

By the same author

The Vogue History of Twentieth-Century Fashion
Costume Jewellery in Vogue
Newport Housees

VIVIENNE WESTWOOD
AN UNFASHIONABLE LIFE

JANE MULVAGH

HarperCollins*Publishers*

HarperCollins*Publishers*
77–85 Fulham Palace Road,
Hammersmith, London w6 8jb

Published by HarperCollins*Publishers* 1998

Copyright © Jane Mulvagh 1998

9 8 7 6 5 4 3 2 1

A catalogue record for this book is
available from the British Library

ISBN 0 00 255625 1

Set in PostScript Garamond 3 by
Rowland Phototypesetting Ltd,
Bury St Edmunds, Suffolk

Printed and bound in Great Britain by
Caledonian International Book Manufacturing Ltd, Glasgow

To Anthony

CONTENTS

ILLUSTRATIONS

Vivienne's childhood home from 1954 to 1957, the post office at 36 Manchester Road, Tintwistle. *Photograph © Jane Mulvagh*

Vivienne at primary school in Hollingworth. *Photograph © Eileen Mellish*

Vivienne in her customised Glossop Grammar School uniform. *Photograph © Eileen Mellish*

Vivienne on the town in 1957 with schoolfriends. *Photograph © Eileen Mellish*

Vivienne's first press appearance, as one of *West One* magazine's 'London Belles', December 1973. *Photograph reproduced courtesy of John Bishop*

SEX 'Tits' T-shirt. *Photograph © Christie's, South Kensington*

The exterior of SEX in 1976. *Photograph © Bob Gruen/Star File*

Johnny Rotten in Paris, 1976. *Photograph © Rex Features*

Johnny Rotten with Paul Cook, Sue Catwoman, Siouxsie Sioux and Little Debs. *Photograph © Bob Gruen/Star File*

Seditionaries 'Destroy' T-shirt. *Photograph © Christie's, South Kensington*

Seditionaries blue cotton parachute shirt. *Photograph © Christie's, South Kensington*

Simon Barker and Jordan.

Vivienne, Johnny Rotten and Jordan, 1976. *Photograph © Ray Stevenson/Retna*

Vivienne is arrested on the night of the Queens' Silver Jubilee, 7 June 1977. *Photograph © Topham Picturepoint*

McLaren and Vivienne leave Bow Street Magistrates' Court following their Jubilee night arrests. *Photograph © Mirror Syndication International*

Vivienne's drawing of a penis on flesh-coloured knickers for 'Pagan V', spring/summer 1990. *Photograph © Robyn Beeche*

Vivienne in tweed crown, barrel dress and Rocking Horse shoes from 'Harris Tweed', autumn/winter 1987–88. *Photograph © Anthony Crickmay*

Soon-to-be-disgraced Italian Foreign Minister Gianni di Michelis meets Vivienne in London, July 1991. *Photograph © Paul Massey/ Frank Spooner Pictures*

Vivienne's guru, Gary Ness. *Photograph © Nic Barlow*

Vivienne as Margaret Thatcher for the cover of *Tatler*, April 1989. *Photograph © Michael Roberts/Maconochie Photography*

Portrait of Malcolm McLaren by Jean-Charles de Castelbajac. *Reproduced courtesy of Jean-Charles de Castelbajac*

Alan Jones, Chrissie Hynde, Vivienne and Jordan promoting SEX in 1975. *Photograph © Rex Features*

McLaren wearing the SEX T-shirt 'Two Naked Cowboys'. *Photograph © G. Wood/Getty Images*

Staff outside Nostalgia of Mud. *Photograph © Robyn Beeche*

Vivienne posing in SEX in 1975, dressed in a pink 'Rubber Johnny' bodysuit. *Photograph © William English*

'Buffalo' gals, autumn/winter 1982–83. *Photograph © Niall McInerney*

The Sony Walkman meets the seventeenth-century brigand. 'Pirates', autumn/winter 1981–82. *Photograph © Robyn Beeche*

Matisse's dancers printed on empire-line cotton dresses for 'Savage', spring/summer 1982. *Photograph © Robyn Beeche*

The Elephant Man inspired McLaren's Foreign Legionnaire's *képi* for 'Savage'. *Photograph © Robyn Beeche*

'Burroughs' suit worn with a hooded sweatshirt for 'Buffalo'. *Photograph © Robyn Beeche*

Vivienne's last collaboration with McLaren, 'Witches', autumn/winter 1983–84. *Photograph © Chris Moore*

The establishment spoof of 'Harris Tweed'. *Photograph © Snowdon*

Vivienne models her 'Love' jacket for 'Harris Tweed'. *Photograph © Chris Moore*

Argyll knitwear for 'Voyage to Cythera', autumn/winter 1989–90. *Photograph © Niall McInerney*

Smart satire – City gent's bowler hat combined with punk bondage trousers. 'Time Machine', autumn/winter 1988–89. *Photograph © Robyn Beeche*

'Mini Crini', spring/summer 1986 – inspired by the Empress Eugénie and Minnie Mouse. *Photograph © Chris Moore*

Susie Bick and Sarah Stockbridge in *commedia dell'arte*-inspired Harlequin bodysuit and Columbine mini crini, from 'Voyage to Cythera'. *Photograph © Robyn Beeche*

Tweed trouser suit with 'Super D.B.' jacket and fedora, from 'Always on Camera', autumn/winter 1992–93. *Photograph © Robyn Beeche*

Harris tweed armour-plating for 'Time Machine'. *Photograph © Niall McInerney*

Sarah Stockbridge cradles her newborn on the catwalk. 'Cut, Slash & Pull', spring/summer 1991. *Photograph © Robyn Beeche*

Susie Bick in hunting pink jacket, 'Stature of Liberty' corset, punk bondage choker and leather codpiece. 'Dressing Up', autumn/winter 1991–92. *Photograph © Niall McInerney*

Vivienne, in see-through Boulle-printed lace dress, meets Princess Michael of Kent at Kensington Palace, June 1992. *Photograph © Rex Features*

Sarah Stockbridge in a polo-necked jumper slashed across the breasts, from 'Dressing Up'. *Photograph © Niall McInerney*

Lady McAlpine dressed in Vivienne Westwood to attend the state opening of Parliament. *Photograph reproduced courtesy of Lady McAlpine*

Vivienne is saluted for the second time by Hanae Mori's Fashion Foundation, Tokyo, January 1991.

Slashed seventeenth-century silk bodice from the V&A. *Photograph © The Board of Trustees of the Victoria and Albert Museum*

Vivienne protests outside the Natural History Museum in fig-leaf leggings, 1990. *Photograph © Solo Syndication Ltd*

Vivienne in dusty tulle wedding dress from 'Dressing Up'. *Photograph © Snowdon*

Vivienne and Andreas at Milan airport, 1994. *Photograph © Mirror Syndication International*

Vivienne and her mother in 1991. *Photograph © Jeremy Young/Times Newspapers Limited*

Ben and Joseph congratulate Vivienne on her OBE, 15 December 1992. *Photograph © Topham Picturepoint*

Vivienne and McLaren on the eve of the 'Vive le Punk!' exhibition, February 1993. *Photograph reproduced courtesy of Roger Burton*

Carlo D'Amario in the Elcho Street studio, 1997. *Photograph © Andrew Buurman/The Independent*

Vivienne's favourite portrait, taken in Battersea Park, 1994. *Photograph © Juergen Teller*

Alba Clemente in a Winterhalter-inspired ballgown which led Barbra Streisand to order several Westwood dresses, with disastrous results. *Photograph © David Seidner*

'The child sees everything in a state of newness; he is always *drunk*. Nothing more resembles inspiration than the delight with which a child absorbs form and colour . . . but genius is nothing more or less than *childhood recovered* at will – a childhood now equipped with self-expression, with manhood's capabilities and powers of analysis which enable it to order the mass of raw material which it has involuntarily accumulated.

Charles Baudelaire, *The Painter of Modern Life*

On the Tree of Knowledge
I have carved 'amour'
The answer's not in looks, but books
If you want Glamour.

Vivienne Westwood, lyrics for 'Choice', 1987

PREFACE

I first met Vivienne Westwood in the autumn of 1983, while researching my book *The Vogue History of Twentieth-Century Fashion*. In the two preceding years I had become accustomed to interviewing successful designers in handsome premises in the capitals of fashion. Each encounter was fairly similar. It would be formal and conducted in impressively sumptuous surroundings, with careful attention paid to the professional etiquette of sound public relations. The ritual of passing through a series of receptionists and assistants was typically followed by a one-to-two-hour conversation with the designer in his well-appointed office. Across an impressive arrangement of flowers, and against a backdrop of photographs boasting his acquaintance with the famous and the beautiful, we would discuss the motivations and influences that had formed his work.

None of this prepared me for meeting Vivienne.

Her two-room second-floor studio was squalid and cluttered. The railings up the communal outside staircase were hung with sodden, hand-dyed clothes. The entrance was blocked by half-packed boxes of late deliveries or returned orders, and the temperature inside seemed lower than the bracing October evening outside. Stepping over a collapsed ironing board and past a rickety trestle table strewn with unwashed mugs and overflowing ashtrays, I made my way to a corner where, surrounded by half a dozen ragamuffins, the designer, dressed in thick, padded, ankle-length layers of greige felted wool, nodded an informal acknowledgement.

To the hesitant tap-tap of a vintage typewriter operated by a flustered youth, we attempted to begin our interview. Pulling anxiously on a Gitane, Vivienne periodically turned to the typist and snapped, 'Can't you stop that noise? It's really distracting me. I can't think.' The typing continued. After half an hour, during which she repeatedly lost her train of thought, she finally said, 'Sorry, I get really bored talking about my past.' We appeared to have reached an impasse, and I was preparing to leave when she unexpectedly turned the conversation to incest. In her latest collection she had used hieroglyphs inspired by incest and primitivism and drawn by the New York graffiti artist Keith Haring. She began to ask me questions. Were there any good books on incest? She was fascinated by it. Did I know that it was commonplace in primitive societies? She liked celebrating taboos; the unorthodox was what interested her, 'to shock, to seduce the public into revolt'.

How had she come across Haring's work, I asked. 'That was my boyfriend, Malcolm,' she beamed. Like a love-struck teenager she repeatedly mentioned Malcolm McLaren as she discussed her work, savouring the enunciation of his name. Finally, as if in confession, she bowed her head, wrung the hem of her heavy skirt between her fingers and confided, 'I don't live with Malcolm any more, you know. I don't see that much of him any more, but he's still my friend . . . and there we are.' She sighed, and added in a voice choked with emotion, 'Maybe we'll work a little more closely in the future.' She was clearly not seeking pity, which made her suffering all the more pitiful. I felt as if I had intruded upon a deep private grief. I was touched by her desperate anguish and her frankness to a total stranger, and could not fail to be curious about such a woman.

Over the next few years I was drawn to Vivienne's extraordinary work, which was like no other designer's. While others conformed to the direction that fashion was taking and tried to please the buyers, Vivienne prided herself on her almost militant resistance to orthodoxy, and had little notion of a customer. In the 1980s fashion celebrated clothes that looked rich and fast. Skirts were short, shoulders were wide, heels were high. Women strove to look hard, thin, toned, masculine, powerful and financially independent. Meanwhile, Vivienne's idiom was the poor, the dispossessed, the anarchic. She promoted a rounded, even chubby, female shape, and dressed it in layered, baggy rags and flat shoes, such as trainers or rubber flip-flops that were fastened round the ankles with bandages. Then in an apparent *volte-face*, she began to produce the 'posh' clothes of an élite, parodying the British establishment and its uniforms of class and tradition. Throughout her creative life she irreverently snatched pieces of fashion history, inspected them, dismantled them and reconstructed them, making something modern and disturbing. As a fashion historian, it amazed me how she could extract modernity and, more surprisingly, sexiness, from a Victorian crinoline or the dowdy garb of the British royal family.

My employer at the time, British *Vogue*, did not like Vivienne's earliest and most creative work. Though occasionally mentioned, she was never lauded. She was a maverick: inconsistent, uncommercial, often unwearable but, most of all, anti-establishment, and that was dangerous. Before the nineties, only her 'Pirates' (autumn/winter 1981–82) and 'Harris Tweed' (autumn/winter 1987–88) collections were extensively featured by *Vogue* or any other mainstream British glossy magazine; both were seen as suitably romantic, British and free of polemic. Italian *Vogue*, by contrast, has been consistently fascinated by her work.

Throughout the first half of the eighties, *Vogue*'s fashion editors were cultivating a delicate relationship with Buckingham Palace, dressing, it was assumed, the future Queen of England. Diana and Vivienne, who in her punk days had been associated with a disrespectful, not to say treasonous, attitude to the monarchy, were two images that did not sit happily together, and the magazine understandably chose to maintain its establishment connections.

But, like Diana, Vivienne is quintessentially English. She could only have emerged from a society that is, on the one hand, steeped in tradition and class deference, and on the other prides itself on being the cradle of liberalism and the tolerance – if not unduly threatened – of eccentric non-conformity and satire. Vivienne needed the taboos and rituals of this relatively small and homogeneous post-colonial society, clinging to its class system and sentimental respect for the monarchy, as a backdrop against which she could create and display her parodic pantomime of dress. Her references and the messages sewn into her clothes were full of meaning both to those who revelled in being irreverent and to those susceptible to being offended by them. The vitriol scrawled across her 'Seditionaries' T-shirts, the gentle irony of her Scottish tartans, royal tweeds, Henley stripes, school uniforms and hunting pinks made no sense without this social context.

Gradually, through the mid-eighties, I struck up an acquaintance with Vivienne. She came to the odd party I gave, accompanied by her teenage son Joseph, and they would always be the first to step out onto the dance floor, while other guests were still arriving. She seemed unself-conscious, even shameless, childlike yet intensely serious. Her dancing was manic; an explosion of energy in which she lost herself in a trance: a rock 'n' roll Shaker, a punk Whirling Dervish.

Sometimes I would receive a call from her assistant, who would tell me that Vivienne wanted to talk about 'serious things – literature, art, that sort of stuff'. Would I meet her for dinner at the Indian restaurant on Westbourne Grove? She usually arrived very late, having cycled several miles from her studio, then in North London. Dinner over a couple of bottles of red wine – I did not drink – would last until the waiters turned out the lights. It was never a conversation, rather a monologue. She would tell me what she had been reading, then deliver a passionate attack on how the modern world was unfair, stupid, orthodox and evil. Listening to her woolly and selective idealisation of the past, it became clear that, for all her barricade agitprop and her position at the cutting edge of fashion, Vivienne was at heart a bitter romantic. Convinced of her talent and aware of her precarious financial existence, I decided to try and help her.

During the spring 1991 collections, Paris fashion circles were buzzing with the rumour that Gianfranco Ferre's five-year contract as design chief at Christian Dior would not be renewed. Knowing that Vivienne harboured an ambition to work in couture, I suggested that I introduce her to the house in the hope that they would either consider her as Ferre's successor (a long shot), or agree to finance and develop her own label.

Armed with her portfolio and as much *chutzpah* as we could both muster, we must have been a strange sight as we set off from Heathrow at the crack of dawn. Vivienne negotiated the newly-mopped floor in her platforms, one hand swinging a carpet bag, the other hitching up the skirt of her cling-film-tight, gold-printed velvet dress to the hem of her tweed jacket. Atop six-inch-heeled court shoes, I was dressed in a black velvet 'Rob Roy' jacket with matching mini and a cavalier's blouse. Vivienne was in full flow, lecturing on the ancients, the failings of democracy, the legitimacy of élitism and wise rule under a philosopher-king. The monologue was not only targeted at me, but at any official – passport controller, bag inspector – she encountered. Questions like 'Did you pack your own bag?' were answered with a snippet of classical political thought. Having been mobbed in the lounge by a crowd of sari-ed Indians who astonishingly recognised her, we finally boarded. Exhausted by Vivienne's antics – the mundanities of reaching the plane were of no urgency to her – I steered my unsteady ward from check-in to touchdown.

Our appointment the next morning was with Christian Dior's Directeur Général, Daniel Piette. Dior, one of the world's truly grand couture houses, occupied a whole block of the wide, tree-lined Avenue Montaigne. The dove-grey façade was punctuated every few metres by a grandiose plaque which tilted down imposingly over one's head and bore the house's initials in classic gold script. The ground-floor boutique was fitted with delicate turned-wood display cases that few contemporary cabinetmakers could equal, set with glistening vitrines – no fingerprints here. In one, a virgin-white organza evening blouse for £800, grander in its simplicity than any embroidered rival; in another, a slim, aubergine silk petersham evening pump for £220. And the *vendeuses*, far too professional to affect Sloane Street stroppiness, snappily dressed in grey or black, were the personification of that Gallic adage, passed from mother to daughter, 'I cannot afford to buy cheaply.'

Vivienne and I ascended the staircase to the couture salons, where the proportions widened, ceilings heightened and clues to trade were hidden. We were led along a silent corridor, past doors marked '*Chef de Cabine*', '*Atelier Flou*' and '*Atelier Tailleur*', to Daniel Piette's office. Once the introductions had been made, the floor was handed to Vivienne. I had been confident that this plucky, loquacious Northerner would present her case convincingly, but she remained tongue-tied, nervously tugging her hem, coiling her ringlets and rubbing the corner of her mouth with her index finger.

Unexpectedly forced to become her advocate, I took over, while a sceptical Piette looked on. After fifteen minutes it was clear that words would not suffice, and the portfolio was enlisted. Did Piette recall Lacroix's great success with the mini-crinoline? He nodded. Well, Vivienne had pre-empted Lacroix by three seasons. And Lagerfeld's corsets for Chanel? Vivienne had led the way three *years* earlier. A list of examples was cited where Vivienne had led and others followed. Piette's head was now bent attentively over the groundbreaking port-folio. Finally I suggested that perhaps he might like to inspect some key pieces from Vivienne's archives. He agreed, and in doing so left the door ajar for further discussions. Vivienne only found her voice again once she was well out of earshot. The clothes were never sent to Piette, due to the bad communications and sheer disorganisation of her office. Ferré's contract was renewed for a further five years.

This book is not about the business of fashion. Though Vivienne has consistently been the first to introduce new looks, she has equally consistently failed to capitalise on her fashion lead. She has absolutely no business acumen. Fashion is not an art, it is a trade, and to survive a designer has to sell. Vivienne has scant regard or aptitude for commercialism. Her survival has come despite this failing.

When John Fairchild, proprietor and publisher of *Women's Wear Daily*, the trade's most powerful publication, cited her as one of the six most important designers of the day – along with Saint Laurent, Emanuel Ungaro, Giorgio Armani, Karl Lagerfeld and Christian Lacroix – she was virtually bankrupt. While her peers collected villas, yachts and art, she did not even own her modest flat. As late as 1993, when she had twice been named British Designer of the Year, and been awarded the OBE by the Queen, she still lived a hand-to-mouth existence in a council flat in South London. The entire annual turnover of her business was a mere £600,000. In contrast to the five other designers Fairchild saluted, Vivienne is neither a man nor born into an affluent, or at least educated, background (Ungaro, though from a modest family, was exposed to the refinements of his craft by his father, who was a tailor). Also unlike her peers, she entered fashion in early middle age, not youth.

Compromise for commercial advantage is not in Vivienne's nature. In her somewhat solipsistic universe, other people (in so far as solipsism may be allowed to admit other people) are mad not to see things her way. She has not succeeded – it's doubtful if she every really tried – in charming or endearing herself to colleagues, peers, the press or those with, as she crudely calls it, 'clout'. André Leon Talley of *Vanity Fair* says, 'Most female editors are just plain scared of her. They'd rather not deal with her.'

For someone notoriously uncouth and undiplomatic, Vivienne has one extraordinary social skill. She can elicit help and sympathy where she wishes, and on her own terms. And yet, no matter what an individual does to help her, she has no sense of indebtedness or loyalty. She can be belligerent, rough, rude and selfish. Yet she commands remarkable loyalty from employees and associates. Time after time, they told me she was mean, cruel, heartless and even vicious towards them. Nevertheless, with few exceptions they are happy to have worked alongside a truly original talent who could habitually astonish them with her powers of creativity. Her creativity cannot be copied, anticipated, second-guessed. It is inimitable.

*   *   *

In 1993, Vivienne asked me to write her autobiography. I refused. I did not want to be put into the uncomfortable position of being a ghostwriter, particularly to a woman with such a strong personality and an uncompromising point of view. I spent the next year persuading her to cooperate with a biography which I would write. My conditions were that it would be authorised by her, and I would have access to her, but under no circumstances would she be allowed to read the manuscript. In August 1994, she agreed.

Within four months, Vivienne told me she had had second thoughts. When I asked her why, she would not, or could not, offer an explanation. In the meantime, she had approached family members, friends and colleagues, past and present, and requested that they did not speak to me. Apart from the conversations with her family that I had had over the eleven years I had known her, I have had no additional access to them. As a result, comparatively little information has been forthcoming about Vivienne's father and her first husband, Derek Westwood. Fortunately, I had already managed to reach some of her school and childhood friends. Equally fortunately, most of her associates and friends disregarded her injunction, and agreed to talk to me (of necessity, the identities of some of them have been disguised). Then, curiously, in 1996 various friends and colleagues still close to Vivienne, such as Gene Krell and John Walford, received her permission to cooperate with me. In addition, others who had originally abided by her request changed their minds and spoke to me candidly. To all of them I am indebted.

Why did Vivienne, for no stated reason, decide not to cooperate with the author she had originally asked to write her own autobiography? While I have been researching this book, some possible explanations have suggested themselves. Firstly, and understandably, she is probably apprehensive. To her mind, she has consistently been misrepresented by the media. And even apart from the risk of misrepresentation, nobody likes to have their character and weaknesses laid bare. What will I find out, and what will I write about her? Secondly, I discovered that many years before I set about my task, another publisher commissioned an autobiography from her. To date, they have seen no manuscript. Thirdly, Vivienne's professional survival is founded on her working relationship with her manager Carlo D'Amario. In return for her complete creative freedom, he runs the business. D'Amario might not wish her to cooperate with a project which did not bring profit to the company nor guarantee favourable coverage. No matter what relationship Vivienne strikes up with an associate, it will ultimately be subjected to the sanction of D'Amario's approval or disapproval. She remains indebted to him and him alone, as attested by the long line of friends and loyal colleagues who have been discarded or summarily dismissed over the years.

Vivienne is a difficult, exceptionally talented and fascinating woman. Her relentless creativity is irrepressible, and its mainspring is her busy curiosity. Her visual inquisitiveness is unusual in its intensity and its scepticism. She dissents in order to reinvent. Although ours is dubbed a 'visual age', with images being instantaneously transmitted around the globe, few today take the time to look and to really see; we consume instead not only soundbites, but vision-bites. What distinguishes Vivienne is that she inspects, questions, dismantles and reassembles – as a teacher she would march her young pupils down to the local fishmonger to study the fish before they drew them. My aim in this biography has been to shine some light on her character, and on the way in which her relentless creativity works.

Jane Mulvagh
London, March 1998

Part One

THE AMATEUR DRESSMAKER

1 THE GIRL FROM THE SNAKE PASS

1941–1965

'As a child, I was in waiting.'

Vivienne Westwood, 1995

'She puts her mother on a pedestal.'

Bella Freud, 1997

Just before Christmas 1938, twenty-three-year-old Dora Ball, a flush-cheeked flirt with a determined gait and a passion for ballroom dancing, journeyed from her home village of Tintwistle, on the border between Cheshire and Derbyshire, to the nearby market town of Glossop, to buy material for a new dance dress. Missing the last bus home, she started to walk to another stop on the outskirts of town, passing St Mary's Dance Hall. There, lolling in the doorway, stood the smooth-faced, dapper Gordon Swire, four years her senior. Dora, wary of his reputation, refused his offer to escort her to the bus stop. He insisted, and they struck up a conversation.

On 19 August 1939, two weeks before the outbreak of the Second World War, they married in Tintwistle's Christ Church, in the county of Cheshire. Gordon was described on the marriage certificate as a fruiterer, living at 96 Market Street, Hollingworth, the son of the late Ernest Swire, a boot and shoe repairer. Dora's address was 25 West Street, Tintwistle, and she was the daughter of Edward Ball, a labourer. The young couple honeymooned in Scarborough, Yorkshire. Their first marital home was number 6 Millbrook, a two-up-two-down labourer's stone cottage in a terrace of twelve, between Tintwistle and Hollingworth on the A57, the major road that leads from Sheffield through the Pennine pass to Manchester. Like most humble British homes of the time, the house had an outdoor lavatory in the back yard. The couple washed in a tin bath filled with water warmed on an open fire.

The Swires' first child, Vivienne Isabel, was born on Tuesday, 8 April 1941. She was a first-born war baby, brought up in the English cotton country; circumstances that were to mark both her character and her interests.

The arrival of a sister, Olga, on 14 January 1944 so infuriated Vivienne that she vowed to 'dead her and put her in the dustbin'. Vivienne recalled over fifty years later that when Olga arrived home from the hospital, 'I was outraged. I didn't know I was going to get her. I was three and from then on I decided I wanted to be grown up as soon as possible.' Vivienne's resentment of the interloper went far beyond the sibling jealousy common in young children; indeed, it was so strong that it may have contributed to the competitive suspicion of other women she was to show in later life. As a child she would rarely mention her sister, and few of her friends even realised that Olga existed. Two years later, in 1946, a brother, Gordon, arrived, further thwarting Vivienne's desire to be the centre of attention.

On the night of Vivienne's birth London suffered the heaviest air raid of the war to date. The Blitz had escalated, and the German bombers were targeting Britain's industrial cities as well as its capital. The Swire family would have watched the night skyline during the blackout for the explosions that pockmarked Manchester, ten miles to the west. During the war Vivienne's father served as a storekeeper in the aircraft manufacturers A.V. Roe at Trafford Park, twelve miles from Manchester. This was an extremely important factory during the war – Lancaster bombers were made there – and the Luftwaffe made several attempts to bomb it. The Dam-Busters' famous bouncing bomb was tested at the Derwent Dam at the far end of the Snake Pass, where Vivienne would wander as a child. Dora, meanwhile, took employment as a weaver in a local cotton factory of the sort typically requisitioned by the government to supply materials for the war effort: for uniforms, tents, camouflage, webbing, parachutes and balloons.

With both parents in employment and the wartime rations supplemented by Vivienne's paternal grandmother's grocery store, the Swires were well fed. Later, Dora and Gordon were to run the store for a time. Gordon could drive the family car – a considerable luxury at the time – to Manchester to stock up on supplies, and would bring home news of the city. Thrift was a pervading feature of Vivienne's formative years, which were circumscribed not only by the modesty of her working-class background, but by the austerity of wartime and immediate post-war Britain. Rationing was to be in force until October 1951, and the Attlee government demanded self-sacrifice to rebuild the nation, deploying slogans like 'make-do-and-mend' as an exhortation to frugality.

Meanwhile, Britain's wartime allies enjoyed a post-war consumer boom, epitomised in France by the fabric-consuming lavishness of Christian Dior's New Look, which most British women could only admire, not wear. Thriftiness, inculcated early on as a necessity, would remain intrinsic to Vivienne's character, serving her well during periods of considerable financial hardship, and even when she found relative affluence in her fifties, she never indulged in conspicuous consumption.

Vivienne has always been reluctant to talk about her childhood. In 1994 she told the local newspaper *Derbyshire Now!* that this was because she 'feared people would find it boring'. Until she was sixteen, the Swires lived in or near Tintwistle, in Glossopdale, which is cut off from Lancashire and Cheshire by steep hills and a river gorge, and lies in the western lee of the Pennines, the spine of hills which divides the North of England in two. To the west of the Pennines, in Lancashire, the nation's cotton industry flourished. To the east, in Yorkshire, the woollen industry was established. Exploiting the fast-running water that flowed down the peaks, textile mills and factories were built in the area from the mid-eighteenth century. Immediately after the First World War, the cotton industry had employed nearly 80 per cent of Glossop's working population. Following severe unemployment during the Depression, when the Hadfield Tintwistle labour exchange recorded a devastating 67 per cent rate of unemployment, the local economy revived once again. The mills which surrounded Tintwistle provided a livelihood for many of Vivienne's relations, and she was to retain a sentimental but informed appreciation of the qualities of traditional English textiles: starched cottons, worsted pinstripes, fine-gauge knits, satin-smooth gabardines and hairy tweeds. They were to inspire the nostalgic strand of fashion that would become one of her signatures.

At the end of the war, Gordon Swire senior took work at the local Wall's ice-cream factory. He supplemented the household income with odd jobs, such as collecting holly from the hedgerows to twist into Christmas wreaths which he sold to the neighbours. The whole family enjoyed the make-do-and-mend habit, turning their hands to simple crafts such as dressmaking or utilising domestic ephemera for decoration. Their Christmas tree, for example, was adorned with the perforated silver tops from salt and pepper pots.

Dora, who now worked in the grocery shop, not only made her own ballroom dresses but clothes for all the family, perhaps using remnants bought from the mill where she had worked. Times were good. In the second half of the 1940s the textile trade continued to thrive as the government fostered an export drive to finance war debts. Production was focused on long runs of cheap cotton prints for the African and Far Eastern markets. Workers were secure in their employment, and took patriotic pride in the posters displayed throughout their communities which assured them that 'Britain's bread hangs on Lancashire's thread'.

Vivienne's parents provided for their family and were loving and kind, but they were not remotely scholarly: Dora took the view that reading was a waste of time. They encouraged physical pastimes instead, such as dancing and rambling. The children kept hamsters and guinea-pigs in the back yard and crafted toys and games out of discarded objects. Describing her childhood, Vivienne was to say: 'what we didn't have at home was any literature. I remember my mother once buying some encyclopaedias but they weren't the right sort where you could look things up.'

What her mother, in particular, did give Vivienne was a forthright bearing, a confidence that invited comment and a sense of style. She chose unusual Christian names for her children, and made a point of dressing them well, buying good-quality clothes at C&A in Manchester or making them herself. Childhood friends recall Dora as 'houseproud', something Vivienne would never be, and caring about her appearance, a trait she retained into her seventies and which Vivienne did inherit. A school classmate, Bob Noton, remembered Vivienne as 'meticulous about her clothes and well-turned-out as a schoolgirl. That's what a lot of people found attractive about her.'

By the standards of the time, the Swires were relatively liberal parents. The three children were often left unsupervised, since both Dora and Gordon worked by day, and in the evening they were frequently left with a babysitter while their parents went ballroom dancing (a hobby they pursued into old age) at the Tintwistle and Hollingworth school halls, Glossop's Victoria Hall and in Ashton-under-Lyne, six miles away. They relied on their eldest daughter to take responsibility for her siblings from an early age. Vivienne has described her parents as being 'in love all their life and devoted to each other'. Perhaps she felt that this love excluded her. A former employee of Vivienne's says: 'Her mother and father were so close. He was star-struck by her right to the end of his life. Dora always came first. *She* was the star of the family.'

Vivienne was required to walk her brother and sister to the Hollingworth village school each morning and to St Mary's Anglican church on Sundays. Although her parents were not zealous members of the local church – they would assure her that they would attend the evening service, but rarely did – Vivienne was captivated by religion. On learning, aged four, about the crucifixion, she remembers being so horrified that she vowed to challenge oppression: 'I felt I had to become a freedom fighter to stop this sort of thing going on. I really did want to do something to change this horrible world.'

Making defiant stands became an early characteristic of this confident and independent girl. On her first day at nursery school in Hollingworth, she saw a queue outside the girls' lavatory. Reasoning that there was no point in waiting, she used the boys' instead. She claims that this was her 'first confrontation with tyranny', and it earned her a slap from the teacher. By the time she was five she was questioning the teacher's example, preferring 'to do my "r"'s round and round like a snail because it looked prettier', rather than copying exactly from the blackboard. Even though she was slapped again, she refused to conform. She had already developed an independent view of mores and manners: 'I have an inbuilt perversity, a kind of inbuilt clock which always reacts against anything orthodox,' she said thirty years later.

At the age of eight Vivienne progressed to the Tintwistle church school, where her mother had been educated, and joined a class of variously-aged pupils of both sexes. Her parents took only a distant interest in their children's academic development, neither harbouring grand ambitions for them nor, according to Gordon junior, discussing what they wanted to do when they grew up. 'We never showed our parents our school reports,' Gordon remembers, though Vivienne's consistently acknowledged her 'creativity': 'It wasn't that they didn't care, they just assumed we were bright and let us get on with it.'

Despite her comparatively uncultured background, Vivienne remembers finding stimulating companionship in books, which nourished her imagination and led her beyond the restricted world of her family. One can imagine her escaping the confines of the small bedroom she shared with Olga and Gordon, spending winter evenings huddled in front of the hearth, or sneaking into her parents' room and, propped up against the door under the scratchy tulle layers of her mother's dance dresses, losing herself in the pages of Enid Blyton's Famous Five stories, the brothers Grimm's fairy tales and Walter Scott's 'Lochinvar'. These first writers were soon followed, according to Vivienne, by Dickens, Buchan, Chaucer and Keats. On summer mornings she scrambled over the wall behind the cottage, passed through a disused quarry and climbed up to the high meadow to read: 'I remember sitting in this meadow in the sun with the dew still on the grass, and I could smell May blossom, and even at that early age I remember saying to myself how lucky I was.'

Vivienne's childhood was secure and happy. She enjoyed exploring the lyrically beautiful nearby peaks and dales. Finding hideaways in the wooded terrain of the Snake Pass and Devil's Elbow towards Cut-Throat Bridge, she would read adventure stories or tuck into a picnic of treats from her aunt's greengrocers, washed down with home-made dandelion and burdock lemonade. It was during these solitary, free-roaming days in this gauzy, rain-softened terrain that she developed what she has called her 'country heart'; her subsequent nostalgia for the English rural idyll and her knowledge of its flora and fauna. Two decades later, money being short, she used her knowledge of edible plants to feed her family; as a designer she would refer back to country pastimes – fell-walking, riding, fishing, shooting – to create clothes that, even though they were worn by the hurried city-dweller, conjured up the unhurried, idealised Arcadia of her childhood.

From 1951, a recession developed in the British cotton industry as competitively priced imports from Hong Kong, India and Pakistan began to flood the home market. Large numbers of jobs were lost in Glossopdale's mills, and while some of Vivienne's neighbours found employment in the new chemical and plastics firms that moved into the area, many joined the ranks of the unemployed or the economic migrants. The hardships Vivienne witnessed left their mark on her:

it would be many years before she placed what she saw as the indulgence of higher education above her anxiety to earn her keep.

Almost effortlessly, Vivienne won a place at Glossop Grammar School in 1952. According to her maternal aunt Ethel Mitchell, who owned a sweet shop in Tintwistle: 'Before her eleven-plus I remember Dora suggesting that Vivienne should be swotting. Vivienne simply said, "Why?" She knew it all, and passed with good grades.'

Glossop Grammar School was three miles from the Swires' home, and was reached by a bus that travelled across Woolley Bridge, which separated Cheshire from Derbyshire, past several cloth mills, under a viaduct and into the market town of Glossop. The handsome stone building, erected in 1899 by Francis Fitzalan, the second Lord Howard, as an art and technical school for mill apprentices, stood on the corner of Talbot Street and Fitzalan Street. In 1903 it became a grammar school, with the brightest local children competing for places. Reginald Barnsley, who was at the school at the same time as Vivienne, recalled that 'science, maths, English were important. Music, PE and woodwork didn't count for much . . . it was a learning school with seven lessons a day.'

Formality and propriety characterised this proud grammar school, which is now an adult education centre. Only teachers and sixth-formers could pass through the main entrance, under a stone-carved plaque bearing the school's motto: *Virtus, Veritas, Libertas* (Honour, Truth, Liberty). Juniors had to use the back door, where they changed from outdoor shoes into indoor pumps. The boys, dressed in grey trousers and maroon-and-navy striped blazers, crossed the black-and-white-tiled hall and climbed the left-hand arc of the rosewood staircase to assembly, while the girls, in grey skirts or gymslips, blazers, white blouses and grey stockings, filed up the right. The staff room and offices had long casement windows which overlooked The Nab, a substantial hill at the back of the building, but the classrooms had high windows to prevent pupils from being distracted by daydreams.

A memorable event of Vivienne's youth was the coronation of Queen Elizabeth II on 2 June 1953. It rained that day, and the Swires attended a celebration tea party at Tintwistle Sunday School, which was hung with patriotic bunting and banners. Waving their Union Jacks, the party then proceeded to a neighbouring cottage where they crowded into the front room to watch the event on television. The image of the royal family and all its tradition and pageantry must have had an impact on the visually alert twelve-year-old Vivienne, for she was to exploit them, both positively and negatively, in her creative life many years later.

A few months after the coronation, the Swires rented a new council house for a year in nearby Hollingworth, and then, in 1954, Dora was given the opportunity to become the Tintwistle village postmistress. The family moved into the building which housed the post office in its flagstoned basement at 36 Manchester Road, at the end of a terrace of five. Dora, exhibiting the distinctive independence of the women of her family, boasted proudly that the post office was 'in her name'. All three children inherited this 'supreme self-confidence' which their maternal aunt, Ethel Mitchell, observed and shared. Vivienne's early role models were matriarchal. Power resided with the women in the family, and Vivienne soon displayed their strident determination.

As well as distributing the post, Dora also ran a little general store in which she sold a few of the cheaper magazines, such as *Woman's Own* and *Women's Weekly*, that disseminated the fashions of the time in a watered-down form, and provided dressmaking and knitting patterns. She also stocked a small selection of clothing, such as underwear from John Smedley, the Derbyshire specialists in fine-gauge knitwear, and traditional gymslips (both of which were to feature in Vivienne's collections in the 1980s – when Vivienne's school uniform changed to skirt and blouse, she insisted on keeping her gymslip).

Young Vivienne was determined to make her mark at her new school, to be 'more extreme' than the crowd. In her attention-seeking manner, she was always first to raise her hand in answer to a teacher's question, to the annoyance of her classmates. One contemporary, Eileen Mellish, remembers Vivienne as argumentative, getting 'a bit humpy' when the biology teacher chastised her, and climbing out of the window when she had been locked into a classroom for detention. With her unusual cast of mind, Vivienne would find tangential solutions to set questions: when the class was given the title 'Bats in the Belfry' for a painting, Eileen Mellish recalls, 'We all imagined a church, but she went psychological and did bats in the head. She was smart.'

Her maths teacher, Jack Holden, however, finds it hard to recall Vivienne: she was 'an unremarkable girl, you didn't notice her'. Vivienne was certainly not a distinguished scholar, though she did reasonably well at English, sports and art, for which she took lessons after school with the art teacher, Gordon Bell. She did come third in the high jump at the school sports day, and when she entered the annual poster competition at the age of fifteen, she was highly commended, 'which, as you know,' says Holden, 'means she didn't quite make it. Looking at Vivienne Swire and looking at Vivienne Westwood, I would just sit there in total amazement. How on earth the one became the other is quite beyond me. But you see, we are nice people. You didn't do outrageous things.'

It was exactly this sense of propriety that Vivienne wished to challenge, with bold actions such as 'always [being] the one who kissed the teacher under the mistletoe at Christmas'. Bob Noton, a primary-school sweetheart, was enamoured of her 'striking' looks, composed carriage and long dark hair neatly tied back in a ponytail. He found her direct and flirtatious. But when the pair went on to Glossop Grammar School, he was summarily dumped: there was 'too much competition by the other boys for Vivienne – she was a hot date and knew she was a good-looking, bonnie girl'. Vivienne is also remembered for making a point of championing an unpopular and lonely boy, a moralising and self-publicising stance.

With the onset of puberty Vivienne, who claimed to have had a boyfriend from the age of ten, began to show an interest in sex which her mother would have dubbed 'fast'. She went with her schoolfriend Anne Shaw to Sunday school dances, and looked forward to rainy days when games were replaced by ballroom dancing in the school gym. She boasted that she had a different boyfriend every week: 'I was straight until I was fourteen. Then I went funny . . . boredom, bad boredom.' Though she says she did not indulge in full sexual intercourse (something her parents had brought her up to believe was only to be enjoyed within marriage) until her late teens, her physical relationships were 'quite heavy, lots of kissing and all that'. A former classmate remembers the fifteen-year-old Vivienne flaunting a ring and proudly announcing that she was engaged.

Thanks to protruding teeth (later straightened) and a flat chest, Vivienne did not judge herself to be pretty, though she anticipated that 'I was going to be.' Perhaps her lack of self-confidence was a result of having a pretty and vain mother. Seeing that Dora was always well turned-out, and the impact that had on her father, gave Vivienne an early belief in the power of beauty and clothes. She determined to make something of herself through her clothing. She would come home from school with a piece of material, cut out a dress, sew it up and wear it that night. At school she wore one coloured stocking and one plain one with her uniform, which she had customised by tightening the skirt round her haunches and cutting a provocative slit up the back. She started padding her bras, longing for the sexuality of a curvaceous female form – 'big tits are what boys are interested in'. Her idols were the hourglass-shaped Sophia Loren, Marilyn Monroe and Jayne Mansfield. The clothes she later designed would challenge sports-honed skinniness with a voluptuousness enhanced by corsets and high heels. She also took to curling her hair, leaving the curls so stiff that it looked as if the rollers had not been removed.

In 1957 Vivienne and a schoolfriend, Maureen Purcell, went for a holiday at Butlin's camp in Skegness, a popular working-class resort. The camp had a libertine atmosphere, and many young boys would work there as 'Redcoats' for ridiculously low wages, in the virtual certainty of sexual encounters with female campers. The holiday opened Vivienne's eyes to the sexiness of shoes: 'There were these Essex girls who were really stylish and wore stilettos. In Manchester I saw these amazing high-heeled stilettos in a shop window and I bought a pair ... I wore them to school with a tight-fitting pencil skirt,' much to her headmistress, Dolly Greenwood's, dismay. Maureen Purcell recalled that when Vivienne stayed overnight on the family sofa 'she'd bring a collection of her winklepickers and line them up near the skirting board'. 'Clothes make you the centre of attention,' Vivienne said in 1995. 'It's like when I was a girl, I thought the difference between jive and rock 'n' roll was that you stuck your bottom out, so I would stick it *right* out and the boys would really laugh at me. But I didn't mind because I thought, OK, I know what I'm doing.'

Vivienne reached adolescence in the mid-1950s, right at the beginning of a dramatic social change – the emergence of the teenager. The urban, middle-class teenage girl disdained adult fashion, preferring casual dress that reflected her own age and musical interests, such as separates inspired by Italian fashion, and full cotton skirts and bobby socks from America. Vivienne, though, was born into the conservative provincial working class, which valued the smartness, 'good taste' and *hauteur* of its social superiors. Retaining the romanticism of the New Look and its glamorous Hollywood exaggerations, a fashion-conscious adolescent from this background would have aspired to the image of an elegant and well-married thirty-year-old woman in neat dress or suit and matching accessories. (One contemporary marvelled at how Vivienne was 'so smartly turned out . . . it was always the complete outfit, the shoes, the bag always matched'.) She would have been unlikely to risk looking casual, which might give the impression of poverty.

Her sartorial icons were the aristocratic mannequins who graced the pages of the upmarket glossy magazines like *Vogue*, *Harper's Bazaar* and *Vanity Fair*, such as Barbara Goalen, Fiona Campbell Walter (later Baroness von Thyssen) and Bronwen Pugh (later Lady Astor), and Hollywood stars like Lana Turner, Marilyn Monroe, Jane Russell, Elizabeth Taylor, Grace Kelly and Audrey Hepburn. The big American film studios spared no expense in the grooming and marketing of these female icons, employing the considerable creative skills of costumiers such as Edith Head, William Travilla and Orry-Kelly, and French couturiers such as Christian Dior, Pierre Balmain and the Paris-based Elsa Schiaparelli. The celluloid goddesses reached Vivienne and her friends through the cinema in Glossop, which they typically visited once a week.

Wherever she went, even to school, Vivienne aimed to dress like a woman, not a girl; she 'could not think of anything more exciting', and was convinced she looked better than anyone else – 'a sensation'. The first items of clothing she chose for herself were a fashionably tight pencil skirt, which she later described as 'so sexual', and a pair of high-heeled shoes. She experimented with her image, dying her hair red one week and bleaching a badger streak in it the next. Her mother recalled that 'even at sixteen she would wear unusual clothes'. In an effort to attract attention, when the fashion for delicate daisy earrings hit Glossop, Vivienne made a pair out of huge marguerites. She was thrilled when, as she entered the dance hall, the trombonist took his instrument from his lips, pointed at her and hissed, 'Look at that girl!' On another occasion, when the other girls were wearing net petticoats, stiffened with sugar, under full skirts, 'she came in a slinky black Suzy Wong dress that she had made – but then, she could carry it off.'

Keenly aware of the limitations of her background, Vivienne determined to elevate herself above it. Quite unfairly, she later boasted: 'I am very happy that I didn't need my family. They were not sceptical or questioning enough for me – too conforming.' Despite her apparent self-confidence, she felt she was 'stupid . . . I thought that nobody around me had enough information to give me.' This conviction never left her, and to it one can perhaps trace her intellectual insecurity and her drive to seek out – usually male – mentors.

Aways alert to an opportunity, at grammar school Vivienne selected as her best friend Maureen Purcell, who came from a slightly higher social level – her family owned the Glossop general store just off the main square. During lunch break the two teenagers would look for sheet music in the town, going back to the Purcells' to sing along to the hits they played on Mrs Purcell's record-player. After school, if she did not take the bus straight home to the dull village of Tintwistle, Vivienne could loiter at the Purcells' or join friends, such as Anne Shaw, and the boys in the café in Glossop. Her mother did not like her to be out late, so she began to stay over at the Purcells', which she still describes as being 'like a second home to me'.

Maureen Purcell was Jewish, which distinguished her from most of her classmates, and she possessed 'a much stronger personality than Vivienne'. Looking at photographs of the two friends in their mid-teens, it is striking how knowing and slickly-turned-out they are compared to their contemporaries; any vestige of innocence is artfully disguised. According to Eileen Mellish, 'the boys thought a lot of Vivienne – she was great fun to be with.' Their confidence probably stemmed from their relative worldliness. The Swires and the Purcells allowed their daughters to go to Manchester on Saturdays to shop or visit the dance halls, something which, Eileen Mellish remembers emphatically, 'my parents wouldn't let me do, full stop!' The two girls were even permitted to go for a holiday at Butlin's; Vivienne claimed that she 'got off with over a hundred blokes'.

In the pre-Profumo era, when moral standards were strict and social ordering was precise, the two girls' antics might have been expected to invite comment. However, it was often the case that the working classes were less hidebound by propriety than the 'respectable' and aspiring middle classes. Furthermore, there was in some urban Jewish circles a progressive, tolerant and playful spirit. Frequenting such circles in Manchester, where some of Maureen's relatives were in the tailoring business – and where both of her parents had worked as machinists in a clothes factory in the thirties – would have given Vivienne a glimpse of glamour. As a contemporary saying (at least among Mancunians) asserted, 'What Manchester thinks today, London thinks tomorrow,' and the city's King Street was proudly claimed to be 'the Bond street of the North'. Vivienne and Maureen also socialised with the Purcells' cousins, the McCofskis, who were Jewish tailors in Leeds.

Vivienne did not excel as a scholar in the competitive environment of the grammar school; she was socially rather than academically precocious. By the time she left the school in the summer of 1957, aged sixteen, she had only once visited an art gallery – in Manchester – dismissed the theatre as belonging to the past, and had read only storybooks and the set texts of her curriculum rather than ranging wider or deeper. Though she claimed to have been 'intellectually curious', she admitted to being unaware that what she called 'the vast lake of knowledge' existed, and never entertained the idea of going to university, which she associated with 'the snobby lot . . . the boys all carried umbrellas, which we considered effeminate'. Her horizons were limited: 'I just wanted to leave and earn my living. If someone had told me I could train to be a librarian, I would have thought, "Great!" But I didn't know. How could I have been that stupid?' Eileen Mellish remembered Vivienne observing that nursing or hairdressing were her only options – both Maureen Purcell and Anne Shaw pursued the latter career: 'I think she wanted to do something different, but I don't think she had any idea.'

In July 1957 Vivienne took a six-week holiday job at Pickering's cannery with Maureen and Eileen. The factory's female employees – dubbed the 'pea pixies' because of their green overalls and caps – worked from 7.30 in the morning until 5.30 in the evening. 'It was horrendous because your hands got really sore with the juices,' Vivienne remembered. 'It was just money.' At first the three girls were employed on the fruit-salad conveyor belt, but they soon irritated the regular staff by working faster than them and creating logjams. They were moved to the pea section, and Vivienne's mother would get angry when her daughter came home with her clothes stained bright green.

Later that year Vivienne's life changed dramatically. Her father was unemployed, and the family, at Dora's instigation, moved to the more affluent South, her parents taking over another post office in Station Road, Harrow, in North-West London. 'We had to move,' says Dora. 'there was no work.' It was a great culture shock for Vivienne. In

Cheshire, as Malcolm McLaren says, 'she dominated her brother and sister, left and right, and was very much in control of her life. When she came to London she lost control. She thought they were not kind, easily accessible people and would cry, "I want to go back up North, I can't stand it here." It was tough on her.' Her horizons were broadening, but she was finding it hard to cope.

The social status of Harrow's residents was clearly defined by the position of their homes on the gradient that led up from Wealdstone, past Harrow town centre and on to the leafy heights of Harrow-on-the-Hill, where the well-heeled lived above the persistent urban smogs of 1950s London. Gordon and Dora's sub-post office and small general store at 31 Station Road was virtually at the bottom of the hill.

Station Road was a main thoroughfare, flanked with terraces of three-bedroom Edwardian houses. Some of the ground floors had been converted into shops, including tobacconists, funeral parlours and bakeries. Number 31 was a modest but adequate home. The Swires lived above the shop in three bedrooms, a sitting room/diner, a kitchen and a small bathroom. After a year Gordon took over another post office and grocery business in nearby Stanmore, while Dora continued to run Station Road.

Vivienne, the bombastic sixteen-year-old schoolgirl from Glossop, was temporarily cowed by her new surroundings, and she felt insecure. She enrolled at the local grammar school but found it difficult to integrate, a fact that she put down to her broad Northern accent. After leaving school she attended a silversmithing and jewellery-making course at Harrow Art School, but she left abruptly after one term, took a secretarial course at Pitman's and began to earn her own living as a typist for a local firm, having seen an advertisement on a tube train. Her favourite pastime was still dancing, and she attended many local dances. At one of them in late 1961 she met a young man called Derek John Westwood, two years her senior. Vivienne was instantly smitten by the handsome Westwood, who was confident, ardent and shared her love of rock 'n' roll: 'When I met Derek he was very lively and ever such a good dancer,' she said later. His family lived on Belvedere Way in Kenton, the next suburb, and his father was a checker in a factory. Derek was working as a toolshop apprentice in the local Hoover factory, supplementing his wages with casual work as a manager at bingo halls and hotels. He longed, however, to be an airline pilot, and not long after meeting Vivienne he secured a job as a steward for British European Airways. His prospects looking up, Derek proposed marriage. Vivienne, who had left her typing job and was now working as a primary school teacher in Willesden, North London, accepted, although she later said: 'I didn't want to marry him actually, but he was such a sweet guy and I couldn't give it up.'

Though the young couple planned to marry in a register office, Dora forcefully insisted that they have a white wedding, in a church. Vivienne made her own dress, which was not unusual in those days, and the wedding took place on 21 July 1962 at St John the Baptist, Greenhill, a large Edwardian stone church half a mile up the hill from the Swires' home. The couple were married by Reverend J.R. Maxwell Johnstone, and honeymooned in North Devon. Vivienne and Derek moved into 86 Station Road, three hundred yards from the Swires' sub-post office. On 3 September 1963 a son, Benjamin Arthur Westwood, was born at Edgware General Hospital in Hendon.

To contribute to the household expenses, Vivienne took a menial job chopping up rolls of print with a guillotine at the nearby Kodak factory ('I was the fastest chopper in the factory,' she later boasted). Despite Derek's kindness and great love for his new wife, she was bored. She felt that her life was frustratingly circumscribed, and she watched with envy as her younger brother Gordon moved into a new and exciting circle at Harrow Art School. It was through him that she was to meet the man who would entice her away from working-class family conformity for ever.

2   MEETING MALCOLM

1965–1971

'I was a coin and he showed me the other side.'

Vivienne Westwood on Malcolm McLaren

Vivienne never fell under the spell of the sixties, whose politics, music and clothes were not to be a significant influence on her. But her life did change during that decade. She met Malcolm McLaren, who, in tune with the times, channelled her latent creativity into fashion, a medium in which the pair could showcase his political and artistic posturings and her campaigning zeal. Manipulated by him, Vivienne evolved from a cussing, church-going housewife into a subversive seamstress of agitprop clothing.

It was within her brother Gordon's circle of friends that Vivienne met Malcolm Robert Andrew Edwards (*né* McLaren) in 1965 at the Railway Hotel, Harrow and Wealdstone, where Derek was now managing the club and she served as hatcheck girl in the evenings. McLaren was amused by her waspish asides to her husband. The dyspeptic child of a broken home, he liked to witness marital discord, and may have speculated that her aggression was for his benefit.

Malcolm Edwards (as he was known until 1971) was born on 22 January 1946 in the family home in Carysfort Road, Stoke Newington, a working-class district of North-East London. His parents were Emily (*née* Isaacs), the daughter of lower-middle-class Jewish diamond-cutters, and Peter McLaren, a working-class Scot who had served as a sapper with the Royal Engineers during the war and then became a motor-fitter. Emily considered that she had married beneath her. They had two sons, Stuart and, two and a half years later, Malcolm. When Malcolm was eighteen months old, Peter abandoned the family. He eventually married five times.

Emily then married Mike Edwards, a tailor (who, probably to

disguise his origins, had changed his name from Levi), and decided to call herself Eve. Eve Edwards was a good-time girl and a flirt, boasting a sexual intimacy with the millionaire tycoon Sir Charles Clore. McLaren loathed his stepfather and felt betrayed by his mother, who was permanently absent, by day helping to run the small family clothing factory, Eve Edwards Ltd, and by night out with her lovers. Her sons were brought up by their grandmother, Rose Isaacs, who lived next door.

Rose Isaacs was born in 1887. Wanting to become an actress, she had taken elocution lessons which made her sound pretentious and affected. She was separated from her husband and, frustrated by her circumscribed life, lived out her fantasies through her grandson Malcolm, with whom she shared a bed until he was ten years old: 'She created her own world and I lived in it and was protected by it,' he remembered in 1996. 'She allowed me to do anything; anything, in her eyes, that was not boring. Her motto was, if you were bad you were good, and if you were good you were boring.'

Favouring Malcolm at the expense of his brother Stuart, Rose established a pattern that he was to repeat as a father and stepfather. He was encouraged to defy authority, particularly that of his teachers – egged on by his grandmother, he lasted only one day at the William Patten School in Stoke Newington. After a short spell with a private tutor, he attended a fee-paying Jewish school called Avigdor in nearby Lordship Lane. His final schooling was provided by the Orange Hill Grammar School in Burnt Oak, where he passed an unremarkable three O-levels in 1961. Spoilt by Grandmother Rose and ignored by his parents, McLaren developed a jaundiced view of family life. He became a troublemaker, attracted to any philosophy that incited anarchy and excused belligerence.

Following in Stuart's desert-booted footsteps, McLaren became a mod, a youth style which by 1958 had ousted the teddy boys' insular little Englandism. The mods were dazzled by sharp Italian tailoring and American casuals, such as windcheaters, check or intasia knitted shirts, and short, close-fitting, single-breasted, small-lapelled jackets. Mod tailoring recalled the sexual tightness of Italian Renaissance court dress: the short jacket, codpiece and hose. The sixties version revealed every flex of muscle. The boxy, waistless 'bum-freezer' jacket with narrow, notched lapels fell from unpadded shoulders. It was single-breasted and three-button (only the centre one being fastened), and ventless, or virtually so. A series of flapless 'ticket' and secret pockets were inserted into its plain dark cloth. The jacket was worn with American import denim jeans or slacks that were tight against the thigh and narrowed to a sixteen-inch hem. Trousers hung on the hips rather than being suspended under the armpits with braces, and the zip relegated the buttoned fly to the fashion scrapheap. A white drip-dry or woollen shirt, desert boots and short socks and short, tidy hair completed the look. The effect was hard, clean and modern.

By the autumn of 1964 McLaren, a puny, aggressive *flâneur*, had run away from home and found work with a vintner in the West End of London. The previous year he had taken evening classes at St Martin's College of Art, and in 1964 he entered Harrow Art School, where he befriended Vivienne's brother Gordon. Thanks to a series of student grants, he remained in higher education (Reigate, Walthamstow, Chelsea, Chiswick, Croydon and Goldsmith's) for the next seven years. McLaren was one of a generation of British art school graduates who were to become prominent in the nation's phenomenally successful pop music, pop art, advertising and media industries, which contributed significantly both to Britain's gross national product and its cultural prestige.

By 1965 Vivienne could no longer sustain her dull marriage. Despite Derek Westwood's kindness, good looks and dancing skills, she was bored. She did not share his simple interests, and resented the fact that, as she saw it, she 'was not learning from staying with him'. A tempting world had opened up to her through her brother Gordon and his friends, five or six years her junior, at Harrow Art School. Despite Derek's pleas, she strained to escape the marriage. After several attempts to leave, she finally broke away in 1965, taking three-year-old Ben to live in her parents' flat above the post office. The couple divorced the following year. (In later life, Vivienne conceded that Derek had been a good husband and a kind man – 'too kind for me'.)

Every day Vivienne would wheel Ben's pushchair past Gordon's Morris Cowley, parked outside the Swire flat, and peer through the steamed-up windows. There, hunched under an old coat, lay Malcolm McLaren, who had taken up Gordon's offer to move from his previous abode – 'under a tree in the Harrow-on-the-Hill cemetery' – into the car. Dora Swire disapproved of this dosser, and refused to allow him into their home, but once she had taken her place behind the post office counter, McLaren would sneak upstairs to take a bath and cadge breakfast.

Vivienne admired this camp dandy in his makeshift home, and he was amused by her fiery temperament and Sunday school ways. His earliest memory of her, as a shy Christian out of *Picture Post* dressed in home-knits and kilt, was a caricature that served his storytelling. She remembered being 'a mess' when she met him: 'I was into the dolly bird look. Wispy hair and fur coats. I looked dreadful.' McLaren loved to expose her provincialism: 'London seemed to her a city of snobs . . . she found the people frightening, arrogant and unkind and she could not deal with it.' Though this curious provincial and this posturing metropolitan seemed poles apart, McLaren's rebelliousness was simply a more aggressive expression of Vivienne's discontent. As well as their fertile imaginations, they shared an inclination to conjure up idyllic notions of youth and childhood; he because he had not enjoyed his, she because she had. They also shared a low boredom threshold, and an unwillingness to mention their fathers. But in other ways they were very different. While Vivienne had an earnestness that bordered on the humourless, McLaren treated life as a game, and adopted an irreverent and sarcastic pose.

Like Vivienne's Glossop schoolfriend Maureen Purcell, McLaren's relatives were Jewish tailors. Just as Maureen had introduced her into new circles in Manchester and Leeds, so Vivienne believed that McLaren could provide access to a fascinating world: 'I felt there were so many doors to open, and he had the key to all of them. Plus he had a political attitude and I needed to align myself.' She sought out his company, impressed that 'he was cultured. His family were Portuguese diamond merchants way back and had a whole cosmopolitan understanding.' But McLaren was afraid of women: they were either unreliable, like his mother, or suffocatingly manipulative, like Grandmother Rose. He was unable to befriend them and, though his friends were lustily experimenting in that dawn of promiscuity, he remained a virgin.

Dissatisfied with her uneducated state, Vivienne determined to improve herself in the company of McLaren and her brother's student friends. But for a time she remained suspicious that artists were 'anarchists, time-wasters or vagabonds', and her nature prevented her from sharing wholeheartedly in their lack of interest in the practical side of life. Torn between the self-improvement promised by higher education and the necessity to find a job, she enrolled for a Diploma of Education course at St Gabriel's Teacher Training College in Camberwell, South London, reasoning that she could always be an art teacher. 'I thought, if I can't find a way to make a living at painting' – which, under the influence of her brother Gordon and his art-school friends she had come to believe to be the most desirable way of life – 'at least I can be a teacher, and teach someone else to paint.'

Gordon left Harrow to study at the London College of Film Technique. He rented a rundown house at 31 King's Avenue, near Clapham North underground station in South London. Two fellow film students, John Broderick and Chuck Coryn, variously described by McLaren as 'American draft dodgers' or 'Vietnam vets', shared the house, and after a few months McLaren joined them.

To McLaren's horror, Vivienne and her son moved in shortly afterwards, compromising his 'boys' domain'. He also found Vivienne attractive, and 'a sexual threat'. But the attraction was not mutual. Vivienne liked pretty boys, and McLaren's rail-thin physique, pigeon-toed stance, unruly ginger hair and rage-red face, which he optimistically tried to disguise under talcum powder (hence his nickname 'Talcy Malcy'), were not conventionally handsome. Looks aside, his pent-up anger would from time to time explode violently, and this disturbed her. But slowly, over the weeks, a combination of boredom, curiosity and sheer proximity to this compelling storyteller broke down her indifference to him. While the others attended film school, they passed the hours hunched over an inadequate bar-heater, sharing beans on toast and tea, or smoking Woodbines and downing whiskies late into the night.

As McLaren lectured her on the political power of art and the appeal of cult fashions, Vivienne assembled the costume-jewellery crosses she had started to sell at the weekend in Portobello market to add to her modest student grant and social security benefit. The jewellery was to be their first joint venture. McLaren would watch his methodical companion set the stones in place – red, then orange, then purple, then red again – before intervening to rearrange the colours. 'She started to be taken by me because of the way I put the beads together and made them less boring, and . . . I was intrigued by her . . . because she hung on my every word,' he recalled, with characteristic egotism. Vivienne readily deferred to his suggestions, which she believed were 'more like exercises, more balanced in the way modern art was, instead of what I was doing . . . all sort of bunged together. His were more artist [sic], mine more crafts. I always thought his ideas were so much better than mine.' During these weeks, their roles were established and set for the next decade: she as the student craftsman, he the opinionated art director.

McLaren, who was obsessed with fashion and style, also art directed Vivienne's appearance. She abandoned the 'dolly bird' look. 'He took me by the hand and made me more stylish. I was twenty-five and got heavily into the school uniform look,' which she bought in the children's department of the Oxford Street department store John Lewis and wore with ankle-socks. This formative lesson in style, and its associations with carefree romance, were to emerge two decades later in Vivienne's collections.

Intimacies were exchanged. McLaren disclosed his hatred for his polygamous and absent parents, who had turned him into 'an odd fish', and his regular nightmares about his mother. 'He had just left home very traumatically, a very Jewish home, and he felt he didn't have any roots outside Jewish society.' Vivienne says, romanticising his background somewhat. She in turn confided her relief that she had escaped her marriage to a 'no-hoper', in which she had been 'saddled to the kitchen sink with a screaming brat round my ankles'.

McLaren's anger was channelled into subscribing to any movement that incited anarchy. According to his first art teacher at Harrow, Theodore Ramos, he was 'playing with art', but Vivienne was intrigued by McLaren's anarchist conceits, which suggested an outlet for her righteous indignation about 'this horrible world'. Nevertheless, she was not in love with this ranting revolutionary, though his manic displays of hysteria did arouse her sexual appetite. 'He seemed quite spectacular at the time, really. He had a very, very pale face [thanks to the talcum powder] and he had very slight hair on his skin and very, very close-cropped hair. But I once remember I said something to him . . . and he suddenly exploded in front of me . . . His lips were very red in the context of his pale face and I remember his mouth — he's got a well-formed, well-shaped mouth, quite pointed it is – well, it just opened up and I could see all the gums inside. I've never seen anything quite like it. I respected this kind of intensity.' No physical detail was missed by Vivienne, whose visual recall is exceptional.

When Vivienne mentioned her attraction for an Italian she had met in a Soho coffee bar and who had promised to take her to Italy,

McLaren's jealousy was excited. Posing as her disinterested friend, he warned her against this 'Italian gigolo'. Couldn't she see that his promises were just a ploy to get her into bed? Many years later he admitted that he 'did fancy her', and had 'an ulterior motive' for his self-serving advice.

Though McLaren felt secure in his mental domination of this awe-struck, to his mind sexually experienced older woman, he was uncomfortable when she provoked him by walking round the house naked. Unwilling to make a direct approach, he deployed an emotional cliché to seduce her – appealing to her motherly instincts. He slept on a mattress in the sitting room, and one morning he feigned a stomach ache, moaning and groaning until Vivienne surrendered her more comfortable divan and went to the chemist for medicine. On her return she nursed him until nightfall when, since he would not return to his own bed, she stripped and climbed in alongside him, unconvincingly claiming that she had no other recourse. Finally they consummated their two-year friendship, the twenty-five-year-old schoolteacher instructing the twenty-one-year-old virgin, who 'refused to get out of bed for days'.

Habitually loath to acknowledge any emotional tie, McLaren jocularly dismissed the incident as the amusing sexual initiation of an innocent lad by a voracious nymphomaniac. Vivienne saw it differently: 'He pursued me aggressively. It wore me out and finally I succumbed.' Lust may have driven McLaren to lure her into bed, but her resistance was hardly staunch.

The loss of his virginity unsettled McLaren. He became possessive, insisting that Vivienne ditch her Italian friend. If a man came to tea or was seen in the street with her, he would 'have a fit'. (He retains an extremely short and violent temper.) On one occasion, in despair, he shaved his head roughly, and theatrically emerged covered in blood. These masochistic poses appealed to Vivienne who, casting herself as the indispensable nurse to this lust-sick youth, reasoned that she could not leave him: 'He thought I'd committed myself, but only because he'd been so confiding in me. He thought I'd just thrown him over and not realised the seriousness of the situation. He'd never had a girlfriend before me. And so I started to – I hesitate to use the right word – not fucking, and not making love, because I wasn't in love with him – I guess you could say I started sleeping with him.'

Their sex life was irregular. Throughout their fifteen-year relationship, McLaren only sporadically indulged Vivienne's appetites, partly in order to retain control over her. Though he became infamous for advocating sexual freedom and perversion, he was remarkably prudish about his own sex life. When pushed, the most he would say was, 'I could never understand Vivienne's attitude to sex,' adding defensively, 'As far as I know we had good sex and she was happy about that.' Their working relationship dwarfed their sexual one.

Within weeks Vivienne discovered that she was pregnant. McLaren's attitude to her changed immediately. He claimed to have been duped into thinking she was using contraception, and the prospect of imminent fatherhood distressed him. Since Vivienne was not in love with him, they discussed an abortion. In Britain in 1967, abortion was illegal. Most women who wished to terminate a pregnancy had to risk illness, even death, either from barbaric and dangerous do-it-yourself methods or at the hands of a backstreet abortionist, at considerable expense. An abortion was strongly recommended by the possessive Grandmother Rose, who disapproved of Vivienne, whom she dismissed both as a gentile and a scheming older woman from the wrong side of the tracks who was already burdened with another man's child. She was determined to end the relationship.

Because Vivienne was close to her mother ('perhaps everyone is except me, so maybe that's normal,' he conceded), McLaren tried to break communications between mother and daughter. Her parents were infuriated, regarding him as wilfully irresponsible. When he saw them approaching the house one day, he jumped out of the window to avoid a confrontation. His 'benefactor', as he referred to his grandmother, offered to pay for an abortion. 'Vivienne was fairly for it,' he says, but the deliberation continued for weeks, right up to the moment when, standing on the porch of a Harley Street doctor, Grandmother Rose's cash in hand, Vivienne finally made up her mind and set off to Bond Street to buy a coat instead. McLaren felt trapped. He warned Vivienne that he would take no responsibility for the child, but by now she was too emotionally entangled to terminate her pregnancy.

In recalling his relationship with Vivienne now, McLaren describes an extraordinary parabola: from cold-hearted refusal that she ever meant anything to him, to the admission of deep fondness and even perhaps, in his own terms, love. What were his feelings for the woman who was carrying his child? 'When she was pregnant I never saw her looking so beautiful ... it was the time that I'd seen her look the most kind, the most open, the most centred and somehow as though she belonged ... it was meant to be. I'll never forget the vision of her being pregnant.' This tenderly remembered vision of her is not typical of McLaren's practised persona of cynical control.

Their child was two weeks overdue, and the stoic mother worked right up to the last moment, selling her jewellery and hoping that the baby would not arrive that day. Finally, she was summoned to the hospital in Streatham to be induced and, after an intense, short labour, her second son was born at teatime on 30 November 1967. She had been hoping for a daughter.

Grandmother Rose dissuaded McLaren from attending the delivery, and it was not until several days later that he went to the hospital to see his son. Having being quizzed about his absence by an officious nurse, he approached Vivienne's bed. She recalls that his initial reaction was, 'He's not mine! He doesn't even look like me.' McLaren remembers, 'I've never seen Vivienne look happier.' Vivienne retains a poignant memory of her lover arriving in a snow-dusted Harris tweed greatcoat – bought on the way to the hospital at a second-hand shop on the Vauxhall Bridge Road – and often includes a description of it when sentimentally recounting her time in the maternity ward. The traditional Scottish cloth was to play an important role in her life nearly twenty years later.

The boy was christened Joseph Ferdinand Corré, the middle name after McLaren's favourite Velázquez portrait, *Archbishop Fernando de Valdés y Llanos* in the National Gallery, and Corré being Grandmother Rose's maiden name. While Vivienne called her son 'Joe', McLaren always referred to him as 'Joseph'. In refusing to confer his own surname on his son he was distancing himself not only from paternity but also from his own parents, the former distance later underscored by Joseph being forbidden to call him 'Dad' or 'Daddy'. The birth strained the relationship for McLaren, but it convinced Vivienne to commit herself to it.

In the autumn of 1967 McLaren had enrolled at Croydon College of Art and Design in South London to study painting, and he and Vivienne moved to a ground-floor flat in Aigburth Mansions, Hackford Road, near the Kennington Oval, which McLaren found from an advertisement in a sweet shop. The flat, in a terrace of three-storey pebble-dashed buildings, was in good condition by student standards, and the family was briefly happy there, entertaining Gordon and friends from Croydon on macrobiotic fare. Six weeks after the birth, Vivienne, needing money, reluctantly returned to work as a teacher, leaving Joseph in a crèche.

One of McLaren's Croydon friends was Jamie Reid, the son of a radical Scottish family. Though his political commitment was temporarily debased by his association with McLaren's disingenuous radicalism, Reid remained active, working after graduation for a community press in Croydon which served black, feminist, prisoner and trade unionist causes. At art school he stood alongside McLaren in the hope of changing the world; his companion was happy simply to play up and dress up.

In 1967, radical elements in the student communities across Europe were enthralled by a new publication, Guy Debord's *Societé de Spectacle*. Debord was the chief theorist of the Situationist International, founded in Italy in 1957, which declared that artists should break down the barriers between life and art and, acting as *provocateurs*, create ridiculous situations in urban environments as a nihilist reaction to the status quo. Developing the Marxist critique that every aspect of capitalist life had been reduced to a commodity, the situationists fused it with the artistic agitation of dadaism, the absurdities of surrealism and the unrestrained hedonism of their times. The setting up of ridiculous spectacles was to be a modern expression of popular resistance.

Debord's bestseller honed the arguments about the rampant commodification of cultural icons, and became the textbook behind *les évenements de Mai* the following year in Paris. From the Situationist International and Debord, McLaren absorbed the manner in which the media could be exploited through the production of manifestos, newspapers, collages and misinformation. Through a British offshoot of the movement, King Mob, he became acquainted with the writings of the Scottish Beat writer Alexander Trocchi and the American anarchist/feminist Valerie Solanas, author of 'The SCUM [Society for Cutting up Men] Manifesto', who gained notoriety by shooting Andy Warhol in 1968. Guided by situationism, McLaren perfected his skills as the great dissembler.

A friend from Harrow Art School, Fred Vermorel, who was living in Paris as a 'hanger-on' at the Sorbonne, corresponded with McLaren during the months preceding *les évenements* of May 1968. Like the 1965 race riots in the black Los Angeles ghetto of Watts and the anti-Vietnam war rallies, these French student demonstrations were vividly communicated on television, uniting the younger generation across the world in its condemnation of what it saw as heavy-handed suppression by governments.

It would be hard to exaggerate the importance of the student risings against de Gaulle's conservative rule in France. *Les évenements* were the culmination of a protest march organised by the student Daniel Cohn-Bendit, 'Danny the Red', which began on 22 March at Nanterre, a university in the suburbs of Paris, and gathered support from students and workers alike until it culminated in fierce riots, centred on the Sorbonne, in the heart of the French capital. The protesters were brutally suppressed by the *Compagnie Republicaine de Securité*, the civil guard. Vermorel sent vivid reports of these events to McLaren and his fellow students who, wishing to claim solidarity, mimicked the French protests.

On 5 June McLaren, Reid, and other art students, including Robin Scott, who was to move into the Hackford Road flat in 1969, barricaded themselves into the Croydon College of Art and Design. Obeying the situationist dictum 'Demand the Impossible!', they issued preposterous demands, such as being allowed to sculpt in pure gold. The outside world was informed of their grievances through a series of press releases, and on 12 June Scott's views were published in *The Times*. It was more fun to revolt than to study, and hedonism, as much as idealism, underpinned many student cries for revolution. The fervour of the protest waned with the onset of the summer holidays.

Participating in such pranks left McLaren little time for his family: 'I was excited by this idea of taking culture to the streets and changing the whole way of life, using culture as a means of making trouble. These were not dead words, this was action!' McLaren's 'actions' now look like mere attention-seeking high-jinx. He joined twenty-four others in Selfridges toy department to give away toys. Their flysheet manifesto read: 'Christmas: it was meant to be great but it's horrible. Let's smash the great deception. Light up Oxford Street, dance around the fire.' On another occasion he pulled on black gloves to 'steal steaks from the college canteen and cook them in the college kitchens late at night – no fingerprints! It was fun. It felt like the best years of your youth.' Vivienne shunned these antics, focusing on the essentials of motherhood and earning a living.

McLaren visited Paris in 1968, and retrospectively exaggerated his role in the 'revolution'. Though he claimed to have marched with *les enragés* in May, he did not actually arrive until August. Accompanied by a friend from Croydon, he inspected the iconic debris of student protest with awe. Not a brick of the façade of L'École des Beaux Arts on the rue Bonaparte was visible under the wallpaper of posters and graffiti declaiming such situationist slogans as 'It is forbidden to forbid', 'Under the pavements, the beach', and 'Imagination is seizing power'. Gallery owners were peeling these mementoes off the walls, aware that posterity would prize them (just as the *avant-garde* London art dealer Robert Fraser was to do a decade later, collecting punk posters and donating them on his death to the Victoria and Albert Museum). McLaren found refuge in the Left Bank cafés, imagining that the waiters 'liked the anarchic idea and believed in it too', especially as they did not present him with a bill. Unlike Vivienne, who was thrifty, he was mean.

Attracted by notions of Algerian freedom fighters and Black Panther revolutionaries, the two students headed south, aiming for North Africa. But prosaic bureaucracy thwarted the budding rebel; McLaren had not been inoculated. He was forced to kill time on the south coast of France, waiting for his friend, who had travelled on to Libya, to return.

It was not love but loneliness that prompted McLaren to miss Vivienne. He began to write to her, describing his life among matadors and gypsies, passing the time, he claimed, discussing communism with the local workers. It is unlikely that his pidgin French would have stretched to philosophical complexities, and after a few companionless days he summoned Vivienne. She borrowed her fare from her mother, left her sons in a crèche and headed south on her first trip abroad.

Together they bought a small tent, pitched it on Le Trayas beach and camped there for a few weeks, subsidised by money sent by Dora to the local post office. Austerity-trained Vivienne made their modest funds last by collecting discarded fruit from underneath the market stalls and cooking cheap sardines in the sand. Alone together for the first time, the couple were happy and relaxed. Vivienne, undistracted by children, was riveted by McLaren's accounts of his imaginary exploits on the barricades in Paris, and he was happy to have an audience. His eccentricities amused her: he would insist she take off all her clothes to keep warm, and would refuse to leave the tent to urinate, preferring to use a bottle he would make her take outside to empty. In years to come, she would nostalgically recount these perfect weeks of happiness. 'When she falls, she really falls,' says fashion journalist and former Vivienne employee Caroline Baker. 'She really loved him and she talked about [the holiday] so romantically. Every little thing about Malcolm impressed her, even the fact that he only had to pee once a day. She said she was in awe of his strong bladder!'

August passed into September. One night, according to McLaren, the lovers under their canvas roof were woken by the thumping and crashing of pots and pans. A strong tide had swept their tent into the sea. They scrambled onto the beach, having lost everything: cooking utensils, clothes, passports and wallets. It was 3 a.m. Naked and shivering, they ran to the local village, where they persuaded the baker to let them crouch by the ovens to dry out.

The idyllic holiday had ended. They hitched to Marseilles, where they sat on the church steps in the main square and discussed how to get back to England. There was no point in contacting Dora and asking her to send the bus fare, it would take too long. Perhaps they should surrender themselves to the British Consul, in the hope that the Foreign Office would fund their return. According to McLaren's implausible account, while they were dithering in the afternoon sun a mini-van pulled up alongside the steps and McLaren's friend, returning from Africa, rushed up to greet them. 'Great! You got my postcard then?' he began. Apparently the friend, assuming that McLaren would still be hanging round Aix-en-Provence, had sent him a postcard, care of the university, instructing him to meet up on the steps of the church in the main square of Marseilles on that very day, 7 September, at 3 p.m. The three piled into the van and set off back to England.

Vivienne and McLaren came home to a shock. Joseph had slipped into what McLaren described as a 'catatonic trance'. They took him to the park and tried to rouse him, cajoling him to react, but he just sat inertly staring into space. Finally Joseph responded to McLaren — 'not to me, because I'd really let him down' (by abandoning him), his guilt-ridden mother recalled. The following Monday she handed in her notice at the school, determined never to leave Joseph again. McLaren supported her decision.

Gradually, penury and McLaren's lack of commitment tore the family apart. When the lease expired in Kennington he escaped back to his grandmother, who had moved into a council flat above South Clapham tube station. Since she refused to shelter Vivienne and the boys, they went to live with her parents, who had now retired and moved from Harrow to a cottage just outside Banbury in Oxfordshire. A former employee remembers Vivienne telling her matter-of-factly that her father made her sleep in the garden shed.

The relationship between Vivienne and McLaren was now, conveniently for him, in limbo, though Vivienne expected a reconciliation. McLaren kept in touch by taking the train to Oxfordshire approximately once a month to see Joseph (Ben does not feature in his recollections). He received short shrift from Dora, who referred to him as 'the interloper'.

Despite her parents' disapproval, Vivienne wanted to hold on to her man. On numerous occasions McLaren attempted to end the relationship. Since they were no longer lovers, he argued, and were not living together, surely it was a sham; and anyway, he wanted 'to fall in love with a student – any student', with whom he could live the free student life in London, rather than be shackled to a working-class single mother living in the country. But within an hour of arriving Vivienne would change his mind, partly because Joseph looked so content, and partly because McLaren could not find another lover: 'It just didn't happen, perhaps because I was rather odd, so the relationship carried on.' Occasionally he got the better of Grandmother Rose and Vivienne would stay for the odd weekend with him at her flat.

In October 1968, while Vivienne cared for her two sons in Oxfordshire and read Thomas Hardy novels, McLaren moved on to Goldsmith's College of Art in South London to study film and photography. There he met Helen Mininberg (later Wellington-Lloyd), a wealthy South African Jewess who became a soldier in his campaign to create havoc through art. Partly to escape Vivienne's clutches, and partly because he was attracted by the fact that Helen was a dwarf, he began an affair with her. He relished aggravating Vivienne by insisting that, although Helen was plain, at least she was more interesting than she was, and taunted her with tales of other infidelities, claiming that, as an artist, he needed to experiment and be free. Neither their relationship nor their child should stand in the way of his destiny.

McLaren's flaming hair and his anti-authoritarian actions at art school had won him the sobriquet 'Red Malcolm'. His behaviour finally attracted the attention of the police, who attempted to arrest him but were barred from entering the college premises by school authorities.

Ben was now six and Joseph nearly two. Sharing the cramped Oxfordshire cottage with her parents became impossible for Vivienne, and so in the autumn of 1969, encouraged by McLaren, she took the children to live in her aunt's caravan at the Tan-y-Rogo Farm caravan park, near Prestatyn on the north coast of Wales, for eight months. McLaren was delighted that Vivienne was removed from her mother's influence, and for the next ten years her formerly close ties with Dora were weakened. It was not until McLaren's final departure that mother and daughter were to be reconciled.

In Vivienne's absence McLaren married Jocelyn Hakim, a Turkish-French Jewish student he knew who wanted to remain in Britain, and who paid him £50 to marry her at a register office in Lewisham (it was to cost Grandmother Rose £2,000 to secure a divorce). The £50 he earned for his troubles was invested in his student project, a loosely situationist film entitled *Oxford Street*. The unfinished film highlighted the dehumanising absurdities of consumerism and fashion.

Vivienne's aunt's caravan was sited in a caravan park two miles from the town of Prestatyn, at the foot of the Clwydian hills. Without work, Vivienne was virtually penniless, save for meagre family allowance payments, and Ben recalls her feeding herself and her sons on 'dandelion roots' and simple fare. Much to Ben's delight, he did not attend the local school, but was given an informal education by his mother, who conducted history and geography lessons in museums and markets and taught botany, geography and art along the beaches and hedgerows, nourishing his and Joe's imaginations and sense of wonder. 'She thought I'd get more from that than [from] a classroom of children. It was legal – she was a teacher,' says Ben.

Released from the interference of Vivienne's parents, McLaren was more inclined to visit Vivienne in north Wales. Here the countrywoman led the town-man and the boys on nature rambles up into the Clwydian hills, where McLaren would sit and sketch while Vivienne played with and watched her children. Away from the distractions of student life, McLaren felt at ease. But for Ben it was 'an awful holiday' as he began to realise the depth of McLaren's antipathy towards him. McLaren had persuaded Vivienne that her first-born was retarded, and referred to him as 'that snivelling little brat who's always holding onto his mum's apron strings'. McLaren also undermined Ben's regard for his natural father, dismissing him as the offspring of a 'no-hoper': 'Joseph's part of me, and Ben's part of someone she never had any respect for.' Vivienne's lack of confidence in her own genes and in her ability to nurture Ben demonstrated how fundamentally unsure she was about her talents and background.

Despite McLaren's behaviour, Vivienne optimistically believed that by sharing a child, at least she had a hold over him. In fact her real hold on him was not his paternity of Joe, but her loyalty and the stable love, denied him in childhood, that she offered. She gradually weaned him from the suffocating hold of Grandmother Rose with steadfast and understanding love, and McLaren came to see that although she was more in love with him than he was with her, she did not pressurise him to make the commitment of marriage: 'I don't remember her ever discussing such matters.' Despite her occasional outbursts of desperation, she gave him a free rein.

McLaren found a flat just around the corner from his grandmother in Nightingale Lane. Vivienne and her sons moved back to London and temporarily into a room McLaren found for them in Balham. After he and his friends had decorated Nightingale Lane, he summoned her, Joseph and Ben to move in. According to Helen Wellington-Lloyd, although McLaren found Vivienne extremely difficult to live with, 'he was concerned to be around for the kid, so he wouldn't be brought up in such a narrow, working-class way, like her family.'

Entering the flat, on the first floor of a thirties council block, was like boarding a train. A long, narrow, windowless corridor, made virtually impassable by stacked bikes, boxes and paraphernalia, led straight ahead. Off this lay a tiny galley kitchen, a primitive bathroom, a boxroom where the children slept in bunk beds, and a reasonably sized bedsitting room. One of the sources of tension between Vivienne and McLaren was household cleanliness. Vivienne was not only messy, but downright dirty – 'The toilets, you know, filthy,' says Helen

Wellington-Lloyd. McLaren, by contrast, was almost fanatically orderly: 'He'd fastidiously take off his clothes when getting into bed, fold them up – the routine was perfect.' Still, McLaren and Vivienne were to live together in Nightingale Lane, with the exception of a few breaks, until he finally moved out in 1980. Vivienne chose to remain, and despite her affluence in recent years, she is still living there in 1998.

On returning to London, Vivienne enrolled in another teacher training course, at Goldsmith's College. She was remembered by a fellow student, Peter Silverstone, as a 'star pupil . . . potentially the greatest primary school teacher of her generation'. While his mother studied, Joseph was left at a local nursery and Ben joined a primary school. McLaren was still a student, so when Vivienne graduated she became the breadwinner of the household. She shouldered the burden of the £3.10s. a week rent and most of the household expenses – McLaren spent the bulk of his grant on himself and his art. At one point domestic finances were so strained that Ben was sent off to live with his father, now remarried and living in Ashby de la Zouch, which he remembers as a bitter blow. Vivienne's stoic practicality kept the family fed and clothed: 'Vivienne comes from the Pennines, and she is one of those English hard-rock people with the ability to survive in the woods,' says McLaren. She scoured neighbourhood gardens, Clapham Common and the local market gutters for herbs, fruit and vegetables: 'I cooked macrobiotically, just rice, vegetables and a few nuts,' she remembered.

As a mother, Vivienne was something of an old-fashioned disciplinarian. McLaren, however, claimed allegiance to the progressive teaching ideology developed by left-leaning educationalists in the 1960s and modelled on the theories of one of his heroes, A.S. Neill, who in 1921 had founded the famous Summerhill in Suffolk. Let down by his mother and mollycoddled by his grandmother, McLaren argued that a mother's influence on a child could only be stifling and detrimental. He preferred a creative environment of chaos, which he believed would break down preconceptions about family life and instil self-reliance and independence from an early age. Dismissing Vivienne's views as puritan, he was rarely around to care for the children or to deal with the consequences of his radical parenting theories.

Joseph was extremely close to his mother, and this affection would manifest itself in gallant gestures: 'He used to want to go shopping for me when he was three,' Vivienne remembered. 'I let him go, but followed him surreptitiously a few paces behind. He was so careful that after a while I let him go by himself.' The following year, Joseph and Ben were dispatched to boarding school. Joseph was four, which even by British public school standards was a harshly early age. McLaren claimed that the decision had been reached in order that the children 'be politicised at an early age', so they could flourish in 'a fascist state'. But was the real reason simply to get them out from under his feet? Under McLaren's influence, and despite her earlier promises, Vivienne had abandoned Joseph again. She witnessed the consequences when they visited him: 'He looked like a little pink pig dressed up in a blazer, navy raincoat and peaked cap. All he would say in answer to any question was, "I suppose so," in a little voice from the back of his throat with his head bowed.' Upon being assured that he would not have to stay at the school 'he burst into sobs and tears of relief'.

Ben pined for his mother when he was dumped at boarding school or banished to his father's new family. Being a loving and faithful son, he insists that he enjoyed a 'really happy childhood', but he does acknowledge his stepfather's hold over his mother at the expense of her sons: 'One thing that wasn't perfect was that Malcolm was her number one.' Vivienne's obsessive love for McLaren, and his disregard for the children, must have felt extremely excluding for the boys. Was Vivienne mirroring her own parents' excluding love, which drove her to early independence?

Though careless of Vivienne's love, McLaren was possessive of her attention. If he came home late at night and found her sleeping in their bed cuddled up to Joseph, he would fly into a rage and kick the boy into his own bunk. Perhaps as a result of the ten years he slept alongside Grandmother Rose, overt familial affection disturbed him.

Vivienne was gradually, under McLaren's influence, adopting the garb of a street-smart Londoner. Indulging his fetish for fashion, he took her down the King's Road to dress up, tutoring her with his mantra 'the beauty of fearlessness': 'Once she had got that, her whole critique and sense of doing things fed through to her clothes.' The rock 'n' roll fashions of her youth that she had worn while with Derek were replaced by parodic retro-chic versions, in tune with the teds' revival.

By the late sixties, hippies dominated the London scene. Fashion had gone limp. Backbones were out. When Ossie Clark scissored Celia Birtwell's flower-strewn chiffons and voiles on the bias and lowered the hem two feet in 1967, wispy, whimsical 'period' dress ousted the strict, short look that had epitomised the energy of Swinging London. Fashion's look moved anatomically south, down the leg from the upper thigh to the lower calf, and geographically west, along the King's Road, from the optimistic, coltish modernism found at Glass & Black, Mary Quant and John Bates to the mawkish and nostalgic tatters of Granny Takes a Trip, opened by Nigel Weymouth in 1966, and Michael Rainey's Hung on You. The name 'Granny Takes a Trip' alluded both to the use of hallucinogenic drugs and to the vintage costume favoured by Weymouth's aristocratic, art school and music-business customers. Over the next two years an assortment of hippie and pop art boutiques, such as Tommy Roberts's Kleptomania and Mr Freedom, and John Lloyd's Alkasura, either moved to or started up in the World's End vicinity of the King's Road (the apocalyptic name derived from a local pub).

Dressed in widows' weeds and under the influence of psychedelic drugs, there was an aura among those in the forefront of youth culture of languor and indolence. But after the high-water mark of idealism reached in the 'Summer of Love' in 1967, disillusionment characterised the end of the sixties. The Vietnam protest movement appeared to have little tangible impact on international politics, de Gaulle had crushed the student riots in Paris, confirming his right-wing regime with a landslide election victory in June 1968, while in Northern Ireland the Civil Rights movement polarised the Province into violent confrontation.

In Britain, Harold Wilson's boom years gave way to devaluation in November 1967. 1970 brought back a Conservative government, and unemployment rose steadily, reaching a (then) post-war peak of 967,000 in the first quarter of 1972. In October 1973 the oil price soared as a result of the Yom Kippur war between Egypt and Israel. An economic malady which the Keynesians had not envisaged, stagflation, ensued. In February 1974 the coalminers demanded a 30 per cent pay increase in the average wage, and went on strike.

Wildcat strikes culminated in the three-day week and an entrenchment of class issues the like of which had not been witnessed in Britain since the General Strike of 1926. The situation was summed up by Brendon Sewill, a senior adviser to the government and special assistant to Anthony Barber, the Chancellor of the Exchequer: 'At the time many of those in positions of influence looked into the abyss and saw only a few days away the possibility of the country being plunged into a state of chaos not so far removed from that which might prevail after a minor nuclear attack. If that sounds melodramatic I need only say that – with the prospect of a breakdown of power supplies, sewerage, communications, effective government and law and order – it was the analogy that was being used at the time.'

Drug-taking youth substituted mind-numbing opiates for the energy-inducing amphetamines they had favoured in the early sixties, heedless of the fact that a number of their pop icons – Brian Jones, Jim Morrison, Jimi Hendrix, Janis Joplin – had died, or soon would, as a result of substance abuse. The energetic optimism of the earlier years of the decade gave way to hapless introspection at its close. Mary Hopkin had a hit with the wistful 'Those Were the Days' in the summer of 1967, reflecting the nostalgia for a better time.

Disillusion bred licence. The law's gradual slackening of its harsh grip on 'acceptable behaviour' reflected, and to some degree fostered, increasing permissiveness. 1960 saw the end of the ban on D.H. Lawrence's *Lady Chatterley's Lover*. Lawrence's biographer Brenda Maddox describes the symbolic impact of the trial: 'the verdict . . . virtually abolished literary censorship in Britain . . . There are those who consider that the circulation of a low-priced edition of Constance Chatterley's discovery of the joys of warm-hearted fucking, to the accompaniment of her gamekeeper's lavish praise for her cunt and arse, launched the permissive sixties all by itself.'

The liberalising process had started gathering steam in the late fifties. In 1959, the ground-breaking Obscene Publications Act ended the Lord Chamberlain's centuries-old role as theatrical censor. In 1967 homosexuality between consenting adults was legalised, and in April 1968 the Abortion Act was passed, allowing women to terminate pregnancies legally. By 1969 the female contraceptive pill was widely available. Family break-up was facilitated by the 1969 Divorce Law, making it possible to divorce after two years' separation if both parties were in agreement, five years' if they were not. The following year, the Misuse of Drugs Act was passed. For the first time, premarital and homosexual sex, recreational drugs and family breakdown were openly discussed.

'Retro-chic' appropriately clothed youth's *ennui*. Originating in New York as 'vintage chic' in the mid-sixties, the term – applied to fashion and films – was coined in France in the early seventies. Retro-chic is Janus-faced: it looks back to the past while keeping a keen eye on today. Retro-chic defied fashion's traditional direction of influence: coming up from the streets and art colleges, rather than down from designers and mass retailers. It took root in disenchantment with commercial fashion, providing a cheap (second-hand), egalitarian alternative. To pull it off required time – foraging in attics or thrift shops – not money, and time was what the young had in abundance.

Style leaders like Catherine Tennant, a fashion editor at British *Vogue*, escaped from the present into an idealised past, ransacking their grandparents' trunks for Cavalier plumed hats and capes and colourful old army uniforms. The impecunious scoured junk shops and markets such as Portobello Road and Petticoat Lane. Anna Piaggi of Condé Nast, Italy, and her companion Vernon Lambert were amongst the first stylists to reject the shoddily produced neophilia of sixties fashion in favour of the antique. They relished the quality and craftsmanship found in Victorian cut and panne velvets, Edwardian plumes, thirties bias-cut *crêpes de chine*, forties furs, and the affordable trinkets of bygone, and apparently better, days. The practice of dressing up in a cocktail of styles and periods spread throughout the youth of the West. By the early seventies, even mainstream designers were showing collections inspired by period costume, such as Yves Saint Laurent's turbaned and shoulder-padded forties molls of 1970, and Thea Porter's tiered chiffon maxi-dresses inspired by Visconti's 1971 film *Death in Venice*.

McLaren and Vivienne, though, had no truck with either the farrago of costumes – second-hand or new – or the philosophical tolerance and relativism of the hippie era. They adopted a form of sectarian dress, the uniform of the teddy boy revival, to distinguish themselves from the hippie creed and to reflect their passion for fifties rock 'n' roll.

The couple's affiliations were doggedly reactionary, not progressive. Allying themselves to the teddy boys, they became customers of Tommy Roberts's Mr Freedom, where they found teddy boy draped jackets, drainpipes, bootlace ties, ram's head belts, 'brothel-creeper' lace-up shoes, circle skirts and cardigans. Unlike the originals cut in soberly smart Edwardian blacks and greys, mimicking their wearers' social superiors' City gent status, these modern impostors were scissored out of vermilion, neon-violet and beacon-orange gabardines and velvets. Yet despite the recolouring into Pop Art's garish hues, they were still charged with the cocky defiance of the fifties: defiance against the restoration of the rigidities of inter-war privilege, against the ineluctably rising tide of American popular culture, and against racial and sexual inequality. Above all, they were indisputably British, working-class and proudly conservative in their sharp, tailored aggression. Set against the prevailing hippie values of inclusive – and, to Vivienne and McLaren, undiscriminating – internationalism, classlessness and tolerance (even this last was not as all-embracing as it seemed), they symbolised a romantic, nostalgic and selective tribalism. Their very tailored construction suggested *macho*, disciplined control, in contrast to the unkempt, unisex and uniclass hippie garb.

Tommy Roberts was one of the most lovable characters of the British fashion scene. This tough, plain-speaking Cockney was – unlike many of the other boutique owners – without affectation. He was there to trade, not to pontificate on possible utopias. As short as a jockey and as wide as a Sumo wrestler, Roberts led fashion into its first flirtations with retro-chic. Parody distinguished his manner, his humour and his creations. Lined up in his shop were the ephemera of fifties rock 'n' roll, the kitsch excesses of thirties Hollywood and the gleefully simple images of Pop Art and American comic-strips.

Among Vivienne's outfits from Mr Freedom were a lurid green dress printed with Pop Art silver stars, which clung to her lithe body from throat to ankle, and a hooped jitterbugger's skirt. Moving along the King's Road to Terry de Havilland, the rock star's cobbler, she bought four-inch-heeled snakeskin sandals and, from Jane & Jane (Jean Muir's first enterprise), a hot-tomato-red jersey baby-doll dress. Taking her cue from Mr Freedom, she would find cheap fabrics in unusually bright colours, such as neon orange and shocking pink, and transform them into teddy-girl circle or pencil skirts and rib-hugging blouses worn with bobbysocks and stilettos. 'She was like a bright peacock, a walking traffic light, though she never thought of herself as beautiful,' said McLaren.

Vivienne's love of drawing attention to herself through dress, which had emerged in her adolescence, was emboldened by McLaren. Cocking a snook at contemporary hippie style, their clothes became more overtly allied to the fifties roots of rock 'n' roll. Vivienne's last vestige of provincial conformity was eliminated in 1971 when she had her hair dramatically cut. Persuaded by McLaren to go to the fashionable Mayfair salon Leonard, at twenty-nine years of age she relinquished her long hair, convinced by her lover that having it cropped would look more sexy, cool and urban. She then peroxided it herself, and razored it into layered fronds down the back of her neck and uneven short spikes which stood erect with hair gel on her crown. Vivienne claimed that she was the first to create the spiky, peroxide-dyed hairstyle, bristling with aggression and artifice, that was to become the hallmark of the punks. Simon Barker believes that David Bowie and his wife Angie copied it: 'I'm sure they got it from Vivienne. Bowie has always been a style thief and she had that look in early 1971 before *Ziggy Stardust* came out. Can you imagine what the hairdressers must have thought? Kids cutting their own hair – brilliant! They [the hairdressers] did do what they called a *"coup sauvage"* after that, bringing it back into the fold and adapting it like that – otherwise they'd have been out of business.' In the space of four years, the provincial aspirant in well-turned-out clothes had evolved into a modish city-dweller in hard cult fashion. The transformation of the girl from the Snake Pass was complete.

Though McLaren had scoffed at Vivienne's rural upbringing for so long, it was the display of her 'country heart', and not her change of clothes, that drew him closer to her. On occasions he would join her, the two boys and the mostly Afro-Caribbean children from the Brixton primary school where she taught on jaunts into the home counties. The countryside was alien to this urban boy, but he accompanied them on their train trips to the green fields and woodlands of Kent. His relationship with Vivienne deepened during the delightful and uncomplicated hours of these idyllic afternoons – she trying to recapture her childhood, he hoping to experience something always longed for.

Gathered round a campfire in a field, the two adults would tell magic tales for the children. Leaping through the long grass like a demonic wizard, McLaren warned his spellbound audience that if they did not keep the fire burning the snakes – poisonous, of course – would attack. He was a mesmerising performer. His oratory could provoke mayhem as he built up the children's natural restlessness, with his flaying arms and fire-bright eyes, into a conflagration of mischievous adventure. Here was an adult who thought like a naughty child. It was a trait he would trade on for many years. Both he and Vivienne would tap into memories of this wild-child Arcadia to create their fashions in the early eighties.

In between her lover's performances, Vivienne enthused the children with her knowledge of flora and fauna. For once, she could be teacher rather than pupil to her lover, guiding him through the natural world and bolstering her feeling of self-worth. 'I was a real rascal with these black kids,' McLaren remembered, 'and Vivienne was in charge of us all. I felt like a child in the childhood that I never had, and that made me care a lot for Vivienne because I felt safe and secure with her.'

Vivienne was deeply and irretrievably in love, but McLaren was emotionally incapable of applying the word 'love' to their relationship, spuriously arguing that 'it was bigger than love'. Though he acknowledged his 'responsibility to the child' (making no reference to Ben), he claimed he was still searching for 'an ideal love', and kept his heart closed and his options open: 'Vivienne, as all women are, was calmer and more collected in her thinking, and hoped that a formula would lay out rules, but we were finding our way and I was a more lonely character; a lot more lost and immature and more driven.' Unlike Vivienne, who relished the chance to disappear into her own world as she crafted her clothes, McLaren feared solitude. But he was not content to settle down to family life, and still sought excitement through 'the chance encounter'.

In the summer of 1971, aged twenty-five, McLaren finally ended his student days by graduating from Goldsmith's, and promptly plunged into a depression. Was it time to grow up? What should he do? In tune with his mood, he painted the hall and floor of their flat black. He became obsessed by the perfection of this floor, and if it was not spotlessly clean when he came home to the flat at night, he would turn on Vivienne. The couple had to make ends meet, but at this stage they had no ambition to enter mainstream fashion. Music was his passion – perhaps he could make a living from it, starting out by setting up a stall and selling his collection of old forty-fives and rock 'n' roll ephemera. And shopkeeping, of course, was in Vivienne's blood. From the age of thirteen until she left home she had lived above her parents' shops.

Sharing Vivienne's knee-jerk aversion to received opinion, McLaren was determined to proselytise the purity and energy of rock 'n' roll's roots. He despised the hugely successful 'super groups' like Emerson,

Lake and Palmer, Yes, Pink Floyd and others, that had emerged in the late sixties. Rock was now big business, and these bands, performing to vast audiences in enormous stadiums, shared neither the lifestyles nor the aspirations of their fans.

Claiming that his wares constituted an 'art statement', as well as a political indictment of the super groups and the glitzy dandyism of glam rockers such as Bowie and Roxy Music, McLaren, a quintessential trader in his winklepickers, posed as a square-toed evangelist, zealously preaching his creed. Since the name Edwards was sullied with a criminal record (he had been caught shoplifting a roll of linoleum, and been arrested for burning the Greek flag at a demonstration), Malcolm changed his name by deed poll back to that of his father, McLaren. In October 1971, wearing his new name, a teddy boy jacket and distinctive lurex-threaded drape trousers which Vivienne had run up for him, he stepped out down the King's Road, in search of a chance encounter that would determine his future.

3 PRANKSTER RETAILING

1971–1975

> 'Be Childish
> Be Irresponsible
> Be Disrespectful
> Be Everything
> This Society Hates.'
>
> Malcolm McLaren, script for the film *Oxford Street*, 1969

After two and a half miles, his optimism flagging, McLaren turned the corner into World's End. There the fashionable King's Road quickly degenerated into inner-urban decay, tower blocks and pubs where drugs could be scored. As he passed number 430, a figure leaning against a bamboo façade beckoned him into the retro boutique Paradise Garage.

'Where you going, man? I dig the drainpipes,' began Bradley Mendelssohn, the Brooklyn-born store manager, referring to McLaren's lurex-threaded trousers. McLaren explained that he was looking for a stall where he could sell his rock 'n' roll records and memorabilia. Bradley suggested the back half of the shop, and an ecstatic McLaren returned home with plans to set up a business with his Harrow Art School friend Patrick Casey, another collector of fifties ephemera. Ever practical, Vivienne initially greeted the idea with scepticism, but as usual she eventually went along with McLaren's wishes.

Pooling their dole cheques and raising additional finance by selling a film camera which McLaren had permanently 'borrowed' from Goldsmith's College – Helen Wellington-Lloyd also lent them £50 – the partners patched up the back of the shop and bought more stock. On the pavement outside they erected a sandwich-board, illustrated with guitars and musical notes, which read 'Let it Rock at Paradise Garage', and commenced trading in November 1971. On the second day Bradley failed to turn up to man his half of the store, so

Casey and McLaren covered for him. After three or four days Bradley still had not reappeared, and the till was bulging. 'What were we supposed to do with the takings?' McLaren wondered. 'Keep the cash in the shop, tuck it under our beds, what?' He requisitioned the shop.

Several weeks later, Trevor Miles, the proprietor who had left his emporium in Bradley's care, returned from a Caribbean honeymoon, walked in and discovered the interlopers. After some haggling he agreed that they could stay, provided they paid a weekly rent of £40. Miles, like many of the young boutique traders at that end of the King's Road, was into drugs, and just wanted some extra cash. McLaren decided to sit it out and claim 'squatters' rights', calculating that even if Miles resorted to legal action they would have at least three or four months in which to trade before the court hearing. But a week later McLaren arrived to find the shop locked. Their stock had been tossed out on to the pavement.

Outraged by this 'injustice', Vivienne turned to their shopkeeping friend Tommy Roberts. 'Oh, Tommy,' she wailed down the telephone, 'the landlord has chucked all our stock out on the street and locked the shop up.' That was illegal, said Roberts, and she should seek redress from the law. He rang his solicitors in the City and made an appointment for Vivienne to see them. She arrived dressed like a slattern in laddered stockings and a mini skirt, with her spiked peroxide hair. After the meeting the non-plussed solicitor – 'an old-fashioned kind of bloke', Roberts remembered – told him: 'Miss Westwood came to see me and we had to walk to court together with her great long winklepickers, the hair, the stockings, the lot!' 'He loved every minute of it,' said Roberts, 'despite the fact that his bill wasn't settled for years.'

Let it Rock was back in business, and now occupied the whole premises. McLaren, Casey and Vivienne (when she wasn't teaching) scoured the unfashionable outer London markets of Hackney, Streatham, Leytonstone and Hendon for merchandise. They amassed old bakelite valve radios, which McLaren restored and displayed on the pavement, a guitar-shaped mirror, of which they had copies made, old records, fanzines, post-war 'skin' magazines like *Photoplay* and *Spick*, postcards of period pin-ups and retro clothing. The booty was hauled back to 430 King's Road.

In imitation of a kitsch fifties front room, the shop was decorated with authentic Festival of Britain-era wallpaper (from a fusty DIY shop in Streatham), a period fridge painted bubblegum pink and black, teak sideboards and formica display cabinets. Rock 'n' roll blasted from a jukebox, and fluorescent pink letters announced the shop's name and creed: 'Teddy boys are Forever – Rock is our business'. Besides vintage records as mainstream as Billy Fury, Little Richard and Elvis Presley, and as esoteric as Hank Ballard and Johnny Guitar Watson, complementary artefacts were sold: Brylcreem, novelty socks decorated with musical notes, plastic earrings and black leather ties with see-through plastic pockets into which were slipped pornographic playing cards. Original, often unworn, fifties clothes were bought from warehouses in the Midlands and on the south coast. Photographs of Billy Fury, James Dean and Marlon Brando were pinned like holy relics onto fake leopardskin, along with Eddie Cochrane's autograph, sent by friends to Shelley Martin, a sales assistant at Let it Rock, but which McLaren commandeered – just as he had taken possession of Paradise Garage, the film camera, books from Foyle's and other people's ideas. He had little respect for the concept of physical or intellectual property, arguing: 'Plagiarism is what the world's about. If you don't start seeing things and stealing because you were inspired by them, you'd be stupid.'

'Hippiedom is dead!' was McLaren and Casey's clarion call. McLaren claimed that he invented retro-chic, but in fact it had emerged back in the late 1950s. There were waves of fifties revivals throughout the sixties, but it was not until 1971 that the look became more than an esoteric backwater. Trevor Miles had traded fifties Americana such as Hawaiian shirts, college jackets covered in baseball or football logos and brightly coloured silk airforce jackets and overalls, some appliquéd on the back with maps of Japan or patriotic eagles. But McLaren's fifties revival was unique in that it celebrated the fifties of Albion, not America. Unlike Americana – the look of the middle-class college kid or the gaudy tourist – McLaren's fifties memorabilia celebrated the working class and the jingoistic instincts of the teddy boy. McLaren himself, remembered William English, one of the shop's customers, looked 'home-grown and working class, not adapted, just like a real old ted'. The merchandise and the accompanying credo had little to do with contemporary fashion. Nevertheless, within two months fashion features on the shop appeared in the *Daily Mirror*, the *Evening Standard* and *Rolling Stone*.

Let it Rock was not only a retro shop, but also a meeting place. Like Ossie Clark and Alice Pollock's Quorum in Radnor Walk off the King's Road in the late sixties, McLaren created a scene in which the like-minded could hang out. Location was vital – 'Harrow or Streatham, forget it! . . . *That* street meant those media people came,' he remembered – along with the popocracy (Jimmy Page, the Kinks, the Bowies, Marianne Faithfull), artists, dedicated followers of fashion and the hard-core teddy boys. Like Haight-Ashbury in San Francisco, Washington Square in New York and Saint-Germain-des-Prés in Paris, the King's Road was a magnet for the young, the curious and the fun-seeking. At that time McLaren was receptive to customers' comments and interested in their lifestyles, and would engage them in conversation rather than subject them to the monologues that were the hallmark of his later trading style. William English was struck that Let it Rock traded 'in complete isolation', surrounded by hippie emporia, and felt that this made them seem 'very fresh, interesting'. He noticed that Vivienne and McLaren clearly felt more affinity with working-class provincials such as himself (he was from Leicester) than with their London neighbours: 'They thought there was more going on in the provinces than in London – they both said as much.' Ben Kelly, a Northern student at the Royal College of Art, was disappointed by the drabness of London until he discovered the shop, which he described as 'a beacon . . . you could become part of their life. You didn't have to buy anything, just get the vibes. It was exciting – better than drugs, really.'

Intoxicated by the attention and the modest commercial success the enterprise was enjoying, McLaren had even less time for family than before: many of his friends were unaware that he even had a child. In the spring of 1972 his grandfather died, leaving Grandmother Rose alone in her flat, only five minutes from Nightingale Lane. When he called on her one day in early December he found her sitting in bed, bolt upright from rigor mortis. His mother, who partly blamed McLaren for not keeping an eye on the old woman, broke off what little contact she still had with him.

Within a few months Let it Rock began running out of original teddy boy clothing, so McLaren co-opted Vivienne, who had made her own clothes since she was a teenager, to run up copies. She was happy to stop teaching, as she had become disillusioned by the class sizes and the conformity demanded by the state system: 'It was impossible to teach anything in such a large class . . . But the naughty children were the smart ones, they've got something. To get out of teaching was not a big jump. I was considered a nuisance when I was a teacher because my sympathies were with the children. If they swore at me, I didn't care, actually. I was already unorthodox in my attitude of what children ought and ought not to do.'

In order to pay for the second-hand sewing machine Vivienne worked on at home, McLaren disconnected the flat's telephone – he could use the one at the shop, and Vivienne, he reasoned, 'was too nervous a person and was used to being alone. She didn't like coming down to the shop and hated having to deal with the phone. It was mostly *my* friends anyway.'

Left undistracted in Nightingale Lane, Vivienne sowed the seeds of her new career, repairing, altering and eventually copying rock 'n' roll clothing. She carefully and methodically unpicked and duplicated original teddy boy garments while Sid Green, an East End tailor whom she regularly consulted, made up the drape jackets in neon colours and fake fur, sequinned or lurex collars chosen by her. With the archivist's exactitude that became her signature, she sourced authentic cloth, buttons and linings and, informed by research in teddy boy clubs, copied and recoloured the look. 'She's a *real* worker,' says Tommy Roberts. 'She was self-taught, taking things to pieces.' What distinguished the merchandise at Let it Rock from the second-hand/ vintage clothing sold at other boutiques was Vivienne's perfectionism. She would restore the clothes to pristine condition, dry cleaning them, repairing the lining and replacing lost buttons with authentic originals.

Despite Vivienne's commitment, McLaren is dismissive of her contribution: 'The fashion industry was in *my* blood, not hers, especially in menswear. My grandparents were tailors. *I* was the Dedicated Follower of Fashion, just like Ray Davies of the Kinks sings, whereas Vivienne was someone who fell into it. I forced her.' He held court at the shop and issued instructions to Vivienne, casting her as a love-slave to his scams, which he amplified into 'a stand against the system'. For many years, when talking to the press he gave the impression that he was the only one involved in the shop – Vivienne did not exist.

Vivienne may have been introduced to the fashion business by McLaren, but it became, in her words, 'a baby I picked up and never put down'. She earnestly taught herself the tailoring craft (McLaren could not thread a needle), and gradually introduced new designs. 'She's quite a formidable force once she sets her mind to it,' one employee recalled. 'She's like a dog with a bone, and she won't give up.' To keep her under his control, McLaren played on Vivienne's insecurities, constantly telling her that she would be 'nothing but a factory worker if it wasn't for me', which was patently untrue.

While Vivienne toiled, McLaren and Patrick Casey reorganised the 'art installation' of 430 King's Road. As Casey was homeless, he dossed on the floor of the shop, hence the musty smell customers noticed on entering. Being a 'speed freak', he would sleep until noon, and consequently the shop rarely opened before lunch. These unorthodox hours amused McLaren, who liked to watch the frustrated customers waiting outside (the practical and disciplined Vivienne would have opened at nine in the morning). To further whet the customers' appetites, McLaren would capriciously announce that a pair of white brothel-creepers, a forty-five or a plastic, guitar-shaped handbag was a 'collector's item – not for sale'. Up to half the merchandise would be teasingly unavailable. McLaren loved to quote Andy Warhol's adage that 'being good at business is the most fascinating kind of art'.

Vivienne would often be summoned at seven or eight in the evening to chauffeur McLaren around in her old olive-green Mini, carpeted with disregarded parking tickets. Sometimes they would go to the Black Raven pub in Bishopsgate in the East End, the venue favoured by the ted revivalists. Dressed as one of them, in a canary-yellow mohair jumper and tight black ski-pants, or a circle skirt and stilettos, Vivienne would mingle with the crowd to research the look or solicit business for the shop. She was adept at ingratiating herself into a scene, particularly in the cause of research; she learnt their dances and shared their enthusiasms. It was when Vivienne was dancing, which she loved, that one could see the unbridled exuberance she had inherited from Dora. McLaren habitually sat in a corner, watching.

Occasionally Vivienne manned the shop, but as yet she was not comfortable with the fashionable King's Road crowd. 'She seemed mumsy and terribly suburban-housewifey, but surrounded by all this incredible gear, to which she didn't seem to relate,' one customer remembered. Vivienne would allow visitors to try on things 'for hours, and it didn't matter if you didn't buy anything'. The hectoring polemicist had yet to emerge.

Given the choice, Vivienne preferred to stay at home sketching, making and thinking about clothes, while McLaren, accompanied by Tommy Roberts, toured the clubs and bars. The two shopkeepers loved to spar, McLaren dismissing Roberts's customers David Bowie and Roxy Music as glam rock *poseurs*: 'I think he got fed up with me,' says Roberts, 'because people used to come into his shop and ask, "Where's City Light Studio [one of Roberts's shops]?" He would charge them ten bob to tell them.'

Let it Rock attracted its own rock customers, including Ringo Starr and David Essex, who ordered clothes for their characters in the rock 'n' roll tribute film *That'll be the Day* (1973), and the cabaret performer Lionel Blair, who dressed the chorus line of his Saturday night television show in fifties copies. Although McLaren was the front man, Vivienne gradually became the stronger personification of Let it Rock, where she was spending an increasing amount of time. For her, the shop represented a commitment to a lifestyle which she disseminated like an evangelical preacher; whereas for McLaren it was simply the stage for a lucrative pose.

Familiarity with the teddy boys soon bred contempt. Claiming that they were disgusted by the teds' racist and sexist tendencies – Vivienne's sense of justice, in particular, was outraged – she and McLaren turned away from it (Casey had left the business). Ethical considerations aside, they were also running out of vintage stock, and were tired of simply copying it. Added to that, the Let it Rock look had caught on. Other local traders were astonished when, having built up Let it Rock's reputation and profitability, Vivienne and McLaren closed the shop in early 1973. But McLaren and Vivienne shared a low boredom threshold, and they now elected, in advance of the pack, to ally themselves to another outlaw youth cult, the motorbike rockers and greasers.

James Dean, the prototypical teenage anti-hero of *Rebel Without a Cause* (1955), and Marlon Brando, the hoodlum biker who terrorises a small town in *The Wild One* (1953), epitomised disaffected American youth. In the spring of 1973, 430 King's Road reopened as Too Fast to Live Too Young to Die (TFTLTYTD), the name having been suggested by their Saturday assistant as a tribute to Dean's early death. Out went the drapes and brothel creepers, in came studded black bikers' leathers, chains, motorcycle memorabilia and oil-stained second-hand Levi's. While many of the Let it Rock clothes had had a tailored elegance, the biker gear was a caricature of fifties rockers. The look (later to be appropriated by the gay community, as epitomised by the American pop group the Village People) was rough and deliberately confrontational.

It was during 430 King's Road's incarnation as TFTLTYTD that McLaren and Westwood began to design slogan-printed T-shirts. They were the first retailers fully to exploit the incendiary impact of these affordable statements of defiance, sales of which were targeted at impressionable teenagers. 'The T-shirt is anti-fashion at its simplest,' they repeatedly declared, intentionally distancing themselves from commercial fashion. It became their core design, serving at the same time as a fashion item, a tool of propaganda and a clarion call to rebellion. In time, the subversiveness and downright scurrilousness of their slogans and designs attracted youthful buyers in direct proportion to the shock and offence they caused to the public at large.

The first T-shirts were relatively insipid, simply advertising Vivienne and McLaren's idols – Marlon Brando, James Dean, Buddy Holly, Elvis Presley – or their affiliations – e.g. 'Vive la Rock'. After unsuccessfully attempting to sell these bland designs at the August 1972 Rock 'n' Roll Festival at Wembley Arena, they converted the lot into knickers. Clearly, the T-shirts needed to be stronger. Vivienne began to customise them, adding tarty marabou feathers and tiny see-through plastic windows, into which a cigarette card of a pin-up girl or a rock idol was slipped. Into others she sewed two zippers which when opened allowed the nipples to peep through. She then came up with a macabre device, evoking a voodoo curse: letters constructed out of chicken bones attached to the T-shirts with chains and spelling out the words 'Perv' or 'Rock'. The bones were collected from Ricky Sky, then a waiter at Leonardo's Italian trattoria opposite 430 King's Road. Vivienne took the discarded chicken carcasses, boiled them to strip them of flesh and gristle, then drilled holes into the bones. Only a dozen or so of these custom-made and highly collectible bone T-shirts were made – the chicken-slaughtering heavy-metal rock singer Alice Cooper bought one – and fakes were to appear on the market in the nineties. Originals now fetch several thousand pounds, and one example hangs today in 430 King's Road, another in Vivienne's Conduit Street shop in Mayfair.

The bone T-shirts demonstrated Vivienne's self-taught, do-it-yourself approach to fashion. Never happier than when sitting alone, immersed in a craft at her kitchen table, she fastidiously drilled, potato-printed and hand-stencilled garments, convinced that she was engaging in the politics of dissent. In customising standard biker wear with Hell's Angel slogans, studs, chains, bones and talismanic rocker motifs such as the skull and crossbones, she had hit upon an approach to clothes design that went straight to the heart of excitable young fans. The formula of customising clothing with slogans became one of her enduring *leitmotivs*

Seething with genuine feelings of protest, fired up by McLaren's invective but frustrated by her own inarticulacy, these didactic clothes became Vivienne's means of carrying their vituperative opinions onto the street on the backs of their customers. Ever the schoolteacher, she crafted clothes to 'instruct' society, and every garment carried an almost sectarian message: the 'Venus' T-shirt, for example, featured horsehair, metal studs and bike-tyre sleeves, while others depicted rock idols made out of glitter. Such tub-thumping pronouncements attested fierce loyalty to a particular style of music and youth culture.

Receptive customers were thrilled by the commitment and zeal of this clothing. The French fashion designer and motorbike enthusiast Jean-Charles de Castelbajac, for example, was so taken with the unexpected juxtapositions of the collaged dadaist T-shirts and their anti-fashion amateurism that he left a note for the proprietor of TFTLTYTD which read: 'I love the things you do. I think we have some common pensives and I would love to meet you.' Coincidentally, he was designing clothes made from domestic rubbish – old floorcloths and blankets – scrawled with phrases from Rabelais. Keenly aware of de Castelbajac's position in France's aristocracy and fashion hierarchy, McLaren was determined to exploit this connection, while Vivienne was thrilled that a 'real designer' had praised her work. Despite their claims to the contrary, both Vivienne and McLaren responded to approval from the establishment. The *Harper's & Queen* style critic Peter York, hearing Vivienne's boasts that she and de Castelbajac were working on similar lines, remembers thinking: 'She was clearly aspiring to be a mainstream designer.'

Several months later McLaren made a trip to Paris and, carrying a huge bottle of Johnnie Walker 'with a label the same colour as his hair' under his arm, called unannounced at de Castelbajac's flat. 'Hi, Charlie!' he began familiarly. 'No one's ever called me that,' de

Castelbajac recalled, and within hours he and McLaren had become firm friends. It was the beginning of a long-lasting alliance.

In August 1973, several King's Road shops were invited to show their wares at the annual National Boutique Show at the MacAlpine Hotel in New York. Feeling hemmed in by domesticity and the routine of shopkeeping, and tempted by a promotional opportunity and the excitement of their first trip to America, Vivienne and McLaren flew to New York. They were accompanied by Gerry Goldstein, a friend of McLaren's from college days. The trio decorated their stall, set up in the hotel bedroom, with an array of T-shirts, teddy boy and rocker clothes and rock 'n' roll memorabilia. Bill Haley and Jerry Lee Lewis hits were blasted down the corridors. Despite amused interest, no orders were taken.

However, Alice Cooper and Sylvain Sylvain, rhythm guitarist for the New York cult band the New York Dolls, paid them a visit. Sylvain and the Dolls' lead guitarist Johnny Thunders had become customers of Let it Rock when they had recently visited London, but they had never met McLaren or Vivienne. Impressed by the retro-dandyism and lewd fifties pin-ups, Sylvain persuaded them to move into the Chelsea Hotel, the dank, downbeat lodgings on West 23rd Street whose residents had included Dylan Thomas, Brendan Behan, Valerie Solanas, and a host of rock groups, artists and writers.

The Dolls introduced Vivienne and McLaren to the heart of New York's rock culture. They found themselves surrounded by a narcissistic hedonism, bent on experimenting with the derangement of the senses. They were interviewed by Andy Warhol's *Interview* magazine about their shop, went clubbing at CBGBs and saw performances by Richard Hell (*né* Myers), the Ramones and Patti Smith, whom McLaren regarded as urban poets. In particular, McLaren was transfixed by Hell and his group Television. Unkempt, degenerate and self-abusive, he wore slashed and safety-pinned clothing. His hair razored into a shag cut and his body daubed with doom-laden poetry, he treated his audience with weary contempt. It was, McLaren felt, as if the very streets of Paris 1968 had come alive in one man, his graffitied flesh like a living wall of protest.

The sardonic, glam rock Dolls – the name referred to their arch transvestism in trashy women's clothes – fused the theatre of the absurd with classic rock 'n' roll anarchy. They feigned sexual ambivalence in order to debunk the *macho* rock star image of success and sexuality. This struck a chord not only among young groupies, but also the older (twenty- and thirty-year-old) art and theatre crowd, Andy Warhol's followers and other musicians like Iggy Pop, David Bowie and Lou Reed. Their act was knowing, louche and dismissive of their fans, but it was not political. It was in New York that McLaren grasped the potential of the disaffected youth market, becoming, according to Sylvain, 'the Dolls' biggest groupie'. Vivienne, however, had not enjoyed the trip, and returned to London declaring that she hated America. She never revised her opinion, later declaring that Americans were 'barbarians' and 'the ultimate philistines', and would not return for two decades.

Back in Britain, economic and social gloom was setting in. Industrial tension escalated into a series of strikes, and following repeated power shortages, a three-day working week was introduced.

Bored with Vivienne, London and the shop, McLaren promptly began an affair with Addie Isman, the wayward daughter of a wealthy New Jersey family who was working at TFTLTYTD. After nights out on the town with Addie, McLaren would return to verbal, and sometimes physical, attacks from Vivienne. Though the affair ended after a few months when Addie returned to America (where she died five years later from a barbiturate overdose), Vivienne became increasingly alert to potential sexual rivals.

Despite McLaren's periodical departures from the Nightingale Lane flat in pursuit of sexual intrigue, Vivienne's tenacity maintained the relationship. She now accompanied McLaren more frequently on his night-time prowlings around clubs and bars. Michael Kostiff, a Northern clubgoer and follower of Chelsea fashions who patronised TFTLTYTD with his spectacularly-dressed German wife Gerlinde, came to know the couple well at this time. During late-night drinking sessions at the Kostiffs', McLaren would hold forth on the ideology of the shop, while Vivienne fed him questions. 'But you know what I think about that,' McLaren would snap. 'Yeah, well I want to hear you say it again,' she would reply. This was her method of learning, parrot-fashion, how to communicate the theories of others, which she would later repeat by rote, with her own idiosyncratic delivery. She was a foil to McLaren, the straight 'man' to his funny man. Having drunk their hosts dry, Vivienne and McLaren would raid the fridge for the last pint of milk, then leave.

The Kostiffs were taken aback that, given the severity of the recession and the duo's avowed allegiance to 'the people', their aggressive didacticism precluded any empathy with or even sympathy for the poor: 'They were big on ideas, and that's a luxury . . . They were unforgiving, not vindictive, but careless . . . and judged the state of the country by the cost of wine or dinner at a fashionable restaurant. Bizarre – not real life!' Michael Kostiff was struck by Vivienne's evident obsession with McLaren: 'She hung on Malcolm's every word. She was quite in awe of him, [his] command of English and his art school and situationist background.' But they were not a loving couple, rather 'hardbitten and definitely not sentimental' towards one another. Tommy Roberts agreed: 'They weren't an overtly loving couple. It was just an interesting twosome. They were strong and ambitious and doing interesting things.'

To McLaren's mind, the presence of Ben and Joe was inconvenient, and they were dispatched to a series of liberal boarding schools. He justified his disregard for them by claiming that he was imbuing them with a spirit of independence. Vivienne, in his thrall, concurred – McLaren was always right. Since the couple could not afford their school fees, the boys would be passed from one school to another once the goodwill had run out: 'They were always being picked up in the middle of the night and shown to another school because they [Vivienne and McLaren] hadn't paid the fees,' says John Rowley, a colleague and flatmate of Joseph's in later life. By the end of the boys' preparatory school education, the couple owed £7,000 in unpaid school fees.

Not yet ten, the boys would have to take their washing to the launderette when they were home from school: 'Vivienne gave me such a free life that I spent most time outside,' says Joe loyally. 'Once I was out very late doing one of my first business transactions, swapping my padlock for a watch. I started to walk home feeling very pleased with myself, when I spotted Mum's Mini. She had been driving around the streets looking for me, obviously worried sick. She jumped out and gave me a real clout.'

Ben was left in no doubt about McLaren's hatred for him. 'He had no time for children,' he remembered, although he did occasionally take the boys on adventures: 'Once we hitch-hiked to Romney Marshes and walked right across a military firing range. Then we hitch-hiked to Anglesey and slept in a barn, and there was this dead sheep with his two back legs chopped off, and Malcolm said there was a madman about and we had to barricade ourselves in.'

Gradually, the boys became more insecure. Joseph was sent to the boarding school Hawkhirst Court in Sussex for two and a half years: 'They were so strict, they just had stupid rules and regulations,' he remembers. 'You had to open all your parcels in front of everyone; the only time you'd get a present was on your birthday. She sent me a Chinese writing set. I've still got it . . . I didn't really like Malcolm, but I didn't hate him,' he continues. 'Once he gave us about fifty comics and a great bag of sweets that kept us going for about five hours.'

For a time Joe boarded at A.S. Neill's radically liberal Summerhill in Suffolk, but even to McLaren's mind 'it was too wild and too free'. He was next sent to St Christopher's. McLaren only realised how lonely Joe was when he came home from one of his schools. He would tease his son by pretending that he, Malcolm, was the King of Portugal (his great-grandparents had been Portuguese Jews), and that Joseph was therefore the heir to the throne. When a letter marked 'Royal Mail' came he'd say, 'It must be for *you*, Joseph.' But despite his entertaining games, the children knew that they were insignificant to McLaren, and that their mother remained under his influence.

They loved their mother, and were fiercely proud of her unorthodoxy. Ben describes her around 1973 as wearing 'really short skirts and having blonde spiky hair. I remember going round to see boarding schools and the other kids were looking up her skirt and I was embarrassed.' If he thought comments by other pupils were disrespectful, he would hit them: 'I love my mum and I loved her then. I used to fight people. They'd say, "Ooh, I like your mum." '

While many of McLaren's friends dismissed Vivienne as no more than his mealy-mouthed and doting girlfriend, those who took the trouble to talk to her alone soon realised that she was a powerful woman who harboured a keen ambition. Gene Krell, a Brooklyn-born Jew who had worked as a doorman at the Salvation nightclub in Manhattan, and who married the Warhol Factory singer Nico, came into the fashion world as a shop assistant at the New York branch of Granny Takes a Trip. By 1973 he was manager of the London boutique (in 1996 he became fashion editor of Condé Nast's *Vogue Korea*). Krell, and Granny Takes a Trip, were the epitome of what McLaren and Vivienne hated – dandy glam rock shopkeepers and their upper-class hippie clientele. But Krell's dress, like his Mr Punch nose and Groucho Marx haircut frizzed out as if by a high-voltage shock, turned heads. He favoured gem-coloured velvet suits, footwear from Gohil, a bespoke cobbler in Camden Town who made patchwork suede Cuban-heeled boots for the 'in-crowd', and garish forties print shirts (made out of material from Pontins, a delightfully dated department store in Kensington). Alternatively, he would wear a multi-coloured kimono printed with overblown chrysanthemums, his three-inch black nails adjusting his unruly squid-black tresses.

Krell was intrigued by the angular creature dressed in a leather, chain-hung mini, with spiked hair, skull earrings and lips painted like a Mondrian grid in three blocks of colour, who occasionally helped at TFTLTYTD (the artist Duggie Fields was inspired by Vivienne's strange make-up to paint an acrylic portrait featuring the tricoloured lips). To Vivienne, other designers and shops were not merely commercial competition, but rival gangs on which to declare war. Didn't they understand that Billy Fury was more significant to the history of pop music than Bob Dylan or the Rolling Stones? Krell would listen amazed as she berated Anthony Price for the glam rock frocks and sharp suits he sold at his King's Road shop Plaza, scoffed at the glitter clothes sold at Alkasura nearby, and dismissed Krell's merchandise, to his face, for its apolitical decadence. A quarrel would ensue, until Vivienne bluntly conceded to Krell, 'Though I hate your look, I really like you.' A lifelong friendship was founded on Krell's admiration for her strength, anarchy and candour, and her love of his loyalty and New York street humour.

Vivienne was clearly beginning to outgrow the shyness that had previously hindered her. 'She was certainly not in Malcolm's shadow,' Krell remembers. 'She looked so visually stunning, whereas he looked like a nerd – a boring rockabilly guy.' Immersed as she now was in the fashion pack, Krell found Vivienne's fiercely anti-fashion stance unique. Despite McLaren's claims to be 'the voice of disenchanted youth', it was commerce and a love of being in fashion that drove him, whereas Vivienne actually believed the propaganda of their cause.

Vivienne's extreme dress and heartfelt haranguing of her customers were beginning to attract attention. On 7 December 1973 *West One* magazine selected her, together with Nell Campbell (nightclub hostess and star of *The Rocky Horror Show*), stylists Louise Doktor and Shelley Martin, and the green-haired Rae Spencer-Cullen (aka the dress designer 'Miss Mouse') as one of the 'London Belles' with the strongest style. John Bishop photographed her for the magazine dressed as a proto-punk in a zippered T-shirt, fishnets and spiked hair. Asked about her ambitions and views, she replied that she wanted to be like a gorilla, her favourite food was brown rice and vegetables, her favourite book was *Summerhill* by A.S. Neill and her favourite song was 'There's No One to Love Me Now' by Shaweez. Vivienne's first appearance in print fuelled her ambition. At a fifties revival concert given by the Shananas, when the band invited someone from the audience up on stage, Tommy Roberts remembers that Vivienne was up there in a flash, 'no messing about, and I knew then she wanted fame. She knew what the game was. She's clever. "She'll get what she wants," I thought.'

The arrival of the New York Dolls in London in November 1973 galvanised McLaren once again, and he devotedly followed them from gig to gig. In January he accompanied them to Paris, where he introduced them to Jean-Charles de Castelbajac. The seeds of punk were apparent in their antics – the rock star cliché of smashing guitars, pouring vitriol on the audience and the press – and their accessories, such as the swastika. Enthralled by the rock world, McLaren nurtured his fantasy of becoming the next Larry Parnes, the Jewish impresario who had managed Billy Fury. To that end he befriended Gloria Jones, the common-law wife of T. Rex's Marc Bolan, and the *New Musical Express* journalist Nick Kent, and started casting about for a band.

By the spring of 1974, class-ridden, economically depressed and seemingly leaderless England was in crisis. Prime Minister Edward Heath called an election on the single issue 'who governs Britain?' Not you! came the overwhelming reply. In this anti-authoritarian political climate, McLaren cranked up his antics. Now bored by youth cults, in April 1974 he closed TFTLTYTD. In New York he had witnessed the extremes of the permissive society. It was there that David Bowie had first openly paraded his bisexuality: 'He would never have had the balls to do that unless he'd been hanging around with Iggy [Pop] and Lou [Reed], because they represented this place across the ocean where things were changing, so fuck all the English hypocrites,' said his wife Angie.

The gradual liberalisation of society set the scene for McLaren, who calculated that one thing that was sure to antagonise the sexually-repressed English was the apparel and artefacts of sexual fetish.

Vivienne and McLaren had first toyed with fetishistic dress when Ken Russell had commissioned them to customise their biker leathers with explicit sado-masochist and Nazi imagery for his musical biopic *Mahler*. (Shirley Russell, the director's ex-wife and the film's costumier, says that neither Vivienne nor McLaren did any work on *Mahler*. The leather-studded S&M costume was designed and made by Lenny Pollock.) Now, in the late summer of 1974, they reopened the refurbished shop under the name 'SEX', brazenly spelt out above the door in huge, spanked-flesh-pink letters cut out of padded PVC, which resembled a malleable Claus Oldenberg pop art sculpture. Naked, headless mannequins were piled, orgy-fashion, on top of one another in the window. Customers passed under the lintel – sprayed with Rousseau's aphorism 'Craft must have clothes but Truth loves to go naked' – and into a sexual romper room. Sheets of elastoplast-pink surgical rubber, as soft and powdery to the touch as a condom, hung down the walls, which were sprayed with quotations McLaren had lifted from pornographic literature, including Valerie Solanas's vitriolic 'SCUM Manifesto' and Alexander Trocchi's *School for Wives* and *Thongs*.

Much of the imagery on the clothes strongly resembled the work of the fifties American artist Eric Stanton, who produced a series of drawings depicting women trussed up in black leather and rubber bondage wear, including faceless rubber hoods, like tethered birds of prey. Labels sewn on to the shoulders of the SEX clothes like epaulettes bore subversive quotations such as: 'The dirty stripper who left her undies on the railings to go hitch-hiking, said, You don't think I have stripped off all these years just for money, do you?' One particularly shocking T-shirt featured a naked pre-pubescent boy provocatively smoking a cigarette – this at a time when the BBC had caused a storm of controversy with a documentary called *Johnnie Go Home*, about a teenager who ran away to London and ended up working as a rent boy. Another bore a graphic image of a naked black man with a large penis.

'French lingerie' (as coy department stores called it) in black or red lace, scissored open for easy access to the sexual organs, left customers in no doubt what game they were expected to play. Displayed on gymnasium exercise-bars alongside the more familiar tools of sado-masochism – whips, chains, nipple clamps, handcuffs and black thigh-high boots – was exotica bought from sub-culture catalogues, such as skin-tight black rubber eyeless masks, the hermetic seal broken only by a tiny breathing tube. These were worn with bodysuits constructed out of two 'skins' of rubber that could be inflated, pressing so hard against the body that they denied it any sight or sound. The focal point of the surgically bleak shop was a huge, grubby double bed laid with a rubber sheet.

'Pornography is the laughter of the bathroom of your mind,' customers were told as they were goaded to disappear behind a screen and dress up in the garb which hung challengingly round the shop. McLaren was greatly influenced by the American 'skinflick' director Russ Meyer, whose films such as *Supervixens* and *Beyond the Valley of the Dolls* were not explicitly pornographic, so much as crammed with camp excess. McLaren and Meyer were two of a kind.

Some of the merchandise, bulk-ordered from catalogues such as 'Scandalous Lingerie & Glamour Wear' from Estelle Lingerie in Walthamstow, which was sent to Estelle's customers in unlabelled, brown-paper parcels, was customised by Vivienne with marabou feathers, lace and leather. Once again, this was not designing, but editing and customising available clothing. Vivienne was not, as yet, a fully-fledged designer.

The couple's attitude to sex was aggressively missionary rather than joyously practised. Like a hectoring Miss Jean Brodie, Vivienne lectured her customers as if in the grip of a disciplined commitment to an idea, rather than a sensuous delight in erotica. She allied herself to McLaren's campaign 'to annoy English people . . . by attacking sexual attitudes, trying to undermine the puritan, philistine basis of our culture', later describing this as 'our first innovation'.

In the context of the time, when sexuality was not freely discussed in any but the most liberal company, to promote what McLaren dubbed 'rubber wear for the street and rubber wear for the office' was astonishingly provocative. *Harper's & Queen* was the only fashion magazine even to refer to SEX's wares, in an anonymous column by Peter York, who jocularly advised readers to avert their eyes when passing 430 King's Road – it was just too shocking.

It is easy to forget just how grey and depressed London – even the King's Road – was in the mid-seventies. Marco Pirroni, the lead guitarist and songwriter of Adam and the Ants, remembers: 'Every day seemed grey, and you still had fog in those days. In my mohair, I'd pull the sleeves down over my hands to stop the cold. You got addicted to the shop. There was nowhere else you wanted to go. Everywhere else was a let-down. It was so tactile; the smell of the rubber, the clothes felt good.'

Viewing the merchandise of SEX from the perspective of the late 1990s, the outrageous edge has been blunted by more explicit images in film, rock videos and fashion, such as the late Gianni Versace's sanitised hooker clothes. But in the context of the relatively naïve mid-seventies, its impact was shocking. SEX attracted curiosity, controversy and custom, and its infamously libertarian crusade was underscored by a series of explicit T-shirts. Classic white T-shirts were bought from Tommy Roberts or imported in bulk from New York in the luggage of Terry Doktor or David Ireland, who later worked at the shop. Never one to leave a classic alone, Vivienne believed that the simple T-shirt could be improved – further simplified. She sat for hours deconstructing it, seeking ways to reduce it to its essence. In the end, she settled on the most basic form. She cut off the arms, ripped the shoulder seams open and knotted them back together, giving the garment the make-do feel of the knotted-hankie 'hat' favoured by the working-class British holidaymaker. Painstakingly researching and experimenting, Vivienne took three days to design a pared-down T-shirt. She cut two simple squares of cotton jersey, and sewed them roughly along the shoulders and down the sides. There was no attempt at attaching superfluous sleeves. It is unlikely that someone with an art-school or pattern-cutting training would have done that. It looked particularly sexy on women, who would provocatively gather the cotton in folds to cup their breasts. After a while, her confidence growing, she turned the T-shirts inside-out to flaunt their home-made scruffiness. The ripping, the customising and the hands-on craft showed that she and McLaren were attacking capitalist modes of production and consumption, and their customers were instructed to live up to the do-it-yourself ethos and the rhetoric printed across their chests.

At first the reconstructed shirts were hand-printed under McLaren's instructions, and after 1975 screen-printed up by his old friend Bernie Rhodes, later to be manager of The Clash, with images and text. Vivienne did not devise the copy on the shirts at this stage. 'She was never someone who could articulate any idea or thought,' says McLaren. 'She did not *have* any ideas. She did not think of herself as being creative, but she was phenomenally good with her hands. She was a great little researcher. She would find a way to make an idea work.'

Vivienne researched into the background of fetish clothing, and became enthralled: 'I had to ask myself, why this extreme form of dress? Not that I strapped myself up and had sex like that. But on the other hand, I also didn't want to liberally *understand* why people did it. I wanted to get hold of those extreme articles of clothing and feel what it was like to wear them.'

It is a common misconception that Vivienne was, or ever has been, interested in street or youth culture *per se*. Rather it was the dress and deeds of any vociferously or militantly sectarian, curiously-dressed or subversive group that fascinated her and stimulated her to spend hours in libraries and museums researching their social and dress history. The groups could be Samurai warriors, the Tolpuddle Martyrs, Shakers or sado-masochists, it did not matter; more important was the chance to study and then emulate the manufacture of their garments.

One of the earliest SEX T-shirts, devised in the autumn of 1974, was a tribal manifesto pinning Vivienne and McLaren's colours to the mast. Entitled 'You're gonna wake up one morning and *know* what side of the bed you've been lying on!', they listed on the left over a hundred 'Hates', starting with 'Television (not the group)' and including Mick Jagger, parking tickets, *Vogue*, 'The narrow monopoly of media causing harmless creativity to appear subversive', the head of the Metropolitan Police, Nigel Weymouth (upper-class proprietor of Granny Takes a Trip), designer Ossie Clark, the rag trade, Bianca Jagger, 'Old clothes, old ideas and all this resting in the country business' and the suburbs (incidentally, the source of most of their custom). In short, the fashionable establishment, the law, the lazy and inert, and all forms of commercial and passively received entertainment. On the right their 'Loves' included Eddie Cochrane, Christine Keeler, SCUM, Great Train Robber Ronnie Biggs, the 1930s Spanish anarchist Buenaventura Durutti, Joe Orton, the band Kutie Jones and his SEX PISTOLS, musical journalist Nick Kent and imagination. In short, rockers, sexual adventurers, rebels, renegades and examples of the do-it-yourself ethos. Peter York was immediately impressed by the T-shirt as 'a very sophisticated insider/outsider thing'. It became a standard editorial device in magazines, to distinguish their caste from others.

Bored once again with Vivienne and dreary London, McLaren

decided that he wanted to 'get the hell out of England', and in November 1974 he announced that he was leaving for New York – never to return. He had set his sights on managing the New York Dolls, with whom he was still obsessed, and chasing Addie Isman, who had returned to the States. In his six-month absence, Vivienne went out with other men, including playwright Jonathan Gems, a decade her junior. Gems was attracted to Vivienne's sci-fi looks, which to him evoked 'the blonde Aryan in *Metropolis*'. Her outrageous creations – be it rubber bondage gear or sexually explicit T-shirt – were now her everyday attire, worn to the launderette, the supermarket and the shop, as well as out on the town at night.

It was clear to Gems that Vivienne was lonely and 'desperate to get involved in things. She felt left out.' On their first evening out together he took her to his new play, *The Dentist*, at the Royal Court in Sloane Square. Coming out of the theatre, Vivienne was silent. Gems assumed that 'she must have hated it, but then she admitted that she had only been to the theatre once before, to see *Oliver!*, the musical.' They moved on to a pub, where Vivienne 'picked up two sailors, which left me humiliated. What she used to do was get really drunk and pick up a guy – just like a man picks up a girl – and she was always into tough types.' On another occasion, Gems invited her to see *Nicholas Nickleby* by the Royal Shakespeare Company at the Aldwych Theatre, but he had to cancel the arrangement. For weeks, Vivienne ignored his calls. Gems asked a colleague of hers what was wrong. 'You don't treat Vivienne like that – it's like a terrible sin!' she explained mischievously. Vivienne, says Gems, regarded herself as 'the diva, the queen, and I'd always been a supplicant to her, which is why she liked me. But as soon as I did anything assertive, I was dumped.' Gems had been useful to Vivienne. He had introduced Vivienne to the world of bourgeois theatre culture, and his girlfriend Jean Seel, a fashion graduate of the Royal College of Art and a designer for the boutique Alkasura, had gone round to Nightingale Lane on many occasions to teach her to cut patterns. But now he was no longer a compliant acolyte, she had no use for him.

In 1975 Vivienne also met Nils Stevenson, an art student who worked on a stall in Chelsea's Beaufort Street market, a few hundred yards up from 430 King's Road. He was attracted by Vivienne's 'dynamic and uncompromising attitude', and describes himself as having had a crush on her. She would drive to Richmond, where he was living in 'a posh house owned by a big-time drug dealer', and they would go clubbing together. 'She was awfully naïve about sex,' he recalls. 'Snogging her was like snogging a schoolgirl. She didn't quite know what to do.'

Though Vivienne had become the powerful embodiment of McLaren's latest wheeze, her role was to be dramatically superseded by an unflinchingly tough shop assistant. The punk icon and actress Jordan, *née* Pamela Rooke, made her first pilgrimage to TFTLTYTD in 1973 from Seaford, a sleepy Sussex town with a large retired population on the south coast of England. She was to become the most eccentric and original character of the punk movement, and usurped Vivienne as its female icon, much to her chagrin.

Jordan's short, sexily curvaceous figure (the antithesis of Vivienne's spiky physique) had been ballet-trained, enabling her to maximise the impact of her modest five foot four inches height. Expelled from school, by 1973 she had created a look, largely culled from charity shops, that was part Bowie, part fifties rocker. She would team, for example, a gold lamé skirt held out with stiff net petticoats with a circle-stitched, conical fifties bra (worn with nothing over it) and gold winklepickers. Her toilette was fastidiously complicated, taking at least two hours to complete every morning. Dramatic strokes of black kohl defined her eyes, recalling the feline maquillage of Elizabeth Taylor in *Cleopatra*, and in contrast to her white peroxided hair, which was swept up like spun sugar into a brittle beehive. A whiff of acrid hairspray hung in the air behind her click-clacking steps.

This astonishing composite was a triumph of artifice over nature. Mainstream fashion was promoting a healthy, natural, outdoor beauty, but Jordan had no truck with such insipidity. Throughout 1973 she made regular pilgrimages to 430 King's Road, acquainting herself with Michael Collins, a homosexual drug addict who managed the shop from 1972 to 1982. Determined to land a job at the cult boutique, she preposterously reasoned that in order to do so, she should train at Harrods. So, despite her appearance, she served as a sales assistant on the fashion floor of the Knightsbridge store, calling in at SEX on her way home to Seaford. 'I went to talk to Michael for ages, and I remember being really precocious, and I tried to sell myself to get the job,' she recalled. Collins fobbed her off, but a few days later he summoned her to start work that afternoon. Jordan became the physical personification of the store in its next two guises – sexual fetish and anarchic punk – and was to be cast as the celluloid icon of punk in Derek Jarman's bleak 1978 film *Jubilee*.

Unlike Vivienne, Jordan was not beholden to McLaren. She dressed sexually in order to educate and arouse, rather than to act as his billboard. She would combine, for example, a T-shirt sloganed 'Venus', the Roman goddess of love, with black knickers and ripped black stockings held up by suspenders against her bare thighs. Every morning, in this state of virtual undress, she proudly boarded the commuter train from Seaford and headed into London. 'I was constantly being harassed or hit,' she remembers with deadpan candour. 'Men would slide too close to me, and one woman threatened to hit me as my clothes were upsetting her child.' Observing the verbal and sometimes physical savaging that Jordan endured every day, one considerate British Rail conductor allowed her to travel alone in a first-class compartment. 'Jordan would take on anybody,' remembers Ben Kelly. 'Robert Plant [the rock star] had a go at her standing there in rubber and underwear – that was a big mistake! Don't try it, she's much too sharp for you. She had a cutting tongue . . . Men worshipped her.'

Just as the infant Vivienne had bemoaned the arrival of her sister Olga, she now viewed this independent and handsome female as a threat to her centre-stage role. Jordan's first impression of Vivienne was of 'an imposing figure who was rather cautious about me'. This was an understatement. 'Intimidating' is the word most often used by those who visited SEX, and it was Jordan, rather than Vivienne, who most powerfully instilled this atmosphere. Standing by the rubber-dressed bed, clad in a studded leather bra, girdle and stilettos, her hair topiaried and lacquered up six inches above her crown, she would knowingly scan the customer through thickly kohled eyes, without a hint of humour or solicitation. What had you come to buy? A spanking? A harangue? A humiliation? 'If you want the epitome of imposing and intimidating,' she says, 'that's what I was. People had to have courage to walk into that shop.'

To be fitted for a bespoke rubber bodysuit demanded bravery. The customer was invited behind the screen, where Jordan or Vivienne took numerous measurements. Men and women from all walks of life – prostitutes, bankers, truckers, fashion-victims – underwent the ordeal. One day Jordan was behind the screen with 'a proper businessman' who was frantically struggling, in a puff of talcum powder (used to ease the body into the rubber), to get his naked body into his new skin when his elbow knocked down the screen. 'He'd only got it up to his knees. Yeah!' says Jordan. 'He was really embarrassed.' The shop was crowded with sniggering youths.

Alan Jones, a customer and later an assistant there, says that a number of customers became so excited by the merchandise that they would disappear behind the screens to masturbate. The staff found this quite acceptable. Once a customer trying on a rubber mask began crying out for help. 'You go, Jordan,' said Vivienne. 'No, you go.' Eventually Vivienne went to the man's assistance, and from behind the screen came whimpers and slapping noises as he tried to unzip his face. When Vivienne emerged, flustered and sweating, the two dominatrixes lost their icy pose and burst into giggles. 'But it was never *at* these people, because we were selling these clothes for a reason. It was serious and a whole new world,' says Jordan. Like Vivienne, she hoped that the gear would provoke a sexual revolution in England, as the repressed discovered the power of deviance.

One regular middle-aged customer, always dressed in a three-piece suit, had a worryingly ruddy face, the veins throbbing through his blood-reddened flesh. Was it stress, high blood pressure or an impending heart attack that caused this flush, the staff speculated. One day while undressing him, Jordan discovered that under his collar and tie he habitually wore a band of rubber around his throat which practically garrotted him. Restriction was his kick. For such aficionados, 'it wasn't a passing thrill, they were just genuinely interested in the clothes. It was serious to them. They weren't leering perverts, and most of them were heterosexual, not homosexual. It might be a sweeping statement, but homosexuals were more into the leatherwear, and the rubber wear was really a specific heterosexual market.'

Utterly uninhibited about either sex or her far from perfect body shape, Jordan became a cult figure, and her following flocked to the shop to admire her performance. Every day she would look different, like a living art object. She hand-painted bold stripes onto a plain Oxford cotton man's shirt, for example, and pinned communist and Nazi emblems onto her clothing – ideas which were copied and developed by Vivienne. Boys from the council estate opposite the shop had Jordan's image tattooed onto their arms. One of her keenest admirers was the television newsreader Reginald Bosanquet. After a liquid lunch he would typically arrive with a bouquet for Jordan, purchase a few items for 'his girlfriend', then stagger down the three steep steps out onto the King's Road.

A coterie of strong women gravitated to SEX either as customers – Siouxsie Sioux (later lead singer of the Banshees), Margi Clarke (television presenter), 'Little Helen' Wellington-Lloyd (artist), Gerlinde Kostiff (club proprietor) and Toyah Willcox (singer and actress) – or as staff – Jordan, Chrissie Hynde (lead singer of the Pretenders), Debbie Wilson and Tracey O'Keefe. Living up to the shop's theme, some of the other, transient young assistants allegedly supplemented their wages by working as prostitutes. But their overtly sexual gear was not worn to pull men – 'We just thought of it as fashion.'

Vivienne, however, did not support her female associates, but regarded them with suspicion. She and Jordan were the most ferocious females in the pack, but Vivienne was jealous of Jordan's sexual power. In pique, she could treat other female staff with condescension, masked as mothering, and on a number of occasions, feeling threatened by or envious of their sexual attractiveness, she attacked and eventually sacked them. She and Chrissie Hynde once went to a Roxy Music concert together. When Bryan Ferry came onstage with a group of backing singers dressed in sexy US Army uniforms Vivienne leaped to her feet and yelled, 'You sexist bastard!' She was thrown out by bouncers, but Hynde chose not to leave with her. To Vivienne, this was tantamount to treachery, and Hynde was summarily dismissed, Vivienne pointing to the door and melodramatically declaiming: 'Go with the flow, and it's going that way.'

Nils Stevenson remembers many similar banishments by Vivienne and McLaren: 'Adam [Ant], Marco [Pirroni], Nick Kent and me were all banned from the shop. It was about your commitment; that was what was awfully attractive about them. It was 100 per cent or nothing.'

Jordan says, 'Vivienne's always been very different with men and women, and I used to think she just looked at people's exterior and what they dressed like too much. But I also think it's to do with how she can mould someone. I had my own mind and vision about how I looked and dressed, I wasn't someone she could mould, and she just likes to treat people like a project, the way she did with Debbie and Tracey and [later] Sarah Stockbridge. She'd send them to Keith of

Smile to have their hair done and then have photos of them taken.'
Looks alone could prompt Vivienne to employ people. Bella Freud,
daughter of the painter Lucien Freud, longed to join her sister Rose
on the staff of 430 King's Road. She was turned down until 1976,
when Vivienne happened to notice her in a nightclub with her hair
shorn, and employed her on the spot.

In 1975 Vivienne boasted to Jordan, 'Me and Malcolm are
eccentrics,' but Jordan had begun to notice how calculating Vivienne
could be: having seen the admiration Jordan and McLaren received
for being different, she determined to work on her own image. Simon
Barker too never believed that Vivienne was naturally eccentric: 'She
just copied Malcolm and developed this persona; but it wasn't her.'

Meanwhile, in New York McLaren had found the Dolls in a miasma
of narcotics and alcohol – their drummer Billy Murcia had died, and
the band was going nowhere. With the help of Marti Thau, the owner
of Flip, the New York and London chain selling American second-hand
'classics', McLaren inveigled himself into the Dolls' circle as their
unofficial and unpaid manager. A new look and new songs were needed
to turn these boys into a successful band, McLaren decided. Their
image rather than their music excited him, and he wanted to exploit
them, to project onto them his Maoist/situationist notions. The Dolls,
for their part, had no interest in politics.

Johnny Thunders, the band's guitarist, had just written a song
called 'Red Patent Leather', and it was from this that McLaren –
acting more as the band's 'haberdasher', according to New York rock
photographer Bob Gruen, than their manager – took his sartorial cue.
Deliberately playing on American Cold War fears of 'Reds under the
bed', McLaren styled the band in PVC jeans and red T-shirts, and
photographed them against a massive red backcloth printed with the
hammer and sickle. McLaren sent the group's measurements back
home to London, and Vivienne ran up the clothes. Even a tenuous
link to McLaren was worth working for, she felt. By February 1975,
the new-look Dolls were ready to perform again. It was a disaster.
After several fruitless months of struggle in New York, McLaren
decided to launch them in Britain. In May he returned to England,
Vivienne and an opportune scandal.

Michael Collins, the manager of SEX, had been interviewed by the
Metropolitan Police following information that the notorious criminal
known as the Cambridge Rapist, who eviscerated his six, mainly

student victims after raping them, had bought his full-face leather mask with the word 'Rapist' on the forehead from the shop, and was living in London. McLaren decided to exploit the rumours that he had bought his mask from SEX – something Vivienne was loath to do. 'I was sure it was one of our customers,' he says, 'so I phoned Scotland Yard and they came to interview me and I wound up in all these newspapers holding the mask and smiling at it. It caused so much publicity that we were inundated with people coming to buy more of them.'

He also asked Vivienne to produce a Cambridge Rapist T-shirt, which showed the notorious leather mask over the words 'It's Been a Hard Day's Night'. (The caption recalled an earlier sexual scandal, the death in 1969 of the Beatles' manager Brian Epstein following a bout of drugs and sado-masochism.) Marco Pirroni remembers Vivienne justifying the shirt to him by saying: 'He was a customer and we thought he should be protected, so we did the T-shirt because ultimately no one is innocent.' This proved to be a publicity stunt too far. 'Wearing something on a shirt was a way of endorsing it – you only wore things you were a fan of,' one customer pointed out. Vivienne was furious about the 'bad publicity', but McLaren insisted that all publicity was good publicity.

With hindsight, Vivienne now praises McLaren for his manipulative skills: 'My reaction was the normal, I'd say stupid, reaction because it had no fantasy to it. Imagine, I wouldn't have anything to do with the press!' She was not to forget the lesson, learnt at McLaren's feet, of opportunistically toying with the press and defying the public's sense of propriety.

The look purveyed by SEX was hardening, and becoming more intimidating. 'It was sadistic,' says Michael Kostiff, 'with a smoked-glass door that was closed. You couldn't see into the shop. Friends would say, "Can I come in there with you?" particularly as it had SEX in huge pink letters above the door. It was very shocking at the time.' Teenagers flocked to SEX in search of any item that would anger their parents, teachers, elders and the public at large. Adolescent girls paraded down the King's Road in Cambridge Rapist T-shirts, cocking a snook at horrified passers-by. 'I thought it was fucking great,' McLaren declared, 'all these kids buying the shirts and going down the local disco wearing 'em. Those ideas really invigorated kids. They saw them as slightly shocking, and that was all that was important, to be shocking, to annoy a few people because they felt so lethargic.' Favouring neither sex nor drugs as an antidote to his boredom, McLaren got his kicks from voyeurism, the outrage of mainstream opinion.

By the summer of 1976, according to Alan Jones, who had now joined the staff of SEX, the shop was taking quite a lot of money, but it was never banked – Vivienne and McLaren simply used it to live and to make more clothes. When two tax inspectors arrived at 430 King's Road one day, Vivienne whispered urgently to Jones, Michael Collins and Jordan, who were serving, 'Just pretend you're customers!'

Jones, who later became a critic specialising in horror films, styled himself in an aggressively homosexual manner. Wearing tight black leather jeans and black see-through rubber T-shirts from SEX, he would apply stage blood to his arms and chest and strap a hypodermic syringe to his arm. Before the curtain went up on the first night of the musical *A Chorus Line* at the Drury Lane theatre, he was approached by the manager and informed that the performance would not begin until he removed his swastika armband.

The first SEX T-shirts had been printed by hand on Vivienne's kitchen table with a child's printing set and stencils. Each was hand-stamped, and many were customised – with marabou feathers, horsehair, lace, studs or shoulderpads cut from rubber tyres – and hand-inscribed with fabric dye. The later T-shirts were screen-printed. As the months passed, other villains joined the Cambridge Rapist in the rogues' gallery of anti-heroes and rebels celebrated on cotton. Whether the eighteenth-century highwayman Dick Turpin, Charles Dickens's Fagin and his Artful Dodger, or modern mass murderers and terrorists, all were lauded as freedom fighters who attacked the confinement of the moral majority.

The irreverent 'Mickey and Minnie' and 'Snow White' T-shirts attacked the Disneyfication of childhood. In Vivienne and McLaren's eyes, the American entertainment industry had robbed children of their imagination and left them dependent on a commercially-driven cartoon culture. 'Mickey and Minnie' showed the Disney icons fornicating, Mickey's ear defaced by an anarchist symbol, while Snow White was surrounded by sexually excited dwarfs.

McLaren sought scandalous material from every source – political, sexual, social. Probably the most notorious of SEX's shock-tactic T-shirts was 'Two Naked Cowboys'. Face to face in Stetsons and boots, naked from the waist down, two men stand with penises drawn – dangling so close that they almost touch. Alan Jones was arrested in Piccadilly Circus in August 1975 for wearing the shirt, and on 7 August the police raided the shop and McLaren and Vivienne were arrested.

A meeting was held between Vivienne, McLaren, Jones, Nils Stevenson and Gene Krell at the Portobello Hotel, where Jones worked as the night porter. Stevenson remembers that Vivienne and McLaren promised to back Jones at his trial, but they failed to turn up on the day. With no supporters in court, Jones pleaded guilty and was fined £30. Nicholas de Jong, then the court correspondent of the *Guardian*, asked him afterwards why he hadn't defended himself and taken a stand about creative freedom. The case made the front page of the *Guardian* the following day, and a number of letters in support of Jones were written to the editor. Jones remains bitter about the whole incident: 'They didn't even pay the fine! I got the shop a lot of publicity, but it did fuck-all for me!'

After a second, farcical court hearing in November, in which the judge insisted that the space between the cowboys' organs be measured in court with a school ruler, Vivienne and McLaren were charged with 'exposing to public view an indecent exhibition' and fined £50. They continued to sell the T-shirts one at a time from under the counter, hiding the rest of the stock in a flat above the shop. The police conducted surprise raids but never found them, because the flat was accessed from the next-door building.

Toying with the theme of sex, Vivienne came up with a strangely surreal design: a pair of naked female breasts printed on a T-shirt's chest. The confusing sexual image, and the shocking displacement caused by seeing it worn by a man, was to reappear in her collections a decade later. SEX clothing was not usually erotic.

By turning S&M gear into a defiant fashion, removing it from the privacy of the bedroom and flaunting it in a juvenile, 'Up yours!' manner in the street, Vivienne and McLaren robbed it of erotic mystery and turned it into combat gear for a post-permissive sexual liberation adolescent army. Passion ended in fashion. The couple's very language was confrontationally righteous rather than alluringly seductive. Nils Stevenson remembers that because the clothes sold at SEX were so 'kinky', many people assumed that Vivienne and McLaren must have had a 'particularly sexual relationship, and that being into a particular

kink or perversion bound them together'. Only later did he realise
how sexually naïve they both were, and that what they actually shared
was an ability to be obsessed by another person. Vivienne became
intrigued, for example, by one client who was a prostitute: 'It was a
strange world to Vivienne, and she became really besotted by her and
what she did to her clients.'

When feminists argued that SEX's sado-masochist accessories
degraded women, Vivienne hit back with the rhetorical question, *who*
was being degraded? Certainly not her dominatrix troops. The threat
– if not the delivery – of sexual ravaging by these teenage harridans
challenged traditional views of the man's role as sexual aggressor.
'We're not just here to sell fetish clothing,' Vivienne claimed in the
pages of the sex magazine *Forum*, 'but to convert, educate, liberate
. . . we want to take it out of the bedroom and onto the streets.' For
McLaren, profit and amusement were the motives, but Vivienne
believed that their campaign would irrevocably alter English attitudes
to sex.

It was not to be. The SEX manifesto had little appeal beyond the
shop's loyal young following, and it encountered the same aversion as
the Rational Dress Movement, founded in 1884 to promote healthy
and appropriate women's clothing, had done a century earlier. A
political manifesto pinned onto a new style of garment rarely persuades
the public to adopt it. It took the alluring oils of the Pre-Raphaelite
painters and, more powerfully, the exotic Eastern promise of
Diaghilev's orientalism to entice fashionable women to loosen their
robes, discard their unhealthy corsets and live a little. Vivienne and
McLaren's support for Valerie Solanas's violent rampage against the
opposite sex was hardly libido-boosting, as the opening sentence of
her 'SCUM Manifesto' suggests:

> Life in this society being, at best, an utter bore and no aspect of
> society being at all relevant to women, there remains to civic-
> minded, responsible, thrill-seeking females only to overthrow the
> government, eliminate the money system, institute complex
> automation and destroy the male.

Many of the young – and most of those attracted to the shop were
still adolescent – were asexual, homosexual or sexually unsure. Their
naïve and playful dressing-up lightened the image of the darker context

which McLaren and Vivienne were dabbling in. Simon Barker, then a shy suburban teenager from Bromley who shopped at SEX, explains: 'We did want to shock, but not in a tacky way. We were really into looking great – we felt great. We didn't want to look the same as everyone else . . . People used to call us street theatre, and we just thought everything else was boring.' McLaren and Vivienne's designs may have been calculated to challenge received opinion, but the kids just wanted to annoy their elders and have a good time. The look was simply the precursor to punk, a singularly asexual style.

McLaren claimed that one of Vivienne's breasts had deflated after Ben's birth, making her 'very self-conscious about that when she was naked'. Whether this was true or not, by now Vivienne's physical self-confidence was blossoming. In the name of free speech and free action she would totter around the shop on high heels, dressed in a totally see-through skin-tight pink rubber T-shirt or négligée, while McLaren, more timidly dressed, sat watching the customers. No one, however, was as fearless as Jordan. While Vivienne never, to Simon Barker's recollection, wore see-through rubber in the street during the day, preferring to dress in leather or PVC jeans and a T-shirt, 'like a tomboy', Jordan dared to wear the most outrageous SEX gear as if it was normal clothing in her day-to-day life: 'Jordan thought she looked great, and she could cope with the admiration and the abuse. She was so sure of herself. I don't think Vivienne would have coped with that.' Barker recalls that on the one occasion when Vivienne did turn up at his flat dressed outrageously in a rubber bodysuit, 'she kept going on about it as if it was a big thing. Vivienne didn't go out like that a lot. Jordan did.'

Will England, a student at the London International Film School, photographed Vivienne in the shop early one summer morning in 1975 while McLaren was out of town. She posed in front of a piece of fetish sculpture, a nail-studded leg (by Lawrence Daniels, later to become a multi-millionaire by patenting the holograms used on credit cards) draped in a black chain-hung T-shirt trimmed with horsehair tails and menacingly stretching a 'blind' black rubber mask. To England's surprise, Vivienne 'volunteered to wear the pink rubber bodysuit – she was not at all shy', and followed his directions like a chillingly blank mannequin. It was an exhibitionist pose, not one that, despite Vivienne and McLaren's claims to the contrary, indicated a liberated attitude.

A woman dressed in this gear, Vivienne argued, was courageously exploring sexual self-determination. This was a poor argument. In the mid-seventies, fashion was under attack from the feminist movement. Fashion, it was argued, simply pandered to the stereotypically sexist image of women. In protest, some feminists adopted an extreme form of asexual, workaday dress.

Neither Vivienne nor McLaren was a feminist, and the appropriation of Vivienne's work by certain writers and commentators in the movement was ill-considered. Ted, rocker and biker uniforms were patently macho and focused on men: their gangs' attendant women were dressed and treated as sexual chattels. Like a Hell's Angel woman, Vivienne's adoption of subversive S&M dress was not remotely feminist. Simon Barker argues: 'Vivienne throughout her career has made women sexy by making them in control of their sexuality rather than suppressing it or playing a passive role. That's what the feminists hate most about Vivienne, because it's much more threatening to them and their beliefs when women want to take control of their sexuality . . . But Vivienne put them in control of those things, and they wear them for themselves and for the power those clothes give them. They can deliver or not, but the choice is theirs.'

This is a strength accorded to Vivienne's work by others, rather than a motive that she herself fixed upon. She was, and has remained, in thrall to a series of manipulative men, from whom she has tolerated disrespect and abuse because she was convinced that it was only through these men that she could transcend her background and make something of herself. One employee remembers Vivienne telling her: 'Malcolm used to kick me and kick me. I think he just wanted to kick me right out of his life. Men get away with so much, don't they?' At the same time, Vivienne failed to develop profound friendships with her own sex, casting weak young women as dolls to be dressed up, and strong ones as sexual and intellectual threats. To view her as a feminist, even a maverick one, is rash.

In the mid-eighties, elements within fashion and feminism encouraged a détente, epitomised in 1985 by the action taken in Paris by the feminist bookshop Maison des Femmes, which devoted its windows to the work of the French designer Sonia Rykiel. Reappraising Vivienne's work, some journalists have attempted to appropriate her antics and clothes to the feminist cause, but they fail to understand (easy to do, since much of her thinking is fractured and inarticulately communicated) that her pronouncements were essentially not liberating. She simply wished to please McLaren, to practise his sensationalist creed and to attract the public's attention, just as she had done as a teenager by wearing her marguerite earrings.

But McLaren's youthful pranks had turned nasty, and he was prepared to go further. Since the New York Dolls had collapsed, and Richard Hell refused to join McLaren's planned London version of the band, the self-styled Fagin had to find his own street urchins to perform his situationist pranks. They had been lurking in the background, approvingly listed under 'Loves' on the 'What Side of the Bed' T-shirt in the autumn of 1974 under the name Kutie Jones and his SEX PISTOLS. Into the limelight stepped four working-class teenagers. The aspiring impresario's first step was to abbreviate their name to the more threatening 'Sex Pistols'.

Above: Vivienne's childhood home from 1954 to 1957, the post office at 36 Manchester Road, Tintwistle.

Above right: Vivienne at primary school in Hollingworth.

Right: The Glossop Grammar School girl proudly turned out in her uniform. She customised the skirt to hug the hips, and sliced a split up the back for added effect.

Below: Vivienne (left) on the town in 1957 with schoolfriends Maureen Purcell (centre) and Eileen Mellish (second from right).

Vivienne's first press appearance: chosen as one of 'London's Belles' for *West One* magazine, December 1973. She wears a pinstripe suit, fishnets and Let it Rock patent boots. Her hair is razored into spikes and gelled to stand erect, a style that David Bowie later adopted.

The exterior of SEX, 430 King's Road, in 1976, just before it was redesigned as Seditionaries. The right-hand window features naked torsos, the left a Karl Marx 'Anarchy' shirt.

Johnny Rotten in Paris, 1976, dressed in the prototype black sateen bondage suit.

SEX 'Tits' T-shirt (1975); best worn by a man.

The decorative potential of safety pins was Johnny Rotten's (via Richard Hell in New York), not Vivienne's idea. Rotten wears a customised school blazer, McLaren's Breton beret and peg trousers. He is surrounded by Paul Cook of the Sex Pistols, Sue Catwoman, Siouxsie Sioux of the Banshees and Little Debs.

The quintessential punk muslin, 'Destroy', from Seditionaries. It features a swastika, an inverted image of the crucified Christ loosely based on one of McLaren's favourite paintings, Mathias Grünewald's *Crucifixion* (1515), a postage stamp customised with the Queen's severed head and the opening lyrics of 'Anarchy in the UK', by the Sex Pistols.

Seditionaries blue cotton parachute shirt with strap harness, printed with situationist slogans such as 'Only Anarchists are Pretty'.

Simon Barker in a hand-made 'Venus' T-shirt from Too Fast to Live Too Young to Die, leather trousers from SEX and bondage boots. Jordan is in Seditionaries string and mohair jumper, bondage trousers and spider boots.

Vivienne, Johnny Rotten
and Jordan, 1976.

Below: Loving every
second: Vivienne is
arrested on the night of
the Queen's Silver
Jubilee, 7 June 1977.

Right: McLaren and Vivienne leave Bow Street Magistrates' Court with Jamie Reid after being bailed out by Richard Branson following their Jubilee night arrests. Vivienne wears her towelling Seditionaries jacket, fastened with rubber buttons, and bondage trousers. Her close-cropped, razored and bleached hair pre-empts Annie Lennox's urchin cut.

Left: American buyers walked out when they saw Vivienne's drawing of a penis on flesh-coloured knickers. 'Pagan V', spring/summer 1990.

Right: The soon-to-be-disgraced Italian Foreign Minister Gianni di Michelis takes time out from the G7 talks in London in July 1991 to invite his tailor to lunch.

Left: The queen of sartorial parody dressed in a tweed crown, the 'barrel' dress and Rocking Horse shoes from 'Harris Tweed', autumn/winter, 1987-88.

Gary Ness: 'one of the last gurus of the Western world', according to his protégée, Vivienne.

Tatler magazine's April Fool cover, 1989. Michael Roberts recognises the similarity between Vivienne and Prime Minister Margaret Thatcher. *Tatler* added the strapline: 'This woman was once a punk.'

4 CARTWHEELING TO CASUALTY

May 1975–1978

'Successful demonstrations are not necessarily those which
mobilise the greatest number of people, but those which
attract the greatest interest among journalists. Exaggerating
only slightly, one may say that fifty clever folk who can make
a successful "happening" get five minutes on TV, can make as
much political effect as half a million demonstrators.'

Pierre Bourdieu

'When music moves from the music section to the front page
of the newspaper, you're in trouble.'

Danny Fields

'Punk is like squeezing spots.'

Jamie Reid to Celia Lyttelton, 1986

Punk is a state of mind, and was a fashion. It had the greatest impact
on Western popular culture – from music to fashion, from graphic
design to politics – of any youth movement since the hippies in the
1960s. Yet the hard-core of the cult lasted a mere thirty months, from
the summer of 1975 to January 1978, and was centred in London on,
at most, two hundred teenagers. It was led by a handful of *agents
provocateurs* in their late twenties and was spawned in a small, highly
stylised shop in West London. Nevertheless, its reverberations
continue today beyond Britain's shores. Culling imagery and slogans
from many cultures and epochs, it was post-modernist in its irony
and fusion of disparate styles, and unmistakably English.

While the roots and impact of punk have excited much debate, it
was a handful of exceptional individuals who made the movement so

influential, idiosyncratic and seductive. And those individuals were all English. In its essential Englishness, punk was continuing a phenomenon seen in the 1950s with skiffle, and in the pop music of the mid-sixties (and perhaps in the 1990s in the worldwide success of 'Britpop'). Colin MacInnes, in his essay 'Pop Songs and Teenagers', identified this Englishness:

> The paradox is that the bearded skiffle singers with their Yankee ballads, and Tommy Steele and his 'rock'-style songs, seem so resoundingly, so irreversibly English. I don't at all deny an [American] *influence* (which, incidentally, has been going on ever since ragtime hit this country before World War I). But the kids have transformed this influence into something of their own . . . in a way that suggests, subtly, that they're almost *amused* by what has influenced them. Put an English teenager beside an American, and you'll see the difference: our vision is less streamlined, less pattern-perfect and more knobbly, homely, self-possessed.

Competing claims − of nation and class − have bedevilled the debate over punk's origins. 'Punk', the word, and 'proto-punk', the style, originated in New York, becoming common currency there when three high-school friends, Legs McNeil, John Holstrum and Ged Dun, set up a magazine called *Punk* in 1975. Its contents reflected their own interests: 'television reruns, drinking beer, getting laid, cheeseburgers, comics, grade-B movies, and this weird rock 'n' roll that nobody but us seemed to like: the Velvets, the Stooges, the New York Dolls . . .'

Those who argue that the movement originated in America cite garage bands and the performers at CBGBs in New York, particularly Richard Hell, the New York Dolls and Tom Verlaine, as the proto-punks. The first, small, British punk coterie − the Sex Pistols and half a dozen rival bands, their earliest fans, the 'Bromley Contingent' (christened by Caroline Coon of the *Melody Maker*) and their hangers-on − claimed that the movement was a peculiarly British, specifically London, phenomenon, and jingoistically downplay any transatlantic influence. Jordan, the female icon at the heart of the movement, insists that 'punk could only have happened in England. I'm a great fan of the British people. I think we're the forerunner in all things that are *avant-garde* in art and, in particular, fashion.' This blunt chauvinism lay at the roots of the movement's appeal, in much the same way that skinheads had drawn upon the emotional lure of 'I'm Backing Britain' in the 1960s. (The country in which punk has retained its strongest following in the 1990s is Germany, where some are still seduced by its most extreme aggressive, anti-liberal yobbishness.)

With the help of his London followers McLaren developed the American inspiration into a British phenomenon, while acknowledging the significance of Richard Hell: 'Here was a guy looking like he'd just grown out of a drain hole . . . covered in slime . . . no one gave a fuck about him. And looking like he'd didn't really give a fuck about you! He was this wonderful, bored, drained, scarred, dirty guy with a torn T-shirt. And this look of this spiky hair, everything about it – there was no question that I'd take it back to London. I was going to transform it into something more English.' The Atlantic crossing transformed the nature of punk: even the title of one of Hell's songs, 'The Blank Generation', metamorphosed into something more violent and dangerous. Whereas Hell used 'blank' to mean merely nameless, the British music press came to interpret it as vacant, or void.

Within Britain, working-class fans underestimated the role played in the movement by its middle-class, art-school leaders; while the largely middle-class commentators who have picked over the bones of punk in their writings have lent it a misplaced grandeur, over-intellectualising the raw, hormone-driven, adolescent instincts to shock one's elders, exclude outsiders, get drunk, get laid and have fun. They have placed too much emphasis on McLaren's half-baked situationist didactics, retrospectively according the movement an inflated political importance, and thereby flattering the pop Svengali's conceit. Johnny Rotten made the point bluntly: 'All that talk about the French situationists being associated with punk is bollocks!' But while McLaren had only a limited understanding of the situationists' philosophy (he could not read French), what he did grasp was the movement's visual imagery.

Compared with their French counterparts, British youth was not attracted to philosophising in cafés. In the sixties, while young Americans protested against the Vietnam war, and the French conflated philosophy and trade union demands to create *les évenements*, the British only tinkered with protest. This absence of intensity meant that punk never acquired real political significance, though many hoped it would.

Boy George felt that 'it became political and all the things it was never meant to be. It was popular to pontificate about anarchy or socialism. All it was about in the beginning was dressing up and looking ridiculous and having fun.' Keith Wainwright, hairdresser to the Bowies, Toyah Willcox and Vivienne, whose salon stood two doors down from punk's shrine at 430 King's Road, also remembered punk as 'Fun. It was youth, it was dressing up,' while Sebastian Conran, the art student who promoted the Sex Pistols' chief rivals, The Clash, was adamant that 'it was *totally* style- not politics-driven.' How could a cult based on political protest ever appeal to the young? 'To talk about depression, the way politicians do, is not a good idea,' says Jordan. 'It doesn't sell! And Vivienne and Malcolm wanted to *sell* . . . Punk wasn't political, it was just mayhem.' Those closest to punk's core were convinced that fun was their motivation, whatever the later tragic outcome.

The essential difference between the proto-punks of New York and the London punks was intellectual posturing. New York's poetic poseurs, such as Patti Smith, Richard Hell and Tom Verlaine, were typically in their mid-twenties, middle class and educated. By contrast, the British punks – mindless of aesthetics, literary references or political prescriptions – were primitive, instinctive and self-destructive rather than self-aggrandising and cerebral. They were also far more aggressive.

One of the major traits of punk was to celebrate 'working-classness'. And though it was the lower-middle-class denizens of the outer London suburbs – rather than solid working class – who constituted its core, it attracted individuals from *all* social strata. What held them together was a common sense of boredom and frustration. 'It was a class mix,' says punk's chronicler Jon Savage. 'You could come from a tower block or be the middle-class person who went to Cambridge . . . the whole point about punk is that it was a group of outcasts from whatever background, and that was the common bond.' Many punks felt that they did not fit in, and 'came together, all the mavericks, in camaraderie and recognition. It was to do with having an attitude and being human, not just part of the system.' While some of the major players may have emerged from the educated middle class – McLaren, Jamie Reid, Glen Matlock, Sebastian Conran – without the raw talent of working-class kids like Johnny Rotten (*né* Lydon), Sid Vicious (*né* John Simon Ritchie, though he later changed his surname to his mother's married name, Beverly) and Jordan, the look and the lyrics would not have been so compelling and potent.

Though McLaren and Westwood were at the helm, they did *not* mastermind – and could not have masterminded – the controversial, runaway success of the movement, or forecast the manner in which the media would respond so hysterically and persistently to their pranks. 'That's one of the great misconceptions, that Malcolm was a great manipulator,' says Sex Pistols drummer Paul Cook. Despite McLaren's retrospective claims in his 1979 film *The Great Rock 'n' Roll Swindle* that he planned and retained Machiavellian control of the whole phenomenon, he too was carried along by the tornado that he had unwittingly unleashed. Most of the scams with the Sex Pistols were accidental. He didn't plan the ones that worked, and the ones that he did plan failed. But the movement was acutely aware of the media, performed in its spotlight, and in the end, for some of punk's victims, it became their only reality.

The image of punk became so internationally familiar as to become an icon: as integral an image of London as the scarlet double-decker bus. Standard postcard images of the capital in the early 1980s included the official engagement picture of Prince Charles and Lady Diana Spencer, the Houses of Parliament and a punk flicking a 'V' sign. The totemic markings of the look were savage self-mutilation, damaged and asexual clothing, a violent rejection of prettiness or naturalness, and a cacophony of clashing visual references, all wrenched from their familiar settings and fused into a shocking juxtaposition. The wearer was always young – 'the members of the new British punk bands squirm if they have to tell you they are over eighteen,' wrote Caroline Coon in *Melody Maker*.

Vivienne's career was to be built on punk. 'The clothes made the music seem more radical than it really was,' believes rock critic Tony Parsons. In creating the Sex Pistols' look – marketed under the label SEX and its successor, Seditionaries – she evolved in a few crucial months from a seamstress who copied past fashions and interpreted McLaren's instructions into a designer. Although she still acted on McLaren's directions, their professional relationship was now more equal. 'Up until the Sex Pistols and punk rock I'd never thought of myself as a designer,' she has said. 'I just thought of myself as helping out Malcolm on his projects; doing research and things like that.' At last her belief in her own creative abilities took root and began to flourish. She had identified her talent, and was determined to leave her mark on international fashion. In doing so, she found a way to bury the provincial girl from the Snake Pass.

Aside from Vivienne's personal development, punk saw the birth of a powerful marketing partnership between music and fashion, sold by the same proprietor. Though the Beatles and Mary Quant emerged simultaneously in the 1960s, no one thought to market them in tandem. The Rolling Stones may have been dressed by Ossie Clark and Granny Takes a Trip, David Bowie by Freddie Burretti, Queen by Zandra Rhodes, and Bryan Ferry by Anthony Price, but no one promoted the clothes with the bands. McLaren brought the two markets together, exploiting the dual demands of youth for a 'look' modelled by their pop idols and a philosophy expressed in their music. 'The Dolls had come into my shop' – he never said 'our' shop – 'several times in London,' says McLaren, 'and they were staggered by the store, because nobody in New York was selling rock 'n' roll culture in the form of dress and music in one particular place.'

'The clothes needed the groups,' McLaren later explained to *The Times*. 'When I went into the music business no one wanted to know about the fashion connection. Now it's the biggest plus you can have. When a pop group signs up with a recording company today there'll be a clause written into the contract that the group will have £1,000 a week to spend on clothes. The Sex Pistols got the ball rolling. As long as a group has the right look today, the music doesn't matter too much.'

Emulating McLaren and Vivienne, the rival King's Road boutique Boy dressed and funded the punk band Generation X, while McLaren's friend Bernie Rhodes backed The Clash, who were dressed by Jasper Conran. In the wake of punk, Gianni Versace, for example, placed his products on the backs of pop stars like Elton John and Sting, while Jean-Paul Gaultier and later Dolce & Gabbana dressed Madonna. The major record labels and entertainment corporations began to merchandise music in tandem with the T-shirt, the cap, the video and the lifestyle.

The Sex Pistols were not only four youths pounding out a frenzied, adolescent attack on the status quo; they were also clothes dummies for McLaren and Vivienne's shop. The lyrics of their hits – such as 'Anarchy in the UK' and 'God Save the Queen', written by Lydon in response to ideas fed to him by Vivienne and Jamie Reid – were printed across their chests, in a masterful stroke of saturation advertising and product placement. The clothes sold the records, and vice versa. Jordan says: 'Malcolm had a great talent to see what he could make of people and to instil enough trust in them, like a very straight ordinary bloke, and dress them up. And it says a lot about [the band] that they put all their trust in Vivienne and Malcolm and let them dress them up.'

Vivienne retained her muddled socialist principles, now combined with McLaren's anarchy. She admired the extremism of the IRA and the Red Brigade, going so far as to tell Nils Stevenson that she'd even understand if the IRA blew up her own children. She wanted to demonstrate that her commitment was so strong that her personal feelings were inconsequential. To McLaren, however, sloganising was simply a means of commodifying revolution: 'Cash from Chaos', 'Destroy', 'Believe in the Ruins'.

For Vivienne and Malcolm, punk was both a continuation of their commercial exploitation of youth culture and a fusion of many previous post-war youth cults – rocker, teddy boy, mod, Rastafarian – into a Molotov cocktail of truculent protest. It was post-modern, borrowing symbols and clothing styles from other tribes to create its own collage, a formula Vivienne continued to use until the early 1990s. In this respect it was a reflection of the pluralism that had already killed the one season/one look of high fashion. 'Punk,' Vivienne explained, 'was a great stand against authority . . . Where did all those things come from? They came from culture! . . . The motives for being anti-establishment were already in the culture . . . When Malcolm and I first started to do clothes before punk rock we were looking at our own lifetime culture and trying to express the rebelliousness while throwing out all the motives. Through our curiosity and research we created a cult of our own.'

In fact, none of the chief signifiers of punk originated from Westwood or McLaren. 'Do-it-yourself' was its clarion call. Drainpipe trousers and jeans were already being worn by those who wished to distance themselves from the hippie flares; the safety pin came from Johnny Rotten via Richard Hell, who also pioneered the shredded and ripped clothing; the 'used' tampon from Sid Vicious; the razor blades, bin-liners and bike or lavatory chain were introduced by punks on the street, as was the later Mohican cut; the dog-collar by Sharon Hayman of the Bromley Contingent; the elements of militaristic dress and the brazenly artificial make-up and hair by Jordan; the customised leather jacket (ideally from Lewis Leathers in Great Poland Street) was appropriated from the Hell's Angels, and became associated with The Clash, not the Pistols, who preferred torn school blazers from charity shops like Oxfam.

Punk dress celebrated the sordid, the cruel, the inappropriate and the poor. If an item smacked of political bad taste (the swastika), sexual bad taste (the used tampon or condom) working-class shoddiness (the paka-mac), cheapness (the black bin-bag, popularised by club entrepreneur Philip Sallon), the macabre (kohl-bruised eyes, inspired by Stanley Kubrick's 1971 film of A Clockwork Orange) or the morbid (the skinny black tie worn as a hangman's noose), it was seized upon. In 1978 Vivienne told the punk magazine Search and Destroy: 'Now that the death penalty has been abolished in England, everyone knows nothing that terrible will happen to them, so you can be as free as you like.'

The most articulate exponents of the punk style achieved a look that instantly communicated all the pain and anguish of the lost adolescent. Their sartorial obscenities celebrated their self-imposed exile from society. Though they did not conceive of it in such terms, their display was reminiscent of the storm scene in Shakespeare's King Lear, in which Lear and the Fool, cast out into the tempest and shivering in their 'looped and windowed raggedness', reflect on the essential nature of man, necessity and luxury. The style's strength lay in its visual embodiment of the unadorned human condition, stripped down to reveal the raw nerves of psychic pain. It was this recognition of suffering that punk unleashed which incited such extreme reactions in the viewer, because it drew attention either to the purposelessness that the young felt or to their ugly, up-yours attitude.

In the mid-1970s, Britain was suffering the worst economic recession since the thirties. Inflation reached 27 per cent in 1975. In 1976, to avoid devaluation, the government was humiliatingly forced to accept financial aid from the International Monetary Fund. Unemployment was climbing steadily, reaching a post-war high of 1.6 million in 1977. The country seemed ungovernable, and it was the uneducated young who bore the brunt of the necessary belt-tightening.

In contrast to their derided predecessors the hippies, who had enjoyed relative economic affluence, the punks cast themselves as figures from the real world of urban decay. They did not seek sanctuary in escapism, psychedelic drugs, utopian politics, rural Arcadias, communes, dreams of outer space, or idealistic liberalism and internationalism. Unemployed, depressed, poorly educated and feckless, how could the punks find solace in such abstract and impossible dreams, such luxuries? Instead they appropriated the rhetoric of crisis, ushering in a period of liberal-baiting, aggressive tribalism and apocalyptic anarchy. With no place to flee to, they stood their ground and fought, in a vague, unfocused manner, against the current system and conditions. But they did not know what they were fighting *for*, and so an inarticulate frustration combined with their demotic hedonism.

Outbursts of rioting at the Notting Hill Carnival of 1976, and in Lewisham, South London in 1977 and Ladywood revealed the bitterness of the prevailing inner-city strife. 'In 1976 it all started falling apart really,' remembers Michael Kostiff. 'There had just been the three-day week, and the country was really going downhill. It wasn't this children's storybook country any more. It was no longer the Queen at the top and the judges, it was all very corrupt, and people started to see the corruption and to question the role of things ... All those people who lived through the war have different views of life, so it was really quite shocking to put a safety pin through the Queen's face.'

The source of punk's vitriol was not only in the reaction to mid-seventies Britain, but also in the psychic damage inflicted during McLaren's childhood, and in Vivienne's overbearing bossiness and her hatred of the complacent establishment. Her emotional responses had a childish fervour to them. She was angry and opinionated without being informed – a dangerous mix. McLaren, on the other hand, was coldly amused, and just wanted to 'dress up to mess up', to take pranksterism to its most irresponsible extreme. The social conditions of contemporary Britain made it an ideal time for him to lead a cavalcade of disengaged, thrill-seeking teenagers, with stories of the romance of anarchy and the opportunities of do-it-yourself stardom or infamy.

Pied Piper McLaren could not play the pipe himself, so he needed someone else to lure his followers. He had realised in New York that because of their age, their chronic drug and alcohol abuse and their indifference to his political ranting, the New York Dolls could not be manipulated to his ends. Back in England, he set about constructing his own band.

Glen Matlock, an art student who worked as a Saturday assistant at SEX, introduced McLaren to Kutie Jones, a band which consisted of Paul Cook and Steve Jones, two working-class teenagers from a housing estate in Shepherd's Bush who were regulars at the shop (Jones had thirteen convictions for theft). They could hardly play – a plus point as far as the anarchic McLaren was concerned – but they had the abusive raw potential that he required. He then cast around for a Richard Hell-like lead singer who would carry his message of trashy revolt with an ironic lack of professionalism. He was seeking a riposte, almost an antidote, to the big-stadium, capital-intensive super groups and their professional sound.

Matlock first encountered the street urchins John Lydon and John Beverly in the Roebuck pub near SEX in the late summer of 1975. Lydon, who hailed from a council estate in Islington, was nicknamed 'Johnny Rotten' by Steve Jones, who commented, 'Your teeth are green. You're rotten, you are.' His clothes underscored his name. Rotten sported cropped hair, a defaced school blazer worn inside out, safety-pinned baggy trousers and open-toed plastic sandals (hence the original London name for punks, 'plastic peculiars'). Matlock took McLaren to meet Rotten in the pub, and after some resistance an audition was staged in the shop, with Rotten mouthing to the jukebox. He was conscripted. According to Nils Stevenson, Vivienne had recommended a teenaged customer of the shop called 'John' to McLaren as a possible singer. McLaren had mistakenly assumed she meant Lydon; in fact she was referring to John Beverly, later to become Sid Vicious.

The original Sex Pistols consisted of Rotten, guitarist Wally Nightingale (replaced by Steve Jones for being too middle class and musically competent), drummer Paul Cook and Matlock on bass. When McLaren first heard a demo tape of their music in autumn 1975, he told Vivienne it was the worst he'd ever heard, 'but it didn't matter. What mattered is that they were so good at being bad.' Every member of the band's final line-up (Sid Vicious, the ultimate Sex Pistol, replaced Matlock in March 1977) contributed to the total image: 'Jones was the lovable Cockney. John was not lovable but had real charisma – much more on stage than off, he came alight on stage. Sid: I loved him, didn't let anything bother him. He never carried troubles on his shoulders. He was happy-go-lucky. He wasn't as worldly as Steve or Paul. Everyone liked Sid,' Jordan recalled.

The relationship between Vivienne and McLaren had been strained for some time, and it became worse as McLaren's public life became increasingly frantic and he devoted more time to the band and less to the shop, Vivienne and the children. Steve Jones lived with the couple briefly, and Paul Cook remembers him remarking on how often Vivienne used to 'bollock Malcolm – she was quite violent'. Nils Stevenson says: 'Vivienne was obviously very tempestuous with Malcolm, and would boast that she'd given him a big slap over something the night before. And she'd lock him in the cupboard. But Malcolm loved that reputation. He got a kick out of it.'

Nevertheless, following a series of rows, in October 1975 Malcolm moved out of Nightingale Lane and into a flat in Bell Street, Marylebone, with Helen Wellington-Lloyd, who had recently returned from South Africa and suggested they share, on condition that he paid his share of the rent and the telephone bill – he lived on the phone. He intended to use Bell Street as an office as well as a home, and for Helen to be his secretary. During his time at the flat, Helen recalls, McLaren 'blanked Vivienne. He didn't want her on his parade with the band. He wouldn't go down to Nightingale Lane for weeks on end.' In retaliation, Vivienne refused to give him any of the shop's takings. Lying alone in their double bed at night, Vivienne's jealousy of women and her resolve to succeed professionally intensified.

McLaren moved back and forth at his convenience, usually spending the weekends with Vivienne, but they never really seemed to be a couple. 'At the time you really thought that she and Malcolm were very separate people,' says Steve Jones, 'and to the outside crowd one didn't feel that he had anything to do with the shop because of what he was doing with the Sex Pistols, which as far as press and media was concerned was much more important. The crossover was the T-shirts, and he was involved there.' McLaren was able to cultivate the impression that not only the band, but also the clothing was his creation.

Vivienne and Jordan were allocated the task of 'grooming' the band and dressing them in clothes from the shop; a hard task, as each of them wanted to look different. 'The band did a bit of input in the style,' says Jordan. 'They got into it, and it was all done with feeling. And as they didn't have to pay [for the clothes], they could mutilate them.' (They were unaware that the cost was deducted from their royalties by McLaren.)

McLaren persuaded the band to write lyrics that promoted SEX, and later Seditionaries, with titles such as 'Submission', and soon they had a full repertoire of songs and he was ready to launch them. The first public venue, on 5 November 1975, was St Martin's College of Art in central London. Cook, dressed in a ted jacket and drainpipe jeans, and Matlock in ted jacket and scarlet jeans with see-through plastic pockets on the bum from SEX, approached Sebastian Conran, treasurer of the union at the Central School of Art and Design, to give them a gig at the college. He booked them to support Brentford and the Nylons. A few days later Simon Barker, then a student in Bromley, South London, chanced upon the band playing at Ravensbourne Art College, his local art school. He was mesmerised, and told his friends that this was what they were looking for, a group of their own age that vocalised their dissatisfaction and boredom.

Within a month the band had a loyal following, centred on this Bromley Contingent, which comprised Barker, Siouxsie Sioux (*née* Susan Ballion) of Siouxsie and the Banshees, Billy Idol (William Broad), Steve Severin (Bailey), Sue Catwoman (Lucas), Little Debs (Debbie Wilson) and Juvenile (Tracey O'Keefe). These visually articulate suburban teenagers, some still at school, others unemployed, were the first hard-core punk fans, liberated by the movement's do-it-yourself ethos. In their dress, wrote Peter York, they were 'works of art – originals', and many of them went on to become performers.

The Bromley Contingent shared a highly developed knowledge of pop culture and style references. Their rock idols had been David Bowie and Bryan Ferry, but once their heroes started dressing more conventionally – Bowie in black trousers and white shirt, Ferry in a tuxedo – they no longer admired them. The rock establishment was becoming richer, older and less accessible, while the plight of the British teenager became poorer and more hopeless. The fans could no longer relate to the stars' gilded lifestyles and expensive dandyism. Hard-nosed confrontation and defiance, not limp foppishness and remote professionalism, were what set the young's adrenaline pumping. Punks were as ironic and self-aware as the glam rock stars, but they found parody in poverty and malnourishment, as a means of condemning their lot within a declining Britain, and as a badge of group identity. To express their common bond they started to make and customise their own clothes, buying for example tight old jumpers from charity shops and striping them with household paint.

'Don't dream it, be it!', originally a line from *The Rocky Horror Show*, was a rallying cry of punk. It was a reaction to the professionalism that had rinsed rock 'n' roll of its hard-edged youthful appeal, and it was urged by Vivienne in particular, and taken up by punk followers and the punk magazines. Danny Baker's *Sniffin' Glue*, for example, published simple instructions and diagrams on how to play two chords, and encouraged readers to go away and form a band. Similarly, Vivienne was delighted if young fans who could not afford her wares went off and copied them.

One of the first venues to host the Sex Pistols, in February 1976, was a massive Thames-side studio rented by the artist Andrew Logan in Butler's Wharf, just across the river from the City. McLaren had learnt that Logan was planning a St Valentine's night party. Logan remembers McLaren ringing him and saying: 'Ooh, Andrew, I've got this group, these boys, they'll be bigger than the Beatles. Do you want the boys to play at the party?' Without asking Logan, McLaren phoned up the whole of London and invited them. 'There were hundreds of people, falling over my sculptures and smashing them. It was a nightmare.'

The band played very late, partly because Rotten was locked out of the building because of the crowds. When he was eventually admitted by Vivienne, who had prised the door open, he smashed her in the face. Applying her idiosyncratic notion of fair play, she did not chastise him or hit him back, but said, 'I can understand how he felt,' rubbing her black eye and bruised face. She did, however, turn on Logan's boyfriend Michael when he asked her not to break the new television. In response, says Logan, 'Vivienne swung round at him and yelled, "You bourgeois git." '

To Logan, Vivienne appeared to be both violent and a scheming opportunist: 'She uses people. I got that straight away, that she's very good at using people. She wanted to create a stir and publicity – that's what she wanted, and that's what she got. She learnt on Malcolm's knee, and she had the best education on that score.'

The studio had a huge metal roof, like an aircraft hangar, and once the band started playing, says Logan, 'the noise was so dreadful, reverberating off the ceiling, that we all of us ran from the group and into a prefab in the middle of the room, the inside of which was covered in gold. All the diehards stayed out there.' In an attempt to shock the audience, McLaren goaded Jordan to go on stage, strip and fondle Rotten.

The early fans frequented Louise's and Bang, two gay clubs in Soho, and Andrew Czezowski's Roxy in Neal Street, Covent Garden, which opened in December 1976. One of Czezowski's most regular expenses during the club's short life was to replace the lavatory chains every night, as they were stolen by customers for adornment. At first, many of the punks lived with their parents. Barker, for example, having spent all his money clubbing, would sometimes walk home to Bromley from Soho in the middle of the night in his threatening, attention-seeking attire. 'You're not scared when you're young.' He admits to undoing the straps of his bondage trousers, which hobbled his knees together, so he could make a quick getaway when he encountered a cackling gang of girls.

In the spring of 1976 Barker, Jordan and David Pavlovic, joined later by Sid Vicious and his girlfriend Nancy Spungeon – moved into a flat in Buckingham Gate, near Victoria Station. Their landlady was a prostitute. Jordan was working at SEX; Barker, her boyfriend at the time, was working as McLaren's assistant; and Pavlovic earned £20 a night looking after prostitutes' poodles while they went out on the game. Unconstrained by the demands of the conventional workplace, their punk attire became a daily uniform, not a dressing-up costume to be hung up when the demands of 'real life' intervened.

Derek Dunbar, later to be an employee of Vivienne's, met this tight-knit group a few months later at their favourite haunt, Louise's. The next day, he paid Barker a visit at Buckingham Gate: 'When I first saw Simon, Jordan and Sue Catwoman, there was something so primitive and tribal. The way that they looked reminded me of Africa [where he was brought up]. It was fantastic. Those people wanted to be different, so much. SEX would have been nothing without their inspiration, especially Jordan's. Vivienne got so many ideas from her.' Dunbar began working as a model, and on one assignment with British *Vogue* was slung out of the building for wearing the obscene 'Naked Cowboys' T-shirt. Condé Nast and punk were never happy bedfellows.

Much of the Bromley Contingent's time was spent with Vivienne and McLaren on the King's Road, or following the band from venue to venue. In September 1976 the Pistols, accompanied by McLaren, the shop assistants and the Contingent – Vivienne stayed behind to look after the shop and her sons – played their first concert abroad, in Paris. Rotten modelled the hallmark punk outfit for the occasion, a black bondage suit with Malcolm's Basque beret. It was appropriate and ironic that Vivienne and McLaren, who claimed to be outside the fashion system, launched the look – albeit informally – in the capital of fashion.

The head-turning Siouxsie Sioux travelled to Paris wearing a bra from She an' Me (a 'marital aids' shop, as they were primly known in those days) which framed her bare nipples, black suspenders and an armband decorated with a swastika. The London punks were frequently jeered and chased down the French capital's streets, and at the concert held at Chalet du Lac, in the centre of the Bois de Boulogne, the bouncers put them backstage for their own safety. Despite protests and hoots of derision from some members of the audience, many of those who were present came again on the following day, having instantly adopted the black clothing and spiky, razored and greased hair. 'They just copied us overnight!' says Barker. 'At first we thought "Shit!", but inside you really felt "Yeah!" ' Imitation was the sincerest form of flattery.

As Vivienne concentrated on designing, McLaren was promoting the Pistols and gaining notoriety. On 21 and 22 September 1976 they played in the first 'Punk Rock Festival', at the 100 Club on Oxford Street, and on 23 September McLaren set up a company, called 'Glitterbest' (the name bought off the shelf for £100), to manage the band, hiring Stephen Fisher as his solicitor and co-director. The following month McLaren rented an office in Dryden Chambers and a rehearsal studio around the corner in Denmark Street, which also served as the band's crash pad. Denmark Street, known as 'Tin Pan Alley' because of its music business associations, had particular resonance for McLaren, because his idol Larry Parnes's headquarters had been there in the fifties. As an additional attraction for McLaren, a member of the seventies rock band Bad Finger had reputedly hanged himself in the studio.

Throughout the autumn of 1976, Vivienne and McLaren encouraged violent scenes at gigs to draw the public's – and, even more importantly, the media's – attention to the band. 'Punk violence was theatrical, but at the same time, McLaren and Westwood were complicit in inciting acts of violence,' remembered one fan, Richard

Boon. Tapping the natural aggression found in disaffected adolescents, they incited them to idolise infamous killers. Sid Vicious, for example, then working in the shop, claimed that Vivienne lent him a book on the mass-murderer Charles Manson.

Pumping up the media interest served McLaren's longer-term motive: to secure a lucrative record deal with a big music company. Throughout the autumn of 1976 he played Polydor off against EMI, and on 8 October he signed with the latter. In exchange for a £40,000 advance (paid to Glitterbest) for a band that technically could not play, EMI would produce and distribute the Pistols' recordings for two years, with a further two-year option. McLaren then tied the four teenagers into a contract with Glitterbest that three of them did not even bother to read, signing them up for three years with an option for another two, and charging them 25 per cent of their earnings for his managerial services. The band's name was also owned by 'the management', i.e. Glitterbest.

McLaren commissioned Ben Kelly, who had recently graduated from the Royal College of Art, to make his new premises in Denmark Street 'slightly more habitable than the kind of pit it was'. As soon as the refurbishment was complete, the band trashed it. This became a standing joke. When Rotten ran into Kelly some months later, he greeted him with, 'Oh, you were the idiot who did that. It didn't last very long, did it!'

Unlike former youth cults, women determined the style and activities of punk as much as men, and shared equal billing with them. Several had successful musical careers, such as Siouxsie Sioux with her band the Banshees, and Poly Styrene (*née* Marion Elliott). Punk women jettisoned conventional notions of prettiness in dress and grace of movement. The distinctive punk 'pogo' dance, for example – jerking up and down on one spot like a power-drill – was robotic and solipsistic, danced in isolation from any partner.

In pursuit of cheap oblivion, punks drank 'snakebites' (strong lager and cider) and the Rastafarian cocktail rum 'n' black, took amphetamines, sulphate (poor man's cocaine), or sniffed glue (hence Danny Baker's fanzine title *Sniffin' Glue*, and the UK Subs track 'Lady Esquire', referring to the solvent in the shoe dye of that name). Unlike marijuana or heroin, these cheap narcotic cocktails did not create inertia but aggressive hyperactivity, somewhat akin to Vivienne and McLaren's natural state. And, unlike the student hippies, many punks had to hang on to jobs, and could not afford to lie around sleepily.

Punk sexuality was characterised by casual encounters, and long-term relationships or bonding were frowned upon. According to Paul Cook, Vivienne and McLaren appeared 'asexual': 'They didn't seem like a couple, sexually anyway. Steve [Jones] used to ask Malcolm, "Do you really have sex with Vivienne?" ' McLaren would protest, unconvincingly, that of course he did. Nils Stevenson believes that the couple's claimed enthusiasm for promiscuity was merely theoretical, and a selling point for the shop: 'Malcolm knew nothing of what was going on. He thought we were all innocent, especially the shop girls who were on the game. We were all fucking each other.'

Fuelled up with aggression, the punks ridiculed overt displays of affection: 'Love snuffed it with the hippies,' declares one of the characters in *Jubilee*, Derek Jarman's 1978 punk film. Indeed, anything that smacked of conformity or permanence was discarded, including relationships. The adjective that summed up the emotional ethos of the movement, according to the novelist and one-time punk David Huggins, was 'loveless'.

Lovelessness and aggression reflected Vivienne and McLaren's personalities. Vivienne was incapable of nurturing a loving environment, or at least unwilling to do so, with either her sons or her colleagues. On a more superficial level, she lacked feminine wiles; she could neither allure nor charm, she simply hectored. 'Vivienne used to harass people,' recalls Simon Barker. 'She wanted to find out the reason they wanted to buy something. She'd go into long discussions about why it was made, the principle behind it, and why they wanted to buy it. She thought that all the people had the same emotional or political reason for buying it. It was almost as if those people had to prove they were worthy to buy it, and I've actually seen people walk out of the shop because they were fed up with all the talk about it.' Paul Cook remembers her constantly questioning complete strangers about what they were wearing: 'She'd interrogate you, wanting to know your motives. She thought you had to have the attitude of "Stand up! Be counted for what you're wearing!" '

When punk broke in the autumn of 1976, Caroline Baker of *Ritz* magazine (later fashion editor of *i-D* and the *Sunday Times*) was one of the most street-orientated fashion stylists in London. She admits that she preferred to interview Jordan than Vivienne, whom she found 'very frightening. She had one vision and one idea, and if you were a little bit shy she would *never* soften up or come down to you. She was very aggressive and daunting. "This is it! This is the sexual revolution! You've got to wear rubber and leather and do this, that or the other!" She never really encouraged you gently to do it. She's not a coaxer.'

It was McLaren, not Vivienne, who seduced their followers. 'Both were incredibly amoral, but between the two Vivienne was the crueller, the harder, the more fanatical.' Even McLaren was sometimes taken aback by her obsessive commitment to the cause: 'She'd take an idea and never saw the nuance, never wanted to debate – tunnel vision. She'd kill them if they did not play her way, they were not in her club, her gang.'

While McLaren concentrated on exploiting the band, attracting the media and shocking the public, the shop was Vivienne's soapbox. Indifferent to money, she did not care whether the clothes sold or not, despite the research and hard work she put into creating them. She continued to underplay her role in creating the style which, as Rotten recorded in his autobiography, 'had a lot to do with Vivienne Westwood. Malcolm took a lot of the praise, but I think she did most of the designs.'

In 1976, high fashion favoured Thierry Mugler and Claude Montana's sci-fi look, Kenzo's bright floral prints and Calvin Klein's casuals and working separates. There was also an undercurrent of radical dress. Helmut Newton was tinkering with sado-masochist and lesbian images for French *Vogue*; in New York Tom Wolfe was chronicling the fascination with radical chic; and in Berlin David Bowie and Brian Eno's followers were adopting fascist styles. Some knowing elements were playing with intellectual, ironic and politically aware dress. Under these diverse influences, fashion was beginning to fragment. Never again was it to coalesce into one commercially determined direction. Vivienne and McLaren contributed to this process.

Rejecting mainstream fashion, Vivienne created 'confrontation dressing', as she dubbed it. She instinctively produced '*bricolage*', a term introduced by the anthropologist Claude Lévi-Strauss to describe artefacts made by primitive people. The object or article of clothing is imbued with talismanic magic by employing basic elements in improvised combinations to generate new meanings. The non-literate and non-technical 'primitive' mind creates a response to the world, arranging ingredients by means of an idiosyncratic logic that is understood by the tribe. A limited range of materials being available, necessity became the mother of extraordinary invention.

The ingredients of Vivienne's *bricolage* included a disparate assortment of cultural, sub-cultural, historical and contemporary symbols and styles, from which she formed a unique collage intended to provoke rage. From David Bowie and glam rock she borrowed narcissism, gender confusion and nihilism. From Bowie and Brian Eno's 'Berlin period', via Sid Vicious and Jordan, she drew imagery from the Germany of the Third Reich. From contemporary New York she borrowed details of Richard Hell's dress. From Dickens's *Oliver Twist* she took the style of Fagin and his ragamuffins, such as handkerchiefs hanging out of back pockets. Jamie Reid introduced McLaren and Vivienne to the dress and slogans of the 1930s Spanish anarchist Buenaventura Durutti, which were added to the provocative catchphrases of the situationists and the aphorisms of Karl Marx. Sexually threatening bondage gear was plundered and fused with dadaism and surrealism. From the inventiveness of the Sex Pistols and their fans, particularly Jordan, Vivienne appropriated black plastic bin-liners, Hoover rings, badges and metal fastenings, and explored the possibilities of Marcel Duchamp's 'ready-mades' by taking everyday, mass-produced objects out of their context.

Vivienne soaked up this plethora of unrelated images and messages and, in the isolation of her Clapham flat – usually in bed – synthesised them into clothing that exhilarated the band and its followers. 'I would work for six months and I'd know it was brilliant, and I'd have to take the phone off the hook. Little naughty bits turn me on,' she recalled with glee.

Lateral, instinctive and unschooled inspiration, as opposed to linear and tutored thought, was and remains Vivienne's greatest strength as a designer. McLaren was amazed by her unbridled and wholly original creativity. One of her most bizarre creations – little-known, as she only made a prototype – was a long-sleeved T-shirt, one sleeve of which featured an image of an erect penis being masturbated and discharging semen over a picture of Marilyn Monroe printed across the chest. On the other sleeve, the spent penis lies flaccid. The sleeves were cut to look like Victorian stockings, with a 'knee-detail' at the elbow and seams at the wrists. Was it sexual jealousy that prompted

Vivienne to deface a female sexual icon in this way, or contrary iconoclasm? A meticulous obsession with tiny elements that could hardly be seen when the T-shirt was worn illustrated Vivienne's extraordinary attention to experimental and seemingly purposeless detail.

Working side by side with Vivienne, Jordan was impressed by her way of seeing. 'She looks – *really* looks. She doesn't take things for granted. In studying and feeling the cloth, she really wants something from it when it's made. She doesn't like and doesn't have this fashion banter, the way fashion designers rave and rave about something. She really means it.' Vivienne's struggle for perfection was manic; 'sloppy mediocrity' appalled her. With her unusual combination of visual freshness – seeing everything as if for the first time – and hard-earned craft, her designs illustrated Charles Baudelaire's definition of the creative mind:

> The child sees everything in a state of newness; he is always
> *drunk*. Nothing more resembles inspiration than the delight with
> which a child absorbs form and colour . . . but genius is nothing
> more or less than *childhood recovered* at will – a child now
> equipped with self-expression, with manhood's capabilities and
> powers of analysis which enable it to order the mass of raw
> material which it has involuntarily accumulated.

Vivienne's enduring gift was that, while accumulating technique and experience, she never lost the child's fresh view of her surroundings.

The quintessential punk outfit was bondage trousers, parachute shirt, mohair jumper (worn by Vivienne since her ted days) and a T-shirt or muslin shirt sloganed with an obscenity, often from a Pistols' lyric. The bondage trousers epitomised the collaboration between Vivienne and McLaren; each detail displayed one or the other's creative mind at work. McLaren had brought some standard-issue cotton army trousers back from the United States, which Vivienne copied in a shiny black sateen McLaren had seen on the back of British Rail clerks' waistcoats and sourced in Manchester. It was McLaren's idea to add the bondage straps between the knees, an extension of the trussed-up sexual look they had purveyed in SEX. They discussed which tribal appendage could be added to these utilitarian trousers, settling on the loincloths worn by primitive tribesmen. Vivienne insisted that their version of this – the 'bum flap' – should be in towelling. She added her characteristically finicky 'couture' details: zips down the legs (allowing the trousers either to flap around the calves or cling tightly to them) and a fetishist zip that ran right under the crutch, from the pubic bone to the coccyx. Despite the hobbled legs, the bondage trousers were easy to move in. Once, when Vivienne was accompanying a punk to hospital, the nurses wondered how she could move freely in her funny trousers. In answer she cartwheeled the length of the corridor into Casualty, to the amazement of the staff, patients and even the drunks.

The trousers were made up by Mr Mintos, a Greek tailor off Camden Road in North London with whom Vivienne was to work for many years. On hearing that Sebastian Conran had sent Mr Mintos some clothes to be made up for The Clash, she called Conran and 'blew me up for stealing her trouser-maker. She was fierce.' All collaborators, to Vivienne's mind, had to remain utterly partisan.

Bondage trousers were worn with a parachute shirt which was hung with four straps attached by D-rings, one to each shoulder, another two from the lower chest. These met in the middle of the breastbone, and were held in place by a large plastic Hoover ring. This suggested not only a military theme, but also bondage and the restraint of the insane in a straitjacket. 'The bondage clothes are ostensibly restricting, but when you put them on they give you a feeling of freedom. They make you want to move your arms around,' Vivienne assured customers.

Male designers rarely create clothes that give priority to the feeling of wearing them, rather than to their visual impact; they prefer to dress a woman in a striking way, no matter how uncomfortable or inappropriate she may feel. Female designers, by contrast, tend to construct clothes on their own bodies, and are consequently alert to the sensuality and freedom of movement achieved by their craft. In some cases the sensation of wearing the garment overrides the aesthetic impact. The Japanese conceptual designer Rei Kawakubo of Comme des Garçons, for example, is so insistent that customers feel comfortable in her clothes that at first she refused to hang mirrors in her shops; this uncommercial but altruistic experiment failed. The British designer Jean Muir was dedicated to the manner in which clothes enhanced a woman's sense of self-confidence; physical freedom was never subordinated to visual effect. Vivienne took this sensual preoccupation of women designers and inverted it. Her abiding design signature became the physical restriction of a woman's body. This, she calculated, would arouse the wearer's sense of sexuality and theatricality.

Though typically tailored in shiny black sateen, the bondage separates were later made in a hard-wearing tartan wool, a material that appealed to Vivienne's patriotism, traditionalism and abiding respect for quality. Jordan had worn a mini tartan kilt, which Vivienne copied, observing in a television interview that it was 'reminiscent of a Greek peasant costume'. No two parachute jackets were alike, but they were typically decorated with one or more of three elements: a quotation from Buenaventura Durutti, such as 'We are not in the least afraid of ruins,' stencilled onto the breast; a portrait of Karl Marx; and the slogan 'Only Anarchists are Pretty' scrawled across the breast pocket.

In December 1976, in order to proclaim the Sex Pistols' message of sedition and anarchy, Vivienne and McLaren decided that the shop's name and image should be changed once again. 'The word "seditionaries", which I used to rename the shop, has always meant to me the necessity to *seduce* people into revolt,' Vivienne explained. The clothes were labelled 'Malcolm McLaren and Vivienne Westwood Seditionaries, Personal Collection', and sold under the enticing slogan 'Clothes for Heroes'. The anarchist symbol, a capital A within a circle, appeared on many garments, along with the tag 'For soldiers, prostitutes, dykes and punks'. The punk army now had a uniform.

Vivienne was determined that the direction she was taking in her designs should be clearly reflected in the shop's environment. Following the commercial success of SEX, the couple were relatively solvent, so they sought professional help to refurbish 430 King's Road. Four people have claimed authorship of the ground-breaking design. Ben Kelly, who had refurbished McLaren's Tin Pan Alley rehearsal room, had recently carried out a strikingly minimalist design for Lynne Franks and Paul Howie's clothing shop Miss Howie, on Long Acre in Covent Garden, which featured high-tech industrial materials like heavy-duty black rubber flooring and a galvanised Dexion plate-glass window. McLaren wanted to style the interior of Seditionaries around the theme of the bombed-out city of Dresden – a typically provocative choice, as the bombing of Dresden is regarded by many as Britain's worst 'crime' of the Second World War. He approached Kelly for designs, but Kelly, saying he was not a draughtsman, recommended a fellow graduate of the Royal College of Art, David Connors, and gave him some preliminary sketches to work from. This allowed Connors to take credit for the final design, although he later acknowledged Kelly's initial input. In fact, Kelly, McLaren and Vivienne came up with the bulk of the inspiration and when Kelly left for New York, Connors executed the brief proficiently.

'I first met Malcolm in a café in Covent Garden,' remembers Connors, 'and I was terrified. He was so weird. For me it was an education, a big influence on my life. I had a formal education and then I ran into these two [McLaren and Vivienne], and they dominated my life for nine months. It was terribly exciting. They really taught me that you were meant to disturb things and challenge everything – it had to be challenged to the limit. Seditionaries was a challenge to the idea of a shop window and promoting the look inside the window. Vivienne's concept was that you have to be brave to walk through the door – one of us, a hero – because you don't know what's behind it, and that only brave people are allowed to wear the clothes. It's retailing madness – don't let people see the clothes!' Connors found the couple's ideas so radical that 'I never got it. I just learnt from it. There's no one like them. I can't predict what they will do. I consider them the most amazing clients. We did Seditionaries for £2,000, and that £2,000 changed the world. It was all ideas. Money had almost nothing to do with it. Intimidation, that was it.'

While McLaren, aided by Connors, focused on the shop's interior, Vivienne and Kelly attended to the exterior. The shop was a hi-tech, futuristic retailing vision of Stanley Kubrick's film of *A Clockwork Orange*. True to character, Vivienne was extremely particular about the shop front, and adamant that a particular kind of opaque, white-flashed opal glass be used. Over the door, a blue fluorescent tube hung at an angle, and alongside it was a brass plaque which read: 'Seditionaries. Malcolm McLaren and Vivienne Westwood. Clothes for Heroes.' All this provoked confusion in the passer-by. Was it a betting shop? A sex parlour? A launderette? Some, seeing the businesslike plaque, assumed it must be a solicitor's office.

The shop was not far from Stamford Bridge football ground, and it soon attracted vandalism, particularly on Saturdays when Chelsea was playing at home. As the glass front was frequently smashed, a wire-mesh screen was put up to protect it. When the vandals started to poke sticks though the mesh to break the glass, the façade was permanently boarded up. 'But that didn't matter, it was part of it – the look,' said Connors. 'And so they wrote all over the boards and really took offence. It was the focus of such aggression, and there were big fights outside on Saturdays.'

As customers entered the shop they stepped onto a grey industrial carpet. The walls to the left and right were hung with blown-up floor-to-ceiling black-and-white photographs of the bombed city of Dresden in ruins, and the back wall was decorated with a massive full-colour photograph, hung upside down, of Piccadilly Circus. This photograph was spliced into sections to allow access to the cupboards behind it. The gymnasium bars from SEX had been taken down from the walls, placed in the centre of the floor and hung with clothes. Austere sixties Adeptus chairs covered with orange nylon served as seating. Powerful film lights provided harsh illumination. Three-quarters of the way down the shop on the right stood a kidney-shaped counter with a hi-tech television suspended above. To one side stood a table made by Connors in which a live rat paced up and down. The stark interior was lit by searing spotlights, placed in jagged holes punched in the ceiling tiles in imitation of bomb damage. The merchandise was hidden behind the boarded-up façade or tucked into boxes – a retailing error that was soon corrected. Though the shop's decor had changed, there was much crossover between the gear available in SEX and in its successor, though Seditionaries was more themed, and slotted more overtly into the then fashionable interest in Berlin and Bauhaus's industrial and streamlined aesthetics.

McLaren's art school hero André Breton famously wrote: 'The simplest surrealist act consists of going out into the street revolver in hand, and firing at random into the crowd as often as possible,' and even the Sex Pistols' name celebrated hedonistic violence. McLaren played with many surrealist notions, and loved to quote George Grosz on dadaism: 'Nothing was holy to us. Our movement was neither mystical, communistic nor anarchistic. All of these movements had some sort of programme, but ours was completely nihilistic. We spat on everything, including ourselves. Our symbol was nothingness, a vacuum, a void.'

More than any club, pub or rock venue, Seditionaries was the headquarters of punk, the meeting point where the Pistols and their fans interacted. Paying homage to the band and the fashions, pilgrims came from all over Britain and abroad. The shop served as an underground headquarters of the cult, from which gig dates and venues could be learnt. Thrill-seeking teenagers, curious art students, the salacious, morally-outraged members of the press and the police were drawn to it. Even Old John, who wore a Beefeater outfit and carried a sandwich-board for the Chelsea Antiques Market, used to visit Vivienne there.

John Egan, a streetwise East End boy who later became a clothing entrepreneur and the owner of another cult clothing store on the King's Road, Demob, could not drag himself away from Seditionaries: 'I loved it. It was really intimidating, in the same way that going into Gucci is intimidating.' Fifteen-year-old George Slattery, another Cockney (later a punk and rock 'n' roll memorabilia trader), visited the shop every Saturday from the autumn of 1976, when he saw the Sex Pistols on television. Determined to become a punk, he and his friends 'bunked off school, went to the King's Road to see it . . . it was absolutely wonderful, probably the most amazing shop I'd ever seen . . . anything shocking was wonderful.' To Slattery and his friends, the clothes were as important as the music – the two were inseparable.

Bella Freud remembers: 'Punk for me was a metamorphosis of my identity. Through her clothes she gives young people the external courage until they have the chance to grow into it. When I wore punk I was terrified of the reactions but I knew I could get away with it because I looked so different from the way I felt inside. It's the opposite to when you grow up, when you might look conventional but you have bolder and more confident thoughts inside.'

Seditionaries' clothes unleashed a more violent reaction than their predecessors from SEX. Marco Pirroni, explaining why they were often 'not in good nick' for the vintage market which later began collecting punk memorabilia, says of their wearers: 'They wore the clothes, slept in them, fought in them. They had no money. The clothes were so strong you got beaten up in them.' A complete punk outfit could elicit 'weird reactions', says Caroline Baker. 'There were some men who were really drawn to the clothes – the hipsters were cut to emphasise your bottom, they were really sexy, and the straps round the knees and the bum flap, you looked really trussed-up; and if there were guys out there into trussed-up sex – well.' Caroline Baker wore the gear in Germany, where she was 'always hassled by the police . . .

people felt threatened. I was also attacked in the King's Road – *Vogue* [for whom she briefly worked] didn't want to know about it at all.' Paul Cook says, 'They were powerful, those clothes, and very different from what was around at the time. People don't realise how straight and conservative things had got. It was dangerous to wear them. They were dangerous clothes. You had to have balls to wear them. You'd get confronted in the street and you'd have to stand up for yourself.'

Many 'customers' stole the merchandise, as they could not afford the shop's high prices: at a time when £25 was a good weekly wage for a young person, a pair of bondage trousers cost £50, a parachute shirt £30, and a T-shirt £7–8. 'I used to nick stuff out of the shop . . . most of the stuff I ever got out of the shop I stole,' George Slattery confessed. Shoplifting from Seditionaries wasn't difficult, as the assistants would sit about reading punk magazines like *Sniffin' Glue*, and couldn't care less if stock was stolen. Slattery's favourite booty was a pair of cock 'n' ball (male genitalia) earrings and a pair of gloves – one white with 'Guilty' printed across the knuckles like a tattoo, and the other black, with 'Innocent' in white. Alternatively, intending shoplifters would loiter, like scavengers, in the shop, waiting for the teds to attack. 'Nine times out of ten we would get the clothes off the teds, who nicked them while smashing up the shop. They didn't want them, they just handed them out,' says Slattery. Since there was no serious attempt at book-keeping, no one knew how much stock went missing each week.

In 1995, Jon Savage observed that many years later the Seditionaries clothes still retained their power to upset and provoke: 'When I put on a mohair jumper I get some extreme reactions. I wore it about five years ago to a media party and people were getting very hostile, and I had to tell them to fuck off . . . clothes of that period have enormous content, and they are deliberately provocative and subversive. You have to be prepared to wear them. I think Vivienne still has something about that in her clothes, which is something I admire.'

Jeff Banks, the British fashion entrepreneur and television presenter, also encountered fury when he bought a couple of T-shirts from Seditionaries. Invited to spend a holiday in 1977 at the home of a Jewish family on Long Island, USA, he and his son went to the shop to buy presents for their hosts' teenaged children. In a rush they grabbed a few wrapped T-shirts and headed for the airport. Gathered in the living room with the extended family, the teenagers began opening their presents: 'Imagine the reaction – a traditional Jewish household – when these images of swastikas and Nazis appeared all over these things. I'd never even bothered to look closely at them! They were in tears. Some holiday that was!'

To Americans, even followers of the cult, the clothes, removed from their British context, were virtually incomprehensible. Terry and Louise Doktor in New York City were sent a parachute shirt by McLaren: 'We didn't know what it was,' remembers Terry. 'What does this mean? This post-apocalyptic feeling was so amazing. Vivienne's clothes were always different, always confrontational. You can look through any rack of clothes and pick hers out – it's got to be hers.'

By the end of 1976, Vivienne was determined to create a cohesive look and control the clothes' designs. Free from McLaren's influence – he was preoccupied with the band – she determined most of the styles that were made and sold. Fashion had become her domain, and the antics of the youths around her was her source book. Many of the totemic accessories popularly associated with punk were borrowed from the young who frequented Seditionaries. Vivienne never used safety pins in her work at this time (though over a decade later she exploited the association for her label). That was Rotten's idea (via Richard Hell), and it was used for the Pistols' album cover, posters and fly-sheets by Jamie Reid, the graphic artist who had organised sit-ins at Croydon with McLaren. Safety pins entered mainstream fashion in the spring of 1977 when Zandra Rhodes used them to hold together a ripped jersey dress. This was photographed in British *Vogue* under the headline 'What a Rip Off', though in fact Rhodes had been designing textiles that were printed with rips and slashes in the early seventies. In 1973 Claire Boyd, a knitwear designer who had graduated from Camberwell Art School and the Royal College of Art, had presented knitwear featuring not only slashes but also lines of raised 'nipples', which moved as the body moved and stretched. Vivienne's 'Witches' collection, six years later, featured similarly skin-tight knitwear decorated with raised 'nipples' and peaked shoulders.

Sid Vicious, working as a shop assistant in Seditionaries, was intrigued by Nazi symbolism, and started to paint swastikas and Third Reich eagles over his body and clothes. For Vivienne, unlike Sid, the Second World War was a personal – if vague – memory, and she must have appreciated how offensive the older generation would find this tomfoolery. Looking back fifteen years later, she said: 'Well, all right. I am with these people and I started actually to put swastikas on armbands. And I am not going to apologise for myself because, to be honest, it was exactly what I was after when I started it. But the way I rationalise it is that we have every right to do it, because what they are saying to the older generation is: "You've mismanaged this world, and we don't accept any of your advice, and what's more, we don't accept any of your taboos, and, you know, we are just going to confront you with all this." '

The original punks (unlike later perversions) stripped the swastika of its fascist associations; punks were not in sympathy with the extreme right, they simply donned the symbol in order to shock. As one punk girl explained: 'Punks just like to be hated.' They wanted the taboo imagery of the swastika without endorsing, or even thinking about, its ideology. In virtually every photograph taken of punks at the time they are either scowling or sneering at the camera. Vivienne, however, rarely managed to look glum or aggressive, and was often caught off-guard beaming with glee. 'You can see how much she was enjoying it,' says Nils Stevenson. 'She was having the time of her life, more fun than anyone! She just loved all the attention.'

Another style borrowed from Vivienne's followers was the crudely-striped shirt. One day Jordan came into the shop wearing an Oxford cotton man's shirt, the sleeves of which she had painted with do-it-yourself stripes. Vivienne took this further, alternating the painted stripes with bleached ones and adding a silk patch printed with the face of Karl Marx (McLaren had found a job lot in Chinatown). Stencilled onto the body was the Iggy Pop lyric 'Gimme Danger' (Iggy Pop's disdainful demeanour and his album *Raw Power* had earned him the sobriquet 'the Godfather of Punk'). Anxious lest McLaren would think it ridiculous, Vivienne hid the shirt at the back of their wardrobe. When he found it, she explained defensively, 'I was just trying to achieve some sort of guerrilla look, like those South Americans.' But McLaren was impressed, and urged her to continue designing in this vein. He also registered that 'she was terrified of designing things that I would not like,' and exploited that fear.

Vivienne and McLaren imitated the teenage nihilists who frequented the shop by, for example, burning cigarette holes in their clothes. 'I loved to *get* holes in my clothes because I felt like I'd been to a punk thing,' says Michael Kostiff, 'and I loved tearing my pockets on a door handle, but it's not something I did on purpose. I'm sure that Vivienne and Malcolm were a bit too mature to do that too. It was something those kids did.'

It was Sid Vicious who came up with the gag of wearing a 'used' tampon as a brooch, felt-tip colouring the end bright red with a pen and hanging it from his lapel. 'Why am I so offended by this boy wearing something that is part of a woman's life?' hairdresser Keith Wainwright remembers asking himself when he first saw it. 'So it did have an impact on me. But I don't think Sid saw it that way. I think he thought it was pretty offensive and a bit of a laugh.' Vivienne was amused by the good-looking seventeen-year-old boy walking around in such outrageous apparel, and appropriated a number of his ideas.

On his first day at St Martin's College of Art in October 1976, Stephen Jones, the milliner, went out for lunch with a girl who was wearing a man's black suit, white shirt and black tie. On her lapel hung a 'used' tampon. They met her friend Johnny Rotten in Soho market. 'I do believe it was the kids who really thought of it. Someone like Johnny really synthesised that look. It wasn't just one individual, but a combination of many elements. They [Malcolm and Vivienne] really pulled that look together.'

Jordan was frustrated when working for the couple, because they 'speak off the top of their heads all the time, and they then change their mind next week. They are like a sponge soaking up people's political and aesthetic opinions. They throw them around and feel quite fervently dedicated to the idea, and then change their minds, which is partly the charm and the fervour of them. They don't get stuck in a rut.' The built-in obsolescence of the fashion industry was perfectly suited to Vivienne and McLaren's temperaments, though both would be reluctant to concede it. Nevertheless, one enduring characteristic of Vivienne is that when talking to her one hears echoes of the opinions held by the last person she held a conversation with. She finds it hard to erase someone's persuasive views until she encounters new ones that are held with equal passion. She has always been extremely impressionable.

Vivienne claims to be inspired by the street: 'For me, street style is something with a content. Establishment clothes are always just about the architecture of garments or a reworking of what's already gone before. The street has always got something to do with support of people who are outside establishment approval, like strippers, Third World people.' To the originality of these amateurs, she added her experimental cut and McLaren's ragbag of slogans. Not all the clothes were made from scratch; some were customised, as she had done before. An example from this time are the black rubber fishing macs with straps inside to attach to the thighs, bought in bulk from factories that were closing down on the south coast and in the North of England.

Jordan witnessed Vivienne creating many of the clothes as they worked together in Nightingale Lane. 'It was dreadful. She asked whether I could use a sewing machine, and I said yes, probably by mistake. It was crazy. What I was good at was the shop and selling. Can you imagine any other designer asking the sales assistant to come along and sew the clothes?' Placed in a tiny room under a bare lightbulb, she had to sew rubber buckles and D-rings onto piles of parachute jackets, and piece together the muslins. 'I was left there all day, and she used to come back and cook really odd meals, putting everything – odd things, including the earth from the potatoes – into the pot that had been used to dye clothes. It was an amazing experience!' Nils Stevenson was served many 'awful lunches' at the flat, made up of 'bits of old sunflowers and herbs from the local park'. They were so inedible that Ben and Joe would rush off to the fish and chip shop, while Stevenson and McLaren slipped away afterwards for a hamburger – something Vivienne would have strongly disapproved of, being (for the moment) a proselytising vegetarian.

Vivienne's favourite rebuke to slackers was to remind them that they had the honour of working for 'The Church of McLaren & Westwood'. When Jordan eventually complained about her working conditions, Vivienne retorted, 'When I took you on, I took you on to do anything I ask. Don't forget, you're on my bandwagon.' Jordan responded by coming to work later and later. One morning she was relieved to find a note on the door which read, 'You're late Jordan. You can fuck off!' Within days, however, she was missed, and was asked back to sell in the shop.

The muslin tops, which looked like bandages, were fastened at the shoulders with a strip of Velcro. Vivienne wore them without a bra. These fabric palimpsests were graffitied with slogans by McLaren and then re-graffitied by the punks who bought, or stole, them. Some sported the anarchist symbol, some a swastika, an inverted crucifix, Lydon's lyric 'I am an Antichrist' or the Queen's severed head. Others bore provocative situationist statements, such as 'Create Hell and Get Away With it', 'The Barrier Between Friend and Foe is Thin', and 'At Certain Times of the Day There are Only Us'. Most of the literary and political allusions were sourced by McLaren or Jamie Reid, for whom punk genuinely was an ideology.

While McLaren, the prankster-voyeur, favoured the pornographic T-shirts, Vivienne, the teacher-activist, was more excited by the political exhortations which, like Reid, she hoped would effect a social revolution. 'She'd take the most cerebral and literal point of view,' said McLaren. 'Her punk T-shirts were cold and humourless. My attitude was, how can I make this represent boredom to the kids? You have to put it in context – a Saturday night context – maybe with a little quotation at the bottom.' Vivienne disregarded the fun; she wanted to bring about social change. 'It was me that did the anarchy things. That's what kids responded to, because they could, but not many of them wore the pornographic T-shirts . . . yeah, I kept doing them as a cause.' Vivienne's fanaticism made her increasingly intolerant of waverers, and more extreme in her methods. 'I'm a great believer in people's commitment to ideas, and if they wear my clothes they have to be committed, because they won't go unnoticed, and they'll arouse comment and horror,' she explained years later. Vivienne argued that the high cost of her creations was 'all part of the commitment. If people can't afford my clothes, they can make their own. Let them chop their T-shirt in half and then use their imagination. I'm all for people doing their own thing.' This ethic, approved of by the lingering teacher in Vivienne, was communicated by slogans such as 'Do it Yourself is King'.

While Vivienne designed most of the clothes, McLaren was the more adept at selecting the T-shirt slogans and graphics. A cultural magpie, he did not create his own political statements or visual iconography but plundered other sources. He designed the graphics on one of the icons of punk dressing, the 'Destroy' T-shirt, one afternoon in his office. At the centre was a swastika and an inverted image of the crucified Christ, based on one of McLaren's favourite images, Mathias Grünewald's 1515 *Crucifixion* (McLaren drew the assorted images on a piece of paper, and the printer dressed Christ in a loincloth, but McLaren insisted on nudity). A postage-stamp image of the Queen's head, severed at the neck by Reid, also featured, and the word 'Destroy' was printed on top, originally in huge block-capitals, but McLaren wanted to communicate a sense of crumbling, and replaced the printed capitals with rough hand-drawn letters.

The anarchic themes on the T-shirts were emphasised by quotations lifted from *The Anarchist Cookbook*, including instructions on how to make a Molotov cocktail. Graphic homosexual images by cult artist Tom of Finland were scrawled on the shop's walls and duplicated on the clothes. One T-shirt that induced horror in passers-by read 'Fuck Your Mother and Don't Run Away, Punk', accompanied by a Tom of Finland illustration of two men fist-fucking.

Reid designed the 'God Save the Queen' image – using a famous portrait by Sir Cecil Beaton – and it was he, not Vivienne, who impaled the monarch's face on a safety pin. Though Reid did not invent the ransom-note lettering that was used as script (it was the consequence of a shortage of cash, when Helen Wellington-Lloyd, unable to go out and buy new Letraset, instead cut out the letters from newspapers and magazines lying around the office), he did recognise its stylistic potential, and exploited it for the Sex Pistols and the shop. The device was to be copied for many years on record sleeves and in magazine and advertising layouts.

For one T-shirt, McLaren took a nineteenth-century George Cruickshank cartoon of street urchins and, with a rough stick and a bottle of ink, wrote on the front and back:

> They are Dickensian-like urchins who, with ragged clothes and pockmarked faces, roamed the streets of foggy, gaslit London pillaging . . . setting fire to buildings, beating up old people with gold chains. Fucking the rich up the arse and causing havoc wherever they go. Some of these ragamuffins gangs jump on tables amidst the charred [turn over to the back of the T-shirt] debris and the burning torches play rock 'n' roll to the screaming delight of the frenzied, pissing, pogo-ing mob. Shouting and spitting Anarchy one of these gangs call themselves the Sex Pistols. This true and dirty tale has been continuing throughout the two hundred years of teenage anarchy and so in 1978 there still remain the Sex Pistols. Their active *extremism* is all they care about and that's what what [sic] counts to jump right out of the

twentieth century as fast as you possibly can in order to create an environment that you can truthfully run wild in.

Oliver Twist

The subversive messages claimed authority through their literary and historical origins. McLaren always asserted that the punk movement was romantic. By placing his band in the tradition of the imaginary characters of Fagin and Oliver Twist, he was attempting to lend a specious legitimacy to the increasing violence he was encouraging in his young followers: if teacher says this is part of the great British tradition, then it must be OK. No wonder some, including John Lydon and Derek Dunbar, came to accuse McLaren of knowingly leading the young astray, in some cases to their self-destruction, and that once the movement turned truly violent, Vivienne, the mother of two teenage boys, sought to dissociate herself from it. Simon Barker, however, believes that punk was no more violent than were the mods and rockers, and that it was the press that created its vicious image.

By the end of 1976, the lives of Vivienne, McLaren, the band and the Bromley Contingent were closely intertwined. Stephen Jones recalls that Vivienne cut a memorable figure dancing at Louise's: 'She had an extraordinary angularity, and those uncoordinated, jerky movements, just like those toy cats made of wood and elastic and you push the bottom and they move jerkily. That's how she danced . . . She really was not considered a star . . . I hadn't heard of her. Jordan was much more famous and terrifying.'

But Vivienne wanted attention. During concerts, she jumped on stage to dance, mimicking the teenagers around her and heedless of her age (now thirty-five). 'She's really anti-bourgeois. There's some streak of rebellion in her which she has never, ever compromised, which is really incredible, because you get a lot of bashes,' says Caroline Baker. Wearing the aggressive bondage clothes with fanatical zeal, she accentuated her hard angularity by partly shaving her hairline back from her temples, because, according to Simon Barker, 'she wanted to look more intellectual, like Vanessa Redgrave with her concentration camp look'.

McLaren, by contrast, faded from a budgerigar-bright ted to a paled-down version of a punk, wearing little other than black leather jeans or bondage trousers except for photo-opportunities.

Self-conscious about his body, as the clothes became more outrageous and attention-seeking, McLaren let Vivienne and Johnny Rotten pose as the label's mannequins. Colleagues noticed that he never took his clothes off in front of others to try on new merchandise. There was also a growing distinction between the couple's body-language: Vivienne, at ease with her shape, happily flaunted it in whatever garb they were promoting, while the more inhibited McLaren dressed to blend in, not to stand out.

Apart from dressing them and creating one of the only original fashions of the seventies, Vivienne had little involvement in the development of the Sex Pistols, or in their music, record contracts or stunts. This was partly because the band didn't get on with her, and partly because she was more interested in the clothes. 'She didn't even listen to the music,' says Simon Barker, although she often attended the Pistols' gigs, and was the first out on the floor to pogo. Astonishingly, she once said to Barker in the mid-eighties, 'Ooh, I listened to that song "Anarchy in the UK" the other day. It's quite good really, isn't it?'

Although he and Vivienne were again living under the same roof, McLaren's obsession with the band precluded any involvement with Vivienne, the boys or the shop. Accordingly, she grew increasingly angry and tired. 'She did all the work while I kept threatening to leave,' he bragged. The couple were not on good terms. Out of frustration and resentment, Vivienne would sometimes lock McLaren out of the flat at night, and when he returned he had to shin up the drainpipe. 'They always made out they were totally broke,' remembers Paul Cook. 'That was one of their tricks.' In fact the shop was bringing in regular profits.

As well as their floundering personal relationship, there were professional reasons for the couple's growing acrimony. All the main protagonists of the movement were pulling in different directions. Vivienne wanted to concentrate on fashion that would have a political impact, while McLaren was into cash, chaos, the band and self-promotion. Meanwhile, Reid was struggling to achieve the overthrow of the status quo, while the boys in the band pursued fun, booze, narcotics and girls. They were paid £25 a week and as much lager as they could consume. Despite all these strains, to some extent Vivienne still remained in thrall to McLaren.

The pair were enjoying increasing notoriety as a moral threat to society. And though McLaren would not admit it, Keith Wainwright felt: 'I think that Vivienne probably helped Malcolm on an intellectual level, whereas Malcolm was more on the street level. They were both ambitious. Yes, they *both* wanted to get on and make money.' One friend observed that the fanatical couple shared 'a workhorse stamina'. Vivienne's tenacity expressed itself not only in her determination to keep her relationship with McLaren going, but in the obsessive attention to detail she applied to her clothes. Once they had been bought they were typically scissored, razored and worn to rags, but there was nothing throwaway or shoddy about them. Vivienne used inappropriately good-quality materials, painstakingly researched and sourced, and crafted each item with a seamstress's neatness. She had no truck with the trash culture of most sixties boutique designers, who in reaction to the *ancien régime* of high fashion lazily offered inexpensive and poorly-made rags. Vivienne did not want to sacrifice quality to cheapness. Like Jean Muir, she was one of the few British designers who valued quality and craft, even if for her customers, more than any others, such attributes were peculiarly irrelevant. And though, unlike Muir, she did not as yet have the technical skills of dressmaking and tailoring necesary to produce well-constructed garments, she always used good cloth.

With McLaren engrossed in his projects and indulging in the odd affair, there was little physical affection between the couple, and Vivienne was lonely and frustrated. Throughout her career it would be at just such times of unhappiness that she produced her best designs, finding solace in her work. Another outlet was experimentation, and she flirted with lesbianism (a fad for heterosexual women in punk circles). McLaren remembers coming back to the flat and finding Vivienne in bed with 'a lesbian in the Bromley Contingent who wore a leather hat'. Vivienne also had periodic crushes on the boys around her, notably Steve Jones and Sid Vicious, whom she would alternately mother and want to sleep with. 'I got so upset, really emotionally upset at such an idea,' says McLaren. 'I was outraged and went blue in the face.'

Gradually, the Seditionaries fashions were getting glossy-magazine and newspaper coverage independently of the Sex Pistols – indeed, the band was sometimes not even mentioned. Miles Chapman featured the clothes in the January 1977 edition of *Honey*, followed in May by both *Elle* and *19*. This recognition was a fillip to Vivienne, whose lack of self-esteem had kept her in McLaren's shadow. She needed the approbation of others for her confidence to blossom, and the result was to put her in direct conflict with McLaren. While she had previously complied with his exploitation of the Cambridge Rapist T-shirt, she now refused to cooperate with his planned publicity stunt of getting *her* to set fire to the wax effigies of the Beatles in Madame Tussaud's, with the Pistols photographed in front of the conflagration. 'He was deadly serious,' she told the *Guardian* in 1992. 'He really tried to get me to do that, but he wouldn't have been anywhere around when it happened. I wouldn't do it because I thought it would endanger public life, [though] I could see what a good publicity stunt it would be.'

McLaren, who was tiring of Vivienne's humourless cast of mind and her commitment to an imagined social revolution, complained that she 'never really got it. I was so urban. Punk was a projection of a much darker childhood than hers, rooted so much in the politics of the sixties, which Vivienne had absolutely no association with.' She did not understand how to be dangerous with style, he said, because she was an illiterate who could not create poetry out of potent symbols. In fact, the gulf between the two was one of intent, not intellect: her seriousness versus his frivolity. What Vivienne lacked was an affinity with the popular culture of the street. As evidence of her lack of comprehension, McLaren singled out a T-shirt she had designed which fused a ditty about the charge of the Light Brigade with the Hell's Angels, another mounted regiment. The juxtaposition failed, not because Vivienne was illiterate, but because she had not injected it with a contemporary reference that would fire up a teenager. The semiotics of the street did not impinge on her isolated sensibilities; she was not 'plugged in', but invented in a vacuum. McLaren had a brazen, feet-on-the-ground, finger-on-the-pulse modernity. He was insincere, glib and witty. Vivienne, on the other hand, was fantastical, shrill and abstruse. She had a romanticised notion of historicism and tradition, but her sincerity was heavy-handed.

The contrasted sensibilities of the couple had made them a good team, but the divergence in their objectives was becoming more apparent. 'They tended to argue quite a bit in a very naggy sort of way,' said Jordan. 'It was never easy. You certainly got no feeling of a sexual relationship, very few outward signs of emotion or affection between them.' McLaren cast Vivienne as the killjoy and nag, and she 'taunted him to get annoyed with her – she wants people to get annoyed with her'. Sometimes this led to physical violence – a theme which was to recur in Vivienne's later relationships, for to her confrontation was preferable to being ignored. As the aggression mounted, not least because McLaren was losing control of the band and the media's demands, the relationship became increasingly vitriolic. McLaren's immersion in his own affairs angered Vivienne, and she was intolerant of his mood-swings: 'Vivienne did not understand why I was so dogged sometimes, why I could not see the wood for the trees. She was much more pragmatic than I ever was. She was extremely stubborn and given to mad outrages.' But it was Vivienne who was single-handedly running the shop and the family: she received no practical help from him. People were often surprised to discover that the couple had children. 'You wouldn't know she had any family,' says Paul Cook, who remembers Joe asking him, 'What's Malcolm actually like, then?' Alan Jones wonders 'what those kids must have gone through' while Vivienne was off hand-picking her 'family' of punks, who would conform to her ideas and become her mouthpieces – 'We were the perfect dysfunctional family,' says Jones. Nils Stevenson says the boys were 'passed by, never involved, sort of invisible'. Joe, he says, was 'mad for his mum, and there are lots of demons in him that are now unleashed by drink. Ben is another kind of victim, who's always been ignored.'

By the late seventies it was blindingly clear that Ben, who had now left school, was emotionally damaged. He sought solace in photography, tinkering on the pornographic fringes. Ben inspired a protective pity in many who encountered him because he was such an affable boy, and was fiercely loyal to his mother. He played down the difficult relationship with McLaren, which had caused him such suffering and had irreparably damaged his feelings of self-worth.

'We always loved Ben,' says Michael Kostiff. ' "The Postman", we called him [he had worked for the Post Office to earn his fare to New York]. He was a very sweet guy.' Kostiff and his wife Gerlinde spent time with Ben while they were all staying at the Chelsea Hotel in New York in 1980. They found him pleasant but strange. One of his pastimes was to take a map of Manhattan, divide it into grids, and systematically walk each block of the city, one day at a time, until he had crossed the island. 'I thought it was marvellous,' says Kostiff, 'but quite weird as well.' Having achieved this, he found a job delivering a car to Los Angeles, and asked if he could borrow the

Kostiffs' credit card. When they refused, 'he couldn't believe it'. But then, Ben's expectations had been set by his mother and stepfather, who habitually imposed on others' generosity or gullibility.

Though it was not obvious to all of those who knew them, McLaren needed Vivienne's practicality and application to make the movement work. 'I wasn't caring, and I had much more sense of humour. She preferred order, I preferred chaos. Chaos made me creative. Vivienne always had to be very serious all of the time. I was never hindered. It was a great counterpoint, and I'll cherish that for all time.' But in public he underplayed her contribution, keen to persuade onlookers and press alike that, as Ben Kelly put it, it was he who was 'making all the moves, and she was slightly quieter in the background. He had a bigger mouth on him.'

It was now Vivienne who had the clearer vision of the look and identity of the shop: 'It became quite apparent that she was driving those sorts of ideas more than Malcolm was. He wanted things to happen, but perhaps he was more interested in the speed of things happening, and not exactly what it was that was happening.' It was Vivienne who meticulously selected the fabrics and images, and welded the elements together to create a look.

While Vivienne's designs clothed some of the band (Johnny Rotten now refused to act as the shop mannequin), and she attended some of their concerts, she never toured with the Pistols, and her life, unlike McLaren's, was not inextricably linked with theirs. Paul Cook had the impression that Vivienne thought McLaren was 'wasting his time with the band. Neither of them understood it. They were naïve about the power of it.' Nils Stevenson, who worked as a roadie for the Sex Pistols, believes that McLaren hated being on tour with the band: 'He wanted to get back to the shop. He felt the money was in the shop.' However, the Pistols' notoriety – to which she contributed – sold Vivienne's clothes. Throughout 1976 the press coverage of the band was moving beyond the music magazines and into the mainstream media. Newspaper headlines reported punch-ups and scraps at various gigs, such as the Nashville pub in West Kensington, where Vivienne tried to knock out a young fan for taking her place near the stage. The band was even denounced in Parliament as 'unbelievably nauseating' and 'the antithesis of humankind'.

But the Sex Pistols reached a new level of notoriety as a consequence of their behaviour on 1 December 1976. It began when the super-group

Queen pulled out at the last moment from an interview with Bill Grundy on Thames Television's late-afternoon *Today* programme. EMI suggested the Pistols as a substitute. Before the interview, the four nervous and drunk youths were wound up by McLaren, who showed them an interview in the *NME* in which a rival punk band, the Stranglers, had contemptuously laid into them. On arriving at the studio, Grundy, inebriated himself, exacerbated the tense situation by making it clear that he had not wanted to interview the Pistols. The inevitable explosion took place in front of millions of viewers when, at the end of an ill-natured interview, Grundy taunted the band by saying, 'Go on, you've got another ten seconds. Say something outrageous.' Steve Jones obliged with, 'You dirty bastard . . . You dirty fucker . . . You fucking rotter!' In the limousine driving them away from the studio, McLaren told the band: 'By accident rather than design, you've seriously made history.'

Though the word 'fuck' had been uttered on British television for the first time a decade earlier by the theatre critic Kenneth Tynan, the tabloids decided to make the incident front-page news. 'The Filth and the Fury' read the headline in the *Daily Express*. 'The Night of the Nasties. Four-Letter Punk Group in TV Storm' announced the *Daily Mail*. 'Why I Did It', Grundy told the *Sun*. The public's outrage was epitomised, according to the media, by the hysterical outburst of James Holmes, a forty-seven-year-old lorry driver who had been so offended he had kicked his television in. 'I can swear as well as anyone but I don't want this kind of muck coming into my home at teatime,' he told the *Daily Mirror*. As a result of the furore, EMI cancelled their contract with the band, giving them a £40,000 payoff.

The following month a member of the band vomited over the floor of the terminal building at Heathrow Airport. This unplanned incident attracted widespread media attention, but when McLaren attempted to stimulate further coverage by assembling a large group of punks to greet the band on their return from Amsterdam, it was a non-event. The band's outrageous behaviour led to their new contract with A&M being abruptly terminated after only one week. McLaren converted the setback into a publicity stunt, claiming that he was 'going in and out of doors collecting cheques': £40,000 from EMI and £75,000 from A&M, the band having delivered nothing.

Obscenities and punch-ups, though, were insignificant compared to the impact heroin would have on the band and its followers. With the arrival in London of ex-New York Doll Johnny Thunders, his new band the Heartbreakers and the promiscuous punk groupie Nancy Spungeon, class-A drugs were introduced to the Chelsea punk scene. 'No shooting up until Nancy showed up,' said Leee (sic) Childers, the band's manager. 'If the Heartbreakers brought heroin to England' – an exaggeration – 'then Nancy brought it to Sid.' Spungeon, a registered heroin addict who had spread her favours through the New York rock scene, was determined to bed a Sex Pistol when she arrived in London in the spring of 1977. Both Jordan and Simon Barker, then sharing the Buckingham Gate flat with Sid, were warned off her by another New York groupie, Sable Star. They were left in no doubt of her ambition, Barker remembers, when they saw a postcard she had written in which she said she 'wanted Johnny Rotten, but he wasn't interested. Sid met her and thought she was the most beautiful woman he'd ever met, but Sid was a virgin, and it was the first woman he'd ever been in love with.'

Spungeon had ensnared her Pistol. Under her influence, Sid became a heroin addict. 'Needles were left lying around the house,' says Barker, 'and some mornings I would go into the bathroom and there would be blood in the sink. But it was punk times, and you didn't want to seem shocked.' Spungeon also encouraged Sid to live up to his adopted surname, which ill-suited this soft-hearted youth, who nevertheless tried to impress his girl by acting tough. The flatmates tried to get rid of her by refusing to speak to her, throwing her belongings out of the window and cutting her heroin with flour and talcum powder, but she was thick-skinned and tenacious. Within weeks Sid had contracted hepatitis, and was moved out by McLaren to recuperate at his friend Gerry Goldstein's London home.

Sid was now aggressively playing up to the public perception of punk as violent. Anaesthetised by drugs, he was able to endure the punch-ups, knifings and self-inflicted razor-slashes. 'You can see the progression in the T-shirts from SEX onwards,' says Simon Barker. 'At the beginning it was a pornographic thing, and it went on to become more political and propaganda about the punk movement. Anarchist, anti-establishment ... anything's destroyable – even yourself. It was Too Fast to Live, Too Young to Die, and Sid was fulfilling that prophesy.' As heroin took its grip on the London punk scene, McLaren's hold on Sid weakened, and the other members of the band, concerned for Sid, began to question McLaren's actions.

McLaren recalled his and Vivienne's dallyings with drugs at the time: 'We took heroin together at a party in Chelsea and were both sick in the toilet and didn't do it again. But we did take a lot of cocaine in New York, and I'd say she didn't hate it at all. She was always curious.' Compared to other members of the movement, Vivienne's drug intake was modest, and she remained ill-informed: 'Vivienne thought that smoking dope was the same as shooting up heroin,' Simon Barker remembered. 'I know in the punk days she had amphetamines, like everybody, but she can't handle booze, and would go right over the top, cartwheeling everywhere.' By and large Vivienne was not involved in drugs, although many of those around her were.

Throughout the 'Summer of Hate' in 1977 (as opposed to 1967's 'Summer of Love') the Pistols' violent reputation led to their being banned from most venues. McLaren encouraged them to indulge in nihilistic and drunken behaviour in order to maintain press attention. He was determined to release the band's anti-royalist single 'God Save the Queen' to coincide with the celebrations of the Queen's Silver Jubilee in early June, but when the contracts with EMI and A&M were scrapped within weeks of each other in March, he had to scramble around for another record deal. He eventually succeeded in signing one with Richard Branson, of Virgin Records.

The single was released on 27 May. Its lyrics dubbed the Queen the figurehead of 'a fascist regime', while the cover featured her face impaled on a safety pin. Within five days Virgin had sold 150,000 copies of the record even though high-street chains such as Boots, W.H. Smith and Woolworth's refused to stock it. During the week of the Jubilee the anti-monarchy anthem reached number one, though the slot was left blank by the chart organisers, as they did not wish to publicise it. 'Top chain stores are refusing to stock the record. Concert promoters have cancelled the Sex Pistols' appearances. But such is the new-found and disturbing power of punk that nothing can stop the disc's runaway success,' reported the *Daily Mirror*.

British society seemed polarised between the monarchist majority who hung out bunting to honour the Queen's Jubilee, and the minority who gravitated towards the anarchic message of punk. While many spent the eve of the celebrations preparing street parties or sleeping under black plastic bin-liners on the Mall to catch a glimpse of the monarch, the punks – also in bin-liners – defaced the Union Jack and screamed obscenities. 'Little boys would come running into my shop,' Vivienne says, 'and say, "Do you really think the Queen is a moron?" If you took away the Queen, the army and all those people, [we] wouldn't have this figurehead to look up to that smiles at them and pretends that everything is all right. Maybe, though, she doesn't know what's going on, the old berk.'

On the night of 7 June, Richard Branson, persuaded by McLaren, held a party for two hundred people on a Thames riverboat which sailed under the banner 'Queen Elizabeth Welcomes the Sex Pistols'. While the Pistols were playing, a scuffle broke out between a photographer and Jah Wobble, a white Rastafarian friend of Johnny Rotten's. In a panic, the captain radioed the River Police, and within minutes their launches were bearing down on the boat. 'The police got really heavy,' John Egan recalled. 'The barges surrounded us, like *Miami Vice*, while we were on board singing "The Jolly Roger". It got really horrid – right out of hand.' A megaphone announced: 'This is the River Police. You will have to stop playing and we will escort you to the pier.' Alan Jones remembers that as the officers boarded the vessel Vivienne defiantly pulled down her white trousers and 'pissed over the side of the boat in full view of the police'. The minor scuffle escalated, and the police began to seize guests.

At Charing Cross pier two officers approached Vivienne and, each seizing a fistful of her hair, dragged her down the gangplank. 'I distinctly heard a policeman say, "There's McLaren. Get him!" ' says Ben Kelly, who saw six policemen knock McLaren down. Kelly leapt to McLaren's defence, but a burly arm caught him around the throat. He was arrested and thrown him into a Black Maria. Tracey and Debbie, the shop girls from Seditionaries, were thrown in on top of him, and 'a policeman or woman put boots across their throats to hold them down'. The punks were taken to Bow Street police station. A few minutes later they heard Vivienne being brought in, kicking and yelling, 'You fucking pigs! Where's Malcolm?' According to Ben Kelly, she was 'thrilled to be arrested, and didn't stop banging on about it. Someone told me she practically threw herself into the black van, yelling, "They've got Malcolm. Fucking bastards!" ' McLaren, who had also been arrested, 'made such a drama about it,' says Paul Cook, 'but the band had spent loads of nights in the cells.' The publicity stunt had been more successful than McLaren could have hoped.

The next day Branson, accompanied by a lawyer, bailed them all out. (Not that they were to show much gratitude: in McLaren's unreleased film about the Sex Pistols' rise to fame, *Who Killed Bambi?*, the title song, written by Vivienne and Ten Pole Tudor, included the line 'Never trust a hippie' – a dig at Branson.) The media gave the whole incident extensive coverage, the *Evening Standard*, apparently indifferent to the contempt with which much of the public viewed the punks, printing the names and addresses of those arrested. To Vivienne's satisfaction, the affair turned into one of the high points of the punk legend. 'The Pistols should have disappeared as soon as the "God Save the Queen" record came out,' says Jamie Reid. Alan Jones agrees: 'It should have ended with the boat trip. They'd done it all – the clothes, the hit. They couldn't get more anarchic. And you just knew it would end in violence.'

Throughout the second half of 1977 the press continued to report on the band's scraps: 'Rotten Razored', the *Daily Mirror* screamed on 28 June. In November and December the *Daily Mail* published alarmist centre-spreads on punk, the degeneration of youth and the rise of moral relativism. While the front pages decried punk violence, the fashion sections celebrated punk style. Three *Observer* colour supplements in 1977 and 1978 featured Seditionaries clothes, and even the establishment British *Vogue* selected Johnny Rotten as one of the 'Successes of the Year'. The *Investors Chronicle* went so far as to vote the Pistols 'Young Businessmen of the Year' in a cover story which praised their acumen in making £115,000 from EMI and A&M in a matter of weeks, while giving them nothing in return.

McLaren resolutely disapproved of cooperating with the mainstream fashion press. When, for instance, the photographer Michael Roberts, who was working freelance for the *Sunday Times* and Condé Nast, came to Seditionaries to borrow clothes for a shoot, he was refused. To get around the ban, Roberts came back pretending to be a customer, bought the clothes, photographed them, then sent them back to the shop requesting a credit note. Vivienne, however, craved mainstream approval. To that end, and behind McLaren's back, she took her designs to Grace Coddington, the influential senior fashion editor on British *Vogue*. Despite the fact that Coddington was wearing a mohair jumper – 'an exact copy of the one I had designed' – Vivienne's clothes were dismissed as irrelevant to the magazine. When McLaren heard about the meeting, he accused Vivienne of having betrayed their ideals.

During the winter of 1977–78, the Pistols' increasingly unbridled behaviour made it clear that they were heading for a fall. McLaren was determined to make his reputation in the United States by importing his extreme interpretation of the New York Dolls' nihilism back to the scene of its initial inspiration. The CBGBs crowd may not have taken him seriously in 1975, but now he would take America by storm. In January 1978 the band commenced a controversial tour in the deeply conservative southern states, where McLaren correctly calculated that they would cause the greatest offence and receive the biggest headlines. Dressed in Vivienne's hate clothes, the band performed under a Warner Brothers publicity poster which read:

> We're the flowers in the dustbin
> We're the poison in your human machine
> We're the future
> Your future

'You cowboys are all a bunch of fucking faggots!' Sid yelled at the Texan audiences. Unsurprisingly, such antics provoked an angry response. McLaren, measuring his success purely in terms of column inches and broadcast minutes, whipped up the antagonism, heedless of the consequences. Sid was by now sodden with heroin, methadone and alcohol. Separated from Nancy Spungeon, and with his mother, also an addict, back in London, he was isolated from any comfort or support. With no one to turn to for solace, and goaded by drunk, aggressive audiences, he took to slashing himself in public to satisfy their lust for blood. Even his friend Johnny Rotten could no longer control him. Sid was in free-fall, and no one could save him.

Disgusted by McLaren's manipulations and Sid's descent into drugged mayhem, Rotten terminated the tour, broke up the band and returned to London in late January. A few weeks later McLaren set off to join Paul Cook and Steve Jones in Rio de Janeiro, in pursuit of another publicity coup. With the fugitive Great Train Robber Ronnie Biggs they recorded 'Belsen was a Gas' and 'A Punk Prayer', dedicated respectively to Martin Bormann and Myra Hindley. Sid, abandoned, was left directionless. Slipping in and out of overdose comas, he returned to London and Nancy Spungeon's arms.

He did not stay there long. Ostracised by his old friends, including Rotten, and after the fatal overdose of their flatmate John Shepcock in August, he and Nancy decided to rebuild his career in New York. They moved to the Chelsea Hotel, where they sank into a drug-induced torpor, funded by the odd stumbling concert played by Sid at Max's Kansas City Club. At dawn on 11 October 1978 Nancy was found dead on their bathroom floor, stabbed in the lower abdomen with Sid's hunting knife. Sid could not recall the night's events, but was arrested for her murder. Though McLaren bailed him out with Richard Branson's money, Sid believed he had nothing to live for, and attempted suicide. Four months later, on 1 February 1979, he was found dead at a friend's apartment in Greenwich Village. An overdose of virtually pure heroin bought for him by his mother had killed him. With self-revealing frankness, McLaren said of Sid's mother: 'I didn't trust her. I never trusted mothers. I still don't.' Sid had vowed, like his hero James Dean, not to live beyond the age of twenty-one. In 1986 his decline was to be inaccurately and melodramatically portrayed in the film *Sid and Nancy*.

Though some members of her circle at the time believe that Vivienne harboured an affection and motherly concern for Sid, the most malleable and naïve of the Pistols, it is difficult to square these claims with her actions. When she heard about Nancy's murder she produced a T-shirt printed with Sid's image which read: 'She's Dead. I'm Alive. I'm Yours!' When Sid died she sat down at her kitchen table and crafted a 'Sid Action Man' dressed in a swastika vest and black jeans, lay it in a coffin and displayed it in the shop. McLaren had taught her well: every event, however tragic, was a trading opportunity, a chance to publicise one's wares. Robyn Beeche, an Australian photographer who met Vivienne at this time, believes 'she felt culpable, but I don't think she'd ever let anyone know that. It's her way of remaining an enigma.'

Seeking refuge in the explanation that punk was ironic, and 'some people just didn't get it', Vivienne never publicly accepted that she and McLaren had any share of responsibility for Sid's self-destruction. Disillusioned and villified in the press, McLaren fled to Paris to stay with Jean-Charles de Castelbajac and cast around for a new project, while Vivienne retreated to the flat to experiment. Not surprisingly, she did not wish to be associated with the violent demise of the Sex Pistols. She was irked by the way in which the classlessness of punk had been compromised: 'They were trying to give this punk rock thing some kind of Marxist frame which I didn't think was correct

. . . punk rockers were never entirely working class or upper class or bourgeoisie. They were always all of them,' she insisted. Punk had become a 'polarisation of something old hat'; by this phrase, typical of her, Vivienne meant that punk was the antithesis of class, class categories were inapplicable. The largely uncomprehending young punks adopted Vivienne and McLaren's poses of nihilism and aggression. Vivienne 'liked the aggression in terms of communicating ideas', but McLaren admitted: 'I do abandon people. I'm a bit like a sculptor, except instead of using clay I use people.'

Though Jordan argues that these were 'happy times' until the tragedy set in, McLaren has described punk as a 'dark subject', having its roots in his 'black childhood', something that Vivienne could not comprehend. When a young person entered Seditionaries he or she 'joined some fraternity, and its rules were different from anywhere else, and it was dark and intimidating and forbidding . . . Punk rock was against the idea of career – even career rock 'n' roll, against the idea of a very organised music industry, against stadium groups lording it over everyone, and against the technology that was dominating the music industry. It was against trying in any way to be technical . . . It was brilliant, anti-professional, and it looked clandestine.'

Peppering his declarations with seductive words – 'fraternity', 'romantic', 'individual', 'rock 'n' roll', 'clandestine' – that were guaranteed to entice discontented teenagers, McLaren incited them to play out self-destructive situations in the glare of the media that he had enlisted. 'Youth has to behave irreverently,' he says. 'It has to take drugs, because of its fundamental belief in its own immortality, which it needs to assert over and over again.' He claimed his actions were political art, but in reality they served his personal pursuit of money and fame. 'I got called many things,' he remembers, 'by journalists, by executives in the music business, sometimes by members of the band itself. I was meant to be a charlatan, a con man, or (most flatteringly) the culprit responsible for turning British popular culture into nothing more than a marketing gimmick.' Vivienne was his knowing accomplice. In their wake they left a string of burnt-out or dead cases.

The carnage was captured in a maudlin documentary entitled *Dead on Arrival* which filmed the last violent Sex Pistols concerts. It ended with Mary Whitehouse, long ridiculed as the chastising voice of the 'moral majority', commenting: 'I'm not shocked by punk, I'm ashamed by it . . . what have we done to our young?' In Derek Jarman's 1978 film *Jubilee*, a personal interpretation of bleak late-seventies London, it was Jordan, not Vivienne, who was cast as the female icon of punk. Vivienne was furious. She had expected the film to be a promotional vehicle for the shop, the band and, above all, her. It turned out to be none of these. Her position as the Queen of Punk had, she felt, been appropriated. Dismissing Jarman as an outsider and Jordan as a traitor, in a fit of jealous pique she printed a seven-hundred-word 'open-letter' to Jarman in the form of a T-shirt, signed, for no apparent reason, 'Vivienne Weekwood', and bearing a one-penny 'stamp'. The text was hand-written in her schoolteacher's script, like McLaren's 'Oliver Twist' T-shirt and others. Vivienne underlined or double underlined certain words for emphasis, and made free use of four-letter expletives and occasionally rambling asides in brackets.

The 'letter', which completely filled both front and back of the T-shirt, began with an announcement that Vivenne had seen the film ('once', she pointed out), and judged it to be 'boring and therefore disgusting'. She did, however, concede that unlike most film-makers, at least Jarman had the 'soul' to deal with the 'absolute relevance' of punk and urban decay in contemporary England.

Turning to one of the leading characters in *Jubilee*, who was dressed in period costume as Elizabeth I (a figure whom Vivienne, incidentally, would one day refer to in her work — indeed, she would even pose as her in one of her advertising campaigns), she vented her fury at the film for lingering on such 'grand stuff', which she concluded was simply an expression of Jarman's gay love of dressing up, and even speculated on whether or not he had 'a cock between his legs'. She went on to take a partisan swipe at the Sex Pistols' rivals The Clash, and to compliment the acting performances of the amateurs Jordan and Helen Wellington-Lloyd. She approved of Jarman's message that 'nationalism is vile' and royalty a 'con trick', but complained that he should have been braver in his critique of contemporary England, and shouldn't have resorted to 'perverse artiness' and decadence. Copies of the T-shirt were sold at Seditionaries.

Despite Vivienne's savage criticisms of Jarman and his 'irresponsible film', in fact *Jubilee* memorably captured the greyness and hopelessness of late-1970s England. Its inner-city streets were littered with refuse, and the urban infrastructure — tube stations, bus shelters, council housing — was rundown and neglected. Large tracts of London lay derelict, peopled by the unemployed, the violent and the aimless. It was against this depressed background that the punks acted out their youthful protest.

Shortly after creating the T-shirt, Vivienne reiterated her passionate criticism of the film in a tirade to the painter Duggie Fields, who she ran into in a café just around the corner from Seditionaries. Fields leapt to Jarman's defence, insisting that he and Vivienne actually had 'far more in common than she realised'. She refused to believe him.

Vivienne has a long memory, and an ability to perform, unabashed, a complete U-turn in her point of view. Ten years after the 'open letter' T-shirt, she encountered Fields again. She reminded him of their earlier conversation, and 'apologised for having been so worked up'. To her credit, she told him that she had, eventually, come around to his opinion: perhaps Derek Jarman was talented, interesting and brave after all. She now regrets having written the vituperative T-shirt, and has requested that the full text not be included in this book as it is 'not representative of her work'.

Whatever Vivienne might argue, it was Jordan who ultimately became the female embodiment of punk, because she was fearless, independent of McLaren's manipulations, and she originated and maintained the strongest personal image. Though she did not intentionally overshadow Vivienne, Jordan was a better communicator: 'tough, front-line, singular, courageous, audacious', says Ben Kelly. 'She really gave society a black eye.' Jon Savage referred to her as 'the first Sex Pistol'. When Jordan announced to Vivienne that she was going to marry Kevin Mooney of Adam and the Ants, Vivienne railed at her: 'You're a symbol! How could you go off and get married?' Jordan realised that for Vivienne marriage was 'a big statement, and she was denying the emotional part. She only saw it as a political statement.' To Vivienne's mind, Jordan was a traitor to the anti-bourgeois cause.

In the spring of 1979, the Buckingham Gate flatmates went their separate ways. The party was over. As Derek Dunbar sat sobbing on packing cases, Simon Barker asked him what was wrong. 'Don't you realise?' replied Dunbar. 'It's all over.' During the next six months, using the excuse that he needed to collect their post, Dunbar repeatedly returned to the flat, climbing four flights of the fire-escape and entering their old home through a skylight. There he would sit remembering dead friends — Sid, Tracey O'Keefe (who had died of leukaemia, although she was dabbling in heroin), John Shepcock – and the extraordinary times they had shared. 'McLaren should take a lot of the blame for what happened,' he now believes. Ever ready to move on to a new shock tactic, McLaren now planned to print IRA T-shirts and to stage a West End musical featuring the various European terrorist groups who were then violently challenging the political status quo: the IRA, ETA, the Red Brigades and the Baader-Meinhof gang.

Though many punks still feel bitter or melancholy when they talk about those days, and though contemporary commentators dismissed the movement as either demonically destructive or, as the establishment couturier Sir Hardy Amies put it, 'a pissy little thing that lasted ten minutes', in its annihilating wake new opportunities in fashion, music, graphic design and advertising were born. Punk was a form of 'social churning' which brought new, young talent to the fore. Many talented people built careers on its anarchic principles, including the journalists Tony Parsons, Julie Burchill and Danny Baker, the various bands, architects, graphic, fashion and industrial designers, music producers, artists and academics. A proliferation of small, independent record labels were established, although, interestingly, the three biggest punk bands – the Sex Pistols, The Clash and The Jam – all signed with major labels. The word 'punk' came to indicate a licence to destroy, giving rise to punk photographers, hairdressers, writers *et al*, who upended the conventions of their trades.

Punk also touched the most unexpected worlds. Jean-Louis Scherrer, for example, a French couturier whose expensive clothes were favoured by ostentatious Middle Eastern and Mediterranean women, kept a postcard of a London punk on his desk 'for inspiration'. Punk's anti-bourgeois rhetoric could be interpreted, according to fashion journalist Suzy Menkes, as 'the great letting-go of England. Vivienne's England, the England she was reacting against, was that of Macmillan: the meanness, the end of Empire, the end of austerity.'

Punk's importance has increased over time. In its heyday it affected only a few people, but its legacy is recognisable in many walks of life, from the increasing sloganising of politics to the elevation of unschooled youth above age and experience. The breaking-down of inhibitions released an astonishing creativity. By dismissing the traditions and sacred cows of the past, the young were presented with a blank canvas on which to scrawl. They no longer felt they had to be musically trained in order to play a guitar in a band, or classically literate to write a poetic song.

Vivienne was a shining example of this do-it-yourself ethos. Self-taught, and unburdened by the conventions of classical dressmaking, she could invent in an idiosyncratic way that would surely have been refined out of her by a fashion college – it is hard to imagine a conventionally trained student creating the 'Marilyn Monroe' T-shirt. She railed against British art and fashion schools, exaggeratedly accusing them of not teaching their pupils the basic practices of classical dressmaking.

Sebastian Conran, later an industrial and product designer, is emphatic that 'punk is to do with breaking the mould, making things slightly provocative and not having things which are perfect. It was conceptually driven, and there was a huge amount of creativity in what people wore. People thought it was a uniform, but each person dressed differently, styling things, stitching them, chopping up clothes, adding insignia.' 'Those kids were absolutely proud of themselves ... They could transform themselves and feel so wonderful,' Peter York observed. 'Malcolm and Vivienne saw the despair in people at the time and had the genius to do something about it, practically.'

For some years, Vivienne determinedly distanced herself from this transformation, in which she and McLaren had played a crucial role. Her denial of punk's importance rests on three facts: a fundamental failure to grasp the influence and power of the movement she helped unleash; a bitter battle with McLaren which led her to disassociate herself for many years from the fruits of their labour; and a sea-change in her attitude towards her career. She was disillusioned that punk had not turned out to be the social revolution McLaren had led her to believe it would be, just an opportunistic craze that had turned violent. She no longer wished to challenge the establishment, but to join it, and her punk credentials did not sit happily with this new ambition. In 1993, however she admitted of punk: 'I do think it's a very, very dangerous thing to do. I wouldn't play with that again, actually ... I don't want to whitewash myself.'

When Jon Savage was researching his detailed history of punk, *England's Dreaming*, he requested interviews with Vivienne but was informed by Simon Barker, acting as her intermediary, that she would

not cooperate unless he paid her £1,000. The request was flatly refused. Vivienne thus wrote herself out of Savage's history, which as
a result accorded a disproportionate importance to McLaren. 'In
retrospect, I think I made a mistake not to be interviewed,' Vivienne
now admits. One suspects that the main reason she did not cooperate
with Savage was not money, but control. Both she and McLaren
preferred to disseminate self-serving myths rather than unadorned
facts, which is one reason why, over time, their version of events
changed.

During the early days of SEX and Seditionaries, Vivienne would
often allow McLaren to claim the credit for things that in fact she
had done. Bella Freud is adamant: 'Malcolm did not do it all . . . She
was the creative one. Yes, she took some of Malcolm's ideas, but she
made them happen. She was the one to graft, to craft and make them
work. And I think that she had a big effect on him, but I don't think
he had any wish to give her credit.' By 1986 Vivienne was stating:
'The thing is, I *invented* punk with Malcolm McLaren. Together we
formulated a master plan for the ultimate rebellion, for one thing
which, like rock 'n' roll, should shake the foundations of civilisation
– it was a total blast . . . I want to promote change in the very fabric
of society. So I am still carrying the torch for punk.'

In the late eighties, though, preferring to align herself with high
culture, Vivienne began to deny her former interest in the street and
'the revolution'. When asked about punk by Gillian Greenwood, who
was producing a 1990 profile of her for *The South Bank Show*, she
snarled, 'I don't want to talk about it. That was all Malcolm.' Simon
Barker was appalled, and protested, 'But Vivienne, you *were* all about
that. It was an important time, and you should get your bit of history
in.' She did not agree. BBC Radio 4 producer Anna Robinson, who
worked with Vivienne on a 1990 broadcast entitled *Opinions*, recalls,
'She completely disowned the thing at the time. She didn't make any
claims for it being anything of interest, and said it was rebellion, and
there was nothing more to it than that . . . I got the distinct impression
it was the pleasure of being contrary, and as punk had become an
icon, that had to go as well.'

But in 1994 she was to boast, 'I'm proud to have been part of it.
It was a heroic time.' By then the movement had reached iconic status.
There were endless punk revivals, some risibly banal. Gianni Versace,
one of the most commercially adept interpreters in the business, offered

a sanitised, kid-glove leather version of the S&M fashions that Vivienne and McLaren had introduced to such shocking effect in the mid-seventies. The original clothing and ephemera became highly collectible, particularly among the Japanese, who, born into a tightly controlled society, were enthralled by punk's xenophobic and iconoclastic power, its fascination with the alien, and the sexual and social deviance it dared to celebrate. Other enthusiastic collectors included museums all over the world, and members of the international rock establishment, including Madonna and Nellie Hooper of Soul II Soul. By the mid-nineties even Vivienne and McLaren were collecting old pieces of their own which they had discarded at the time.

With collectibility came problems of authenticity and provenance. In the mid-eighties, Vivienne, desperate for cash, had leased the printing screens of all her T-shirt designs to the rival King's Road shop Boy (they were never to be returned) for a mere £200. Her stipulations restricting their use were ignored, and originals became difficult to authenticate as the shirts flooded the Japanese market. 'They paid her a small royalty and just did hundreds of them ... Many were sold to the Japanese, but Boy scrubbed out the penis entering Minnie and the anarchy symbol on the ear [on "Mickey and Minnie"],' says Simon Barker. The most valuable T-shirts were the early ones that had been hand-dyed and hand-printed with a school 'John Bull' printer on Vivienne's kitchen table or McLaren's office desk. These were distinguished by the fact that the colours ran, so the shirts could not be machine-washed. 'There are a lot of collectors now,' says Barker, 'who, for the right thing, will pay thousands. The "Venus" T-shirt with studs, bike-tyre shoulder caps and horsehair tresses; the one with "Perv" spelled out in chicken bones and hung with chains; and the one with the plastic breast pocket into which was slipped a pornographic playing card. Some girl sold a "Venus" T-shirt to Acupuncture [a London specialist store] for £600 in 1994. It was in bad condition and they got double that. I was offered £5,000 for a bones T-shirt by a Japanese.' These T-shirts were all hand-made by Vivienne on her kitchen table, each one taking at least a day. There are no more than half a dozen of each in existence.

The punk period was a watershed in Vivienne's personal and creative development. In the eighteen months during which she created the Sex Pistols' look, her confidence in her own creative abilities now took root and flourished. She had identified her talent, and was determined to leave her mark on international fashion. In doing so, she found a way to bury the provincial girl from the Snake Pass.

Part Two

THE GROUND-BREAKING DESIGNER

5   WORLD'S END

1979–1983

'Life is an adventure, so I make clothes to have adventures in
. . . They give you power over rich people, because you can
look more chic than they ever can.'

Vivienne Westwood, 1981

Vivienne was alone again. Unencumbered by children and undistracted
by McLaren, who was still in Paris, she retreated to Nightingale Lane
to conjure up a new style of sartorial rebel. Leaving the well-trodden
path of post-war youth cults behind, she found inspiration in a book
of nineteenth-century fashions showing the raiment of *les Incroyables*
and their female counterparts, *les Merveilleuses*. She decided that these
post-revolutionary French republicans could be updated.

The original *Incroyables* had worn defiant dress in reaction to the
political upheavals of the late eighteenth century when, as the
privileges of class and aristocratic birth were challenged, style emerged
as an alternative means of social stratification. Their dress celebrated
both the new republican politics and the romantic hero. Consequently
it appealed to ardent republicans and disaffected aristocrats. Over 150
years later, Vivienne Westwood was attracted by the flamboyant
dissent and eccentric dandyism of these peacocks.

On McLaren's return to London after a year's sojourn in Paris,
Vivienne showed him the designs for her next series of clothes. 'But
eighteen-year-olds just aren't going to get it. It isn't rock 'n' roll,' he
complained. 'I've got a much better idea. Get rid of the black, get
the gaudiness of pirates. You see, pirates are another form of punk.'
Once again, McLaren had lent a contemporary appeal to Vivienne's
efforts. His role as an originator of ideas was vital to her. With his
fashion instinct, he provided focus and topicality to her meanderings,
bringing to her attention the music, the gadgets and the issues that

would excite the young. Vivienne, with her tangential logic and diligent experimentation, was able to fuse these themes into the cut and decoration of her clothes, creating magical and truly original collections. Their best work was done in partnership because, like Janus, the couple faced in opposite directions. She, with her heightened sense of wonder, looked back, and marvelled at the shifting mannerisms, modes of sexual communication and peculiarities of dress of the past. He looked to contemporary street life and towards the immediate future, turning her costume into fashion.

McLaren half-heartedly returned to Vivienne at Nightingale Lane, but while their working partnership flourished over the next few years, their emotional relationship floundered. In his absence, reflecting her new interest in historical design, Vivienne had softened her personal look, replacing the harsh, sexual dominatrix dress with baggy layering. Her peroxided crop had grown out into hennaed tresses which she wore in girlish plaits, framing her fresh-faced complexion, now scrubbed of make-up. Moving her lithe body with characteristically erect gracefulness, and gesticulating expressively with her long, slender hands, she presented a pretty picture of a girlish ragamuffin. But McLaren was immune to this softer exterior – and at heart, Vivienne remained as belligerent as ever, easily riled by his infidelities. Jordan remembers: 'It was never very easy, their relationship. She's naggy. You certainly got no feeling of a sexual relationship, very few outward signs of emotions or affection between them.'

McLaren was often embarrassed by Vivienne's uninhibited out-bursts, and still belittled her by calling her 'a hick from Snake Pass'. Although he liked to present himself as a rebel, he was essentially conventional, and was squeamish about her excesses. 'You could see his eyes on her at the table,' remembers employee Lorraine Piggott, 'watching to see what she was up to, whether she was going to be OK, talking about being a designer, or whether she was going to be absolutely revolting.' Too much red wine or whisky could turn her into a bawdy exhibitionist.

Indulging in sexual dalliances when it suited him, in the name of 'artistic freedom', McLaren spent the next three years extricating himself from Vivienne's embrace. After twelve years, he found her a heavy-going and humourless companion, and wanted another mate. To Vivienne, life was a crusade, to McLaren it was a game. That was the nub of their incompatibility. 'I found it difficult to have fun with

Vivienne,' he now says. 'She never allowed us to relax, particularly in the company of friends. It depressed me, and I stopped going home.'

To bolster the shaky relationship, and to prove her love, Vivienne invested all her energies in pleasing McLaren through her designs, but she felt that nothing she did was good enough for him, and feared that without him she could not achieve anything – 'I needed Malcolm's ideas,' she said. McLaren exploited her dependency, maintaining control through intellectual browbeating and the threat of sexual infidelity: 'She eventually fell so much under my spell that she was working for me.' McLaren consistently cast Vivienne as a mere executor of his ideas during this period: 'You couldn't have a better soldier in your army, and she was so loyal. It breaks my heart to think I was not loyal too.' To those around them, including Caroline Baker, who shared their flat, sleeping in the corridor, it was evident that McLaren did not really care about anyone but himself: 'He knows how to flatter you and get what he wants. He's horrific, Mr Manipulator in person.'

The link between clothing and music would continue to be essential for the couple's business. At the beginning of each season, McLaren would provide Vivienne with a theme which related to the music he was promoting, and he would cull any designs he regarded as thematically extraneous, sexually incomprehensible or poorly executed. 'He's plugged in,' says Simon Barker, 'she's in a vacuum and never sees anything that's happening around her. That's why they were such a good team.'

By the closing months of 1979, escapism – from the persistent British class system, the deepening recession, the alarming rise in unemployment and the nation's flagging prestige – was epitomised in the emergence of two distinct and extreme groups of disenchanted youth: the fogies and the new romantics. The fogies posed as bookish, tweed-wearing, rural-loving reactionaries, affecting the manners, dress and politics of their fathers' generation. The new romantics, urban-based art students and their imitators, eschewed sexual distinction in dress, preferring to astonish and delight with lavish costume, cavalier locks and vivid facial make-up. They gathered at such London clubs as Billy's, Blitz and Club for Heroes, 'spinning forward in a whirl of eyeliner and ruffles. Getting a reaction was the ultimate goal,' according to one of their style leaders, the pop star Boy George.

Led by bands like Spandau Ballet, Visage and Adam and the Ants, and clubbers such as Philip Sallon, Steve Strange, Toyah Willcox and Chris Sullivan, the new romantics decked themselves out in the flamboyant historical dress of Jacobites, the velvet livery of operatic valets, the frogged mess-dress of Tolstoyan officers or the doublet and hose of Shakespearean courtiers. Typically, they made their own costumes or combined articles from street markets and theatrical costumiers – Adam Ant bought his distinctive charge of the Light Brigade frogged jacket at the closing-down sale of theatre outfitter Charles Fox in Covent Garden. In 1998 the designer John Galliano was to say: 'Vivienne is constantly innovating, but her work during the punk and new romantic periods defined the era. It's impossible to think of the bands, the music and the spirit of both punk and the new romantics without Vivienne's work.'

In general, the mainstream fashion scene was unadventurous, epitomised by the polite beige separates and classics of American designers such as Calvin Klein and Ralph Lauren. Some designers were tinkering with punk, and there was a general softening up of the silhouette, but without thematic direction. Gaudy disco clothes, as depicted in the 1978 film *Saturday Night Fever*, were also in evidence. Responding to the burgeoning new romanticism, Vivienne and McLaren came up with their own romantic character, a modern pirate. Vivienne's brief from McLaren was 'sun, sea and piracy'. Her designs were an inspired reaction to the familiar fashion landscape. If fans expected a tight, black, minimalist and bleakly modern uniform, she would give them a loose, multi-coloured, multi-layered and historically romantic look. Like a Jackson Pollock of fashion, she splashed colour onto London's drab canvas.

Initially, the Pirate look was worn by Adam Ant, formerly the lead singer of Bazooka Joe, the band which the Sex Pistols had supported at their first concert, and a character in Jarman's *Jubilee*. He was a regular customer at 430 King's Road, and was casting about for an image for his new band, Adam and the Ants. McLaren charged him £1,000 for a restyling, drawing a streak of white paint across his cheeks, Red Indian style, dressing him in Pirate-cum-Apache-Indian costume and giving him a spaghetti Western guitar and some African drums from Burundi. The Apache imagery was lifted from 'a fantastic book in Foyles that I stole', McLaren casually confessed. Within a few months, McLaren had taken over the management of the band, replaced Adam with a fourteen-year-old schoolgirl, Annabella L'win (of

Burmese origin, her real name was Lu Win), and renamed it Bow Wow Wow. But it was Adam's interpretation of the pirate/highwayman, epitomised by his 1981 hit single 'Stand and Deliver', that caught the popular imagination. Remarkably, in view of the expensive fiasco of their brief involvement with the Sex Pistols, McLaren secured a recording contract with EMI for Bow Wow Wow.

The Pirate theme was not pulled from thin air; McLaren had a music business prank to promote. He wanted to undermine the domination of the recording industry giants by the use of pirate radio and personal stereos. Pirate radio inevitably attracted him, as an illegal expression of the power of pop music. When the Sony Walkman was introduced to Britain in 1979, he was quick to grasp its potential, and devised a campaign to flout copyright law by encouraging young people to record hits from the radio. At the time, a long-playing music cassette cost about £4, a blank cassette only £1. In July 1980 Bow Wow Wow released a single on EMI entitled 'C30 C60 C90, Go!' (the name referring to the amount of recording time on blank cassettes). One of the verses ran:

It used to break my heart
When I went into your shop
We're out of stock
So I don't buy records in your shop
I tape 'em all.

The British Phonographic Industry, the industry's trade association, was infuriated, claiming that home taping was costing it over £200 million a year in lost sales. It issued a High Court writ claiming damages from the Japanese hi-fi company Toshiba, who had run an advertisement encouraging people to tape directly from albums and the radio without paying copyright fees. McLaren watched from the sidelines with glee. To heighten the appeal of his incitement to plunder the airwaves of pop music's treasures, he dressed Bow Wow Wow and its followers in pirate costume.

The lyrics of the band's track 'Work (Oh no my Daddy don't)' attempted to persuade fans that 'the demolition of the work ethic leads us to the age of the primitive'. In a period of high unemployment, McLaren was encouraging the young to drop out. This was a paradoxical standpoint for him to espouse, as he himself adhered to the work ethic. Even less could the workaholic Vivienne be expected to subscribe to this point of view.

Cries of child pornography greeted the launch of Bow Wow Wow's first album, the cover of which showed the nude, pubescent Annabella in a photographic reconstruction of Manet's *Déjeuner sur l'herbe*. McLaren's art history background was evident once again – he wanted to repeat the scandal caused by the original painting in 1863. 'Malcolm was a great person for taking something and abusing it,' Vivienne observed, though she appeared not to notice that he also abused people's friendship and trust. To ensure Annabella's emotional dependency, McLaren goaded the reluctant virgin to have sex with the boys in the band, whom he also pressured to visit Soho prostitutes, paying for them and waiting outside to hear their accounts of what had happened. When he realised that the gay scene was becoming fashionable, he suggested they feign homosexuality.

Just as the Pistols dressed in Seditionaries clothes, Bow Wow Wow promoted the Pirate look, which had developed into an amalgam of the pirate of costume history archives, comic books and Hollywood, made more savage and striking with facial make-up and decorative detail borrowed from Apache Indians. In its detail Vivienne had created an emotionally charged, composite figure of international appeal, dressed in a vivid palette of African Gold Coast colours: saffron, chrome yellow, orange (dyed five times for intensity), vermilion and lapis lazuli, highlighted with a bold serpentine print – copied from an old scarf that Jean-Charles de Castelbajac had given McLaren some years earlier – that writhed across the flounced cottons.

Vivienne's Pirate had taken over a year to devise, and like all the collections to which she devoted time and concentration (such as 'Sex', 1974–75, 'Harris Tweed', 1985, and 'Portrait', 1989), it was one of her best. The intensity and extent of her research was one of the most distinctive aspects of Vivienne's designing. 'The sourcing behind everything! It was less imagination and more research,' observed Richard Torry, who was to work with her in the early eighties.

The real importance of the 'Pirates' collection was that Vivienne became the first modern-day designer to exactly copy the cut and construction of historical dress. 'In the nineteenth century,' she explained in 1996, 'Worth was passionate about past fashions, but he was content to adjust the details and adapt the proportions to

contemporary patterns, rather than explore the original cut. I was a
pioneer, the first to introduce that into fashion. At the same time I
was also the first to explore ethnic cuts to obtain a great number of
shapes.'

Vivienne employed the same approach to design as she had when
instructing her class of infants on making a fish mobile, marching
them down to the fishmongers to study fresh fish before they attempted
it. After three months researching the original patterns of dress and
images of pirate attire in the National Art Library of the Victoria and
Albert Museum, the designs emerged 'out of chaos, really. But that
chaos is something you're continually piecing together and
discovering,' she explained, linking McLaren's punk clarion call,
'Chaos!', to her own meticulous working process.

In the eighteenth century, clothes tended not to follow the lines of
the body, but were seductively folded and draped around it. 'Their
priorities were really different,' said Vivienne. 'They didn't want to
cut a trouser that neatly defined the two cheeks of your bum . . . They
were interested in sexuality in a totally different way . . . And I only
find it out by research really; the stimulus is always academic.'

The low-slung seat of the Pirate trousers was the antithesis of
modern trousers, which cleaved to the buttocks. Anthony Price had
accentuated this hugging, superhero silhouette, as epitomised by Mick
Jagger's dancer's body, by cutting a horseshoe seam across the outline
of the haunches. Perversely, Vivienne wanted to create the opposite
effect: 'I'd seen a picture of a man whose trousers were too big, and
they were all kind of rumpled around the crutch, and all the pockets
were baggy. I wanted to do that, but I couldn't pull that trouser off
until I found a book which showed how people made breeches in
those days, and I found that the shape of the trousers was quite, quite
different . . . I wanted that rakish look of clothes which didn't fit, and
I was into that for quite a long time, and I splurged off a whole thing
of English terrible tailoring.' Vivienne delighted in the extraordinary
appearance of her trousers. When her loyal customer Michael Kostiff
complained, 'My arse will be hanging down round my knees,' she
retorted, 'Well, go to Anthony Price then!'

Just as in her make do and mend childhood Vivienne had loved
simple crafts – potato-printing, dyeing cloth in the bath, or staining
it with teabags – so she set about crafting her new look. Laying aside
British youth styles, she began to seek inspiration from international

cultures. References were brought to her by McLaren, who, unlike her, travelled regularly. She had a particular aversion to his favourite source of inspiration, the streets of New York. To Vivienne's mind, her Pirate was a classless member of the global village: the 'new intelligentsia who relates more to a man in New Guinea or Africa or somebody in the Third World than they do to the idea of an English gentleman and his offspring'. To contrast him with this English gentleman, whose suits were tailored close to his body, she cut the clothes in an anarchical manner, making them swing loosely away from it, creating a feeling of action. Instead of running the Pirate trousers' flies vertically, she swung them to one side. Inspired by the pop singer Ian Dury, who was crippled by polio, she shifted the neck of a T-shirt so that it rucked up under one armpit.

The trousers, breeches or petti-drawers and asymmetrical T-shirt were combined with a voluminous squiggle-print shirt cut with one sleeve longer than the other, matching stockings, a sash ending in tassels tied around the waist or forehead, a Medieval tailored satin jacket slashed to reveal a contrasting fabric underneath, soft leather boots fastened with buckles up the leg, and a Napoleonic bicorne hat pinned with a tricolour rosette. Gilding the lily, the pirate's face was decorated with gold (by the make-up artist Yvonne Gold) and a distinctive streak of white paint daubed horizontally from cheekbone to cheekbone in imitation of the Apache chief Geronimo. Finally, to suggest the pirate's primitive origins and greed for booty, one front tooth was covered in gold (in fact gold foil taken from the lining of a Benson & Hedges cigarette pack, in imitation of Caroline Baker's Rastafarian boyfriend, who could not afford gold caps and used foil instead).

Vivienne was striving to alter not only the wearer's appearance but his stance, by changing the feel of the clothes on the body: 'My clothes . . . make you stand in a different way. For a start, you don't adopt the same postures. You can't be anonymous. You have to sort of strut about . . . as if you own the street. I do believe that appearances are everything.' This was the beginning of a long experimentation with clothing and footwear's effect on posture and movement – the impact of clothing on the wearer, rather than on the onlooker. Vivienne's Pirate look was the beginning of a process by which she changed the way people looked at covering the body. Though her clothes were extreme, they affected mainstream fashion, reappearing, for example,

Above left: Portrait of Malcolm McLaren by Jean-Charles de Castelbajac.

Above: Alan Jones, Chrissie Hynde, Vivienne and Jordan promoting SEX in 1975.

Left: McLaren wearing the SEX T-shirt 'Two Naked Cowboys', that resulted in Alan Jones' arrest in August 1975. Despite promises, McLaren failed to turn up in court to support Jones.

Right: Staff outside Nostalgia of Mud, including Michael Collins, Horace Carter-Allan, make-up artist Yvonne Gold and Gene Krell. The St Christopher's Place Trading Association vowed to close the shop down.

Above: Vivienne posing in SEX in 1975, dressed in a pink 'Rubber Johnny' bodysuit.

Above right: The exuberance of the 'Buffalo' gals, autumn/winter 1982-83, featuring the bra worn on the outside, a look popularised by Madonna and Jean-Paul Gaultier.

Right: Pirating on the radio waves. The modern technology of the Sony Walkman meets seventeenth-century-inspired brigands of the high seas. 'Pirates', autumn/winter, 1981-82.

Far left: Modern art on fashion: Matisse's dancers are printed on empire-line cotton dresses with a wraparound train. 'Savage', spring/summer 1982.

Left: John Hurt's costume in *The Elephant Man* inspired McLaren to include the Foreign Legionnaire's *képi* turned backwards, the neck-guard slit for the eyes, in the 'Savage' collection.

Below: Sportswear marries tailoring: 'Buffalo' boy 'Burroughs' suit (named after the godfather of punk, writer William Burroughs) worn with a hooded sweatshirt.

Left: Vivienne's last collaboration with McLaren, 'Witches', autumn/winter 1983-84. Peak-shoulder jacket, lined in marbleised cotton in imitation of the endpapers of old books; huge, heavy wool skirt printed with Keith Haring's imagery and bandaged around the waist; and triple-tongued trainers.

Above: British *Vogue* loved the establishment spoof of 'Harris Tweed'. Lord Snowdon underscores the tradition by flanking Amanda Pays with the Household Cavalry outside his sister-in-law's palace.

Right: Smart satire: the tradition of a hunting pink wool double-breasted jacket, City gent's bowler hat and brown brogue shoes, combined with punk bondage trousers. 'Time Machine', autumn/winter 1988-89.

Far Right: 'Mini-Crini', spring/summer 1986. This collection, based on the circle and inspired by Empress Eugénie's nineteenth-century crinolines and Walt Disney's Minnie Mouse, was originally designed for Vivienne's business partnership with Giorgio Armani and entitled 'World School'.

Vivienne models her 'Love' jacket, twinset, pearls, breeches and Rocking Horse platform boots for 'Harris Tweed'.

A best-seller: Argyll knitwear manufactured by John Smedley for Vivienne, from the 'Voyage to Cythera' collection, autumn/winter 1989-90.

Susie Bick and Sarah Stockbridge in the *commedia dell'arte*-inspired Harlequin bodysuit and Columbine mini crini from the 'Voyage to Cythera' collection.

Tweed trouser suit with 'Super D.B.' double-breasted jacket and fedora from 'Always on Camera', autumn/winter 1992-93. As classic as Yves Saint Laurent.

Harris tweed armour-plating for 'Time Machine'. The armour in the Wallace Collection and Richard Torry's designs a season earlier inspired this cut, worn here with a 'knockout' tweed skirt and frill.

Real life on the catwalk: Sarah Stockbridge cradles her newborn in the finale of the 'Cut, Slash & Pull' show, spring/summer 1991. Gary Ness was given Ben Westwood's trashed paintbox to colour in Fragonard's *putti*.

Above left: Vivienne returns to the Paris catwalk with her 'Dressing Up' collection, autumn/winter 1991-92. Susie Bick wears a hunting pink jacket, leather 'Stature [sic] of Liberty' corset, punk bondage choker, *La Goulue* boots and the season's accessory, a leather codpiece.

Above right: Vivienne and an unamused Princess Michael of Kent at Kensington Palace for 'Court Couture', an exhibition of royal dress in June 1992. Vivienne claimed she did not realise her Boulle-printed lace dress would be see-through under harsh light.

Left: Things happen to a girl in a polo-necked jumper slashed across the breasts. Sarah Stockbridge, 'Dressing Up'.

two years later as Rei Kawakubo's ripped black knitwear, and a decade later in the Belgian deconstructivism of Martin Margeila and Ann Demeulemeester.

To prepare for the release of the clothes, Vivienne and McLaren decided that 430 King's Road needed a refit – the refurbishment was reputedly financed by EMI's advance to Bow Wow Wow. McLaren deliberately heightened anticipation by boarding up the shop for several months during 1979–80. Punks who had made the pilgrimage to what they thought was still the movement's Mecca could be heard outside saying, 'Well, I'm sure it was here somewhere . . .'

Initially McLaren approached David Connors, who had helped create Seditionaries, but his designs were deemed both too expensive and not sufficiently hard-edged. Having admired Roger Burton's shop PX in Covent Garden, which had been constructed out of air ducting salvaged from the old MI5 building in Conduit Street and styled to look like a ship's engine room-cum US Army store, McLaren summoned Burton to a meeting in the Nightingale Lane flat. After pushing his way down the corridor, past sagging clothes racks and unravelled bolts of cloth, Burton entered the book- and record-strewn bedroom, and the meeting commenced on the bed. 'I want Ye Olde Curiosity Shoppe,' McLaren explained, adding that they had no budget. 'Vivienne was in the background fiddling with clothes,' remembers Burton, 'and Malcolm was constantly on the phone trying to have two conversations at once, so I could never wholly get their attention.'

Such distractions enabled him to have a relatively free rein. He based his designs on an old pub, the Crooked House at Himley in the Midlands, whose floors sloped due to subsidence caused by the intensive local mining. But how was he going to achieve this effect artificially in the heart of Chelsea, and escape the wrath of the council's Planning Committee? Ignore the bureaucrats, McLaren advised. The sloping floor was constructed with a series of wooden pallets, stacked four high on the right-hand side of the shop and gradually descending to a single one on the left, roped together and covered with decking salvaged from an old boat. The effect was like being on board a ship at sea, and the assistants, having to brace themselves against the tilt for several hours a day, began to suffer back pains. A solution was found by Derek Dunbar, who later worked at the shop: behind the counter he placed a wooden box tilted in the opposite direction, so restoring at least that part of the shop to an even keel. Most of the staff spent their time perched on it.

'I want to challenge time!' McLaren announced, so two clocks which ran backwards and had thirteen-hour faces were installed; a large one outside and a smaller version inside. They were the most expensive fittings, made by a special effects craftsman. Burton found an electrician to wire up the shop through the listings magazine *Time Out*. On the appointed day a gargantuan man with a massive belly, chest-length hair straggling down from a bald pate, and National Health glasses – one lens smashed and held together with plaster – arrived, dragging a tartan shopping trolley and an old dog. In a posh accent, he announced himself as Andy Newman, former singer with the sixties band Thunderclap Newman. The lighting was to be an old chandelier made out of copper pipe which Newman tarnished with chemicals. This verdigris effect was echoed on the crucifixes that were lined up along the right-hand wall which, once draped with clothes, Vivienne thought resembled medieval martyrs. Finally, Burton bought a leaded window from a do-it-yourself shop and fixed slates precariously onto the gable that extended over the Chelsea pavement. Vivienne was to become so attached to the design that she refused ever to change it.

The new shop, evoking a storm-tossed galleon, was to be called Worlds End, a name derived not only from that part of the King's Road, but also from the title of an eighteenth-century Hogarth print, in which the grim reaper indicates man's destiny with his scythe. The shop reopened in the autumn of 1980. Customers marvelled at how the number 11, 19 and 22 buses were labelled with the destination 'Chelsea, World's End', as though McLaren and Vivienne had enlisted even London's red double-deckers to publicise their wares. At noon on the day of opening, crowds of punks, regular customers and fashion journalists pushed into the tiny shop, only to flee a few minutes later following an explosion; Newman had blown the fuses.

Vivienne, not caring if she lost sales as a result, would subject customers to an aggressive interrogation as to why they wanted to buy these clothes. She was more accommodating to those who were elegant or rich enough to gain her approval, among them Bianca Jagger: 'That lady is so much more pretty in real life than she ever was in photographs,' she enthused, apparently forgetting that Mrs Jagger had been on the 'Hates' list of the 'What Side of the Bed'

T-shirt. 'She had such feeling for the clothes, and she just put those things together, and I was just gasping with admiration . . . and of course I gave her a reduction. The richer they are, the bigger their discount, really.'

The early customers witnessed the first chaotic unveiling of Vivienne's Pirate. Though this pretty, colourful and unisex figure was visually very different from his predecessors, the hard-edged teddy boy and the punk, his style derived from the same philosophy. 'The hobo, the pirate, the punk rocker – they're all the same,' Vivienne insisted. 'They're all part of the dispossessed, defying laws and creating their own.' She also wanted to parody the traditional British role of the colonial plunderer, adept at 'presenting other people's ideas well'. Her pirate was an escapist, a new romantic fleeing from the 'banana republic' she and McLaren believed Britain had become, a mere colony of American cultural and commercial imperialism.

Vivienne sported the Pirate suit night and day, often draping it with a tartan car rug from the John Lewis department store. She elongated her eyebrows with an orange pencil, and daubed her eyelids with gold paint. As well as at Worlds End, Pirate clothes were sold randomly at nightclubs. On the opening night of Philip Sallon's Planet, in Piccadilly, Vivienne set up a shop balanced on the fire escape. 'I think she sold two T-shirts all night,' Sallon remembers.

In March 1981 Vivienne and McLaren decided to show the 'Pirates' collection formally on a catwalk. The idea, initiated by McLaren, represented a conscious decision to participate in the mainstream arena. Despite her claims to be an anarchic rocker who hated the fashion world, Vivienne wanted to prove herself within it, and to reach a wider audience. Fashion's system of shows demanded that they present a new collection every six months, rather than simply changing their designs and the decor of the shop when they felt so inclined. By joining the rigorous and unrelenting schedule of an autumn/winter collection shown in March, and a spring/summer one in October, Vivienne and McLaren stepped onto a treadmill. They were ill-prepared for the discipline demanded.

The system was unknown territory, and to introduce them to it the couple employed Marysia Woroniecki, a persuasive and energetic twenty-two-year-old public relations officer, and the show's producer Mark Tarbard, a sculptor-turned-pattern-cutter, both of whom they met through Jeff Banks. But Vivienne mocked Marysia for being a 'toff', claiming that she did not need a PR. 'You're too straight,' she used to complain whenever Marysia suggested anything. Vivienne's class envy and parsimony soured the relationship – as they were to strain her relations with the press throughout her career.

The preparations were chaotic. At the Nightingale Lane flat on the eve of the show, Jordan was presented with piles of voluminous cotton Pirate shirts to press with an antiquated iron, while Vivienne, with finicky precision, hand-pleated silks over tampons rather than just buying furnishing tassels. Meanwhile McLaren talked manically on the telephone, pausing occasionally to cast out or accept Vivienne's offerings with a grand sweep, 'coming in at the last minute and firing the last cannon', as Vivienne described it.

A buzz of anticipation for the show swept through the London club, music, fashion and art school scenes, and there were fights to get tickets (on which, incidentally, the title 'Pirates' did not appear). It was held at the Pillar Hall in Olympia, the West London exhibition centre, and it started late. Right up to the first bar of the Bow Wow Wow soundtrack that accompanied it, assistants and friends were hurriedly sewing garments together. 'It was complete mayhem,' remembers Marysia, 'and half of them were totally out of their brains' with alcohol or narcotics. As Simon Barker scurried out of the nearest tube station, he was intercepted by a middle-aged woman laden with bags who asked him, 'Are you going to Vivienne Westwood's show?' 'Yes, I'm really late,' he replied. 'Oh, don't worry,' she said reassuringly, 'I've got the clothes here in the bag.' The woman was a freelance seamstress named Maureen, from Mitcham in South London, who had been delayed because her dog had escaped and she had spent the morning chasing it round the neighbourhood.

Once the clothes had arrived, Vivienne piled them onto the floor backstage and asked the models to choose which ones they wanted to wear, since she had prepared neither a list of outfits nor a running order, which most designers plan to the last detail. Fortunately, although most of the models were amateurs, she had hired some experienced and inventive professionals, such as Nick Kamen, later a pop singer and actor, and the Rastafarian singer Horace Carter-Allan, and everything was designed to mix and match. It was a measure of Vivienne's relaxed approach that she simply surrendered the clothes to the models, allowing them to wear them with their own stamp of individuality. A do-it-yourself vibrancy infused the show. Each model came out with a different hairstyle: Mohican, plaits, bunches, etc. None of the shoes or boots fitted, as the last had been based on Vivienne's exceptionally narrow feet, so the models either kept their own shoes on, went barefoot, or wore the show shoes two or three sizes too long, so that they flapped around like a clown's.

In the early eighties, the catwalk was typically a functionally plain, raised white oblong stage with a white backdrop onto which the designer's logo was fastened or projected. Vivienne and McLaren were determined to change the fashion show into an 'art happening', a theatrical performance; the more haphazard and impromptu the better. Few designers, whatever their budget, decorated the auditorium. McLaren covered the massive pillars of the hall with Worlds End wrapping paper, printed with the McLaren & Westwood logo of an arm brandishing a cutlass and the words 'Born in England'. The models, wearing Walkmans lent by Sony, skipped down the catwalk through dry ice and the sound of cannon fire.

Michael Kostiff recalls that the show 'blew you away, it was so glamorous'. The audience of several hundred people included Mick Jagger, Adam Ant, Boy George, many club scene leaders, ex-punks, customers of the shop and art school students. When Mark Tarbard explained to Vivienne that professional designers remained backstage during their shows, she was astonished. 'You mean they don't watch it? I think that's awful!' She did not want to miss the fun.

Tony Glenville, a freelance journalist, could still feel the euphoria fifteen years later. After the show, he and a group of journalists and students 'were still drawing on the tablecloth at two or three in the morning, and arguing whether it was the most important collection we had ever seen in our lives or the most ridiculous'.

The powerful American trade magazine *Women's Wear Daily* proclaimed: 'Westwood is the hottest designer of new look', and said the show had 'some of the eccentricity of Kenzo's old extravaganzas'. Though there was some confusion as to whether it was a summer or a winter collection, Tommy Perse of the Los Angeles store Maxfield Bleu predicted that while parts of it were 'too wild', there was much that would be 'imitated everywhere'. The Henri Bendels buyer Jean Rosenberg commented: 'I know she is trying to make some kind of complicated social statement with this collection, but it doesn't matter. Under those layers and ideas are some of the youngest and prettiest clothes in Europe.' To a buyer, that was what mattered.

But at first, few mainstream fashion editors dared venture into Worlds End. Liz Tilberis, for example, a fashion stylist on British *Vogue*, balked at the idea of going to 'that punk place where the windows get smashed', but when she overcame her reluctance she was astonished by the clothes, and recommended them to Grace Coddington, the senior fashion editor at the magazine. Anna Piaggi, editor of Condé Nast's *Vanity* magazine in Milan, one of the most forward-thinking journalists in the business, commissioned an illustrator to capture the pantomimic vibrancy of 'Pirates'. It exploded from the pages of the magazine.

In August 1981 British *Vogue*, which had previously deemed Vivienne's work irrelevant to its readership, endorsed the establishment's growing approval of her new look with a four-page feature on 'Pirates' as a celebration of London's romance. Ever since Let it Rock, Vivienne had designed for both men and women, and she was delighted by the sensitivity with which Coddington, one of the world's most celebrated fashion editors, had styled the unisex clothes on the male and female models, and had accessorised the collection with sympathetically nostalgic Fair Isle knitwear. McLaren, however, was furious that the editor had, as he saw it, diluted and sanitised the 'Pirate' look. Their disagreement led to a bitter row.

In the short term, 'Pirates' caused a much greater sensation in the fashion world than punk had, because the commercial fashion press judged the clothes to be accessible and pretty, rather than confrontational and barbarically ugly. As dream-carriers, they transported their wearers to a better time and place. In Vivienne's opinion, 'fashion is the strongest form of communication there is,' and her antennae served her well, for at that time fashion was, for some sections of Britain's youth, supplanting music as the source of their greatest excitement. For the first time, youth's icons now included designers as well as rock stars, who, to some minds, had become bland and over-commercial.

As Vivienne and McLaren did not expect 'Pirates' to attract wholesale custom, they did not bring ledgers to the show to take down orders from retailers. But the chief fashion buyer of the New York department store Bloomingdales, who rarely attended the London shows, happened to see 'Pirates', and placed a tiny order for clothes from the collection, which were featured in the windows of the store. Joseph Ettedgui, of the fashion retailer Joseph, was the first

London shop apart from Worlds End to sell the collection. Vivienne and Caroline Baker, who was now working as her assistant and living at Nightingale Lane, arrived at his offices with three large suitcases, and emptied the contents out before him. 'The clothes looked absolutely incredible, but very theatrical and difficult to sell,' he remembers. Then he spotted the squiggle-printed 'Pirate' shirts they were wearing, and asked if they were part of the collection. On being told that they were, he bought fifteen white and fifteen printed. He found himself reordering every week to keep pace with demand: 'It was one of the most successful shirts I've ever sold in twenty-five years of retailing. You could have been a Saint Laurent customer and you would have worn it.' Macys and Henri Bendels also placed small orders, but at this stage, according to the New York nightclub hostess and boutique owner Suzanne Bartsch, 'They didn't go mad for her here. The Americans are very straightforward.' The fact that Vivienne and Baker had not realised the saleability of the shirts was indicative of their business naïveté.

The 'Pirate' clothes were not cheap: the shirts retailed at £25, stockings £7, sashes £15 and waistcoats £30. Consequently, Vivienne faced a barrage of criticism from journalists and some customers, who argued that she was pricing her fashions beyond the pockets of the very people she claimed to champion. 'I can't put myself in the role of the social services,' she argued. 'If the kids really want them, they'll find the money' – and so they did, or simply stole them.

The customers were far more numerous than Vivienne's former rebel and art school constituency, and in May 1981 the *Sunday Times Magazine* noted that the look was even 'catching on with the Hooray Henriettas of Chelsea'. 'Pirates' appealed to them partly because its catwalk debut coincided with the marriage of one of their own, Lady Diana Spencer, to Prince Charles. Lady Diana's wedding dress, designed by Elizabeth and David Emmanuel, was a saccharine-sweet interpretation of new romanticism. Its petticoated and ruffled volume conjured up the sentimental idyll of a fairytale bride, and tapped into the public's yearning for escape.

Despite the beginnings of recognition from the establishment, Vivienne still liked to rail against it, declaring with republican fervour to the *Sun*: 'I don't know that I'd like to design clothes for the Princess of Wales. I am against all royalty. I mean, Princess Diana to me is just lamb dressed as mutton. I don't like her clothes. What would I dress her in? Probably a potato sack. I wish royalty would corrode away, because I'm against all leaders and authority which prevents people grabbing the potential they were born with . . . But I suppose Prince Charles is a bit stuffy and Princess Diana adds a bit of smartness to him . . . It's just that I don't believe in the establishment. They put the seal on a lot of hypocrisy . . . I just feel her clothes are aimed at provincial people – like the churchgoing lady in Pinner.'

Mainstream recognition was confirmed when the perceptive curator of twentieth-century dress at the Victoria and Albert Museum, Valerie Mendes, quick to realise that 'Pirates' would launch a thousand looks, requested a custom-made outfit for the permanent collection. This was a brave move for such a traditional institution. Vivienne readily obliged, despite her precarious financial state. Notwithstanding her iconoclastic pose, she could not contain her joy: 'Of all the things I am proud about more than anything else, it's that my clothes are in the V&A,' she said in 1983. Similarly, the young Christian Lacroix, then designing for Jean Patou, was struck by 'Pirates': 'It was a new glamour, both modern and nostalgic at the same time.'

While the clothes were a critical – and, modestly, a commercial – success, Bow Wow Wow proved to be a failure on both counts. Spurred on by the acclaim she was receiving, and by the increasing acrimony of their relationship, Vivienne distanced herself from McLaren's music, insisting that her clothes be judged independently of it: 'I'm doing it on my own, you see. I am the best designer in the world,' she boasted, 'but I'm also, by that definition, an enormous fool because I've never got the juice out of what I do . . . because, being so good, it's just a shame . . . I just don't want to see myself as a fool – in this commercial world, anyway.' Having felt subjugated for so long, she found the praise and the widening custom a potent cocktail. Rightly, she observed of McLaren: 'I know he needs me, he needs my head.'

'Pirates' represented the turning point for Vivienne. In her official *curriculum vitae*, drawn up in 1993, she commenced the chronology of her career with it, disregarding her punk years. When quizzed about this, she explained, 'It was in the days of "Pirates" that I first decided to be a designer. Before that I was more interested in street culture. I realised then I had something . . . I wanted to present myself on the proper fashion level by going through all the right channels seriously as a fashion designer. I wanted to do that because I'd have felt stupid if I hadn't. If I'd have given up then, it would have been a silly thing to do, and I would just have been an underground sort of person. I hadn't finished.' Now Vivienne was at pains to explain that the definition 'underground', once worn as a badge of honour, was a pejorative association to be avoided. 'I don't want people to think, "Gosh ... if I wear these clothes I've got to be part of the underground." They are definitely overground clothes. They're for chatting in aeroplanes in, not in tunnels.' In September 1997 Vivienne again described 'Pirates' as a turning point in her career, enabling her to 'step out into the world'. The fully-fledged designer now emerged with confidence.

Robyn Beeche, who Vivienne invited to take pictures of 'Pirates', was struck by her need to control: 'Vivienne really wanted to do everything herself. I set the camera up so that she could take the pictures. These were her own ideas, whereas SEX and Seditionaries were more about McLaren and his music.' Vivienne's sense of professional independence from McLaren had clearly taken root.

It was during the creation of 'Pirates' that Vivienne evolved her *modus operandi*. Instead of simply watching young people on the streets or in the clubs, she scanned anthropological textbooks and cuttings from the *National Geographic* sent to her by her New York friend Terry Doktor, and listened to McLaren's descriptions of encounters with ethnic peoples as he travelled in Africa and New York in search of tribal music. She then created a synthesis of peasant costume and street-gang wear. Though this use of ethnographic dress seemed original to Vivienne's fans, in fact it was in tune with the sartorial globetrotting of the Parisian couturier Yves Saint Laurent, who had turned to the street as early as 1960, while he was still at Dior, and had later shown North African, Russian and Chinese collections. The Japanese ready-to-wear designer Kenzo was also recolouring ethnic dress, from Hawaii and the Far East to Slavic peasants, throughout the late seventies.

The difference was that Vivienne's interpretations were raw and primitive, rather than glossy and Westernised. Unlike the established designers' prettified versions of folkloric dress, Vivienne did not strip it of its status as an anti-fashion. By celebrating people who cobbled clothes together by recycling discarded trash, whether they were Africans making necklaces out of old hubcaps or punks fastening garments with safety pins, she implied a criticism of unthinking

consumerism, and celebrated the demise of European cultural
supremacy.

The elation Vivienne felt at the success of 'Pirates' was short-lived.
McLaren finally left Nightingale Lane after the show, moving in with
his new girlfriend, a fledgling German designer called Andrea Linz:
'I took another apartment and took other girls, and I knew it would
end, because Vivienne would not tolerate that under any
circumstances.' Whatever lip-service she might pay to promiscuity,
Vivienne was at heart conventional and jealous. Unlike McLaren's, her
code of sexual behaviour had been formed in the fifties, with the
example of her parents' traditional, monogamous marriage. McLaren
and Vivienne would never live together again.

He had been bad-mouthing her to other people for some time:
'He'd come in and tell us about his sex life with Vivienne, which was
nil. He'd say what a fuckin' 'orrible bird she was and how he hated
being in bed with her, and we found it very offensive,' recalled Lee
Gorman and Dave Barbe of Bow Wow Wow. Despite McLaren's
departure, it was not a clean break. The couple continued a professional
partnership for another five years, and, periodically, an intimate one
too. 'Though we kept going back and forth,' says McLaren, 'I could
not feel affection and care a great deal, and that's what stopped me.
Even after 1983 I went back several times, a weekend here, a week
there, but no.'

The great love affair of Vivienne's life was over. McLaren may have
lost the convenience of a compliant partner, but a door closed in her
heart forever. From then on she was to invest all her considerable
energies in a determined pursuit of recognition within the fashion
world, albeit on her own terms. Tommy Roberts observed how the
end of the relationship damaged Vivienne: 'It should have broken up
five years before it did. She would have been a bit younger, and it
would have given them both a chance.'

Yet despite McLaren's public desertion of her, Vivienne would not
fully relinquish her emotional and sexual rights over him, convincing
herself that this was just another inconsequential dalliance, and that
sooner or later he would return to her. Although she claimed, 'I'm
no longer the woman who loves and waits for crumbs,' she admitted
that she was 'in agony' when he left: 'I felt so emotionally distraught
by it all I went through a sort of door, as if I died. In the end, I was
watching myself in this other place. I hadn't realised before I was

capable of such passion . . . I think I cared so much because I had put so much into the relationship.'

Vivienne put McLaren's departure down to 'a terrific fear of women'. There was an element of truth in this. Sexual confidence had never characterised his relationships, and his manipulative and cold-hearted ways were, in part, a reflection of his insecurity. He had been ignored by his hedonist mother, smothered by the overpowering Grandmother Rose, and overwhelmed by Vivienne's bossiness and ardent demands. Gasping for liberation from this sequence of domineering females, it is small wonder that he wished to escape.

Despite her rejection, to acquaintances it seemed that Vivienne did not lose her physical self-assurance. 'Sexually, she had such a high opinion of herself, her look and her body, and she did not think anyone else was her equal,' says Robyn Beeche. But her public image as a strong, confident woman was paper-thin. She had suffered years of careless and abusive treatment from McLaren, and regarded every other woman as a sexual threat. She considered herself 'much more intellectual than most women that she met', according to Robyn Beeche, and was incapable of feeling respect for them. On the other hand, she was often to be influenced by mediocre men, particularly if they voiced their opinions forcefully.

After McLaren's departure, with characteristic self-regard Vivienne focused on her career at the expense of her children. 'Work is her whole life,' says Caroline Baker. 'They were completely secondary.' Marysia Woroniecki, who worked closely with her during these days, was struck by the fact that Vivienne 'rarely interacted with her children, in fact she never seemed very genuine in the way she reacted with people in general . . . she's not good at relationships. She's a slightly spooky character.' On one occasion Vivienne's eldest son Ben, then aged about twenty, arrived in her studio carrying a bunch of daffodils. Rocking nervously from foot to foot, he tried to catch his mother's attention, but was ignored. Eventually, he interrupted her. 'What do you want? I'm busy,' she snapped. 'These are for you, Mum. It's Mother's Day.' 'I hate daffodils,' she responded, dismissing him. She was, albeit harshly, merely making the point that she would never subscribe to a convention, particularly one that had been commercialised and Americanised as much as Mother's Day.

Ben, rejected by both his mother and his stepfather, is brave-faced and conciliatory when discussing the break-up: 'Malcolm was number one with my mum. I always resented that, but I benefited from Malcolm myself. I didn't really like Malcolm, but I didn't hate him.' Sensitive to the passion with which his mother regarded McLaren, Ben did not want to seem disloyal to her. In 1994, though, he said: 'I didn't care if he came or went. I never called him Dad. He was a bastard as well, when he went for us. We used to try and jump out of the window.' The fifteen-year-old Joseph, who had always been treated as McLaren's favourite, felt especially abandoned by his desertion, and never recovered his affection for his father.

In her grief, Vivienne immersed herself in design, committing herself to a show every six months. 'It was very hard for her to get to grips with that, since she was used to two- or three-year cycles,' says Marysia. Nor did Vivienne make particularly efficient use of her creative output. She was a fiendish worker, but unlike most designers she did not refine an idea and exploit it over several seasons. At this stage of her career she tended to devise a virtually new look, and complicated constructions, every season.

'Savage', her 1982 spring/summer collection, shown at Olympia in October 1981, extended her anthropological explorations of the tribes of the Third World and the modern metropolis. Inspired by primitive Africans, Vivienne clothed models – their limbs crudely painted and their hair mud-plastered – in the garb of many eras and places: Napoleonic, Red Indian, Peruvian, Dickensian. Experimenting with squares of fabric shaped with gussets and worn as unconventional layering, she played with displaced costume. McLaren kicked the mix into the future with the final addition of three neon 'go-faster' stripes, inspired by the fashionable Adidas sports shoes, and prints of famous images from modern art. The models set off down the catwalk in togas which they opened out to reveal copies of Matisse's cut-outs, Picasso's *Guernica* and *Crying Woman* and Andy Warhol's *Campbell's Soup Can*. These were McLaren's, not Vivienne's, favourite images.

The audience had barely digested this celebration of modern art when other styles and motifs followed: patterns taken from Aztec saddlebags, huge Peruvian felt hats, shredded chamois leathers, domestic bric-à-brac and Victorian frock-coats. Though there was a limited number of clothing shapes, they were mixed into endless permutations. Vivienne was equally eclectic in her use of fabric, juxtaposing knits, stonewashed leathers, cottons, felts and tweeds. To create a 'kitchen sink' cardigan (a reference to the post-war British art and theatrical movement), Vivienne cut a square out of a crudely dyed open-weave dishcloth, sewed it with exposed seams, and fastened it with three huge burnished buttons made by the young jeweller Tom Binns from the lids of Vim kitchen scouring powder. The intention, according to Vivienne, was to 'undermine the status system of fashion'. Her mix was astonishingly inventive and overwhelming when seen as a whole, but it was only when the pieces were isolated that they could be fully appreciated. 'Savage' was another step up the ladder.

Valerie Mendes of the Victoria and Albert Museum recalls the impact of the collection: 'I could kill myself. We [the museum] had a very small budget and I remember going down to Worlds End and seeing them on the rails and thinking, my goodness, they are so strong. I wasn't earning much, but I wanted one for myself as a piece of art to put on the wall because it would be so stunning. I should have had the courage of my convictions and got one for myself and one for the museum.'

Vivienne's approach to construction was anarchic and instinctive. She would stand for hours in her flat, ankle-deep in discarded pieces of calico, pinning, tucking and scrunching samples of cloth onto her body, then rushing to her sewing-machine to make them up. She usually worked alone, sometimes assisted by Mark Tarbard. Free from technical training, she regarded anything as possible. These sessions could last four, six, eight hours, in a frenzy of creative trial and error.

Nothing was rigid or fitted in her next collection, in March 1982, 'Buffalo' (autumn/winter 1982–83), which conveyed an air of wild abandon. As the young models danced along the catwalk to the 'scratch' single 'Buffalo Gals' (which introduced the New York DJ technique of scratching records to Britain) in clothes cut deliberately big, they constantly had to shrug them up onto their shoulders or hitch them up their waists, gestures that to Vivienne's eye seemed provocatively sexy: 'There's more to clothes than just comfort,' she explained. 'Even if they're not quite comfortable and slip and have to be readjusted now and again, I don't mind, because that's some sort of display and gesture that belongs with the clothes.' Some years later she was to artfully employ this visual trick to divert attention from McLaren to herself by wriggling and tugging at the hem of her skirt when she appeared on television with him. And in her 1988 'Time Machine' collection she would intentionally leave the white lingerie ties of her blouses and petticoats trailing, inviting the anticipation of an imagined (or actual) revelation with their unfastening.

'I saw a picture [in a book] of an Indian chief who came to England to see the Queen,' she explained, 'and he had put on my "Pirate" shirt, but half on, and the sleeve draped around him – the idea of clothes falling off. Savage people are just so inventive.' This notion of disarray communicating a subtext established Vivienne as the originator of a narrative, storytelling approach to fashion, an approach that John Galliano was to adopt three years later for his Central St Martin's degree show.

In reaction to the vivid colours of 'Pirates', Vivienne painted her 'Buffalo' gals and boys in a sombre palette of mud browns – 'but I was really into dyeing at that stage, to make life shine through the dullness of the colour'. For the public at large, the most distinctive pieces that demonstrated this were knitted singlets and matching cardigans with a border that combined the Manhattan skyline and a tribal rug decoration. The single most memorable item from 'Buffalo' was a satin 1950s bra (copied from one at the royal corsetières Rigby & Peller) which was worn *outside* a tunic. Adept as ever at promotional catchphrases, McLaren dubbed the look 'underwear as outerwear'. It was designed in imitation of the women of black South African townships who wanted to parade their Western lingerie. Jean-Paul Gaultier took Vivienne's prototype and commercialised it, and Madonna made it her own on her 1989 'Blonde Ambition' tour.

Like 'Pirates', 'Buffalo' challenged the figure-hugging clothes of American designers which exhibited to advantage the sports-honed body. Vivienne delighted in 'big women . . . who live in a space of their own, waiting for the world to grow up'. Her emphasis on the skirt rather than on trousers owed its origins to the Rastafarian mode of dress. Punks had a great affinity with Rasta culture, and their style was made familiar to Vivienne by Caroline Baker's boyfriend. The layers of heavy, midi-length skirts created a bulky line which was almost crinolined in its bell-shaped massiveness. In imitation of the tufts of raw wool that sheep leave on branches and fences, Vivienne designed a rough and shaggy underskirt which was printed with a border of folk images lifted from an album cover of Bolivian music that McLaren had found. She then embroidered another pattern on top of this border. The skirt or trousers were worn with a hooded jumper and a tailored double-breasted jacket or a shaggy sheepskin called the 'Chico', after Chico Marx. Echoing tribal *bricolage* by making personal decoration out of the debris of modern life, Tom Binns attached broken knives, forks and spoons to lapels and earlobes.

With his finger on the contemporary pulse, McLaren drew in references from contemporary films (Vivienne rarely went to the cinema), such as black kohl stripes painted across the eyes in imitation of characters in Ridley Scott's *Blade Runner* and Allan Moyle's *Times Square*. Both the shoes, which looked like leather bags tied round the ankle, and the Foreign Legionnaires' hats turned back-to-front with peepholes cut in the neck-guard, evoked David Lynch's *Elephant Man*.

'Buffalo' was a joyous collection. It conjured up an imaginary and enchanted wild place, which recalled, McLaren says, the tender period in his and Vivienne's relationship in the early 1970s, 'those mad times we had with those kids in the woods. The idyllic free moments when I was very happy.' It also reflected Vivienne's bookishness – one series of dresses was made from cotton printed with a marble effect, in imitation of the endpapers of an old book. McLaren concedes that by the time of 'Buffalo', 'Vivienne was contributing at least 75 per cent . . . I guess she was desperate by then. She really did not want to be known as a partner of mine, but a designer in her own right.'

A new look required a new shop, and when McLaren and Vivienne heard that the lease was due for renewal on ground-floor and basement premises in St Christopher's Place, off Oxford Street, they summoned Burton again. He was given the vague brief: mud, Peruvian women and scratch music. Casting around for ideas, Burton bought an architectural magazine and was 'blown away' by the work of SITE, a Californian group of post-modernist architects who had built a chain of supermarkets in Texas. Playing with distress and recalling the work of the artist Christo, they had veiled the buildings with material to disguise their inner function, and buried old vehicles in tarpaulin and concrete to create a motor car mausoleum.

Developing the theme of buried plunder, Burton designed the shop's entrance in an austere Regency manner, and created surprise by means of a collapsed floor, as if the building had been struck by an earthquake, revealing another, secret world of darkest Africa below. Using scaffolding, he transported the customer down into an 'archaeological dig', towards Vivienne's treasure. In the cavernous interior below ground, an elliptical copper chandelier, spiked with fifteen-inch-long halogen bulbs, illuminated a cracked 'lava' floor (made from a cement sealant used for walkways by London Underground) and a pool of bubbling mud (powered by a fish-tank pump, which kept breaking down) from which rose a slimy verdigris column. Caves along the sides of the room were stuffed with skeletons and 'jewels'. Original World War Two camouflage tarpaulins draped the ceiling and the entrance.

When the shop, Vivienne and McLaren's second London site, opened in the summer of 1982, it looked to passers-by as if it was still under construction. A driftwood map of the world was fastened above the door, on which was pinned the name Nostalgia of Mud (from the French expression *nostalgie de la boue*, meaning the bourgeois inclination to seek out low-life). In Vivienne's customary make-do-and-mend fashion, she had created mannequins with 'character' faces made out of roadwork lamps and hair made from household dusters. They resembled McLaren.

Nostalgia of Mud aroused extreme reactions. On one occasion a middle-aged man in a three-piece suit and bowler hat walked in and, after looking around in astonishment, summed up his feelings by crouching down on all fours and roaring like a lion. The shop also became a favourite stage for drag queens to perform their Vivienne impersonations, but the most extreme reaction came from the St Christopher's Place Trading Association. Its members were livid that the tone of the exclusive shopping street was being lowered, and determined to close Mud down. They were to succeed two years later.

Vivienne's clothes were now influencing Paris-based designers, principally Jean-Paul Gaultier, Rei Kawakubo and Yoji Yamamoto. McLaren, persuaded by Jean-Charles de Castelbajac, decided that they should present them in the capital of international fashion. 'Buffalo' was shown there in March 1982 at Angelina's, a gilded rococo tea room on the rue de Rivoli close to the Cour du Louvre, the official site for the Paris shows. The venue was organised by Pierre Benain, whom McLaren had met when the Sex Pistols played at the Chalet du Lac in 1976.

Vivienne and McLaren were as ill-prepared for showing in Paris as they had been in London, and as they were flat broke, everything was done on a shoestring. They slept in a tiny hotel bedroom around the corner from Angelina's, with rails of thick sheepskin coats surrounding the bed. The following day these were precariously wheeled to the tea room, many of them falling to the pavement on the way. Sylvie

Grumbach of the PR agency Deuxième Bureau, for whom Berain worked, handled the public relations with exemplary calm amid the chaos, which included a catwalk that collapsed. 'Lots of dancers and people of all ages modelled the show, but there was no question of getting paid,' says the model Katie Braine. 'Buffalo' was received with wonder and excitement by a select few of fashion's *avant-garde* – Japanese designer Issey Miyake gave it a standing ovation – and there was interest from American *Vogue*, the Japanese press, designers and buyers such as Roberta Wagner of Bloomingdales. 'Suddenly I had a client that everyone wanted to be involved with,' Marysia Woroniecki recalled. Critical acclaim was one thing, but they only took £500 in orders, which McLaren complained wasn't enough for the airfares.

'Pirates', 'Savage' and 'Buffalo' had a considerable effect on high fashion in 1982 and 1983, particularly on the Japanese designers Rei Kawakubo of Comme des Garçons (for example her autumn/winter 1982–83 'Lace' slashed knitwear collection) and Yohji Yamamoto, both of whom visited Worlds End, as well as Issey Miyake. Dubbed 'the yellow peril' by journalists in the West, the Japanese took Paris by storm, and temporarily usurped the fitted and tailored Gallic silhouette. Onto their own loose-fitting kimono tradition they grafted androgyny – a feminist critique of overtly sexual Occidental dress – together with Vivienne's asymmetrical bagginess and distressed fabrics, to create an austere hybrid disparagingly referred to as 'post-holocaust dressing'. The Oriental designers' work was rinsed of all colour and pattern in order to communicate a sense of cleansing and high seriousness. The results were thought-provoking but glum, where Vivienne's clothes were playful.

Some of the more jingoistic British commentators thought Vivienne was insane to show her iconoclastic clothes in Paris. The fashion establishment there was not yet familiar with fringe or 'youth scene' designers on the catwalk, and was flummoxed by 'Buffalo'. 'The French could not see that this was the way of the future,' says Gene Krell. 'They were dealing with conservative houses. They just didn't know where to place her work or how to deal with it. Should they condone or condemn?' Cannily, the Chambre Syndicale, the French fashion industry's ruling body, reasoned that it was better to welcome the foreign *avant-garde* onto the Paris catwalk, so emphasising the city's status as the centre of international fashion. The Japanese had originally opted to show their collections in London, but because the

British Fashion Council failed to seize the opportunity, the French stepped in and persuaded them to come to Paris instead. Vivienne was invited to show the following season in the Louvre tents, but although she accepted the invitation, she continued to dismiss the Paris establishment, like all establishments, as 'fucking boring'.

Nevertheless, showing in Paris galvanised her ambition: 'When I went to Paris it was really good for me. It made me want to get better, because people do things so well, the way they execute themselves [sic], the detail.' She could see that the Japanese had taken her ideas and improved on them, 'making them graphic and strong. Sometimes my things are a little close to the street, a little bit ordinary, and I want to make them kind of caricatured in a fashion sense. I sometimes think to myself, what would the Japanese do here?' This competitive instinct was encouraged by McLaren, who Caroline Baker remembers as being infuriated that the fashion establishment accorded greater respect to the Japanese than to Vivienne, who had originated the asymmetrical 'unfit': 'He was so angry that Vivienne wasn't as clever as Comme des Garçons, because Rei Kawakubo was getting all the press and she wasn't.'

In 1997, explaining the popularity of Vivienne's designs in Japan, which accounted for nearly three-quarters of her company's turnover, one buyer, Yasuhiro Tanaka, said: 'We Japanese do not have our own modern culture. We were not taught to be individual and original. We have no great self-confidence . . . we take from other cultures and copy them. Vivienne was in many ways a leader, a teacher, and we were her pupils. Each generation discovers her anew. That's why I can sell things designed twenty years ago. They are still new and more original than anything we have here.' A young Japanese customer said: 'I know that fashion is superficial, but in Japan it is the only thing I can use against the system.'

'Buffalo' was a high street as well as a critical success. Watered-down versions of Vivienne's clothes appeared in many British chain stores, including Miss Selfridge, who McLaren threatened to sue for copying the 'Pirates' collection. However, not all the fashion establishment understood Vivienne's creations. 'Why are you making clothes for us to look poor in? We want to look rich. We *are* rich,' McLaren was told by an editor of Italian *Vogue*. He replied, 'You know the story of Robin Hood? You make the rich look poor in order for the poor to look rich.' The exchange highlighted a fissure that was developing between McLaren and Vivienne. While she aspired to enter the inner sanctum of the fashion establishment, he wanted to upset it – although he was also eager to turn a profit from it. 'Why were we in Paris making clothes for Italian editors?' he asked rhetorically. 'It's just another game, another business, and you become a footsoldier of the corporate machine selling that gear. I'd been against that – and the music business – years before, so I quit.' While McLaren posed as a rebel against the system, his sights were increasingly set on another corporate machine – Hollywood.

Vivienne had presented her designs in Paris in order to reach a wider audience. But the decision, initiated by McLaren, although he subsequently disclaimed responsibility, attracted bitter criticism from her hard-core followers. 'It was *his* doing,' says Gene Krell. 'She *never* wanted to do a runway show. People thought of her as a sacred cow, and that's why they felt betrayed when she went to Paris.'

Vivienne had moved her workshop out of her flat and into a couple of cramped rooms in Kingly Court, on the southern edge of Soho, in the heart of London's fashion quarter. The studio looked out over a central well, on whose wrought-iron balconies clothes were hung to dry.

The amazement aroused by Vivienne's clothes did not pay the bills, and Marysia Woroniecki struggled to translate it into press coverage and sales. Vivienne, however, proved almost impossible to manage because of her total disregard for punctuality and decorum. On several occasions Woroniecki arrived at Kingly Court on an appointed morning with an important journalist, only to find Vivienne sleeping in a corner under a sheepskin coat. Unabashed, she would shake herself down and, turning her muddied face (she frequently used cosmetic masks) towards them, ask if they wanted a 'cuppa'. She would model the clothes by brazenly stripping off – 'wearing no underwear and showing her varicose veins and all', says Woroniecki. This was not intended to shock: Vivienne simply never wore underwear, and having spent months at SEX dressed in see-through rubber, she had little remaining sense of modesty.

Despite her odd behaviour, Vivienne's enthusiasm and spontaneity were infectious. Journalists found her and McLaren 'good copy', but few of them took her designs seriously. Her frankness could be disarming – she could trail off in mid-sentence and admit, 'Sorry, sometimes I get a little bored talking about this topic.' Occasionally

McLaren was in town to promote the music and the clothes. Concentrating on the task at hand – to inform the media of *his* genius and, incidentally, of Vivienne's clothes – he would begin in a conspiratorial fashion by leaning up close to his interlocutor, sharing a prejudice or point of view. Having seized their attention, he would construct a utopia, scene by scene, item of clothing by item of clothing. His arms would begin to flail, his complexion to redden, his eyes to assume the manic stare of the possessed as he rose to his feet in an exclamatory crescendo. It could be a mesmerising performance. He was now spending much of his time abroad pursuing world music. He had also set up a company called Matrixbest for his film interests, and was working in Hollywood with Julian Temple and Russ Meyer.

At her first shows Vivienne did not want to appear on the catwalk to receive the traditional applause, but McLaren insisted, telling her it was part of her job. The ecstatic embraces between the pair as they accepted the audience's acclaim were misleading. They were now at loggerheads, and their ambitions had diverged, although Vivienne was still smitten. While McLaren immersed himself in the popular music business and aspired to film production, Vivienne was tiring of throwing sartorial incendiary devices at the fashion establishment, and wished instead to join it. Now in her forties, she had finally progressed from doting accomplice to opinionated designer. She was being pulled two ways; on the one hand she was desperate to remain emotionally close to McLaren, but on the other she wanted to distance herself from him professionally.

She was now determined 'to do it alone, because I found he was too dictatorial, and sometimes – not always – my ideas were better than his. I wanted to pursue them, and not get thwarted.' To allow her own ideas to flourish, and to shield herself from McLaren's overpowering influence, she refused to show her collections to him until a fortnight before the show. Gradually Vivienne was becoming more confident of her own abilities, but as she gave no thought to commerciality, some of her pieces were unwearable. 'She was designing things that were more and more difficult to wear,' says David Ireland, who was working in Worlds End at the time. 'One pair of shoes were impossible to keep on one's feet, never mind feel comfortable in, but she would not alter them, as she felt that was a compromise and a criticism. She was not open to criticism.'

By the spring of 1982, Vivienne and McLaren's relationship was so acrimonious that their rows often ended in physical fights. McLaren was angered by Vivienne's emotional and financial demands, but for Vivienne, rows were a means of gaining McLaren's attention. He claims that she used profligacy as 'a form of blackmail. She just spent money – *my money* – on ridiculously expensive fabrics.' In front of the staff Vivienne would provoke fights, swiping at McLaren or crashing a chair across his back. 'I bashed her very hard,' he says, 'and I knew that was what she wanted. Weird, that. She's violent in that way . . . She would take me to the very edge of my patience.' Physical violence did not frighten Vivienne. In fact, she was excited by it, and McLaren concluded that it served as a sex substitute: 'it was a relationship with me that she did not have on a physical level.' As quickly as these fights erupted, Vivienne would return to normal with 'Anyway, what were we talking about?'

Jordan says: 'They had quite a stormy, no-frills relationship where they would say exactly what they thought about each other in front of other people.' Vivienne would regale staff with accounts of her battles with McLaren in front of customers. On one occasion David Ireland was trying to serve 'a bunch of Sloanes' as she described, at the top of her voice, how 'he grabbed my head and pushed it towards his cock and told me to suck it off. I just grabbed the vase in the bedroom and emptied the contents over his head and told him to get out.' The customers stood agog.

Jordan remembers that Vivienne continued to find solace in hard work: 'Nothing was too hard, and no time was spared to look for the right buttons and all those tiny things – the details – that make up Vivienne's clothes. She wouldn't give up.' Caroline Baker would be sent out time and time again to get *exactly* the right shade of yellow thread. When total immersion in her work did not distract her from her heartache, Vivienne could snap. Once she telephoned McLaren from Kingly Court at the flat he was sharing with Andrea Linz, a ten-minute walk away, to complain that she had run out of money. After a protracted row, in the course of which she demanded, 'You meet me at Centre Point in ten minutes or I'm leaving the business,' she slammed the phone down, returned to her sewing-machine and, head down and shaking with fury, started to sew maniacally. A few minutes later she stood up, screamed, and marched out of the door. After an hour she returned with a huge smile across her face. McLaren and Andrea had been in their first-floor sitting room when a brick came flying through the window, followed by a stream of abuse. Rushing to the window, he just caught sight of the hem of a 'Buffalo' coat disappearing round a corner.

Unwilling to accept that he had left her, Vivienne insisted on referring to McLaren as 'my boyfriend'. This was partly explained by the fact that he kept her dangling; every once in a while, according to Lorraine Piggott, 'if she got too difficult, he would fuck her and then he'd get what he wanted.' Most of Vivienne's relationships with women were adversarial rather than sisterly, and McLaren's departure heightened her sexual jealousy. No longer young, and with a confrontational character that few men relished tackling, she did not have a queue of admirers, and her sexual frustration was vented on her female employees: 'Just mention that you had a relationship and she would turn green,' says Piggott. 'She'd be quite vicious . . . she wants 100 per cent loyalty, and she's the centre of the universe. She's dangerous! It's a good thing she didn't have any daughters.'

As McLaren was often abroad, and Vivienne had no commercial acumen, the accounting and stocktaking procedures were non-existent. The firm did not even have a business account, simply trading through Vivienne's personal account at the National Westminster Bank in Beaufort Street, Chelsea. Vivienne seemed oblivious to the fact that Michael Collins, who managed the Worlds End shop from 1972 to 1982, was now controlled by his addiction to heroin, and funded his habit by stealing clothes and cash from the shop. He would sell large amounts of stock for cash at retail prices, registering them as wholesale deals and pocketing the difference. Receipts were hand-written, and the shops' takings were just stuffed into an old Burroughs till. Thousands of pounds' worth of 'Pirates' clothes were being bought by the Japanese, Jordan recalled, but 'the shop was not geared up for that sort of business – cargo listing, weights, export papers. We could hardly cope with the ordinary customer, let alone an export one.' 'Pirates' clothes were selling so well that Collins could not close the till drawer, as it was overflowing with money. 'Michael did pinch a lot of money,' says Jordan, 'but it was funny, when Vivienne needed a loan and he lent it to her it was only ages later that the penny dropped and she realised where he'd got it – it was her money all along! How else could he have so much money on those wages?'

Collins would be absent from the shop for days on end. On one occasion he failed to arrive for a ten o'clock meeting. It was pouring with rain, and six hours later a moped pulled up outside Kingly Court and Collins dismounted, saturated and wearing only his underpants, having been absent-mindedly riding around all day. It took Vivienne many months to acknowledge Collins's addiction and his related thefts. Eventually, the evidence became so overwhelming that she sacked him. He had embezzled many thousands of pounds over the years. 'Aren't you going to have him busted?' one employee asked. 'No. I just told him to fuck off.' 'But if you don't, they'll all rip you off. It's a signal for everyone else to do it.' With astonishing optimism, Vivienne reasoned: 'All the while he was stealing from me, I was making money. So I wasn't losing money after all.' Such positive thinking remained one of her most remarkable traits, sustaining her against all odds.

After leaving Vivienne, Michael Collins went to work for the young designer John Galliano. Collins introduced him to Mr Mintos, Vivienne's Camden Town tailor, and Galliano started using the same fabrics as Vivienne, such as Madras cotton for his 'Afghan Bankers' collection. Suzanne Bartsch, who sold Galliano's designs in New York, says of him, 'In the beginning he was very influenced by Vivienne, and he admitted it to me. He was a big fan of hers.' Tom Binns also went on to work for Galliano, and Patrick Cox to design shoes for him.

Clearly, Vivienne required a proper accountant, and she finally hired one. One day Lorraine Piggott and Gene Krell were in Worlds End when Vivienne telephoned asking for the accountant. 'Not here,' Piggott replied. She rang again fifteen minutes later. 'Look, where is he?' While Piggott was explaining that she had not seen him all day, Vivienne interrupted, 'Hang on, there's a noise,' and put down the receiver. Loud banging could be heard down the line, and after several minutes Vivienne returned to the phone, yelling, 'Bloody hell! That stupid accountant's set the toilet on fire.' He had gone to the lavatory to shoot up, and had inadvertently set the toilet paper alight, then nodded off to sleep astride the pan. Vivienne had to break down the door and extinguish the flames. However, she would not sack him, simply saying, 'He's got a bit of a problem. He's just got to sort himself out, and he's promised he will.'

Amid the chaos, and despite her own penury, Vivienne could be spontaneously generous. When Michael Collins was fired, his flatmate David Ireland was left homeless, and she paid for him to stay in a hotel until he found a place to live. Similarly, when Gene Krell fell under the influence of heroin, Vivienne never failed to support and try to help him. Tolerant as she was of aberrant behaviour, Vivienne could also be very hard; Richard Torry says she was 'definitely tougher than Malcolm', and could be 'dreadful to people who were good to her'. Her loneliness, frustration, impecuniousness and sense that she had not received the recognition she deserved could be expressed as aggression towards others. All her favourites shared one quality – they were malleable, and she could treat them, as Jordan put it, 'like a project'. Loyal staff, however, were seldom rewarded with a financial bonus or even a thank you. On a whim she would put one employee's wages down while raising another's, even though they worked side by side. Some were amazed by her capacity to trust 'the scummiest people in the world', though this may have been due to an unwillingness to confront business matters, leaving others to sort out practical problems while she immersed herself in her work, convinced that she was in the vanguard of a heroic crafts movement. Chaos was also a means of securing McLaren's attention.

As the business began to falter, unpaid staff took to stealing the shops' stock in lieu of wages. Sometimes she borrowed money from her employees without repaying them, or devised elaborate 'solutions', such as suggesting to one astonished assistant that rather than paying him £125 a week she pay him £25, and take him off the staff list so that he could sign on for unemployment benefit: 'It would save me a hundred quid. Don't you think that's a good idea?' By 1983 most of the assistants in Nostalgia of Mud were drug addicts, and it was widely known in London club and student circles that for £50 in cash one could walk away from the shop with any amount of clothing. Since there was effectively no stocktaking, who would ever know?

In October 1982 Vivienne's next show, 'Hobo-Punkature' (spring/summer 1983) – dubbed, together with the Japanese versions of the style, 'bag lady chic' by the press – was a fusion of 'Buffalo' and punk, and her first collection to be shown at the official Chambre Syndicale venue, at that time tents pitched outside the Louvre Palace. Many of the models, most of whom had been discovered in the nightclubs and bars of Paris by Sylvie Grumbach and her assistant Pierre Benaim, were on heroin, which was rife among Parisian models at the time. Their 'smacked out' look – some even sported scabs – was exaggerated by their staggering progress down the catwalk in silver make-up that turned bruise-grey under the lights. Dressed in layered and distressed rags, the effect was ghoulish. Some of the models could not even make it out onto the catwalk, they were so incapacitated.

The few staff who accompanied Vivienne to Paris were double- or triple-booked into the same humble hotel rooms. 'You'd come back late at night exhausted and find all these liggers in your room,' recalls Lorraine Piggott. 'They'd say, "Oh Vivienne said we could stay here". It was ridiculous.' One of the meagrely-paid waifs who worked for Vivienne lived in an East End squat 'roofed' with tarpaulin. Since she could not afford to buy Westwood clothes she wandered about shivering in calico toiles that she picked up in the studio – 'That's all Sharon had!' – but she was such a fervent fan she would not wear anything but Westwood.

'Hobo-Punkature' featured extremely distressed fabrics fastened with acid-tarnished buttons. To Vivienne's eyes they looked 'as if they'd been used, to give them even more of a story'. The clothes required complicated piece-dyeing and printing, involving up to five processes. However, with no clear line of authority, contradictory instructions from Vivienne and Lorraine Piggott confused the dyers. To make matters worse, Vivienne insisted that the garments be made up *before* they were stonewashed, as there was only a week before a large order had to be shipped to Japan. After a day of wrestling with half-dyed, sodden garments, the East End stonewasher telephoned the office and bellowed: 'Get down here right now. Your bloody rags have clogged up my machines and it's costing us thousands!' Hundreds of tie-waisted skirts were dragged, sopping wet, from the machines and transported back to Kingly Court, where four assistants spent days untangling them and hanging them up to dry on the railings of the communal stairwell. The staff, standing precariously between large vats of toxic and inflammable acids, then had to pack the half-dry clothes into cardboard boxes. The smell was overpowering. It was into this chaos that a *Women's Wear Daily* journalist walked to interview Vivienne, who was at home in bed designing.

As well as selling the clothes in their own two shops, Worlds End and Nostalgia of Mud, Vivienne and McLaren had acquired a few wholesale customers – two boutiques in New York, two in Italy and five in Japan, controlled by the wholesaler and retailer Astore Robot, and an independent retailer, a Japanese fan who had rechristened herself Berni Vinyl and opened a tiny shop in her flat in Fukuoka, on

Japan's south island. But the orders were meagre: between five and twenty outfits, often only intended for arresting window displays. Finances were so stretched that often Vivienne could not even afford the fabrics to make up the orders. One guest invited to dinner at Nightingale Lane was offered fried parsley and garlic, such was the shortage of money. Gift hampers from business associates were saved to feed the staff, and a tuck box sent to Joseph at school in Herefordshire consisted of a Pirate shirt and some soggy oranges. The Italian agents were concerned that any money they sent would be swallowed up by Vivienne's huge overdraft, and that they would not receive their orders. Instead they persuaded Lorraine Piggott to travel to London with £10,000 worth of lire strapped to her waist – an arrestable offence under the rigorous Italian exchange controls.

Employees were astonished that despite the debts, the addicts, the violent relationship with McLaren and her loneliness, Vivienne's tenacity never faltered. She thrived on tension, one employee explaining: 'She loved the feeling that everything was just about to collapse ... It's a kind of detachment which is quite chilling'. 'Nothing gets her down,' says Simon Barker. 'I don't think I can say that I've ever seen her depressed. She's a real fighter.'

The whole set-up at Glitterbest was a textbook case of the ills afflicting the British fashion industry: a lack of professionalism and business planning, and a contempt for customer demands, combined with a passionate commitment by people working night and day for next to nothing. The Canadian shoe designer Patrick Cox, who was sharing a flat with Vivienne's Irish personal assistant David Staines, observed the collapse of the company at close quarters when he was invited to design the shoes for the autumn/winter 1984–85 'Clint Eastwood' collection while he was still at the Cordwainers' College. Cox remembers being appalled by Vivienne's precarious relationship with suppliers and outworkers – he had to pay one shoe manufacturer out of his own pocket to have Vivienne's shoes made for the show, and it was a long time before Glitterbest reimbursed him.

The 'Witches' clothes (autumn/winter 1983–84), designed to slide seductively off the body, were inspired by a book Vivienne had found on voodoo practices in the tropics, and her curiosity about incest. To the sounds of *Duck Rock*, McLaren's album of African music, 'Witches' opened with an exquisite series of fuchsia, Aegean blue and cinnamon wool capes with huge peaked hoods, and shin-length pleated and wrapped skirts hung from a bandaged waist and worn with wedge-heeled, triple-tongued trainers. As the models unwrapped their Capuchin monk capes, some revealed tight, hip-length cardigans featuring peaked shoulders, and matching tube skirts in a range of low-key terracottas or peat browns. The peaked shoulder was repeated in huge, cream macs. The show revealed Vivienne's sensitivity to colour, and her originality in using it. The whole collection was an interplay between fit and non-fit, the baggy cape shapes and the clinging fine knits. It seemed astonishingly modern, playful and sporty. Sensuousness was achieved by the apparently haphazard way in which the body was wrapped and draped. The collection's innocent sense of fun was accented by a range of navy blue horn-buttoned gymslips (of the sort Vivienne had worn at school) and thick sweatshirting that was so warm and cuddly it felt like fur. The models wore little make-up, and their hair was roughly plaited.

The collection's active sportswear, inspired by New York gangs, was based on simple elasticised tubes of fluorescent ciré acrylic jersey which delineated the body, worn with the giant trainers. The tube skirt was to be made memorably fashionable by Madonna. Vivienne commissioned designs from the New York graffiti artist Keith Haring, whose naïve and exuberant cartoon characters McLaren had used earlier on the cover of *Duck Rock*. Vivienne utilised Haring's work like hieroglyphics, playing with the imagery of pagans and incest.

At the end of the show, which was designed almost entirely by Vivienne, McLaren stepped out into the lights to receive the applause. Vivienne tentatively followed in his footsteps. Illuminated by the spotlights on the catwalk, the body language between the two spoke volumes. McLaren, conservatively dressed in shirt and tie, corduroy trousers and a Jermyn Street-style mac, approached Vivienne and pecked her perfunctorily on the cheek. Vivienne, wearing clothes from the collection, seemed delighted by even that cool show of affection.

The impact of 'Witches' came not from the production or staging, but from the joyful vibrancy of the happy clothes and the jaunty spirit the models exuded. The Japanese designer Kansai Yamamoto stood riveted throughout, his face lit up with wonder at the festival of clothing before him. Polly Mellen of American *Vogue* declared it 'a major collection, very important', and one fashion editor said, 'You had to miss Givenchy to see Westwood, but it was worth it.' The collection took £250,000-worth of orders from Italy alone.

McLaren had little to do with 'Witches'. His professional interest in fashion was waning, and two men stepped into the void created in Vivienne's life by his absence: Carlo D'Amario and Gary Ness. The former promised to fulfil her ambition to become a recognised figure in the fashion establishment, the latter inspired her intellectual conceits.

Vivienne met Carlo D'Amario after 'Witches' in Paris. Like McLaren, he was five years her junior. A thick-set Italian with an over-familiar manner, D'Amario had earned a living travelling along the hippie trail to Afghanistan, dealing in rugs and other commodities. On returning to Italy he had sold a job-lot of painted glass backdrops from 1950s pinball machines to the pop fashion designer Elio Fiorucci, and he had also worked for the Italian company King Jean and set up a public relations company, 'Casanova'. He was now casting around for a new project, and his glass eye (the original had been lost in an earlier misadventure) fell upon Vivienne. He introduced her to Fiorucci, for whom she did some freelance designing, but his plan was to manage her Italian business and to manufacture her clothes in Italy.

By May 1983 Vivienne was sexually and professionally involved with D'Amario, and admitted that her relationship with McLaren was 'more off than on'. Like McLaren, D'Amario was a storyteller, capturing her imagination with colourful aphorisms such as: 'The establishment is a car that's going one hundred miles per hour, and if you try you might be able to slow it down, but you'll never stop it. In the end the car will go faster with your energy. What you have to do is go *two* hundred miles an hour.' With his mantra '*Dai* [go!], *Dai*, Mrs Westwood! Promote! Promote!' D'Amario persuaded Vivienne that McLaren's anti-establishment posturing was slowing her down, and that he could help her gain a place at the heart of the fashion establishment. Lorraine Piggott says of D'Amario: 'He certainly saw [Vivienne's] business potential first. I think she was just very, very flattered by this man who was coming on to her sexually, but also fed her this yarn . . . He desperately flattered her, and knew exactly what her vulnerability was.'

McLaren was enraged by her defection: 'I just didn't like that man. I felt let down by Vivienne's choice, I just could not deal with him. Vivienne clung to him, and she was trying to get at me when she thought she'd lost me.' Lorraine Piggott believes he was incensed that 'this man who was so repulsive was going to take his place . . . most people thought he was a bit of a joke, but he also recognised that he could be dangerous . . . but she didn't want to see that.' McLaren, who for so long had undervalued Vivienne, was furious that D'Amario would now profit from all the work he believed he had invested in building her reputation and her career: 'He hated Carlo for what he stole from him.'

Gary Ness, the other new man in her life, cut a chilling figure as he peered at the world through a permanent cloud of Gitanes smoke. His phlegmatic demeanour and laboriously enunciated Anglo-Canadian accent recalled Vincent Price. A trio of acute angles dominated his face: a pronounced widow's peak of steel-grey hair combed back from prominent temples, a sharp goatee beard, and a large, hooked nose, its nostrils flared with disdain. Ravaged by drink and tobacco, his slate-grey pupils scanned his surroundings malevolently.

A homosexual in his fifties, Ness could not charm Vivienne with sexual promises. Instead he promised education and inspiration. Once again, Vivienne had found a mentor. Ness took her by the hand and led her into a world of books, art galleries and high culture. 'He took me back from punk to culture,' she said in 1997. 'Without him I would not have become the fashion designer I am today.' 'Instead of having me as her bible of ideas,' grumbled McLaren, 'she had these books. She didn't want to be part of this rock 'n' roll mentality any more, and all my stuff was about music. Books were a way of breaking away.' Ness claimed to be the son of a wealthy Canadian family that had denied him his inheritance. In 1954, after having spent four years designing the scenery and costumes for a touring Canadian repertory theatre, he won a place at the École des Beaux Arts in Paris, where he studied portraiture, specialising in miniatures. He had introduced himself to the characters at 430 King's Road in 1977 by offering portrait sketches. Initially he was more interested in capturing Jordan on paper than Vivienne, as she had the stronger visual image. He also helped Roland Penrose edit a critically acclaimed biography of Pablo Picasso, and claimed to be working on a book on Anglo-American philistinism. Ness's mental hold on Vivienne began when he introduced her to the anthropological writings of Claude Lévi-Strauss, which she was to allude to in her work from 'Buffalo' onwards. He was Henry Higgins to her Eliza Doolittle, and she started to refer to him as her 'guru'.

Ness lives in a squalid flat at the top of a crumbling white stucco house off Westbourne Grove, West London, among chaotic piles of books, records, paintboxes and newspapers on which balance overflowing ashtrays. His bed is a worn foam mattress on the bare floorboards, covered by a threadbare blanket. No cooking is attempted, and until recently there was not even a fridge, so milk was stored on the windowsill, where it soon soured.

Ness began to rely on handouts from Vivienne, who from 1982 visited his flat once a week for a 'tutorial', for which she was prepared to pay a fee. Her poorly paid staff soon became aware of the arrangement: 'She used to put money aside for him every week,' says Lorraine Piggott, 'and we used to wonder, who is this person? People hadn't got their wages, and yet who was this old git who was coming into the shop?' Since Vivienne did not tell her staff of her mental dependence on Ness, it was not surprising that they viewed him with contempt.

Eager to acquire knowledge and to appear educated, Vivienne devoured the books introduced to her by Ness. Through him she became aware of the salons that had enriched Parisian social and intellectual life in the eighteenth and nineteenth centuries. She began to regard the salon as the perfect form of society, and to fantasise about garnering a circle of intellectuals – preferably men – in her own modern salon. This ambition was to become such an obsession that it eventually rivalled her interest in fashion.

Despite the attentions of Carlo D'Amario and Gary Ness, Vivienne was still tormented by memories of McLaren. Relations between the two had completely ceased by the winter of 1983, exacerbated by the collapse of their business and McLaren's suspicions about D'Amario and his associates. McLaren, his attention now occupied by ambitions to produce films in Hollywood, and unwilling to throw good money after bad, stopped paying the bills.

The unique creative partnership of Westwood and McLaren had finally broken up. For many years, largely due to McLaren's talent for self-promotion and Vivienne's inarticulacy, the world had regarded McLaren as the instigator of their innovative fashions, perceiving Vivienne only as the compliant girlfriend in the background, carrying out his instructions. In the late eighties an equally extreme – and equally fictitious – view was to emerge, that Vivienne was the unacknowledged genius from whom all this extraordinary creativity had erupted. She played on this perception of herself as the undervalued talent manipulated by her Machiavellian partner. In fact both Vivienne and McLaren were talented, original, hard-nosed, ambitious and exploitative, and both gathered fawning acolytes about them.

An incident arising out of the Victoria and Albert's acquisition of a 'Pirates' outfit for its permanent collection was symptomatic of the acrimony between the couple, and an apt summing-up of their work together. The museum had labelled the garment 'Westwood', but amended it to 'Westwood & McLaren' in 1993, after McLaren sent a solicitor's letter demanding an accreditation. This was fair: neither could have realised the collection without the other. But according to McLaren, 'Vivienne had a certain kind of enjoyment in doing that, and she knew it would hurt me. It's a lie, that label.'

McLaren was instrumental in creating Vivienne. He not only convinced her of her ability and focused her talents on fashion, but he provided a rationale, a point of view under which they could market their designs to the public. He gave her the courage to challenge conventional fashion. Perhaps most importantly, he engaged her in society, to what was happening on the streets and inside the heads of the young, thereby extricating her from the fantasy world of high-sounding ideas, words and history that she preferred to inhabit. After his departure she was to gradually slip back into a more rarefied, more disconnected world, and her collections suffered as a result.

McLaren also gave Vivienne a clothing philosophy. He believed that looks should not change every six months to suit the fashion calendar. Instead they should be introduced as and when a designer had something new and relevant to say; perhaps once every two years or so. It was in this informal way that they had evolved their fashions, restyling the shop every time they introduced a new look. But once Vivienne had stepped onto the fashion bandwagon, she had to comply with its rules and calendar. Once she had been abandoned by her great love, Vivienne chose to dismiss him as 'the perfect orthodox rebel' – to her, 'orthodox' was a pejorative word.

Pursued by creditors, she was also under attack from McLaren, who had not only abandoned her emotionally but was now attempting to pull the business out from under her. He did a masterful job of undermining her prestige, persuading the press that she was in the grip of a dubious Italian, and that it was he, not she, who had originated the innovative designs that had emerged from 430 King's Road over the past decade. Apparently defeated, it seemed to Vivienne that her world had come to an end, and that there was little to keep her in England. She turned to D'Amario for solace, and to Italy for professional opportunity.

6 'WITHOUT ITALY, I WOULDN'T EXIST'

1984–1986

'I may be a rebel, but I'm not an outsider'
Vivienne Westwood, November 1983

Italy's post-war economic boom owed much to the conviction of many of its leading manufacturers that good design was an intrinsic element of consumer goods, and not merely a decorative afterthought. These manufacturers correctly calculated that if the nation's economy was to improve its status from a source of cheap labour like Spain or Portugal to a much more profitable supplier of value-added goods, like Britain or Germany, they must apply top-class design to their products. Exploiting the traditional Italian aesthetic flair, leading designers such as Ettore Sottsass, Sergio Pininfarina and the Castiglioni brothers were hired to create desirable consumer goods like Fiat cars, Zanussi household products, Olivetti office equipment and B&B, Cappellini and Kartel furniture. This enlightened attitude was also reflected in the Italian fashion industry, where leading textile and clothing manufacturers such as GFT (Gruppo Finanzario Tessile), Aeffe and the Genny group invested in leading-edge Italian and foreign designers, including Giorgio Armani, Romeo Gigli, Valentino, Emanuel Ungaro and Jean Paul Gaultier, producing and marketing their collections.

Collaborating with innovative and experimental editors at Italian fashion magazines was a further aspect of the manufacturers' and designers' success. Italian *Vogue*, for example, was widely regarded as the most daring example of the magazine, while Anna Piaggi, editor of another of Condé Nast's Italian titles, *Vanity*, consistently provided a platform for inventive and modern clothes. Italian editors and manufacturers pioneered the *quid pro quo* of editorial pages for advertising revenue, and by the 1980s this had helped the nation's top designers, such as Armani, Valentino, Krizia and Ferre, to secure a global following. Clothing and textiles became the nation's largest industry, and by the end of the decade Italy was manufacturing approximately half the fashionable ready-to-wear created in the West, including the profitable American labels Calvin Klein, Ralph Lauren and Donna Karan.

It was in Italy that Vivienne found not only critical acclaim but, more crucially, financial backing. She turned her back on London where, except for a few lone voices, she was ridiculed. Keith Wainwright recalls that in Britain she had been 'knocking her head against a brick wall. Vivienne and Malcolm were doing the most inventive things, no one else was coming anywhere near them to change things or move fashion on, and yet no one was taking notice, least of all [British] *Vogue*, which is supposed to be the arbiter.' (In fact a gradual transition had been taking place, and in 1983 British *Vogue* had named Vivienne and McLaren the 'chief engineers of contemporary style'.)

In retaliation, Vivienne repeatedly criticised the British for their cultural conservatism, entrenched class system, lackadaisical attitude to work and preoccupation with street culture, which she now dismissed as too 'underground'. 'My inspiration will not be the outsider in future,' she said in 1983. 'I'm on the inside. I may be a rebel, but I'm not an outsider.' Having emerged from McLaren's shadow, Vivienne was determined not to let him have the Worlds End label. She would take it herself, and fight her way to the centre of the fashion world.

Burdened by debt, threatened by inspection from the Inland Revenue and bedevilled by McLaren, Vivienne filed for personal bankruptcy, and fled to Milan at the end of 1983. Over the next six months she shuttled back and forth between Britain and Italy, before settling in with her new lover and business adviser Carlo D'Amario in Milan for nearly a year, while his mother housed the sixteen-year-old Joseph nearby. Ben, now twenty, remained in London.

D'Amario vowed to realise Vivienne's potential, and would produce her collections in hi-tech Italian factories. 'I will work in Italy,' Vivienne insisted. 'All I'm asking for is people's professional help. I have a super-fantastic situation there.' It was principally career rather than love that prompted Vivienne to emigrate. She rightly reasoned that production success in the fashion industry could be attained by Italian manufacture. For his part, D'Amario saw a profitable opportunity. According to Bella Freud, 'He realised that she had talent – Italy is a country that understands the value, quite literally, of ideas and design. He thought, "Wow! we could be rich." Carlo's skin is as thick as a horse. He doesn't care what people say or think about him, as long as he gets the money.'

D'Amario, recognising Vivienne's unique talent, adroitly won her over. Vivienne, always vulnerable to flattery, was thrilled that this man – although not a dashing figure – was attempting to seduce her. According to D'Amario, when he first met Vivienne he assumed that as she was so famous she must be 'a multi-millionaire . . . I was very shocked when she said how little money they made. Luckily she seduced me.'

Like McLaren and Ness before him, D'Amario communicated with Vivienne in fables. He would, for example, describe himself as the engine that would pull her train to success. 'He desperately flattered her and knew exactly what her vulnerability was,' the Worlds End production manager Lorraine Piggott observed. Terry Doktor described D'Amario's tactics simply as 'sex'. Gene Krell, a loyal friend of Vivienne's, says, 'She didn't have an alternative . . . and anyway, over business she's not terribly concerned.'

Vivienne's next collection, 'Hypnos' (spring/summer 1984), was designed in Italy and shown at the Cour du Louvre in Paris in October 1983. It featured active sportswear cut from fluorescent nylon prints contrasted against white. In an oblique tribute to the sexual freedom and paganism of the ancients, she printed the clothes with erotic Greek figures, such as a satyr fornicating with a cloven-hoofed beast and a Medusa-like figure whose head was decorated with penises rather than snakes. Miniature phallus-shaped buttons fastened the clothes. *The Face* dubbed it the 'Porno Olympics' collection. It was manufactured in Italy, much to McLaren's chagrin, as this confirmed that he had lost control of Vivienne.

'Hypnos', reputed to have cost £30,000 to stage, was well received by the American buyers from Macy's and Bloomingdales. Although the wholesale prices of Vivienne's collection had doubled (from $70 a skirt wholesale to $140) because it was now being manufactured to a higher standard in Italy, the Bloomingdales buyer Mary Wong and her colleague Kal Ruttenstein, Vice President of Fashion Direction, intended to place orders for the range and to feature it in the store's windows.

However, persistent rumours were circulating that Worlds End was on the brink of bankruptcy, and some buyers, fearing that the clothes would never be delivered, were reluctant to place orders. The Italian pop art clothes designer Elio Fiorucci, who had previously employed D'Amario for seven years, was planning to buy the label. Since Vivienne and McLaren's designs from the 1970s had become collectible modern classics, he hoped to gain ownership of the patterns and reproduce them on a commercial basis. Thanks to D'Amario, Fiorucci had already hired Vivienne on a freelance basis to design part of his spring/summer 1984 collection, for which she was paid a much-needed and handsome fee.

Vivienne's move to Italy did not end her bitter dispute with McLaren. James Fallon, *Women's Wear Daily*'s London bureau chief, summed up the situation: 'Malcolm, being Malcolm, was envious. She was getting too much attention. She was no longer controllable as he had expected her to be.' McLaren began courting the press, systematically impugning Vivienne's professionalism and persuading journalists that he was the true originator of their work, while she was merely the seamstress who executed it. He said that she should remain in her home country, the source of their inspiration, and predicted that the company would collapse if it was severed from its source of inspiration: 'Worlds End was born out of English fashion, in particular our street fashion . . . What we create on the streets out of the dustbins of England is an extremely exportable commodity. If Vivienne wants to go down a more bourgeois road, fair enough. But she owes some consideration to the partnership here. I'm afraid she'll end up making some verbal agreement with the Italians . . . I'm not going to throw it away easily.' Some of Vivienne's fans agreed with McLaren; Philip Sallon said, 'her lack of loyalty to the British really pisses me off. She got a free education here and all that support from fans and customers and then she starts criticising the British for having no culture.' Since McLaren was by far the more adept media manipulator of the two, and in any case Vivienne, mainly living abroad, was unable to defend herself, his point of view held sway in Britain for a number of years.

McLaren also attempted to damage Vivienne by informing the

Milanese company which was producing 'Hypnos' that she had stolen the patterns from their workroom. The directors understandably panicked and ceased production. 'He would ring up factories and tell them not to work with her,' recalls Bella Freud, who was by this time studying fashion design at the Academia di Costume e di Moda in Rome, and who saw Vivienne from time to time. 'Not only did he break her heart, but he also wanted to stop her succeeding.'

Back in London, McLaren had new locks put on the studio doors to keep Vivienne out, and changed the company bank account. He instructed his assistants to remove items from their past collections that had been stored in the studio. Vivienne believes he did this in order to 'prove how unimportant I was'. To this day, she is having to buy examples of her early work from auctions and dealers to fill the gaps in her archives. McLaren also turned a number of their staff against her, splitting the company into two camps: those who had worked at Nostalgia of Mud, who largely supported McLaren; and those from Worlds End, who remained loyal to Vivienne. Gene Krell, from the latter camp, believes that 'McLaren tried to impugn her in any way that he could. He talked about her having too many "spaghetti dinners" ' – a reference to D'Amario.

Worlds End started to fall apart. Vivienne, briefly back in London, yelled at McLaren in the studio and hit him with a chair in front of an astonished *Women's Wear Daily* reporter. Over the winter of 1983–84, the power and water supplies were disconnected from the King's Road shop, the Kingly Court studio and the flat in Nightingale Lane because of non-payment of bills. David Ireland, manning the darkened shop on his own in candlelight, could only accept cash. Meanwhile Vivienne's personal assistant, David Staines, was forced to make long business calls on his and Patrick Cox's home telephone, running up enormous bills. 'He'd come home and make a two-and-a-half-hour call to Australia about an order for three and a half pairs of socks', Cox complained. 'I'd be presented with a £2,000 phone bill that Vivienne couldn't pay, and I was a student! So our phone was cut off.' Kingly Court was abandoned, and sackloads of clothes were distributed to be stored in employees' homes across London. 'All these black bin-liners were stacked up in the flat,' says Cox, 'filled with stinking, rotting clothes, and loads just went straight into the bin.' In July 1984 Ireland refused to work at Worlds End any more, and left. He was briefly replaced by Patrick Cox and then Horace

Carter-Allan, but the shop was closed down in the autumn. 'People's wages had pretty much dried up,' says Ireland. 'I was working there six days a week for nothing . . . I'd become disillusioned with the whole scene. There was a lot of backbiting, drugs, unpleasantness and a lot of heroin.' Watching the collapse of the business at close quarters, Patrick Cox concluded that Vivienne's lack of commercial acumen and disregard for the practicalities of organisation were 'a textbook case of what was wrong with British designers. Everyone was working day and night for nothing, just because they loved it. It was so unprofessional.'

Bailiffs removed property from the shops, to be sold at Harvey's Auctions Ltd, 'by order of the Sheriff re Vivienne Westwood and Malcolm McLaren', on 25 July 1984. Eleven lots of clothes were listed – for example, 'A selection of fluorescent orange and yellow garments of Italian manufacture' – plus trunks, pouffes and fans. On the eve of the sale, however, David Staines was sent to the auctioneers with cash, and retrieved the goods.

It rankled with McLaren that his former partner had found another lover/manager, particularly as he was an Italian. He still smarted at the memory of a previous Italian sexual rival who had attracted Vivienne's attention in the mid-1960s, and he felt it diminished him that Vivienne had transferred her affections to someone he thought an unworthy successor. He began to disparage not only D'Amario, but the whole Italian fashion industry. 'This is the same story all over Italy,' he said. 'Carlo D'Amario is from that school – not an unusual character in the world of mainstream fashion. None of them are savoury people.' Predicting that the Italians would 'rip Vivienne off', he declared that the loose verbal agreements scattered around on her behalf by D'Amario were worthless, and vowed to prevent Vivienne from tying their label up with an Italian associate.

Disputes erupted over who would assume financial control of Vivienne's designs. Despite her bankruptcy, she was still a potentially profitable designer. McLaren insisted that he and Vivienne were still in partnership, and that they should take up offers for the clothes to be produced by Japanese manufacturers and licencees. At the same time he declared himself 'not incapable of designing the next collection myself'. Meanwhile, Elio Fiorucci was referring to Vivienne as his 'fashion consultant', and McLaren told *Women's Wear Daily* that Fiorucci intended to take over Worlds End. However, Worlds End's Italian agent, Alberto Raffaelli of the Milanese company GLR, who manufactured the 'Hypnos' collection, insisted to the newspaper that *he* had worldwide rights to license, manufacture and distribute any products created by Vivienne Westwood, under her own name or any other, including 'Worlds End'. To substantiate his claim, he showed the reporter contracts, dated 11 November 1982 and signed by both Vivienne and McLaren, giving him legal control of any design agreements concerning Vivienne. He also stated that he was the 'first creditor' of the company, and that the debt owed to him was 'not a small amount'. Raffaelli threatened court action against Fiorucci if he persisted in calling Vivienne part of his team.

According to Luigi Bastigli, the manager of GLR, only 10 per cent of the orders for Italian customers for the previous year had been delivered by the British manufacturers, and only 40 to 50 per cent of $20,000-worth of American orders. 'They are not bad-intentioned people – they just didn't know how to run a business.' Throughout late 1983 and early 1984, the future of the Worlds End label hung in the balance as Vivienne and McLaren threatened to sue one another over who actually owned it. In a last-ditch bid to salvage the partnership, McLaren flew to Rome in the spring for discussions with Vivienne, D'Amario and their Italian colleagues. 'They wanted to keep the partnership,' he recalls, 'but my lawyers advised me against it. It was only a partnership, not a limited company, and so as we didn't know what these Italian guys were like, and if we started to manufacture and nothing sold, I'd be liable.' He claims that Vivienne deliberately destroyed the company out of sexual pique. 'She broke it over my head. She knew that she couldn't have me and she couldn't be in business with me so she smashed the business to smash me.' This self-serving version that did not fully explain why the couple were now £250,000 in debt.

Eventually, McLaren gave up the fight and moved to Hollywood, to pursue a brief career developing ideas for Twentieth Century-Fox and live with the model-turned-actress Lauren Hutton. (According to Nils Stevenson 'it was Lauren Hutton who turned him on to sex. It was through her, not Vivienne, that he discovered sex.') Attributing the end of the partnership to a clash of ambitions, McLaren suggested that Vivienne 'needed to be a designer in her own right and she needed people who were more . . . sincere . . . There's no question that I only did fashion with her, but I wanted to break the mould. I wasn't enamoured with fashion. I was always interested in the media side of it whereas Vivienne wanted to be involved in the Paris mainstream.'

In the short term, the split professionally and personally benefited McLaren and devastated Vivienne. In the long term, however, it was the painful catalyst that enabled her career to flourish. No longer misled by his self-publicising cant, the fashion world eventually came to recognise the fundamental role she had played in their creative partnership. The price she paid for the separation was that, in matters of the heart, she never trusted again with the same intensity. The price he paid was a decline into comparative professional irrelevance.

Discussing her work with McLaren, Vivienne said that 'it was the culture he gave me . . . that's what excited me so much'. Her designs had been inspired by 'an aesthetic dialogue I have with Malcolm'. From him, she said, she had learned to divide styles into warm and cold: 'The warm and cold vocabulary helps you understand where the essential vitality is. Mod fashion, for instance, is cold. Malcolm would say that is for bank clerks. It's not generous, it's cold-arsed. You know, with those little hats and cool shades. But if you have a rocker, a guy who will stand out in the rain on Chelsea Bridge in a leather jacket with studs all over it and a T-shirt with his big belly hanging out – that is warm. And the way the rockers dance with big boots on – there's more generosity in that. It isn't precious.'

Despite the disruptive and occasionally violent relationship between Vivienne and McLaren, they had created their most exciting and innovative work as a team. 'The influence of the pair cannot be overstated,' according to the style commentator Peter York. The partnership was greater than the sum of its parts. Vivienne was the experimental craftsman, McLaren the art director who suggested the themes, gave each collection an of-the-moment and popular appeal, and refined the final selection. McLaren needed Vivienne. 'Malcolm needs a good collaborator, otherwise he's useless,' say Nils Stevenson. 'Punk needed the binary opposition of Malcolm and Vivienne to work.' Nevertheless, McLaren continues to dismiss Vivienne's contribution, reducing it to the merely mechanical: 'She was never someone who could articulate an idea or thought. She did not have any ideas. She did not think of herself as being creative but she was phenomenally good with her hands. She would find a way to make an idea work.' And yet, despite the predictions of McLaren, the press and customers, it was Vivienne who was to emerge as the more dynamic and creative of the two, qualities she combined with disciplined application and fierce ambition.

Free from McLaren, Vivienne worked on her 'Clint Eastwood' collection for autumn/winter 1984–85, designed as a spoof on spaghetti westerns. Under huge fluorescent belted macs, nylon and wool jackets and short-legged bondage trousers were decorated with famous Italian logos such as Fiat and Olivetti, trimmed with fluorescent flashes and fastened with belts closed with Velcro. Some items featured huge, box-like pockets in a gesture to supersede handbags.

A few weeks before the show, Vivienne realised that she had not designed any shoes. Two styles already drawn by McLaren were fine-tuned by Patrick Cox: a thick-soled black patent shoe with a prominent tongue and a version of the 'Witches' triple-tongued sneaker. In addition, Cox proposed five pairs of platform shoes raised three inches off the ground at the front and four-and-a-half at the back. When he pulled the prototypes from his bag to show Vivienne, she dismissed them with the cry, 'Ugh, platforms! They're hideous – so seventies!' Since there were not enough shoes available backstage before the show, Cox offered the platforms to the models, who loved them. John Galliano and John Flett were in the audience, and both commissioned him to design shoes for their collections. Vivienne revived the platform, in a more elegant court shoe, for her 'Portrait' collection in March 1990, and it became a house signature.

The staging of 'Clint Eastwood' at the Cour du Louvre in Paris in March 1984 was shambolic. Since the clothes did not arrive from Italy until two hours before the show, and many of them were unfinished, Vivienne dragooned her assistants, the stylists and various members of the audience into sitting backstage at portable sewing machines and literally constructing the garments. Meanwhile, Gene Krell had to placate the infuriated audience, who were kept waiting for over two hours.

As little of 'Clint Eastwood' was actually manufactured, and Vivienne no longer had any retail outlets in London, it was an unprofitable collection. Nevertheless, D'Amario continued to support Vivienne, and arranged a bank loan in order to rescue the Worlds End label. Then, once Vivienne's contract with Fiorucci had expired, he began unsuccessful negotiations for her to create collections for Zamasport, the company which produced Romeo Gigli.

D'Amario also held discussions with Sergio Galeotti, Giorgio

Armani's partner. Galeotti masterminded Armani's business and dealt with the practicalities of production, teaming up with Italy's leading designer fashion manufacturer, GFT, to produce the line. He was also developing a stable of designer brands for Marco Rivetti, the chairman of GFT. Galeotti recognised Vivienne's talent and proposed that the Armani Group draw up a contract to produce and distribute her collections. While the negotiations were taking place Vivienne was temporarily in London, and was so broke she could not afford the airfare back to Milan. In desperation, she turned for a loan to David Connors, the architect who had helped design the Seditionaries shop. 'Just imagine,' Connors recalls. 'Here is Giorgio Armani offering her worldwide domination, and she can't afford the air ticket – not even a bus ticket!' (Several years later, Vivienne offered Connors either £200 in cash or £400-worth of clothes in settlement of the loan. He took the clothes.)

The impending Armani/Westwood deal was announced on 16 January 1985 in *Women's Wear Daily*, who dubbed it 'one of fashion's stranger couplings'. Nevertheless, it made commercial sense. While Armani's discreet and grown-up clothes were the epitome of sleek minimalism for modern working women, Vivienne's work was colourful, youthful and attention-seeking, and young Italians longed for British *avant-garde* fashion. By the mid-1980s, fashion had reached a fork in the road. Would it turn back to the conventional, ladylike quality associated with Gallic designers, or would it take the more experimental path of deconstruction pioneered by Vivienne and taken up by the leading Japanese designers? Galeotti had constructed a deal that would embrace both ends of fashion's spectrum, with two designers who epitomised and led the field in their respective, starkly contrasting, images of modern woman.

The agreement was to involve a seven-year contract with Vivienne, with a further five-year optional extension, and gave Armani the exclusive right to the Vivienne Westwood name worldwide. As well as 'substantial' financial backing from Armani, who would produce and market her collections, Vivienne would receive royalties, retain complete creative control and manage all promotional matters, such as fashion shows. The first was to be presented in Paris in March 1985.

Giorgio Armani was happy to be associated with Vivienne. Having seen a video of one of her collections, he declared that she had 'a style and grace in her collection – a tenderness'; perhaps what Vivienne might have called 'warm' fashion. 'There's something ancestral about it,' he continued. 'There's a somewhat primitive air in her clothes but what I liked was that they weren't at all aggressive.' Vivienne, who only met Armani once, welcomed the deal: 'We both have very clear formulas. Armani gives status to relaxed clothes. He will always look like Giorgio Armani and I will always look like Vivienne Westwood.'

While Vivienne was working on her first collection under the aegis of the Armani group she lived at the modest Elizabetta Hotel in Florence, liaising with the GFT factory in Tuscany. Occasionally she made trips to Rome, where she met up with her one-time shop assistant Bella Freud, who was sharing the house of the British artist Brian Clark and going out with Prince 'Dado' Ruspoli, the head of an eminent Roman family. Freud was somewhat wary of her old boss. She had been commissioned by Keith Richards of the Rolling Stones to make a coat, but recalling how anti-establishment Vivienne was, particularly about the superstars of the rock firmament, she expected her to 'think that it was really naff to work for him'. But to her surprise Vivienne was affectionate and friendly, and helped her design the coat.

Vivienne confided to Freud that she was lonely in Italy. Her isolation was presumably increased by her inability to speak Italian. Though she talked excitedly about her new affair with D'Amario, 'like a teenager who keeps going on about their compatible star signs', she was surprisingly detached when describing her heartache over McLaren. 'She was never self-pitying. It was almost as if she was sitting outside herself, describing her pain as "like a smarting feeling in a part of my body", rather than doing what most women would do and calling him "that fucking bastard".' One afternoon they were walking along a street when Vivienne turned to Freud and said, 'You know, if that car came and ran me over now, I'd just say bye to Mum, and there's no one else.' No mention was made of either of her sons.

Bella Freud introduced Vivienne to a privileged and rarefied world habituated by the rich, the aristocratic and the artistic, such as the Ruspolis, the Earl of Mulgrave, Baroness Francesca von Thyssen-Bornemisza, and artists such as Brian Clark, Cy Twombley and the photographer Alastair Thane. They gathered at Dado Ruspoli's castle, Cerveteri, to the north of Rome, or at a farm nearby belonging to Ruspoli's cousin, Paola Igliori, and her husband, the artist Sandro Chia.

Amid the Renaissance fountains of the seventeenth-century gardens of the Chia home, Vivienne played charades with this gilded young set. It opened her eyes to another lifestyle, sensibility and mode of dress. Finding herself out of her familiar setting and in such confident and carefree company, Vivienne tended to be reserved and observant rather than opinionated. Paola Igliori described her as 'low-key, not very loquacious', but she was enchanted by her seriousness and her 'unusual outlook on things'.

At the time Vivienne's appearance was distinctive, and virtually the same every day. She wore a short, princess-line jacket and a corduroy midi-skirt printed with a woodgrain pattern (used in her next collection and worn by the singer Cindi Lauper). She believed that the wood print, which figuratively represented part of her surname, was a talisman and would 'bring her luck', remembers Dometilla Getty. Her hair, held by medallions in thin plaits, was garishly tinted with henna, and smudges of pirate-gold make-up were wiped across her eyelids and brows and a dark line drawn around her lips.

Professionally, it seemed that Vivienne's star was in the ascendant at last. Her recognition within the fashion business had been underscored when, in November 1983, she showed her collection in Tokyo as one of the 'Best Five', Hanae Mori's global fashion award, along with Claude Montana, Calvin Klein and Gianfranco Ferre. However, early in the spring of 1985, just before Vivienne's new collection was scheduled to be launched in Paris, Sergio Galeotti died of an AIDS-related illness. In mourning for his close friend, and concerned that his business was left without a manager, Giorgio Armani retrenched, and cancelled the presentation and production of the Westwood line. Rumours abounded that the factory working on her collection had complained to the Armani group that Vivienne was impossible to work with. She had failed to present properly graded patterns and was accused of being temperamental and incapable of sticking to a system.

What struck Gene Krell most about Vivienne's response to the collapse of the Armani deal, which had promised to be the fulfilment of her dreams, was her resilience and determination to carry on regardless. In the short interval between Galeotti's death and the cancellation of her deal with Armani, samples for Vivienne's new show had been made up and invitations sent out to the press and buyers. She opted to tell the audience in person that the show had been called off at the eleventh hour. It must have been extremely humiliating for her to have to advise the guests of her professional demise, but with characteristic *chutzpah* she stood at the entrance of the Cour du Louvre tent in a cap decorated with a fist holding a huge felt hammer that she had bought from a tourist shop, and told everyone that the show was off.

The Armani débâcle postponed the unveiling of one of Vivienne's most extraordinary collections, the 'Mini Crini' (originally entitled 'World School'). Contrary as ever, she had elided two of the most extreme, controversial and apparently irreconcilable of women's fashions: the encumbering, floor-length crinoline worn by the matronly woman of the respectable 1860s, and the girlish short skirt worn by the ostensibly liberated and sexually promiscuous young woman of the 1960s. Vivienne delighted not only in the juxtaposition of the exaggeratedly concealed and the exaggeratedly revealed but also in its timing. She introduced this wide-hipped, knee-length skirt in utter defiance of the unisex, snake-hipped silhouette of 1980s power dressing, hoping that her crinoline would 'put the boot into that Italian look, which is so ugly. Women want to look feminine again.'

In the mid-1980s, mainstream fashion idealised the adolescent boy's silhouette. Women's clothing was cut along wide-shouldered, narrow-hipped, long-legged and lean lines. Feminine curvaceousness and fecundity were masked by a hard-edged androgyny. The nineteenth-century crinoline, by contrast, drew attention to women's hips, and celebrated fecundity. What better way to fly in the face of the contemporary concealment of the childbearing potential of woman than to reintroduce the crinoline? Vivienne's first mini crini sat right out on the hips and swung down to just below the knee (shorter versions followed). It was teamed with a narrow-shouldered, waist-defining short blazer or bow-fronted little jacket, and wooden or white foam-rubber platformed Minnie Mouse shoes, in imitation of the childlike attire of a cartoon character. The ensemble was a curious hybrid, including the vulnerably feminine upper torso of Dior's New Look, the girlishness of the mini, the fulness of the net-petticoated skirts of Vivienne's youth, the lampshade dresses designed by Leon Bakst for Diaghilev's ballets *Petroushka*, *Narcisse* and *Carnival*, and the crinolined hoops of the French Second Empire.

Over the past four hundred years, an extremely exaggerated line in women's clothes has prevailed three times: the whaleboned body and farthingale of the fifteenth century; the stays and hooped petticoat of the eighteenth century; and the corset and crinoline of the nineteenth century. The original crinoline, popularised by the Empress Eugénie of France, held sway between the 1850s and the 1860s. As the skirt became progressively wider it provided a fund of ridicule for satirists, who lampooned it for being ludicrously impractical and dangerous. Fashionable ladies were depicted taking off like umbrellas into the sky with the slightest gust of wind, and in 1858 *Punch* discussed the fashion's impact on architecture ('staircases must be widened and porticoes enlarged') and the female brain ('a narrowness of waist betrays a narrowness of mind'). It was also a source of frustration for men, who were forced to keep their distance from women ring-fenced behind garments of nine to twelve feet in circumference. Nevertheless, the crinoline was adopted not only by ladies of leisure, but by factory workers, shop assistants and servants. Though it was bulky, the crinoline freed women's legs from tight, heavy petticoats, enabling more active pursuits. The Empress, for example, took up strenuous walking in it, and by 1865 the *'jupe passe partout'* was introduced, incorporating a system of pulleys to raise the skirt's hem while its wearer practised active pursuits such as rambling, archery or croquet.

The nineteenth-century crinoline rested on a horsehair petticoat (*crin* is French for horsehair) stiffened with watchspring steel wire, whalebone hoops, plaited straw or even inflatable rubber tyres. Vivienne pointed out to critics that her contemporary version, suspended on plastic 'whalebone' hoops, was comfortable and practical. 'It just collapses around you, so you don't even notice it . . . you could sit on a tube train and not really know you've got one on until you get up and it just bells out. Even if you're on a crowded tube, it always springs back after being squashed.' Attracted to the crinoline's exaggerated proportions, she believed it gave the wearer 'an immense sense of presence. It really makes you want to preen.' To Vivienne's mind, the crinoline was 'one of the most sexual garments that ever existed because of the way it sways and slowly displays little bits of flesh and underwear'.

Its archaic quality also intrigued her. 'I take something from the past which has a sort of vitality that has never been exploited . . . and get very intense, as if I were writing a piece of music or a painting. Dior was forever in museums and some assistant would try and find him and he'd be right underneath one of the big dresses, trying to find out how they were constructed. The thing is that you take something that already exists and you get so involved with it that, in the end, you do something original because you overlay your own ideas.'

It is rare for a designer to articulate her working method so methodically and revealingly, but traces of the teacher she had been still lingered in Vivienne. Though she was not eloquent, the manner in which she explained her *modus operandi* was straightforward and informative. She described fashion designing as 'almost like mathematics. You have a vocabulary of ideas which you have to add and subtract from in order to come up with an equation that's right for the times.'

Vivienne's sense of timing was acute and canny. She told Simon Barker that she had initially explored the crinoline in 1978, but had decided to shelve it until she had developed the concept fully, and could introduce it at a more opportune moment. Although Vivienne's crinoline brought her great acclaim as an innovator, she was not the first designer to want to bell out the skirt. In 1977 Chrissie Walsh (the architect Ben Kelly's girlfriend) featured it in her MA degree show at the Royal College of Art, as did Rifat Ozbek for his BA show at St Martin's. Vivienne knew them both. Philip Sallon was also experimenting with the crinoline, as his college sketchbooks at the time show. Also, all fashions end in excess, and it was inevitable that the snake-hipped mode would be challenged.

Vivienne's mini crinis were based around the circle. She combined the round-faced and round-bodied figures of Mickey and Minnie Mouse with the wheel-like circle of the crinoline. The cottons and denims from which she cut her skirts were printed with giant polkadots or stars, and the models' round-toed platformed shoes, she believed, gave the impression of 'an old prostitute pretending to be fourteen years old'. Straight lines were banished. To bring home the importance of the curve, Vivienne showed her small collection on buxom young English models.

Thanks to a bank loan arranged by D'Amario, the mini crini's debut took place in October 1985 at the Cour du Louvre. Three versions were shown: a pannier, a sphere, and a beehive with hoops on the outside. A few weeks later Suzanne Bartsch took over the Limelight nightclub in New York to show the new line, which the Americans christened the 'Pollyanna' collection. Bartsch, an exceptionally *avant-garde* German émigrée, was an important contact for Vivienne in New York. Her first boutique, opened on Thompson Street in SoHo in 1981, provided a unique showcase for 'New London in New York', selling BodyMap, Leigh Bowery and Rachael Aubin clothes, Andrew Logan glass jewellery and Tony Gross's spectacles. Initially the look was dismissed as merely a lark, but within months the *New York Times* reported that Bartsch's boutique, 'among others, has been hard-pressed to keep its *avant-garde* clientele in hoops lately, so popular has the skirt proven'.

The liaison with Bartsch did not end amicably. According to Bartsch, Vivienne had demanded substantial down-payments for orders that never arrived: 'I gave her $15,000 or $20,000, and I never got anything.' In retaliation, Bartsch, it was alleged, requisitioned the 'Mini Crini' samples shown at the Limelight. 'If I'd had deliveries, I'd have done really well,' says Bartsch. 'It flew out of the window, her stuff.' For many years the two women did not speak, their relationship made more difficult by the fact that deliveries of the Westwood collections to Bartsch's boutique were sporadic, haphazard or non-existent.

Since the 'Mini Crini' collection had been prepared while Vivienne was working in conjunction with the Armani group, her patterns had been left at the Tuscan factory commissioned to produce the range. She was desperate to retrieve them, and according to Bella Freud, Carlo D'Amario 'stole them back from the factory' for her. This deed, combined with D'Amario's support and the bank loan he had raised to save her company, left Vivienne feeling hugely indebted to him. It was a debt that she would not forget. Simon Barker, however, considers that she 'exaggerated Carlo's saving role. Italian *Vogue* would have featured her anyway, and Fiorucci was keen on her. She had a future in Italy whatever happened.'

During Vivienne's absence from London, Gary Ness, who had become dependent on her handouts, was abandoned. He sank into a torpor, awaiting his benefactress's return. His influence was to dramatically affect Vivienne's work.

7   RULE BRITANNIA!

1986–1988

'I've never been happier than when I'm parodying the English.'
Vivienne Westwood, 1987

At the beginning of 1986 Vivienne was in straitened and precarious circumstances. Her seven-year contract with Armani had been abruptly terminated, and the tempestuous affair with Carlo D'Amario was over. There was little to keep her in Italy now. Without man or money, she arrived back in London, where the £250,000 debt she had incurred in partnership with McLaren remained outstanding.

The architect David Connors ran into his former client in Chelsea soon after her return. When he asked about the Armani deal, she complained, 'In Italy they take cheap cloth and make it look expensive, and I take expensive cloth and make it look cheap. They just don't understand what I'm trying to do!' Despite ridicule, penury and loneliness, Vivienne was determined to carry on: 'She has an extraordinary ability to close off failings,' her friend Gene Krell observed. 'She's not cognisant of things like adversity.'

Perhaps because of her exposure to Italian views on smartness, Vivienne now abandoned her ragamuffin clothes in favour of strictly prim English suiting. She took to ceaselessly extolling the fine tailoring of Savile Row and the tradition and craftsmanship to be found in Scottish and English tweeds and English gabardines. She had not abandoned sexuality in dress, but was simply playing with another form – suppressed sexuality. She toyed with the eroticism latent in national clichés: the bespectacled schoolteacher, or the nanny going about her business dressed with precision and propriety. Only a British designer, intuitively alert to this comic element in the British character, could have celebrated it.

Vivienne's parents had moved to Teignmouth in Devon, and on 8

September 1985 her father died of heart disease. His estate of just over £4,000 was shared out equally among the three children, but he had named only Olga and Gordon as trustees, although Vivienne was the eldest. Vivienne welcomed the company of her recently widowed mother, who moved up from Devon to live with her for a while in Nightingale Lane. Dora's robust constitution, girlishness, frankness and love of dressing up had clearly been inherited by her daughter. She was a crazy dresser, favouring flashy, peacock-blue satin jackets or pillarbox red 'Love' jackets from Vivienne's collections. But Dora was happier and less complicated than her daughter. Her cheeks were flushed and her aquamarine eyes glittered with anticipation of life's next thrill.

Vivienne's relationship with her mother had had its ups and downs, but with the departure of 'the interloper' (as Dora styled McLaren), the two women became closer. Dora, however, still could not accept what she regarded as her daughter's lewd behaviour — the excesses of punk, an illegitimate child and pornographic designs. She encouraged Vivienne to make use of nostalgically English items, such as Smedley woollen combinations and the gymslips she had sold in the Tintwistle post office. Once when Simon Barker came into the shop and bent down to inspect some 'Witches' oddments for sale in a basket, Dora warned him, 'Ooh, don't look in there! She's got some tops with those funny buttons in the shape of penises. I really don't know why she has to do that sort of thing.' Her mother's censoriousness had irked Vivienne during the punk period, but now Dora agreed to help her rebuild the business from scratch, with nothing but Vivienne's reputation and her own modest savings. As she had done with Let it Rock, she invested in her daughter's new venture.

Vivienne returned to Worlds End to begin the long climb back to solvency and critical acclaim. As a registered bankrupt, she was unable to trade under her own name, so her mother and her son Joseph signed as directors of a new company, Casnell Ltd (the name was bought off the shelf from a failed company). Vivienne's morale was low. She refused to discuss why the Armani deal had been summarily terminated and she had lost trust in her past associates. McLaren had abandoned her; D'Amario, though still ardent, was an unreliable ally; Michael Collins, now an incapacitated heroin addict, had embezzled thousands of pounds from her; and most of her staff, fed up with not being paid, and Vivienne's bad management and selfishness, had deserted her.

Nevertheless, Vivienne was still convinced that she would become a great fashion designer, and utilised her considerable persuasive powers to elicit loans, advice and unpaid assistance from her family and a few loyal friends.

Though she had been forced to close Nostalgia of Mud, and had abandoned the Worlds End shop when she fled to Italy, she had never relinquished the keys to 430 King's Road, which had stood empty for a year. In July 1986 she simply reopened the front door and took up where she had left off. At first it was a gloomy struggle. The electricity and gas supplies were still cut off. Helped by her sons and her mother, Vivienne mopped the floors, cleaned the windows, laid out the few specimen pieces of her aborted Armani and 'Mini Crini' collections, and commenced trading – quite literally – in the dark. Customers had to shop by torch and candle-light. Holly Johnson, the lead singer of Frankie Goes to Hollywood, visited the shop at the time: 'There was no lighting or electricity by which you could look at the rails of printed denim clothes. An old woman [Dora] sat in the corner sewing buttons on things in the dim light, while another middle-aged, redheaded woman [Vivienne] rummaged about, apologising for the lack of lighting or electricity.'

In the darkness, the colours of the mini crinis, little blazers, shirts and denims were poster-paint bright. Stars and polkadots as large as tennis balls were printed onto the cotton in radiant contrasts of scarlet and white, navy and white, scarlet and apple green or sunflower yellow and black. They were also printed onto denim, as 'Spot Jeans'. The Mini Crini collection, which had been shown on the Paris catwalk and at the Limehouse nightclub in New York the previous autumn, had such an impact that by the autumn of 1986 many of the world's leading designers had interpreted Vivienne's crinoline line, a line that determinedly flew in the face of twentieth-century functionalism in dress. The most acclaimed rendering of the silhouette was made by Christian Lacroix when he launched his couture line in 1985, featuring his version of the mini crini. As well as couture versions by Lacroix and Karl Lagerfeld for Chanel, glossy copies were available in New York from Oscar de la Renta, Bill Blass, Donna Karan and Calvin Klein, and in London from Miss Selfridge. 'It has always been the case that when others have copied me they lifted me up with them,' says Vivienne. 'I never begrudge people copying me – as long as they don't mess it up.' However, although she may have felt vindicated at seeing her design lead being followed by international high fashion, Vivienne received no financial reward.

Jordan, now divorced and back in Seaford, received a plaintive telephone call from Vivienne in the summer of 1986, asking her to come back and run the King's Road shop as, she claimed, she could not find anyone else who wouldn't steal from her. But having found peace in her home town breeding Burmese cats and working for a local veterinary practice, Jordan declined. It was a measure of Vivienne's thick skin that she could approach Jordan, having been cutting and catty to her on so many occasions; she had vilified her for taking a 'bourgeois' and weak action when she married Kevin Mooney of Adam and the Ants in 1981, and labelled her a traitor for appearing in Jarman's 1978 film *Jubilee*.

Ambitious to restore her reputation in high fashion circles, Vivienne was determined to get her clothes back on the catwalk. Two men consistently stood by her during these dark days: Keith Wainwright, who owned the hairdressers Smile, two doors down from the shop, and Jeff Banks, the proprietor of the fashion group Warehouse and later the presenter of the BBC's *Clothes Show*. 'It was absolutely desperate,' Wainwright remembers. 'We were feeding her, and I went to dinner parties at Jeff's home, and we talked about things just to keep her spirits up.' Wainwright coiffed the models in all Vivienne's shows for no charge for the next five years, while Banks succeeded in making her listen to criticism, and virtually single-handedly placed her business on a firm footing.

Banks had originally heard about Vivienne's predicament from Wainwright. When a mini-cab company instigated court proceedings against her over an unpaid £800 bill (much of which had been run up by McLaren), thereby threatening her with bankruptcy and the closure of the shop, Wainwright rang him and asked: 'Could you help Vivienne? She's desperate. It's all caving in on her.' Banks agreed to help her, provided that she constructed a viable business plan. Having dealt with the creditors, he then insisted that Casnell be separated into small divisions, so that if one area, for example Japanese customers, failed to honour its debts, the rest wouldn't be dragged down too. He generously lent her between £15,000 and £20,000 (he cannot recall the exact figure), and stood as guarantor for her new bank account.

One of Banks's toughest stipulations for the reconstructed business was that it would not accept any wholesale orders unless a 50 per cent deposit was placed with the order and the remainder was settled *before* the goods were delivered. There were to be no exceptions – not even powerful American department stores like Bergdorf Goodman or Nostrums. He then set about tutoring the nineteen-year-old Joseph in the accounting techniques he would need to manage his mother's affairs. The boy, being a natural trader, learnt quickly, and relished the opportunity to assume this role. The next step was to introduce Vivienne to Jean Bennett, an experienced public relations officer, and John Walford, a show producer (his sister Thea had made leather underwear for SEX). They also agreed to waive their fees until she was on a firmer financial footing.

Without Banks's skilful guidance, it is unlikely that Vivienne would have survived on the fashion scene. He was prepared to invest considerable amounts of time and money into her venture, because he believed 'there was no reason why this superb talent should get drowned under the bailiff's papers'. Nevertheless, he was amazed by Vivienne's selfishness: 'She's *incredibly* self-centred, and doesn't think about anyone else. Her whole life and being is Vivienne Westwood. Her drive is egoism – she has a massive ego – not financial gain or acquisitions, but [she] requires the satisfaction of being held up as a font of knowledge and creation and a raconteur.'

Vivienne was sustained in her adversity by the conviction that she was as talented as her newly discovered heroine, Coco Chanel. 'I *am* Coco Chanel [and] Yves Saint Laurent,' she told a journalist in 1986, 'but I don't particularly want to do couture in that sense. I have strong ideas that can filter into a whole classical background . . . men's suits, women's suits. I'd like to click into all that.'

The American fashion trade journal *Women's Wear Daily* was the first influential publication to champion Vivienne's talent, and she nurtured its interest. Boasting to its London bureau chief, James Fallon, in 1985 of the innumerable ideas she intended to bring to the marketplace in the next twelve months, she assured him: 'My prestige has never been as high as it is at the moment because I have such a lot of innovations under my belt . . . I know where I'm going and what I'm doing, I'm just not sure how I will get there. I'm keeping to a definite pace and am being very businesslike about everything.' She explained that most of the manufacturing for her forthcoming collection would be done in Britain, but that she would not commit herself to a show and a wholesaling business until she had secured suitable production capacity. She was, she claimed, 'back to a strong base. If I had had that before I wouldn't have had to stop, but could have continued in a small way.'

Partly in reaction to her experiences in Italy, and partly because of her deep-seated patriotism (she always referred to 'England' and 'English', not 'Britain' and 'British', just as women were always 'ladies'.), Vivienne became overtly nationalistic in her choice of cloth, manufacturers and themes for her clothes. She had always loved good-quality English wool (many of her punk bondage suits had been made of it), and she resolved to exploit the fine and largely neglected traditions and crafts of England: 'Because of its history of industry you can get things here that you can't anywhere else, and at good value.' She cited Fair Isle knitting as an example of something that could not be produced in Italy, where modern machinery had virtually eclipsed craft knitting, and where fashion forecasting determined the colours and fabrics of each season, allowing little variety. It may have been after seeing the work of Tai and Rossita Missoni in Italy that Vivienne reassessed craft knitting. In the early sixties the Missonis found some abandoned 1920s knitting machines which could knit up to twenty different coloured yarns in a row, and had gone on to revive intricate decorative knitting.

It was the quirks of English dress, both that of the upper classes and the Royal Family and their vernacular parody in the form of the Cockney Pearly Kings and Queens, that inspired Vivienne, and which she gently spoofed in her 'Harris Tweed' collection (sometimes called by her the 'Aristocratic' or 'Royal' collection). Once again she was using the techniques of collage between high and low culture she had learned from McLaren. 'Harris Tweed' was shown at the Apex Room in Olympia in March 1987, exactly a decade after her venomous attack on the royals at Seditionaries.

In 1987 she claimed that her favourite designer was the royal couturier Sir Norman Hartnell, who had designed heavily embroidered, multi-petticoated gowns for the Queen. 'English tailoring and tradition have always been a big influence on me, it's my mark, my roots. It's not possible to have technique without tradition. Technique is always a borrowing from what other people have done ... I take influence from the street but I give more influence back than I take,' she insisted to *Women's Wear Daily*, perhaps in response to McLaren's jibe that she had lost touch with the street. Now they were playing the same game – making the past fashionable in a provocative and original way: he by adding souped-up rock to famous operatic arias, she by making fashion out of traditional Scottish tweeds and arcane accessories.

The small 'Harris Tweed' collection, Vivienne's first back on home turf, was put together in the front room of her flat, 'without an ironing board or trestle tables, nothing! It just manifested itself from nowhere,' a temporary assistant who helped to machine samples recalled. It incorporated such staples of upper-class dressing as tweed schoolgirl/ nanny coats inspired by images from the thirties and forties of the young princesses Elizabeth and Margaret (although McLaren claimed he thought of the idea years before, while researching in the children's department of John Lewis, and had dressed his new girlfriend, Vivienne, in the look), twinsets and pearls, hunting coats, jodhpurs and black velvet. These were accessorised with pantomimic headgear – a crown, a John Bull hat, Pearly King's and Queen's titfers. The St Trinian's-style models, chosen for their English schoolgirl looks, chewed gum and smeared lipstick across their mouths in imitation of the photographs in the society magazine *Tatler* of debutantes snogging their beaux at dances. Vivienne liked to imagine, she said, that 'they were good girls and didn't take the boys home'.

At the time of the show, Harris tweed, the epitome of traditional, romantic British cloth, was out of fashion. Modern lifestyles did not require rough, heavy cloths. Affluent urban men and women preferred layers of light, easily packed mid-season clothes for their centrally heated, air conditioned lives. Harris tweed had been made by hand for 150 years on the bleak Outer Hebridean islands of Harris and Lewis. The stout, thorn-proof, water-resistant cloth was so hard-wearing that a man's coat would outlive him. To wish the wearer longevity, the weaver chanted a Gaelic song over and over in time to the beat of his pedal and the to-ing and fro-ing of his shuttle across the loom:

Mayest thou wear the cloth to shreds,
Mayest thou wear the cloth to rags,
Mayest thou wear the cloth
With food and music in every way,
As we would fain have thee.

Such folkloric detail would have been immensely appealing to Vivienne, who searched for a story behind every fabric and garment. Strict rules, laid down by the Harris Tweed Association, defined an authentic Harris tweed, which had to be 100 per cent virgin Scottish wool, woven at home by the islanders.

The intense and varied colours of the cloth (up to seven different hues, for example, were woven into a 'black' tweed) were drawn from the weaver's surroundings: the grey-purple of a sea mist, the black-purple of a sloe berry, the piercing yellow of a peregrine's beak, the reddened umber of the sodden earth. Vivienne loved the tweeds because of these colours, which were 'so intense, they're like jewels'. Jewels fitted her royal theme, and the Windsors had worn Harris tweed for generations.

Vivienne was reminded of this evocative cloth when she was shown it by Elliott Little, the London agent for Kenneth MacKenzie, one of the two mills licensed to produce it. The firm's managing director, Harris MacKenzie, travelled to London to meet her. When he showed her his colour chart, he found her 'very explicit in what she wants . . . demanding, yes, demanding' – she even sent swatches back with instructions to 'make it more hairy'. Vivienne used nine eighty-metre pieces in the collection. The order was hand-written in her bold, looping, schoolmistress script, giving only a home telephone number and a promise that the bill would be settled – she was clearly accustomed to suppliers refusing to open accounts with her.

As Vivienne's relationship with Kenneth MacKenzie Ltd developed, she became increasingly experimental in her use of the traditional cloth. Unlike other designers, whose clothes were produced in modern, automated factories, her small collection was hand-cut and assembled on domestic sewing machines. Consequently, she could work with the single-width (75-centimetre) traditional tweed which could not be cut on industrial cutting machines designed for double-width (125-centimetre) cloths. Robin Huggan, the firm's art director, found her 'forceful' and constantly innovating, suggesting a tweed based on the Prince of Wales check or, on being shown a sheet displaying a multitude of samples of different tones and grids, proposing that they be amalgamated into one patchwork tweed. Huggan replied that this was impossible, but Vivienne was adamant, and the multi-coloured tweed was painstakingly woven inch by inch on many shuttles.

Since 1911 the Harris Tweed Authority's trademark has been the royal orb – a symbol once known to virtually every child who owned a tweed school coat and every man who wore a sports coat. On the backdrop of the catwalk for her 'Harris Tweed' show, Vivienne used a huge orb encircled, Saturn-like, by a ring, and this became her logo. The reason she chose it, she explained, was that she had 'always worked in a very traditional way, and the step into the future is the Saturn ring around the orb . . . and of course I've often, just peripherally, been associated with the Queen, as in "Queen of Punk".' This blatant appropriation of the Harris Tweed Authority's trademark caused some rancour, but as Ian McKenzie, chief executive of the authority, says, 'On balance, it would probably do more good than harm, so there was no point in making a song and dance about it.' Casnell was not taken to court by the authority, and Harris tweed did benefit hugely from its association with such a fashionable designer. Having adopted the symbol as her trademark, Vivienne was advised by Banks to develop it, and to 'polish that orb, look after that orb until it's really shining, and then people will come to you, and a satellite ring will start to turn up.' A pattern was developing, in which the men who knew Vivienne best – McLaren, Ness, D'Amario, Banks – communicated with her in fables, as if they were talking to a child.

Another sentimental attraction to a traditional, quality cloth overlooked by rival designers was demonstrated in Vivienne's use of John Smedley's fine-gauge knits. The material evoked her childhood – Dora had sold Smedley's 'hygienic' woollen undergarments in Tintwistle. Smedley had been producing these wools since 1765 in a stone-built mill in the nearby Derbyshire hills, and as a family firm that was ticking over comfortably, it was not inclined to change. Then, one dark, wet autumn day in 1986, Vivienne arrived. She was met at the local station by the firm's designer, Craig Alexander, who accompanied her across the old bridge, between dry-stone walls and past employees sitting out on the royal-blue-painted benches eating their sandwiches in the bracing air. The clattering of the looms contended with the roar of the water-wheel. Vivienne must have felt that she had stepped back a century as she passed through the doorway which bore a modest brass plaque announcing the firm's name.

Vivienne had long worn Smedley's garments, and knew exactly what she wanted: the classic twinset, in four blatantly unfashionable colours – Saxe blue, camel, ecru and tomato. The traditionally English, but now dated look of twinset and pearls had been brought to her attention by Jordan's ironic wearing of it – she appeared in it as the character Amyl Nitrate in Derek Jarman's punk film *Jubilee*. It amused Craig Alexander that Vivienne 'always chose the colours we were about to drop because nobody had been buying them for ten years'. To these she added her distinctive orb buttons and motif, embroidered by Halls of Mansfield. She insisted that the waist-defining ribbing be raised tight around the ribcage and up under the bust, for a sexier effect. This body-hugging silhouette became a distinctive Westwood signature – incidentally, it flattered her own figure of narrow shoulders, a small upper torso and a high waist. At a time when other designers were promoting loose knitwear, it was typical of Vivienne to propose the opposite.

For subsequent collections she added a greater range of colours, and challenged Smedley's skills by commissioning intricate intasias – pictures and images knitted into the pattern – depicting love-hearts and multi-coloured 'Harlequin' Argylls. Her Argyll leggings became a bestseller, and over the next three years Smedley's supplied between three and four hundred pairs a season – in sea-island cotton for summer and in wool for winter. From the time when she designed clothes for SEX, Vivienne had repeated successful designs from one collection to another. Just as Saint Laurent had his 'classics' – the pea coat, the smoking suit – so Vivienne developed hers.

On the few occasions that she visited the Smedley's factory, Vivienne would work hard all day, joining the employees at the pub for a lunch of chips and whisky. In their presence, Craig Alexander remembers, she loved to hold forth, boasting that she was 'reading something in depth – Greek history or whatever'. Whether or not her audience was interested, 'she just kept talking' – about her childhood, or shocking her mother by walking around the countryside in her bizarre outfits. Her father was never mentioned.

Many traditional British clothing manufacturers would not be diverted by the vagaries of fashion. Tony Langford, the managing director of Smedley, admits: 'Fashion frightens me.' He cites two difficulties in working with fashion designers: 'They are designers first and business people a very, very poor second, so for people like ourselves, who are pragmatists, designers seem fickle, head-in-the-clouds. And when it comes to the nasty subject of finances, there can be difficulties.' And so it was to prove with Vivienne. Smedley were 'always chasing money' from her. However, in the end

Smedley were indebted to her for attracting more solvent designers
to them, including Paul Smith, Margaret Howell and Rei Kawabuko
of Comme des Garçons. The collaboration, Langford concedes, also
encouraged Smedley 'to become aware of the bigger world, because
tucked away in this beautiful valley, it is very easy to become
self-centred. It has broadened our horizons', in turn leading to new
markets. For him, what distinguished Vivienne from the other
designers was her decisiveness: 'Westwood knew *exactly* what she
wanted.' Compared with major retail buyers, who might choose
twenty-six different colours because they were unable to make up their
minds, Vivienne was single-minded in her choices.

The 'Harris Tweed' show mattered a great deal to Vivienne, because
it was her coming home. It answered her fans and McLaren, who had
criticised her for abandoning the London catwalk in favour of Paris
and then Milan. All the clothes were made in England, and Vivienne
invested every penny she could lay her hands on in this handsome
collection which, she believed, would seal her professional fate. She
later admitted that 'it was a very, very tight squeeze . . . because I
had no capital to work with. I was kind of gambling really, doing
fashion shows that cost an awful lot of money was something I
shouldn't have been doing.'

This was also Vivienne's first London show without McLaren, and
to differentiate it from the ones they had presented together (and
perhaps as a demonstration of her new-found cultural seriousness), she
instructed the models not to walk quickly, and instead of rock music
chose pieces from Tchaikovsky's *Sleeping Beauty*, Debussy, Ravel, Lotte
Lenya singing Kurt Weill, and some sentimental British tunes, such
as 'My Love is Like a Red, Red Rose', played by a Yorkshire brass band.
It is possible that in this collection Vivienne was giving imaginative
expression to certain evocative early experiences and memories she had
as a war baby, recollections of waving Union Jacks under celebratory
bunting in Tintwistle village on VE-Day, or later for the coronation
of Elizabeth II. Keith Wainwright executed Vivienne's idea of styling
the models' hair stiffly into large cylindrical shapes as though the
rollers had just been taken out, a look taken straight from Vivienne's
childhood.

On the eve of the show, Vivienne's mother turned up on her
daughter's doorstep with a new boyfriend in tow, and demanded that
Vivienne surrender her double bed to them. Vivienne offered them

Joe and Ben's old bunk beds instead. A huge row ensued, and Dora stormed off, leaving Vivienne extremely upset. One of Vivienne's assistants remembers: 'Dora didn't give a fuck about her daughter and the pressure she was under.'

The Apex Room in the Olympia Exhibition Centre was bursting for the show's opening. The audience included McLaren, ranks of the curious fashion press and Japanese film crews. The show was two hours late. As was now customary, Vivienne, regardless of the time, was backstage sewing petticoats. The milliner Stephen Jones had been hauled from the audience to give last-minute assistance. When Lynn Franks, a senior organiser from the British Fashion Council and a leading PR, came backstage yelling, 'Get this fucking show up and running or it's off!' Vivienne calmly turned to John Walford and said, 'I don't think there's any need to talk like that,' and carried on sewing. Walford, his pulse-rate rising, negotiated with Vivienne that she finish that one petticoat, and then she must begin.

The models had arrived up to six hours before the show started. Thanks to the cases of champagne that Joseph had brought backstage, most of them were too tipsy to get dressed. As usual there was no running order, and the clothes hung in a disorderly fashion on the rails. For Walford, creating a show with Vivienne was 'like working with a student', and he was maddened by her persistent impracticality. One of the highlights of the show was a 'Stature [sic] of Liberty' corset, which became a Westwood classic. Vivienne wanted virtually every girl to wear this one corset, and suggested to Walford: 'We'll have it on the first girl, and then she'll change and give it to the second.' She gave no thought to the amount of time it would take a model to remove the corset and pass it on to the next, who would then put it on, come forward and begin her walk down the catwalk – during which time the catwalk would have been empty.

Gary Ness was partly responsible for this corset. The garment was introduced to European courts, particularly the French, Italian and Spanish, in the fifteenth century, and was known as a 'divorce' because it separated the breasts, pushing them up and out to form a provocative balcony. Ness had shown Vivienne a nineteenth-century version, made of tiny panels of black velvet and ivory silk faille, that he had found in a market. She then borrowed an eighteenth-century copy from a theatrical costumier to use as a template, photocopied patterns from a book, and described the details over the telephone to a self-taught cutter and tailor, Sandy Gordon, who made the prototype.

Karl Lagerfeld was so impressed by the 'Stature of Liberty' corset that not only did he copy it for Chanel in 1990, but in 1994 he described it as the most important fashion (re-)invention for years, and part of the fashion canon. Sceptics, however, questioned whether such a structurally complicated garment could ever take off in ready-to-wear, as it required the fitting techniques of couture, and could not, it was assumed, be commercially exploited. However, once Vivienne had inserted elasticised sides in later versions, the corset was a commercial success. Madonna popularised it, and Jean-Paul Gaultier did a conical version in 1983, publicly acknowledging his indebtedness to Vivienne's creative lead. From the same collection, the combination of recycled denim (thriftily bought second-hand from American Classics, around the corner) and Harris tweed was also copied by Lagerfeld for Chanel.

As well as the twinset and pearls, another important item from the 'Harris Tweed' collection was inspired by Derek Jarman's *Jubilee*: the crown, as worn by the character 'The Bod', who called it 'high fashion'. The artist Andrew Logan and the club host Philip Sallon, both of whom Vivienne knew, had also made a habit of wearing crowns. Unusually for her, Vivienne had doubts about her cloth crown, and the morning after she had made it she showed it to her assistant Bella Freud, whom she regarded as 'very useful to me because she's got real snobby taste' ('snobby' being a compliment in her view). After receiving Freud's approval, she went ahead. Stephen Jones was briefed to make the crowns out of Harris tweed, and he completed some sketches and a toile – a calico pattern of the garment – which he took to Vivienne. There ensued 'much discussion about money', as Jones pointed out that it would be a time-consuming process to cut up countless strips of tweed. The penny-conscious Vivienne took Jones's toile, cut out enough tweed strips for six or seven crowns, and sent them back to him to assemble. The finishing touches were added by Jones, such as 'ermine' trim, made out of white 'fun fur' bought from Berwick Street market in Soho, the black spots added with marker-pen.

Jones attached his 'Stephen Jones, London' label to each crown and returned them to Vivienne, who promptly ripped them out and replaced them with ones which read 'Worlds End'. Jones was angry when he saw this, but decided to let it go. Few of the young artists

and craftspeople who contribute to collections are ever publicly
credited, and Vivienne quickly adopted this practice. The
multi-coloured tweed crown became a collectible piece of Westwood
memorabilia.

Another accessory from this collection also became a Westwood
classic. Back in 1984 Patrick Cox had presented Vivienne with the
idea of reviving the platform shoe, and she now designed her own
idiosyncratic version. The stout, platform-soled, lace-up 'Rocking
Horse' shoe and ankle-boot caused people to point in the street. The
name derived from the motion it forced its wearers to adopt: a nick
cut in the back of the heel made them rock back and forth from heel
to toe. The shoe was introduced at a time when the neat, flat ballet
pump, the court shoe and the trainer prevailed in fashion. It was
typical of Vivienne's perversity to design items of clothing that ran
counter to the prevailing orthodoxy. 'Even when something's
unpopular, she wouldn't compromise,' says Simon Barker.

To bring home the utter Englishness of the 'Harris Tweed'
collection, Vivienne hired a model who epitomised the raunchy,
seaside-postcard beauty queen. Sarah Stockbridge, introduced to
Vivienne by her talented design assistant Murray Blueit, was a
model-cum-actress from South London who styled herself as a spoof
fifties B-movie starlet, with a bleached blonde Diana Dors perm and
a sex-kitten 'mockney' accent. She had modelled for Boy (the King's
Road rival to SEX and Seditionaries), but was reluctant to do the
'Harris Tweed' show until John Walford persuaded her. She was to
become the public face of the Vivienne Westwood label, and was
possessively referred to by Vivienne as 'my beautiful Sarah' (in the
same way that she would call her assistants 'my treasures'.

Sarah Stockbridge was not just pretty, she was a witty and
compelling performer. Knowingly veering between come-on gestures
and a peekaboo coyness, she generated an electric tension in the
audience. Vivienne loved her because she was so English, right down
to her name, and because she moved 'like a real old stripper and yet
[was] very classy looking'. Sarah had mastered the hooker-duchess
performance, and was a stranger to embarrassment. Even in front
of aggressive crowds whipped up to jeer at Vivienne's clothes, she
could brazen it out. Without inhibition, she shocked but never
alienated. She would be thrown unrehearsed out onto the catwalk and
instructed either to striptease or to carry herself with the decorum of

a tongue-in-cheek queen. She was the perfect vehicle for Vivienne's clothes, the personification of her dream woman, in many ways her alter ego.

The 'Mini Crini' and 'Harris Tweed' collections highlighted Vivienne's love for playing with British taboos and parodying their conservatively elegant dress. With McLaren, she had taunted her public with violent displays of fetishism and republicanism. Now she gently teased them about two British hang-ups: class and nudity, including fig-leaf tights, corsets that left the nipples exposed, a revival of the naked breasts T-shirt. Her appeal to her public was this playfulness with such prickly subjects. The British loved her for daring to be funny about their taboos. They had always loved the comedy of embarrassment.

The Japanese had been particularly intrigued by the teddy boy, mod and punk themes in Vivienne's previous collections, and they were now drawn to the elaborate and romanticised notions of an older and grander Englishness in her clothes of the mid-eighties. They loved the way in which she played with the uniforms of a traditional society which, like their own, was formal, hierarchical and ritualistic. For those Japanese who sought to differentiate themselves from their conformist and xenophobic fellow countrymen, Vivienne's clothes served their purpose well. Like the other Western labels they favoured, such as Chanel and Moschino, her clothes could be read easily at a distance. Japanese fans made pilgrimages to Worlds End to buy in bulk, and some even brought scrapbooks lovingly filled with press cuttings and photographs of their heroine. Assistants in the shop were quizzed not only about the outfits or the staff featured in an article, but also the names of anyone accidentally caught in the background of press photographs.

For Berni Vinyl, her first sighting of a Vivienne Westwood piece of clothing was tantamount to an epiphany. As a fifteen-year-old girl in Fukuoka she saw a video of Annabella, the lead singer of Bow Wow Wow, dressed as a pirate. 'It was something raw, something special,' she remembered. 'I wanted to know what it felt like to wear the clothes and be different to other people.' At that point Vivienne's clothes were unavailable in Japan, so she travelled to England to buy them. So began her biannual pilgrimages to Worlds End: 'Her clothes give me some energy and make me feel strong. I never felt like that before. I couldn't find any clothes in Japan that made me feel like that.' Within a few years Berni had set up a little shop called Round the World in her minuscule flat in Fukuoka, stocked with clothes she bought at retail prices from London, and Japanese fans would come to her home to buy old and new Westwood clothes. Berni studied the stories behind the clothes and relayed them to her customers. For the Japanese, the most collectible items were punk originals, John Bull hats, 'Pirate' shirts, the 'Mini Crini' collection, the 'Harris Tweed' crown and a 'Witches' cardigan with dog buttons and pointed shoulders. Although Astore Robot had an exclusive deal to distribute Vivienne's clothes in Japan, Vivienne turned a blind eye to Berni's dealings.

Superficially, it may have seemed that Vivienne's idiom had changed dramatically in the mid-eighties, from egalitarian street clothing to elitist costume that displayed an archaic elegance. In fact her style had gradually evolved, and she was still using similar working methods and inspirations to those she had explored in partnership with McLaren. 'Vivienne's clothes have always been untraditional but elegant, right from the start,' says Terry Doktor. Whether it was a heroic pirate's blouse, a queen's tweed crown or a Peruvian peasant's shirt, they all bore a romantic, idealistic message, inspired by Vivienne's idiosyncratic research and the juxtaposition of apparently unrelated elements. And whatever form they took, her clothes remained attention-seeking rather than subtle, reflecting the choices she had made in dressing as a teenager.

Though Vivienne's *modus operandi* may not have altered, what did change at this time were her themes. She gradually shifted from retro-chic to revivalism, and from the proscribed to the prescribed. This shift reflected both her changing aspirations and a new target market. Under McLaren's influence, her clothing had been an irreverent parody of the vernacular dress of the young since the war, which cocked a snook at the establishment. Her new fascination with aristocratic clothing was partly the result of snobbery. Whereas most fashion commentators assumed that Vivienne was sardonically commenting on the social élite and their way of life, at heart she harboured a wistful nostalgia for their values and lifestyles. Yet she could be vitriolic towards them. Derek Dunbar was struck by the way in which she would interrogate him about what clothes regular 'posh' customers had bought from the shop and what they were wearing them to. On one occasion, Dunbar told her that the customer intended

Establishment custom at last. Lady McAlpine dressed to attend the state opening of Parliament, wearing Vivienne Westwood with her tiara.

Above: Vivienne is saluted for the second time by Hanae Mori's Fashion Foundation, Tokyo, January 1991. On the sofa: Christian Lacroix, Vivienne, Isaac Mizrahi and Franco Moschino. Back row, centre, Hanae Mori; fourth from right, Victoria Fernandez.

Left: Museums increasingly became the source of Vivienne's inspiration. She copied the slashing on this seventeenth-century silk bodice from the Victoria and Albert Museum.

Right: Cultural protest outside the Natural History Museum, London, 1990. Vivienne wears her fig-leaf leggings in order to remind the passer-by that 'those Greeks were civilised, but we're not'.

100 JO
LOST

PLEASE SUPPOR
DO NOT VISIT T
MUSEUM TOD

Left: Snowdon captures the pathos of his sitter's life. A lonely Miss Havisham in the dusty tulle wedding dress, the first Vivienne had designed, from 'Dressing Up'. It was worn with a golden chastity belt forged in Austria by Andreas's blacksmith father.

Above: Vivienne, aged fifty-two, and her husband Andreas, aged twenty-eight, at Milan airport, 1994. Were they *en route* to the fertility specialist Dr Severino Antonori, as the tabloids speculated?

Vivienne with her mother, Dora, in 1991.

Two devoted sons. Ben Westwood and Joseph
Corré congratulate their mother outside the studio
in Battersea before she goes to Buckingham Palace
to collect her OBE, 15 December 1992.

Vivienne and McLaren on the eve of Roger Burton's 'Vive le Punk!' exhibition, London, February 1993. This was the moment at which she realised she didn't love him any more.

Carlo D'Amario, Vivienne's business manager, in the studio at Elcho Street, Battersea, 1997.

Vivienne's favourite portrait, taken in Battersea Park by Juergen Teller in 1994 . Her dishevelled appearance is the consequence of a sexual encounter with Andreas earlier that morning. A ten-by-twelve-foot print of the photograph adorns one wall of her Davies Street boutique.

to wear a tweed jacket and shirt while falconing on horseback. Vivienne launched into an attack not on blood sports, but on what she saw as upper-class pursuits.

From Seditionaries onwards, Vivienne's designs became much more than a cheeky façadism that merely toyed with history; by 1987 she had become too reverential about the past to be light-hearted with its fashions. By contrast, McLaren treated history as something to be ironically exploited. Vivienne argued that dressed in her new style, 'you look as though you've got power and culture. It's a long way from middle-class bourgeois culture, but it was also a move away from the underground . . . there's no status in it . . . You have a better life if you wear impressive clothes.' Her insistence that elegance should usurp street wear reflected the times, the consumer-driven and aspirational values of the eighties. The greedy yuppie had replaced the idealistic rebel as a role model for the young. Glossy magazines trumpeted the return of class. Their society pages celebrated debutantes and the *nouveau riche*, while their fashion editorials featured expensive outfits, most notably the suit. Extravagant amounts were spent on designer ready-to-wear. Vivienne approved: 'I know someone who spent his university grant on a Yohji Yamamoto jacket to wear with jeans every day,' she cooed admiringly.

She was 'tired of looking at clothes from the point of view of rebellion – I found it exhausting and after a while I wasn't sure if it was right'. This divergence of views with McLaren, she said, was the reason they had separated: 'I was not so concerned with attacking . . . I'm more concerned with jumping over . . . I don't have great faith in youth or politics, the way I did when I was doing punk. The jungle beat was supposed to rock the establishment and threaten the puritan ethic and all that sort of thing, and I realised that it didn't . . . Elegance is my favourite word at the moment, because it has to do with culture, and the only thing I really do believe in is culture, civilisation. If someone looks elegant, that suggests that that person is interested in cultural things.'

Fashion was now on a par with pop music as the obsession of the young. Designers became their idols, lauded and granted god-like status by fawning journalists who pandered to their egos by seeking their opinions not only on fashion but on ecology, love, politics and contemporary *mores*. This allowed them to attach modish philosophies and gesture politics to their merchandise, making them seem more desirable. When Katherine Hamnett covered her T-shirts with slogans such as '58 per cent Don't Want Pershing' or 'Oppose Clause 28', or Valentino embroidered the word 'peace' in twenty-seven languages on a couture evening gown during the Gulf War, they were guaranteed media coverage. Why pay for advertising when a pliant press, eager to interview star designers, would flock to your door to hear your voguish sloganising and ideology?

Vivienne's work carried a literary as well as a visual text; indeed, to her and some of her acolytes, the messages were as significant as the aesthetic effects. She used clothes to attack received ideas, dismissing the masculine 'power suit' for women – epitomised by Karl Lagerfeld's designs for Chanel and Armani's designs, and championed by Anna Wintour, then editing British *Vogue* – as 'bourgeois'. Sloppy sports clothing, she maintained, was worn by 'hyperactive idiots'. 'I'm not interested in the perfect body,' she said. 'People with perfect bodies make me suspicious about what's in their heads. I hope my body is in some way a tribute to my brain.'

Vivienne ranted against the philistinism of the twentieth century. She was selling an alternative vision, drawn from the past. Her approach was the antithesis of, for example, Yves Saint Laurent, who strove to achieve in his designs *'le silence des vêtements, le meilleur silence des vêtements'*. She preferred the tub-thumping didactics of dress to its aesthetic impact. This was partly a product of her nationality, in that the English have a literary rather than a visual culture.

Attacking the cartoon-like *Dynasty* female silhouette of wide shoulders and thigh-gripping short suits – once again reflecting her hatred of imported American culture – Vivienne wished to reassert femininity by narrowing the shoulder, tightening the waist and loosening the skirt. Under her influence, Romeo Gigli and Christian Lacroix promptly took up the cause. But despite their efforts, it was the 'working woman' suit, upholstering a rail-thin figure honed in the gym, that prevailed to the end of the decade, along with Azzedine Alaïa's curves sucked into skin-tight stretch Lycra jersey.

Determined to assert her independence from McLaren, Vivienne now made few public references to him. He, meanwhile, was facing a legal challenge from the surviving members of the Sex Pistols, who were claiming profits from the band's activities that they believed he had withheld from them. Vivienne didn't think the case was worth fighting, and though it went to court, McLaren eventually capitulated.

The defeated Svengali walked away, saying, 'Those who have been the puppet-masters have to accept that sooner or later the puppets will rebel.'

Vivienne did, however, maintain contact with McLaren while he was living in Hollywood with Lauren Hutton. She periodically telephoned him in the middle of the night seeking advice and comfort: 'I'm over forty! I've got to prove a point and become a great fashion designer,' she told him. They discussed the best plan of action, and decided that couture, not street fashion, was the route to the prestige she craved. Their interpretation of 'couture' was not strictly accurate: they did not mean handmade clothes crafted on the body for individual customers, but rather a refined version of ready-to-wear.

Vivienne had become attracted to couture while she was researching the history of dress at the Victoria and Albert Museum, partly because of its élitism and partly because of its superior craftsmanship. McLaren liked to claim that it was he who set her on this path, but she was simply moving with the times. By the mid-eighties 'couture' had become the buzzword in high fashion, largely because of two entrepreneurs, Bernard Arnault and Alain Wertheimer, who had invested millions in this glamorous though anachronistic loss leader in order to promote their licensed and branded fashion goods. Arnault, the chairman and chief executive of the luxury-goods conglomerate Louis Vuitton Moët Hennessy, had bravely launched, from scratch, a new *haute couture* house under the talented design direction of Christian Lacroix, whom he had hired from Jean Patou. The Wertheimer family, who owned the house of Chanel, had hired the German designer Karl Lagerfeld to revive the brand through the medium of couture. Consequently, the original designs of Coco Chanel, Christian Dior and Cristobal Balenciaga, three of the century's greatest couturiers, were brought to the close attention of those in the industry.

If any one person could be said to have encouraged Vivienne in this high-fashion direction it was not McLaren but her 'guru', Gary Ness. He was instrumental in redirecting her ambition and fostering the apparent shift in her design style. Symptomatic of this transmutation was her changing vocabulary: 'culture', 'elegance' and 'civilisation', rather than 'rebellion', 'rock 'n' roll' and 'youth', now peppered her conversation, reflecting Ness's, not McLaren's, preoccupations.

Now that his benefactress was back in town, Ness immersed himself

again in Vivienne's life, grateful to receive her weekly handouts of
£100 or so. Usually they met on Wednesday evenings. Dressed in
wire-stiffened polkadot crini, Rocking Horse platform shoes, flared
Harris tweed Princess coat and, if the weather required, a tweed crown
to keep her head warm, Vivienne would cycle to Ness's flat on Hereford
Road, off Westbourne Grove. She believed that her attire 'caused a
sensation'.

Despite his penury, Ness refused to prepare food in his flat, and
though Vivienne would have been happy with a banana sandwich or
a take-away pizza, he insisted that they eat out, usually at her expense.
And so this dusty dandy with a fresh flower in his buttonhole and a
silk scarf, not worn around his neck but melodramatically pressed
with his hand against his throat, would escort his tweed queen round
the corner for curry at Khan's or noodles at Lee Fook.

After having moaned about the service and the decline in
gastronomic standards, Ness instructed his eager pupil and laid plans
for her fashion renaissance. The relationship between them was not
entirely one-way. Ness may have secured a paymaster and a willing
mannequin on which he could hang his idiosyncratic thinking, but
in return Vivienne was given a version – albeit a polemical one – of
the education in high culture which she had craved since her twenties.

The burden of Ness's argument – an argument that Vivienne was
to parrot over the next decade – was that the twentieth century was
culturally worthless, that contemporary youth was 'brain-damaged'
thanks largely to the impact of American cultural imperialism, and
that Vivienne's prestige could only be established through élitist
clothing that displayed wealth and was scattered with overt cultural
references. Having worked for four years as a theatrical costume and
set designer, Ness led her away from fashion towards costume.

One of his practical pieces of advice was that she should engage
professional staff, because her clothing was badly cut. This was a fair
criticism: Vivienne had by now acquired a reputation for producing
shoddy clothes. A make-up artist, John Gustaffson, who worked on
Vivienne's shows, warned Michael Rosen, a PR who was putting on
an exhibition of British designers for the International Wool
Secretariat, to 'check the Westwood stuff for missing buttons and
unfinished hems'. Ness urged Vivienne to exploit the redundancies
on Savile Row and to snap up an experienced pattern-cutter and
tailor. With predictably poor judgement, she settled on a man who,

frequently inebriated, preferred to chase her assistants rather than cut clothes.

Vivienne now needed a proper studio, and immediately after having shown 'Harris Tweed' she settled on some rooms in a rambling warehouse in Greenland Street, off Camden High Street. Jeff Banks guaranteed the rent. Within a year she was employing ten people at the studio, which D'Amario disparagingly dubbed 'Bombay', as it was staffed with what he inaccurately described as 'hippies'. Along with Bella Freud and Ben's Franco-Persian girlfriend Yasmin Eslami, both of whom had independent means, Vivienne employed several gay men in their twenties who eked out a hand-to-mouth existence on the meagre £50–£100 a week she paid them. They helped keep Vivienne, who was now forty-seven, in touch with nightclubs and youth culture.

A visitor to Greenland Street would be left in no doubt about the state of Vivienne's finances. Turning off Camden High Street, with its rundown shops selling speciality records, New Age ephemera and ironmongery, he would enter a squalid, draughty and overcrowded building. Having climbed three flights of concrete stairs, he would pass through a pair of solid timber warehouse doors into a long, concrete-floored hall crammed with trolleys laden with unravelling bolts of fabric. Neither a receptionist nor a sign indicated where he should go. Wandering through a rabbit warren of half a dozen tiny rooms, furnished with sewing-machines, trestle tables and shabby utilitarian wartime cupboards, he might eventually find Vivienne in one of them, standing in her sloppy reindeer slippers, a cardigan safety-pinned closed across her chest, furiously draping and tucking cloth on a dummy.

The squalor of Vivienne's workplace was in stark contrast to the studios of other top designers. Gianni Versace's head office, for example, was based in the heart of Milan, off the fashionable via delle Spiga. Having passed ranks of receptionists and personal assistants in the marble reception hall, the visitor climbed an imposingly austere staircase. Lest he forget that Signor Versace was a man of high culture, marble busts of Roman gods and emperors looked down on him from halogen-lit alcoves. Any evidence of the company's actual business, such as messy papers or swatches of cloth, was carefully hidden from sight, leaving the designer's immediate vicinity tidy and apparently innocent of work.

Visiting Valentino in his private office overlooking the Spanish Steps in Rome was like having a rendezvous with Il Duce. At the far end of a ballroom-sized office, the master-dressmaker sat behind a desk so large that he virtually disappeared from view, and so weighed down with ormolu that it dug deep into the thick pile of the Persian rug underneath. On either side the floor was scattered with pug dogs snuffling between cushions, tusk-legged banquettes, button-backed conversation chairs and pouffes, all upholstered with lavish Islamic and Oriental cloths. In order to speak to Valentino himself, the visitor was forced to stretch over a barricade of silver-framed photographs of him embracing celebrities.

Even the more modest three-storey workplace of Vivienne's compatriot Jean Muir was antiseptically clean, orderly and whitewashed, bearing a greater resemblance to an operating theatre than a workroom. Miss Muir was as fastidious as a Shaker always prepared to meet her God. Her staff were forbidden to eat oranges, for she could not abide the smell.

By contrast, Vivienne's office was 'a dump', recalled one fabric merchant who, even when he had an appointment, rarely found her there. Vivienne preferred to work from her bed at Nightingale Lane, and Craig Alexander of Smedley would ring her there for decisions. On one occasion he got the impression that she was not listening, and asked, 'Are you all right? You sound awful.' No, she was not all right, she replied: 'I've got the council here, and I'm really upset. They say they've come to put in central heating, and I don't want it. But they insist I have to have it.' With little concern for her own comforts, Vivienne regarded the council's intrusion as an infringement of her rights.

When Carlo D'Amario followed Vivienne back to London in 1986 he initially moved in with her, and they revived their flagging affair, much to the irritation of Gary Ness, his rival for her attention. Some of Vivienne's associates downplay the importance of her affair with D'Amario, but others who witnessed the relationship at close quarters, including Derek Dunbar, John Walford and Simon Barker, believe that at one point they were genuinely in love. One afternoon while working on a corset, Sandy Gordon mischievously put it on. 'Ugh! Take it off, you look like a monkey,' screamed Dunbar, revolted by the way in which the hair on Gordon's back and shoulders sprouted from under the velvet. 'Ooh no, I think it looks great,' said Vivienne.

'It really reminds me of when Carlo was in the shower and the soap suds were all over his hairy body. It was brilliant.'

One of D'Amario's first acts was to persuade Vivienne to file a suit against Giorgio Armani SpA in the civil court in Milan, charging them with breach of contract. According to *Women's Wear Daily*, who reported on the case, D'Amario claimed that under the contract Vivienne had been guaranteed a $3 million fee. But Gabriella Forte, the Executive Vice-President of Armani, responded by insisting that Vivienne herself had broken the agreement by failing to provide designs that could be commercially produced in a factory (it is interesting to note that at first Alberto Biani of Staff International would not take on production of Vivienne's line for similar reasons). Armani agreed to refer the dispute to an arbiter, as was provided for in the contract, but it has still not been resolved.

Gradually D'Amario's relationship with Vivienne became confined to business, although he was still mainly based in Italy. They did, though, occasionally fall back into bed together. When, for example, they were staying in Berlin in 1988 for 'Dressed to Thrill', a showcase of international fashion, Barker, who was with them, knocked on the door of Vivienne's hotel room. D'Amario answered, doing up his flies. Vivienne was lying on the bed, wearing only a vest.

Despite occasionally having sex with D'Amario, Vivienne was lonely. Unable to find solace in books and Gary Ness's lectures, she developed crushes on colleagues whom she knew to be homosexual. Simon Barker recalls his embarrassment when she declared to her staff that she had fallen in love with him. She fell for Sandy Gordon, impetuously proposing marriage to him. Such incidents, Barker believes, were a symptom of Vivienne's emotional uncertainty: 'She spends time with men and she thinks she's in love. She's very dependent.'

Insisting that work took precedence over love, Vivienne claimed that she did not have time for a boyfriend: 'I'm quite happy to have spent the first part of my life having sex, bringing up children, and all that stuff, but now I'm too busy working. I'm interested, though – put this in your article,' she instructed one journalist. 'If anyone wants to have a relationship where we just meet for sex once every two weeks or something, I'd like that.' She later admitted that, notwithstanding some offers, she was 'quite conformist, to be honest – I didn't take any of them up'.

It was a combination of this candour, her astonishing drive and her ability to innovate that inspired tremendous loyalty from Vivienne's staff. They were swept along by her infectious enthusiasm for designing and her capacity for hard work, and would happily toil through many nights to finalise a collection, snatching the odd catnap on bolts of cloth in a corner of the studio, just like their boss. 'She can be a complete monster, and whips people to work, but she doesn't ask anyone to do anything that she wouldn't do herself. She's completely driven,' says John Walford. Bella Freud, her closest associate during these years, says: 'She can be so generous, but on the other hand she is so catty that it made you wonder why you were loyal to this person. But in the end her work was so amazing that you stayed . . . She's a marvellous teacher. She knows how to get the best out of you. Her skill is fascinating.' Although Vivienne often seemed totally disorganised, her employees were amazed at her astonishing powers of recall. Even the most unimportant instruction issued to a member of her staff would be remembered by her several days later.

No task was too menial for Vivienne, and she would pick pins off the floor and use up rancid milk in her tea to save money. One of her favourite catchphrases to her staff was, 'I don't accept the easy "No". I want the difficult "Yes".' Vivienne created an extended family whose home was Greenland Street. Even when she lost her temper, under financial pressure or looming deadlines, she rarely bore a grudge. But despite the tremendous loyalty she inspired, she seldom returned it unless it suited her. Both Jean Bennett and John Walford were abruptly ousted, though they had offered their services for free at a bleak time in her career. In Bennett's case, Vivienne decided to employ an in-house PR whom she could control more, and a few years later Walford was replaced by a series of more fashionable show producers (he was to be reinstated in 1997).

Despite pitiful and eventually non-existent wages, Vivienne's personal assistant David Staines was unflinchingly loyal to her. It was not reciprocated. On one occasion after she had returned from Italy, she and Bella Freud were walking up the stairs of a nightclub when they spotted Staines. Vivienne caught his eye and started to wave her hand from side to side at him. He was surprised by her warm greeting and returned it enthusiastically. Vivienne coldly repeated the gesture and explained, 'I'm not saying hello, I'm wiping you out.'

Demanding of friends as well as staff, Vivienne thought nothing of imposing on them and their families. At one point, for example, she singled out Walford to be her confidant, and would telephone him at seven in the morning, waking his whole family, to discuss her career. Jeff Banks was irritated by the way in which she would arrive unannounced at his home late at night and, without waiting to be invited in, would wheel her bicycle into his hall and stay until five in the morning talking about her work. Her lack of consideration could be unbearable. Virtually every company which dealt with her during these years tells the same story: it was impossible to get Vivienne to pay her bills, and she brazenly expected her fabric and trimmings suppliers, machinists and out-workers to bankroll her business.

Bella Freud remembers: 'If a woman had a problem she was irritated, but if a man had a problem, she was interested. The only thing that interested her about women was the power of their appearance.' One female employee in her early twenties discovered that she was pregnant in 1987, and was uncertain whether or not to have an abortion. Unwisely, she sought Vivienne's advice, and was roundly admonished: 'You're far too young to have a baby! What about your work? Your career?' Vivienne went on to tell the story of how she had been on her way to have an abortion when she saw a coat and thought: 'Shall I have the abortion or the coat? And in the end we had Joseph!' Joseph was standing next to her at the time.

Vivienne's bluntness could be comic as well as cruel. On receiving a present, she had a habit of scrutinising it and saying, 'Thanks very much, but I won't be able to use it,' or, 'Thanks, but I don't like it.' She regarded such responses as 'being honest'. This 'honesty' could be startlingly unprofessional. In 1987, when she was being interviewed by the music channel MTV at the shop on the King's Road, she disappeared behind the curtain to put on her tweed crown and crini, came out slowly, sat down in front of the camera and calmly began: 'Let me tell you about my clothes . . .' She then sighed, shuffled in her seat, said, 'I'm bored now,' and got up and left.

Vivienne felt no obligation to credit those whose designs she had 'borrowed', and she was to copy the work of many young designers, including Stephen Jones, Georgina Godley, Leigh Bowery and Richard Torry. On one occasion in 1986 Jones invited Vivienne to his showroom on Lexington Street and, charmed by her compliments about his hats, made her a miniature green velvet tricorne. 'It took forever to make, and I never got a thank you note. Then the next season, all these miniature tricornes came out on her catwalk.'

Time and again, craftspeople who collaborated with Vivienne remarked that she was masterful at getting the best out of them through a combination of impossible demands and her technique, observed by Stephen Jones, of 'coming to you like a complete innocent and forcing you to feel you have to take care of her. But you're aware that she has complete judgement and control.'

The annual fireworks party at Nightingale Lane in November was eagerly anticipated by the staff. Berni Vinyl, who had become a feature in the audience of Westwood shows, dressed in the most extreme fashions of her heroine, would also be invited. On one occasion she arrived inadequately dressed for the weather in a 'Love' jacket and mini crini. Seeing that she was cold, Vivienne took her by the arm and said, 'Come with me and I'll give you some woolly knickers.' Under her bed were boxes of Smedley knickers printed with ionic columns. In later years, when the numbers of Vivienne's staff had increased, this party, which had been an important way of bonding her team, was no longer held.

Vivienne seemed incapable of showing physical affection towards anyone. 'I never saw her stroking her sons' hair,' Derek Dunbar observed. 'She's not a natural mother.' Once, when she was visiting Barker and Dunbar, a three-year-old girl was told not to pull the cat's tail. As the child pursued the animal across the room, Vivienne snapped, 'I'll just slap her! She's a little bugger!'

Vivienne's preference for Joseph over Ben was evident. Ben, unlike his brother, was not selected as a model for her catwalk shows, and on a video recording of one show he approaches to give her a congratulatory hug, only to be shrugged off. Meanwhile, Joseph was proudly treated like her escort, and always given credit for his help. 'He's wonderful!' Vivienne would gush. 'The nearest I've ever had to a husband in terms of help.' When she was invited to be interviewed by the *Sunday Times Magazine* with a son, she chose Joseph, not Ben. In fact, Ben worked hard for his mother, taking on difficult tasks such as finding a manufacturer for the Rocking Horse shoes, but he was rarely thanked for his pains.

Ben was struggling to become a photographer, but his mother had little respect for the mechanical arts, and even less for her elder son's abilities. She encouraged him instead to spend time with her brother

Gordon, who was now making films on travel and other subjects for large corporations. Despite his rejection by Vivienne, Ben continued to maintain relations with both his parents, though he was fully aware of how his father had been hurt by his mother. 'Everything my Mum does is fine with him [Derek, his father]. He's not going to say anything. He didn't want to split up with her. She's not interested in his lifestyle. He's married to a normal woman, living a normal life in the Midlands. She doesn't phone him up, he phones her up. They do speak about certain things. He's welcome to any of her shows . . . My family is very close, very loving, open. They treat me like an adult, not like an idiot,' he unconvincingly maintained.

Despite Vivienne's open favouritism towards him, Joseph found it virtually impossible to reveal his feelings. Much of his bitterness stemmed from his father's departure. For many years McLaren ignored his paternal duties, until his girlfriend Lauren Hutton alerted him to them. When Hutton was visiting London in the late eighties she took Joseph out to dinner, and asked him straight out if he felt rejected by McLaren. Taken aback by the directness of her question, he confided the incident to Derek Dunbar: 'Joe was stunned. She came straight through with the main question, but he couldn't express his emotions.'

Focusing on her ambition, and encouraged by Gary Ness, Vivienne gradually isolated herself from emotional contact with anyone. Ness snorted with derision whenever she mentioned affairs of the heart, dismissing them with the Freudian phrase 'the future of an illusion'. He chastised her for allowing her sons to live with her, as he thought they distracted her from her work; during 1988 both of them left Nightingale Lane, renting flats elsewhere in London.

So convinced was Vivienne of Ness's genius that in 1986 she made an appointment to see the publisher Dan Franklin, then a senior editor at Heinemann. Franklin had believed that Vivienne would be offering him her autobiography, but instead she turned up with Ness, and proceeded to try to sell him the idea of publishing Ness's long-promised and as yet unwritten masterpiece on Anglo-American philistinism and the failings of contemporary culture. 'The theory was that we should return to Matthew Arnold and a nineteenth-century vision,' Franklin remembers. 'Both of them were making speeches about the horrors of modern culture, and I was surprised, in that she's at the cutting edge of the horrors of modern culture!' He recalls being struck by Vivienne's ordinariness. He had expected an outrageous, McLaren-influenced punk, not a middle-aged woman who bore a greater resemblance to the prime minister, Margaret Thatcher, than to a rebel (he was not the only person to notice the similarity). He was left with the impression that both visitors were 'completely barking', and dined out on the story for the next fortnight.

Vivienne was determined to display the knowledge and 'culture' she had acquired from Ness in her clothes, and her collections were now treated like blank sheets of paper onto which she could transcribe the teachings of her tutor. But despite her intellectual reliance on him – she told Franklin, 'Silly little me, because I knew nothing until I met this man' – Vivienne was loath to refer to Ness in public by anything other than his Christian name, or as 'one of the last gurus of the Western world'. This anonymity suited her ambition to present herself as an oracle on cultural matters.

Fashion had became Vivienne's vehicle to promote her and Ness's views on art and culture, and in 1987 she decided to start a rock group in order to communicate them to the young. With her instinctive skill in touching a nerve in this audience, she named the band 'Choice', explaining, 'it has that element of choice, like tasty, and the people's choice, and it sounds very international, very big'. On hearing that Madonna had written to tell Vivienne that she was her favourite designer, Carlo D'Amario suggested that the star could be the lead singer of the group, which would be launched at Vivienne's next show. With the help of Robin Scott (whose band 'M' had a hit in 1978 with the single 'Pop Musik'), Vivienne later sent a demo tape of songs she had written to Madonna, but she got no response. Unperturbed, she assumed that this was only because Madonna was 'busy getting married' to Sean Penn, and settled on Sarah Stockbridge to front the band instead.

Choice, Vivienne explained, was devised as a platform for the promotion of 'fashion and art', and 'a chance to control a visual image which is very good for me'. Sarah Stockbridge was to be her 'sacrificial victim. I'm going to pile all the culture I know onto her, just as you would if you were going to kill somebody; you put everything that the tribe knew onto that victim, all the motifs and totems. And then you torch it.'

The lyrics of the proposed first single, 'Bride of Fortune', also known as 'The Mini Crini Song', demonstrated Vivienne's talent for simplifying (perhaps oversimplifying) an idea gleaned from Ness, and giving it a more popular appeal:

Swing the Crini
All round the world
Swing the Crini
Ring the bell.

On the Tree of Knowledge
I have carved 'Amour'
The answer's not in looks, but books
If you want Glamour . . .

Meanwhile in the grotto
Dionysus wakes
Stars and spots are in his head
I will cure his aches.

The song was first performed at the Fridge nightclub in Brixton. As Tommy Roberts had noticed a decade before, Vivienne loved the chance of being in front of an audience. 'The stage was eye-high,' Vivienne gushed. 'Rows and rows of people looking up at me. It was brilliant. Just like being a pop star.' Vivienne wrote six songs for the band, although none was ever recorded. Song-writing was not new to her – she had written 'Who Killed Bambi?' for the Sex Pistols and 'I'm a Teenage Savage' for Bow Wow Wow's first album. Too busy to meet up with Simon Barker, who was writing the music, she would sing into a tape machine or down the telephone to him. She liked to fuse her favourite striptease song, 'The Stripper', by David Rose, with hits from the teds' era such as 'Woolly Bully' by Sam the Sham and the Pharaohs, or the folk song 'Cherry Ripe', remembered from her childhood.

Barker found the eccentric collaboration frustrating: 'She can't sing. She used to change key in the middle, and when I said, "Look, Vivienne, you've changed key," she'd say, "No I haven't! I just started and then I couldn't get the high note, so I changed – but I didn't change *key*!" When we were singing karaoke songs in Berlin she didn't know any of the words. She only knows songs from her childhood.'

The spring/summer collection 'Britain Must Go Pagan' (also known as Pagan I), shown in October 1987, was the first of five collections in which Vivienne explored the styles and *mores* of the ancient world rather than those of Albion. These were initially brought to her attention when Ness took her to an exhibition of ancient Greek jewellery at the British Museum. What particularly thrilled her – and proved, to her at least, that her provocative designs for SEX had an august provenance – was the ancients' amoral and libertine attitude to sex in all its forms, and to pleasure-seeking generally.

Part Three

THE CELEBRATED
OUTSIDER

8   WEAR YOUR BRAIN ON YOUR SLEEVE

October 1988–December 1989

'I use fashion as an excuse to talk about things in broader cultural terms, because that's where my interests lie.'

Vivienne Westwood, 1993

'He who says collage says irrational.'

Max Ernst, 1948

'I pick the brains of clever people,' was how Vivienne frankly described her research technique. As well as displaying her new-found knowledge, her clothes became blackboards on which she chalked up criticisms of her times, and her solutions to them: 'The best accessory is a book!', 'Discrimination will come back', 'I believe in élitism.' Unlike the T-shirts of the 'green' designer Katherine Hamnett, these statements were not printed on the clothes, but were woven into the construction and the styling of her collections, and appeared in texts which accompanied her collections. She also explained them to the public whenever she was interviewed about her work. Vivienne made intellectualism a fetish. In this respect, her designing technique was the opposite of Issey Miyake, who said: 'I make clothes, not package ideas.'

Gary Ness was the source of these messages. Like Malcolm McLaren, his predecessor as Vivienne's mentor, he provided her with a book list, from which she gathered her ideas and devised the titles of her collections and the pithy quotations she attached to them. Ness's fiercely-held opinions were justified by a welter of quotations from Matthew Arnold, Aldous Huxley, Bertrand Russell, La Rochefoucauld and Marcel Proust. Ness became vital to Vivienne's development –

he was her one-man university. While others ridiculed her for her lack of culture, he bolstered her confidence and offered her 'a passage to an extraordinary world of culture', as Gene Krell observed.

Inspiring Vivienne with the image of Proust alone in his cork-lined room, Ness insisted that creativity demanded solitude, and that emotional commitments were 'non-stop distractions'. Having persuaded her to remove her lover and her sons from her home, he urged her to focus on her work. There was, however, a self-serving motive for Ness's determination to isolate his pupil. He wanted to keep her for himself in order to prevent any alternative views from encroaching on his influence. The next few years, like those between 1979 and 1982, when McLaren had effectively abandoned her, would prove to be among Vivienne's most creative.

Ness, the lonely misanthrope, sat in his tiny flat off Westbourne Grove and waited for Vivienne's calls. Rather than engage in conversation, he preferred to conduct monologues which veered between sardonic contempt for humanity and agitated suspicion of those in power – right and left wing alike. If Vivienne interrupted him with a half-baked notion, he would snap, 'Shut your cakehole, Hilda Ogden,' ridiculing her for sounding like the character from the TV soap *Coronation Street*. She might laugh at his camp putdowns, but she would not tolerate correction from anyone except him or D'Amario.

The only time Ness's pallid complexion took on any colour was when he was outlining some new conspiracy theory. In full spate he could be fearsome, but he was erudite rather than original. Any originality in the application of his ideas came from the way in which Vivienne adapted them. She had a voracious appetite for knowledge, and at times Ness felt besieged by her as she picked out the morsels of culture that she craved, which would later be regurgitated to the media or her impressionable assistants back at the studio. She was surrounded by fawning flatterers: her young employees, in general not equipped to question her cultural pronouncements, marvelled at their 'intellectual' boss. Above all, Vivienne loved unorthodox opinions: she had always been attracted to the contrary and the shocking, and now Ness gave these preferences a pseudo-intellectual underpinning. If anyone challenged her, she simply quoted their hero, Bertrand Russell, who had warned that 'orthodoxy is the graveyard of intelligence'. It became her mantra.

Ness's impatient student would often arrive at his flat, usually on a Wednesday evening, with a specific question. 'What's a good title for the next collection?' or 'Tell me about technique in seventeenth-century painting,' she would demand, expecting an easily assimilated summation to add to her stock of instant knowledge. This piecemeal culture, when applied to her clothes, led to some amusing and original designs. But Vivienne only superficially understood Ness's tutorials. This was not surprising, as she had little time to study, and yearned for the free time to just sit alone and read. Consequently, when she tried to discuss an aspect of her 'culture' with a journalist or her fans, she came across as incoherent and pretentious. Vivienne had a unique facility with materials, but was far less assured with words. Nevertheless, she was so desperate to appear civilised and educated that she could not help attempting these debates, rather than confining her discussions to fashion. Misguidedly, she accorded little respect to her own achievements as a designer, preferring to be regarded as an intellectual. 'Fashion was not my first love,' she said in the late eighties. 'I made a conscious decision to study and read literature.'

Though Vivienne alternated between protection of Ness and irritation at his dependency on her financial handouts, Gene Krell believed that she would never let him 'slip through her fingers'. Whether she was thinking up a theme for a collection or being asked for her views on current affairs by the media, Ness would be consulted, like a political speechwriter, about what she should say. Athough he was now costing her about £200 a week, she regarded his 'tuition fee' as good value for money.

For a long time, their friendship was kept private. Though many in the studio had heard of Ness, few had met him, and he refused to visit Greenland Street, which he believed was staffed by 'brain-damaged idiots'. Vivienne's determination to conceal his role from the public demonstrated a calculation that belied her reputation – possibly cultivated – for scattiness and naïveté. When asked by the journalist Duncan Fallowell in 1990 to identify her intellectual mentor she replied evasively, 'Perhaps I shouldn't tell you his name. But I've never yet met a wise person before in my life. And such a scholar, too.' Vivienne wanted to keep the limelight for herself.

Though Ness was not publicly acknowledged, Vivienne did admit to him: 'I need you more than I need anybody. I've talked to you in the past twenty years more than I've talked to anyone.' Ness thrived on these crumbs; they lifted him out of his neurotic sense of dependency on her. Vivienne cunningly played on his neuroses by periodically withholding the handouts, failing to turn up for appointments with him and seesawing between confidante and paymaster.

Anne Barr, features editor of *Harper's & Queen*, had observed Ness's methods over many years: 'He's always making excuses about being penniless . . . He just latches on to you and wants money and to be taken out.' For a time she had worried about his welfare and helped him out, but gradually she learnt his ways. One day she walked into an expensive restaurant and saw the allegedly penniless Ness sitting alone eating a lavish dinner with a bottle of good wine and joking with the waiters. He was clearly a regular customer. She became inured to his pleas of poverty and his complaints that 'everyone drops me in the end'. One of his most objectionable traits, to her mind, was 'his unpleasant snobbery, which has mixed up with Vivienne's freshness and has really had an effect on her work'.

Just as McLaren had purged Vivienne of her well-meaning gestures (typified, for example, by her donation of her meagre savings to Oxfam as a young woman), so Ness caused her to shed much of her ingrained egalitarianism and to imitate his élitism. Under his influence Vivienne's sympathies shifted from the young and the 'ordinary' to members of the establishment – particularly of the academic, social and fashion worlds. She adopted her teacher's prejudices, one moment feeling uncomfortable in the company of her 'betters', the next denouncing the common man and his tastes.

Ness argued that his solitary and cerebral existence should not be sullied by the demands of earning a living, and that he should be supported in order to have the leisure to formulate his important ideas. Vivienne was impressed by what she saw as his romantic stance against bourgeois conformity. She had never been driven by a desire for financial gain, and Ness's professed disdain for Mammon (although he liked other people to pay for his consumption of the finer things in life) appealed to her. She decided to cast herself as his patron, shielding and funding her unworldly intellectual.

Ambitious to meet and gain the approval of certain people, Vivienne clumsily tried to engineer introductions to members of the great and the good: aristocrats, especially those with what she crudely described as 'clout', and members of the cultural and intellectual élite whose views she found sympathetic. On meeting strangers, she would quickly ascertain whether they could help her in her quest. Among those she courted most assiduously were Lord and Lady McAlpine. Alistair McAlpine was the treasurer of the Conservative Party, and an enthusiastic collector of contemporary art. His wife Romilly was a contributing editor to *Vogue* and one of the most daringly dressed women in the British establishment. Lady Henrietta Bathurst, the daughter of the Earl of Bathurst, Jamie Sainsbury, scion of the supermarket family, and Dometilla, wife of Mark Getty of the Texan oil dynasty, were also favoured contacts. Bella Freud, who worked for Vivienne, was valued for her 'snobby taste' and because she opened her employer's eyes to 'the world of toffs', as Simon Barker put it, 'like Lucy Ferry [Bryan's wife] and Dometilla Getty, and how they dressed'.

For her next five collections, Vivienne's work shifted from an exploration of the dress of the British establishment to that of the ancients. In celebration of the Greeks' uninhibited delight in physical pleasures, she offered winged sandals and draped chitons (tunics), and advocated a return to the ways of these heroic people: 'Britain must go back to the ideas of Greece and Rome. Their morality was more sane, it wasn't about sin . . . it's a question of the sceptical point of view. They knew you have to keep an open mind.' Later, out of admiration for Proust, to whose work Ness introduced her, she proposed that young men wear the fashions of the *belle époque*. As a criticism of democracy, she championed the pre-democratic dress of eighteenth- and nineteenth-century élites. Every opportunity was taken to persuade her followers to question received opinions and to follow her back to an idyllic past. Just as Vivienne had assimilated McLaren's versions of situationism and dadaism, so she now adopted Ness's classical antiquity. 'She'd read a book and a collection would be based on that idea,' said McLaren. 'She'd bash you over the bloody head with the book till you die!' Vivienne insisted that 'everything about this century is based on myths. Like the idea that love is something that should be continued; this idea of love we've got is simply too orthodox . . . that's why I'm interested in the pagans. They didn't have any of these myths.' It is easy to see why such an attitude appealed to the broken-hearted Vivienne.

The five collections from spring/summer 1988 to spring/summer 1990 were known as the 'Pagan' series, and entitled 'Britain Must Go

Pagan', 'Time Machine', 'Civilizade', 'Voyage to Cythera' and 'Pagan V'. The series displayed Vivienne's extraordinarily creative mind to remarkable effect, as she fused her technical skill with her childlike freshness of vision. It was as if, free from preconceptions, she was seeing a style or decoration for the first time. Her approach exemplified Baudelaire's description of the creative process as 'childhood recovered at will'. A typical example of this naïve eye was her use of the bestselling American toy, the 'Care Bear', on a corset in the 'Britain Must Go Pagan' collection. She returned to the Greenland Street studio one afternoon to announce, 'I've found this stunning teddy bear.' Her staff could not believe that she was attracted to this kitsch soft toy, but when she applied the image to the front of a corset, using the two claws of the bear as cups for the breasts, they had to concede that it was clever; and it became a hit.

Being virtually immune to the advertising and marketing machines that steered Western consumer taste, Vivienne had been unaware of the Care Bears' international success, and could therefore see it, and other popular images, with fresh eyes. In this instance her immunity was an asset, but at other times it prevented her from exploiting her work, since, having no interest in designing to please the market, she had little notion of or interest in her customer. She would stand before a finished garment and marvel, 'Isn't that beautiful?' If a member of staff asked her, 'But who will wear it?' she would simply respond, 'I don't care, but it's beautiful anyway.' Her faith in her own creativity was so strong that she boasted, 'Anything I put on the catwalk will sell in my shop; my fans will love it.' This was a refreshing change from the 'informed' designers, such as Donna Karan or Giorgio Armani, who boasted that they knew their customers, and consequently rarely surprised them.

Bella Freud was astonished by the number and originality of Vivienne's ideas. Together they would go and source fabrics at merchants or textile manufacturers: 'I'd wonder, "What on earth can she do with this sample?" I'd look at it two or three times in wonder, thinking, "How can she make *this* work?"' She did, to magical effect. Vivienne could not stop creating. 'Even if she was on a desert island she would continue her work in a searching, pioneering way,' believes Freud. On the eve of a show pattern-cutters would be set to work on a brand-new idea, regardless of the impending deadline. Each new show would not just present a few new ideas, but dozens of them –

too many for fashion editors and buyers to take on board. 'What was extraordinary,' according to Freud, 'was that she could hold in her head such a vast amount of detail,' without proper sketches, a running order or planning. 'She would create something in her head and it was dead right. It was like a puzzle fitted together in her head, and the whole collection was absolutely incredible.' Vivienne would utilise the most mundane sources: for example, the 'Galaxy' print of stars, planets, comets and lions printed on velvet and cotton for the 'Britain Must Go Pagan' collection at Olympia in October 1987 was lifted straight from the endpapers of an astronomy book belonging to her son Ben.

As had happened in Vivienne's earlier shows, a number of the models in 'Britain Must Go Pagan' were drunk, including a budding model and actress, Patsy Kensit. Having been told to take off the Smedley pillar-printed underwear because it did not flatter her figure, Kensit forgot that she was wearing nothing under her skirt. Romping down the catwalk, she drunkenly lifted it up and down, unaware of her nudity. Some detractors wrongly assumed that Vivienne had set her up, but in fact she was simply tipsy.

The next catwalk collection, 'Time Machine' (autumn/winter 1988), shown in the British Fashion Council's tent outside the exhibition centre at Olympia in March 1988, was named in tribute to H.G. Wells's 1895 science-fiction novel, which was on Ness's reading list for Vivienne. A series of check tweed double-breasted suits was intended to conjure up the imagined youth of the septuagenarian amateur sleuth Miss Marple, heroine of Agatha Christie's detective novels. Only Vivienne could have chosen such a frumpy schoolma'am as a sexual ideal. The men's and women's suits were so successful that they became mainstays for many seasons. The Miss Marple suits were comically worn with fur Davey Crockett hats, pulled down over the crown of the head in a topical spoof on the wayward Duchess of York's headgear for the ski slopes. Other suits were worn with exaggerated Charles II wigs, handmade by Vivienne on her kitchen table in her quirky do-it-yourself manner.

Vivienne introduced the collection with charming storylines: 'Miss Marple was once a young lady and wore her knockout skirts' or 'Sunday tweeds keep on knocking us out' read the programme, as tweed skirts, their hems kicked out with peekaboo petticoats, came down the catwalk. 'Love goddesses go to market' and 'She wore black velvet and her twin wore grape' were the texts that accompanied a series of black and purple velvet separates.

Classical Greek statues were viewed afresh by Vivienne, with the help of Ness. Having read the American costume historian Anne Hollander's book *Seeing Through Clothes*, and researched the attire of the classical world, Vivienne became convinced that drapery was the mark of a civilised cast of mind, and urged her followers to wear it once again. 'I'll tell you something,' she began, as if nudging them in the ribs with a salacious piece of gossip, 'those Greeks wore this drapery – if you've got something that's draped on the body, that's constantly moving, you will play with it and it will play with you – and they believed that the barbarians were not sensual because they weren't experiencing their own bodies through drapery.'

Draped gowns had been given prominence by Madame Grès and Augustabernard, two French couturiers of the inter-war years who admired classicism. Vivienne, on the other hand, used drapery to lend seductive movement to otherwise functional and close-fitting clothes. She swung diaphanous swags from the shoulders of tweed suits and across the bodices of eighteenth-century-style corsets, creating a modern and original hybrid. There were allusions to the ancient world not only in the stage setting for the show, which included a Grecian frieze as a backdrop, but in the accessories, such as Smedley's knitted vests and shorts printed with images of Ionic columns, ram's head wigs and white platform sandals trimmed with wings, reminiscent of Hermes.

Jumping back and forth through costume history and conflating styles from various periods, Vivienne created astonishing combinations. In an attempt to be 'shocking and original', for example, for the 'Voyage to Cythera' (autumn/winter 1989) collection, named after Watteau's painting of Venus's birthplace, she designed flesh-coloured leggings appliquéd across the pubis with a green perspex fig-leaf: 'It's very difficult to come up with something shocking and original,' she said of this garment. 'I surprised myself by making a garment that shocked me.' Noticing that Greek statues of Adonis invariably enhanced the sensuality of his nudity with drapery, she saw a parallel with *les Incroyables* from the Napoleonic era, who had inspired her 'Pirates' collection in 1980. To her mind, these dandy rebels had worn tight, light-coloured trousers (typically cut in nankeen, close-woven cotton or fine doeskin leather) in order to draw attention to their genitals – she believed 'those men were trying to look like those Adonis figures'. Vivienne's fig-leaf leggings were worn either with loose shirts, 'so it looked like a guy just about to rape you, but it was worn on a woman', or with long double-breasted jackets. She hoped the collection proved it was possible to 'be in your underwear and yet be noble at the same time'.

Trying on her new look in front of a mirror, Vivienne shrieked with amusement: 'It looked pornographic. It was terribly sexy, just because it was the reverse of what was fashionably sexy. Sexuality is always really an interplay between the polarities of masculine and feminine.' When Sarah Stockbridge wore the fig-leaf leggings and bodysuit to the Sex Maniacs' Ball that summer, although other guests arrived virtually naked or trussed up in sado-masochist rubber and leather, she caused a much greater stir, despite being covered from top to toe. Vivienne's harlequin-print leggings were inspired by Leon Bakst's costumes for Diaghilev's Ballet Russe, to which Gary Ness had introduced her. The press and public were initially shocked at the thought of women wearing just leggings under their jackets, but within two seasons the look had become a fashion staple, known as the 'Principal Boy' look.

Vivienne was determined to do battle with what she regarded as England's lingering puritanism. 'Before I say anything about vanity,' she told a journalist in 1989, 'I'd like to note the brilliant observation of the American humorist H.L. Mencken, which I have often heard quoted: "Puritanism is the haunting fear that someone, somewhere, may be happy." Keeping this definition, I'd like to use the word "puritan" anachronistically and say that my first feeling about vanity – which comes from the Latin word for "empty" – is that if it was not coined by puritans, then it has been used by them as a sin to berate us with, up to the beginning of this century. Since then organised religion has been replaced by national idolatry, and the berating seems to have stopped.'

As Ness's influence on her strengthened, Vivienne's collections were presented with pontificating manifestos which read like incoherent collages of the controversial views and quotations she had garnered from her 'tutorials'. For her 'Civilizade' show at Olympia in October 1988, for example, the programme read:

We believe in scepticism, argument and elitism as pagans valued intellectual freedom and mistrusted belief. Death is so Gothic; life is so Greek, as Oscar Wilde said. There is talk of Victorian values, but Victorian values were an insistence on interminable argumentative dinner parties, not middle-class puritanism. Not Pecksniff's [in Dickens's *Martin Chuzzlewit*] business but [Thomas Love] Peacock's. As was said, 'We don't want a Crusade: we want Civilizade.' The French revolution destroyed aristocracy because it ignored other classes. English aristocracy destroyed itself because it became middle class. Anglo-American philistinism is total stagnation, summed up recently by a well-known judge as the 3 C's: Complacency, Conservatism and Conformity. We add two more: Convention and Consumerism. Ideas and Art are kept alive only by argument. Scepticism engenders ideas and belief kills them. Elitism is not power and money; it is the cultivation of ideas and art made possible by power and money.

Despite her enduring reputation for originality, Vivienne was not averse to copying other designers. She picked up ideas from what might be described as the '*avant-avant-garde*', such as underground, student or relatively unknown designers whom she encountered on the London nightclub scene. The 'Time Machine' tweed 'armour plating' jackets, for example, were clearly influenced by a Richard Torry design that had been presented a season earlier. Torry, who had worked for Vivienne for two seasons, and briefly shared her studio, had been inspired by armour at the Victoria and Albert Museum and the Tower of London, while Vivienne took her inspiration from the Wallace Collection. In imitation of the interlocking articulated metal plates that composed a medieval suit of armour, Torry lay sections of tweed side by side along the sleeve and across the breast of his high-waisted jackets. Wearing one of them as he queued outside the British Fashion Council tent at Olympia for the second showing of Vivienne's 'Time Machine' collection, Torry was approached by a friend who said, 'You'll get a shock, Richard; she's done your armour jackets.' In the summer of 1989 Vivienne's Harris tweed version of the jacket was to become uncool virtually overnight when Al Berlin, the stylist who dressed the teenybopper band Bros, put the brothers in them. 'You just couldn't sell one after that,' says Simon Barker.

Torry went on to become part of the late designer, performance artist and model Leigh Bowery's pop group Minty. Vivienne was also influenced by Bowery, and greatly admired his work. When the Victoria and Albert Museum, for example, hosted *Blitz* magazine's exhibition 'Designer Denim' in 1986, while Vivienne submitted a denim jacket prosaically decorated with her orb on the back, Bowery's contribution was a jacket bristling with thousands of Kirby hair-grips. Vivienne singled it out as exceptional; the time-consuming craft that had been invested in it would have appealed to her.

As Vivienne's profile rose, thanks to a curious and sceptical media, the public became fascinated by her comical mannerisms and speech patterns. In front of an audience she would fumble verbally, as if scrolling down a mental dictionary to select the most exact, most impressive word, regardless of how long it took her to find it. Inevitably, malapropisms peppered these performances. Trying to communicate a complicated theme of one of her collections, such as the Greeks and their drapery, she became visibly tense. Wrapping her legs tightly around one another, hunching over and – with one hand nervously tugging the hem of her skirt and the other apparently pushing imaginary spittle back into her mouth – she would screw her eyes shut and embark on a monologue, rocking faster and faster in her chair as if in pain. Barely pausing for breath as the thoughts tumbled out, she desperately deflected interruptions or pleas to stick to the point by snapping, 'No, wait, don't interrupt . . . no, I don't want to talk about clothes . . . no I'll come back to that, I must tell you about those Greeks.' She gave the impression that she was delivering her 'Garyisms' by rote. She had no ability to argue closely, so if an interviewer contradicted her, she simply veered off at a tangent to another topic.

This manner of delivery, and her startling *non sequiturs*, cruelly exposed Vivienne's thought processes and the flimsiness of her arguments. When interviewed by the journalist Brenda Polan in front of a large audience at the Institute for Contemporary Arts in London in June 1993, for example, she was determined to mention a work by the French novelist André Gide. Deliberating over whether to say the title in French or English, she seemed unabashed: 'I won't say it in French, because my accent's not very good, but anyway, I could try if you like – no. Anyway – why not? Yeah! Well, anyway . . .' Such unsophisticated eccentricities, combined with her extraordinary appearance, won her the affection of much of the British public – it was pantomime. To the media, however, she was an easy target for ridicule.

In March 1988 Vivienne was invited to appear on the prime-time BBC chat show *Wogan*. It was hosted by Sue Lawley, the epitome of Middle England, dressed on that occasion in navy-and-white polkadot suit and peep-toed white slingbacks. The other guests were Janet Street-Porter, a champion of *avant-garde* youth culture and a long-standing fan of Vivienne's work, and the literary critic and television compere Russell Harty. Vivienne looked pretty in her scarlet 'Centaurella' dress, inspired by the mythical centaur, and her platform Rocking Horse boots.

Throughout the interview, Vivienne was systematically lampooned by Lawley and Harty, who encouraged the audience – largely made up of old-age pensioners, as the programme was recorded on a weekday afternoon – to laugh at her expense, despite protests from Street-Porter that her designs were important. At one point in the middle of the fashion show, modelled by Sarah Stockbridge and the dancer Michael Clarke, the laughter and jibes became so intense – egged on by Lawley's disingenuous interjection, 'Are people supposed to laugh? Because they're laughing' – that Vivienne warned, 'If they don't stop laughing, I'll tell the next person to stop coming on.' At the end of the farcical performance, Lawley patronisingly turned to Vivienne and, patting her on the knee, said, 'We haven't upset you?' Stockbridge and Simon Barker were astonished when Vivienne remarked backstage, 'Well, that seemed to go all right.' Perhaps fortunately, she was oblivious to ridicule. A few months later, on being told of Harty's death, she bluntly responded, 'Serves him right! He's a bugger anyway.'

Vivienne could be disarmingly vernacular. If ill at ease, she sought comfort in deflating formality with familiarity. When, for example, she entered a formal, classically appointed drawing room filled with art historians and publishers – with 'clout' – she would begin, 'Cosy here, isn't it. Anyone want a cigarette?' When Brenda Polan began the ICA interview by asking her to comment on the institute's founder, Herbert Read, she responded, 'Sorry, Brenda, I've got to find me matches.'

The manner in which Vivienne smoked revealed both her intensity and her girlishness. She smoked like a novice, pouting exaggeratedly as she snatched frequently at the end of the cigarette and blew out the smoke without, it seemed, inhaling. The whole procedure came across as the theatrical gesture of a teenager who was only smoking for effect.

'Deep down she feels uncomfortable, and reverts to that down-to-earth Northernness,' according to John Walford. Valerie Mendes of the V&A, who observed Vivienne over two decades, recognised her social unease, partly because she shared it: 'I came from the North too. I know that kind of background she will have come from. It was a very difficult time for her, and to move into a very sophisticated world from that Northern background which didn't have communications, TVs etc., one simply wasn't aware . . . She has worked hard at surviving, and she has known poverty, and though she never went hungry, presumably she has known what it is to be without. And if you've known that, then it's always difficult. It's always part of you. You never forget.'

Vivienne's po-faced solemnity when interviewed on television meant that she unintentionally came across as camp, and she inevitably became a figure of fun. Her pursuit of the serious was unrelenting, and at times comically inappropriate. When, for example, she interviewed Holly Johnson, the lead singer of Frankie Goes to Hollywood, for a glossy magazine, after some minutes of banter she interjected, 'We haven't said anything crunchy yet, have we?' Johnson assumed that by 'crunchy' she meant something sexual, and so asked if she'd ever had a lesbian experience. But in fact Vivienne had been hoping for a philosophical tussle. They then discussed the salacious tabloid newspapers. Vivienne asked why Johnson refused to give an interview to the *Sun*, since, as she naïvely saw it, tabloid editors 'were there just to be exploited when artists have ideas to sell'. The interview was never published.

While Vivienne's clothes appealed to her clients' theatricality, their extreme styling could make them seem like articles from a dressing-up box, to be worn by children playing at being grown-ups. After McLaren's departure, her work began to incorporate a stronger and stronger homosexual element, to such a degree that by the early nineties it began to resemble transvestite costume. This camp styling was most unlike the clothes created by other successful women designers. If there was one trait that distinguished women's designs from their male counterparts' it was realism, not fantasy. Comparing Vivienne's work with that of the foremost women designers of the twentieth century, the contrast was extreme. They tended to design practical uniforms which communicated the desire to feel comfortable and to command respect. Designers like Coco Chanel, Jean Muir, Jil Sander and Donna Karan, for example, offered clothes that could be worn with propriety by professional women, like themselves, and that drew attention to the wearer's personality by acting as a flattering backdrop to the individual. On the other hand, flamboyant male designers – and Vivienne – favoured fancy-dress. They enabled the wearer to masquerade as someone else, someone better, someone more interesting. 'You have a better life if you wear impressive clothes,' Vivienne often remarked. In their theatricality, her clothes reflected not only the tastes of her homosexual employees and friends, but her unease with her own persona. She clearly felt the need for a disguise that would arouse interest and comment. It is little wonder that she had become an icon in the gay world. Transvestites would queue for her clothes, and stores in Los Angeles could not stock enough pairs of her high, platformed shoes in men's sizes.

Also unlike other women designers, who tended to play down sexuality in their clothes, Vivienne flaunted it. But her idea of what was sexy was idiosyncratic in the extreme. She gave greater priority to feeling than to appearance. When she described an article of clothing as 'sexy', she did not necessarily mean sexy to behold, but sexy to wear, referring to the physical and emotional sense of constriction or discomfort experienced by the wearer in their tight corset, toe-numbing platform shoes or sensuously swaying crinoline. By being constantly reminded of the body because of the way it was tightly packaged and held erect, the wearer felt compelled to move in a sexual manner. It was an autonomous sense of sexuality: if the wearer *thought* she was sexy, then she was. Some men found this knowingness attractive, others were repelled by it. In this respect Vivienne's clothes expressed extreme self-confidence, and time and again customers emphasised how sexually powerful they felt in them.

Some feminists applauded this aspect of her designs, but Vivienne was not a feminist, and dismissed the movement for being 'too puritanical'. She had never felt a strong allegiance to her own sex, which she denigrated as 'the most conservative section of society', an instinct which she believed Margaret Thatcher had exploited. Vivienne declared that she would 'rather promote or defend homosexuals than women, because they've contributed much more to society'. She did not have a talent for friendship, regarding people either as her superiors or her inferiors. She was particularly harsh on other women, few of whom she regarded as being as strong as her. Since they were not her equals, she failed to develop any significant companionships with them. She preferred to collect 'girls', such as Sarah Stockbridge, Ben's girlfriend Yasmin Eslami and the model Susie Bick, whom she would dress up and mother, particularly if they had complicated private lives and could be cast as 'victims'. This was not simple benevolence on her part, but merely a love of projects, of 'to-dos'. As soon as one of her 'dolls' showed signs of independence or ambition, such as Sarah Stockbridge wishing to develop her acting, or Jibby Beane, a shop assistant and unofficial house model, developing her career as an art curator, Vivienne promptly dropped them.

By contrast, Vivienne developed crushes on well-educated or aristocratic women whom she considered had 'clout', such as Bella Freud, Lady Henrietta Bathurst, Lady Romilly McAlpine and the well-connected Amanda Knight (briefly a shop assistant at Davies Street). She cultivated these women, says Simon Barker, in the hope that they would act as unofficial ambassadors who would 'attract the sort of customers that she wanted: posh ones' – and so they did. But as a rule Vivienne did not get on with women, especially if they had the gall to contradict her, or failed to be impressed by her. She was also ungracious toward her defenders. For example, when Janet Street-Porter stood up for her against Sue Lawley and the baying studio audience on *Wogan*, she failed, despite the urgings of Barker and Derek Dunbar, to thank her by post or telephone.

Vivienne was indebted to Carlo D'Amario for rescuing her from bankruptcy and was a co-signatory on a bank loan he had secured to restart her company. He was 'always there for her' says John Walford, 'perhaps because he had been rejected by her' when she left Italy. Since then he had secured his position as manager of the Italian operation, and together with her son Joseph owned 49 per cent of the British arm of the company, Vivienne Westwood Ltd, and 51 per cent of the Italian arm, Vivienne Westwood SpA. Gradually, he persuaded her to manufacture more and more of her clothing in Italy, where he could control both business relations and finances.

Whatever some of Vivienne's long-standing associates may have thought about his lifestyle and activities, there is no doubt that without D'Amario, Vivienne's business would have collapsed. One of his most important functions was to secure a manufacturer who would invest in producing Vivienne's collections, and thereby ensure the stability and continuity of her fashion label. D'Amario was friendly with a small Italian manufacturer, Alberto Biani, who with his partner Sandro Dal Pra had set up Staff International in Noventa Vicentina, in northern Italy. Biani designed Staff International's own three labels – New York, Industria and Alberto Biani womenswear – while Dal Pra dealt with the finances. In due course they went into partnership with the Italian designer Valentino, producing his diffusion range (an inexpensive, mass-produced line bearing – or sometimes purporting to bear – a designer's signature), going on to manufacture Costume Nationale, Martin Margiela, Missoni, Balmain, Bella Freud and Stephen Sprouse.

When Vivienne was designing her 1987 'Harris Tweed' collection, D'Amario approached Biani about the possibility of Staff International manufacturing her range. Vivienne's reputation for financial unreliability, and for impossibly demanding and complicated patterns, went before her, but D'Amario declared her to be 'a genius', and the opportunity of producing her work 'a great commercial opportunity'.

To Biani's credit, he agreed to take on the contract, but 'Harris Tweed' proved to be virtually impossible to manufacture commercially. Not only did Vivienne insist on using single-width traditional tweed, she presented Biani with far too many design permutations and complicated patterns. The resultant difficulties were repeatedly pointed out to her, but she refused to streamline her designs to accommodate the commercial demands of production. A Staff International employee remembers: 'All she had in mind was the show, not the reality of production. She was totally inflexible. She also only wanted to use John Smedley. Alberto soon realised it was impossible to interfere with her designs, she was so strict in her attitude – no compromise!'

Nevertheless, in D'Amario Vivienne had found a rarity, a fashion manager who was prepared to tolerate her flights of fancy, her 'uncommercial' designs and her total disregard for marketing or for the customer. D'Amario controlled Vivienne in two ways. Firstly, he provided her with creative freedom, by relieving her of all administrative concerns. This arrangement suited his pocket and her temperament. And secondly, like McLaren, he was able to manipulate her – he once confided to Simon Barker, 'Whenever I can't get my way with Vivienne, all I have to do is flatter her.' To her face he respectfully called her 'Madame' and gradually the studio adopted this title, but behind her back she was dismissed as the mad 'La Westwood'. Attempting to erase all memories of McLaren, whom he hated, D'Amario rewrote Vivienne's history. Any references to her work with McLaren were removed from her 1993 *curriculum vitae*, and even the mention of McLaren's name was banned in his presence.

Vivienne was an extremely difficult designer to manage, and though she was delicate in movement and gesture, she was far from delicate of mind. D'Amario was usually patient with her infuriating idio-syncrasies, but occasionally he resorted to bullying her (Bella Freud has observed Vivienne's tendency to 'surround herself with men who put her down'). Some of Vivienne's staff regarded D'Amario as a mere opportunist, but notwithstanding his unconventional accounting and business practices – which were hardly unusual by the standards of Italian commercial and political life, including the fashion industry, where bribes and backhanders were commonplace – he shared an emotional bond with her. 'He would have been very happy to have stayed with Vivienne and been a father to her children – he really would,' says Walford. 'He loved her – still does. I don't think his motivation with Vivienne is just money. I do think he still loves her. Gay guys – and most of the guys in that company are gay – don't like Carlo because of his love for her.'

Another way in which D'Amario influenced Vivienne was by trying to keep Joseph on his side, although he was eventually unsuccessful in this. D'Amario had little respect for Joseph, and nicknamed him 'milky', suggesting he was like a suckling child who could not be parted from its mother. The animosity between the two men was exacerbated by the fact that Joseph, as McLaren's son, was a constant reminder to D'Amario of Vivienne's great love.

Contradictions are inherent in human nature, but in Vivienne's case the inconsistencies were unusually extreme. She was both reactionary and radical, mean and generous, tender and insensitive, canny and naïve. Happily immersed in work for hours on end, she would not eat, but just drank endless cups of tea made with rancid milk she did not want to waste. If dining with friends in the evening, she would claim that she was on a diet and order only a salad, then maddeningly scavenge from her companions' plates. Once, at tea with Barker and Dunbar, she was asked to leave the cake alone until they had made the tea. When they returned from the kitchen they found a huge, cartoon-like bite had been taken from it. Vivienne feigned innocence. Gary Ness would find half-eaten bananas in the fruit bowl, the skin neatly folded back to make them look as if they were untouched.

Colleagues complained that Vivienne had an annoying habit of 'bumming' cigarettes while claiming that she did not smoke. Once, when she was stopped at customs for carrying too many duty-free cigarettes, at first she denied that she smoked, then claimed that the cigarettes were not hers, but belonged to her travelling companions. When the customs officer insisted that she would have to pay duty or the cigarettes would be confiscated, she began an interrogation. What was the point of that? What would happen to the cigarettes? Would he smoke them himself? No, they would be burnt, he replied. What a waste! she protested. Why couldn't she burn them instead, by smoking them? Like a terrier, she would not let the matter drop. On leaving the customs desk, defeated, she turned on Sarah Stockbridge, who was wearing a pair of Rocking Horse shoes, and snapped, 'If you hadn't got those stupid shoes on, we wouldn't have been stopped.'

Vivienne's health was so robust that she rarely fell ill, and as a result she had no sympathy or tolerance for staff taking days off for sickness. Disdaining modish gyms and dance studios, she inadvertently kept fit by travelling on her pushbike in all weathers, and at all times of the day or night. The daily journey from Nightingale Lane to her studio was four miles each way, and she would often make detours to museums, her shops or Gary Ness's flat. Dressed in her own designs, she cut an extraordinary figure as she pedalled furiously across London. Heads would turn as this middle-aged woman cycled past wearing a tweed crown and mini crini or Argyll twinset, matching leggings, kilt and Timberland boots. On days when she was due to appear in public, she would leave home with her pink plastic rollers 'hidden' under a fluffy white angora scarf. On reaching the studio, the boots would be swapped for her favourite pair of cosy reindeer slippers.

Vivienne was a winter person. She liked wholesome stews, red wine, whisky, tweed, wool and the rain and wind. She seldom took a holiday, devoting herself entirely to her work. On the few occasions when she did take a break, she was more likely to go for brisk walks on English fells than to loll on the deck of a yacht in the Mediterranean, like the archetypal fashion designer. It was hardly surprising that her winter collections were considerably better than her summer ones.

During these years, the intensity of Vivienne's work, and absence of a lover, led to a sloppiness in her own grooming and dress. Day after day she would wear 'Spot' jeans from her 'Mini Crini' collection and a baggy cardigan held together with safety pins. When her old schoolfriend Maureen Purcell visited Vivienne at her flat she was surprised by the ordinariness of her surroundings and her scruffy attire. Now well into middle age, Vivienne began to fill out, and the combined effect of weight, age and shabbiness gave her an appearance, when off-duty, altogether at odds with her status and image as the high priestess of outlandish design.

When Vivienne was asked about her solitary existence, she dismissed the idea of love with such declarations as: 'I believe that all knowledge is in books, and all love is in art.' One morning, having seen an advertisement for a dating service in the Underground which read: 'Don't let life and love pass you by,' she complained to her colleagues that this was a stupid statement: 'As if they're the same thing! I think a love affair would go a long way to helping life pass you by.' She claimed that 'at this point in my life I am prepared to sacrifice all that – relationships, everything – for brain stimulation.' It is possible that her attitude simply reflected her disillusionment. Over the years, she had invested considerable amounts of love and energy in unsatisfactory men. Only Derek, her husband, had been true to her.

Focusing on her work, Vivienne displayed the rigour and self-criticism of a perfectionist. For seemingly trifling reasons, she would throw out entire collections that other designers might have considered their best. This rigour was combined with absolute belief in the final design. Like most passionately creative people, she enjoyed the total immersion in her craft. This intensity could also be channelled towards a person. Vivienne could become mesmerised by an employee, singled out not for his (or, less frequently, her) professional skill, but for his smile, his style or his desirable connections. As long as her adoration was reciprocated the relationship was happy, but as Simon Barker puts it, 'like Margaret Thatcher, she didn't want a word of dissent in her cabinet.'

The photographer and stylist Michael Roberts exploited Vivienne's remarkable resemblance to Margaret Thatcher by mischievously casting the opinionated designer as the opinionated Prime Minister for the cover of the April fool edition of *Tatler* in 1989. Initially, Vivienne was reluctant to play along with the spoof, Roberts remembers, because she hated Thatcher, 'but she did it so well it was creepy'. As she posed in a wig, pearls and a conservative Aquascutum suit, Vivienne imagined herself to be leaning over a child in a hospital and telling herself, 'I care, I *really* care,' and she put the resultant likeness down to 'my great acting ability'. But the two women, both of whom had climbed to success in the second half of the seventies, and both of whom came to epitomise the 1980s, shared a fierce drive and ambition, an ability to attract and command acolytes, and a ruthlessness that scythed through opposition. If anyone stood in Vivienne's path, Barker observed, 'Wow! Did she have a temper. It's dangerous.' If words failed her, she resorted to the threat of physical violence, such as taking off a Rocking Horse shoe (they weighed five pounds each) and threatening to throw it.

Throughout her life, Vivienne was convinced that compromise was weakness, and so she consistently took the line of greatest resistance. She revelled in being contrary. Since customers expected white clothes for summer, she designed black and grey ones. If a colleague expressed admiration for a book, painting or bolt of cloth, she would deprecate it. It became so predictable that Barker would preface any comment with: 'I know you're going to disagree with me, Vivienne, but . . .'

In October 1989 Vivienne showed 'Pagan V' at the Duke of York's Barracks in the King's Road, where the British Fashion Council had moved British Fashion Week. Like many of her spring/summer collections, it was weak, save for a series of striped cotton pyjama suits for men. The collection, shown to the accompaniment of Debussy's 'L'Après-midi d'un faun', was inspired by pagan erotica, and included a series of cotton separates and leggings printed on the crotch with an erect penis crudely drawn by Vivienne herself. Some American buyers sitting in the front row were so shocked that they walked out in disgust.

The models were led out onto the catwalk by a grinning Joseph Corré, roped together with twinkling diamanté chains as if they were animals on leads. Amanda de Cadenet, the wild-child television presenter of the late-night pop music and chat show *The Word*, was among them. When she confided to Vivienne that her bottom was too big for her to be put in anything revealing, Vivienne, with predictable perversity, made her model the skimpiest swimwear. Vivienne wanted to make the point that she approved of buxom women; she had not lost her appreciation of the body shapes of the female icons of her adolescence, Marilyn Monroe and Jayne Mansfield. If the fashion press and buyers were unimpressed by the show, the tabloid picture editors loved it. But tabloid approval does not necessarily translate into sales.

As well as voluptuous women, Vivienne used older and ordinary-looking models. Bertie Hope-Davies, a wry and characterful sexagenarian 'City gent' and socialite she had met through Bella Freud, was one of her favourites. Vivienne was making the point that 'averagely-shaped' people, rather than just unusually thin and tall models, deserved admiration. Within a few seasons other designers, notably Jean-Paul Gaultier, were following Vivienne's lead by using 'ordinary people' rather than professional models to promote their clothes, and by the mid-nineties mainstream cosmetics and fashion companies, such as The Gap and Levi's, were celebrating – and thereby wooing – the common man and woman.

Though there were some original ideas in 'Pagan V', it was a poorly edited and overlong show, and Vivienne's clothes were not suited to large, impersonal catwalks like the one at the Duke of York's Barracks. The show was a critical failure, and as not enough orders were placed for the clothes, the Italian manufacturers refused to make them. Ignoring Joseph and the show's producer John Walford's advice to create a smaller and less costly collection, Vivienne had incautiously invested far too much money in the 'Pagan V' range, and she was left financially struggling.

In the past, no matter how the press and buyers reacted to her designs, Vivienne herself never had any doubts. But Walford believes that ' "Pagan V" really hit her, as commercially it was an unmitigated disaster. It should have been a real moment of glory, and if she had taken it to Paris five years later people would have been screaming in the aisles . . . There followed a period of retrenchment; she was very down.'

Despite four years of hard work following her return to London, commercial success, and even financial stability, still eluded Vivienne. Critical acclaim came and went, but rather than bringing her money, it only resulted in her being copied. Others profited from her originality, which was watered down into more commercial versions. She, meanwhile, eked out a hand-to-mouth existence. Rarely were visitors invited back to her scruffy flat, which resembled a student's digs, decorated only with a couple of posters: a detail of a beautiful boy's head taken from a Piero della Francesca painting, and a Titian.

Unlike her mother, Vivienne was not house-proud. 'Whenever neighbours come round she won't let them in because it's too messy,' says Simon Barker. The tiny flat was cluttered with rails of clothes, bolts of fabric and a collection of 'Mistress of the Universe' dolls, sci-fi toys dressed with great precision and detail in interchangeable outfits, which were an inspiration behind her spring/summer 1989 'Civilizade' collection. What furniture there was was utilitarian rather than decorative, Vivienne having neither the money nor the inclination to acquire anything else. One thing which saddened her was that she did not have examples of all the clothes she and McLaren had designed together. She claims that during their tempestuous break-up McLaren sent some sidekicks round to Kingly Court to take the samples, and 'he got rid of them, because they were to do with me, and he didn't value that any more'.

Vivienne's flat had become so crowded with clothes, unwashed crockery, pans of dyes and years of accumulated paraphernalia that she was completely unaware that she still had Keith Haring's original artwork for her 'Witches' screen prints under her bed. With his untimely death of AIDS in 1990, at the age of thirty-two, they became extremely valuable. Keith Wainwright remembers that whenever he visited the flat Vivienne would greet him with, 'Have a cup of tea, Keith. Wash your cup up!'

Such were the strains on Vivienne's finances that she had to juggle payments and delay deliveries even to afford the cloth to make up into clothes. Although she could not honour her debts, Joseph was unable to control her determination to design larger and larger collections. Vivienne was simply not getting enough orders from retailers. Most of her custom came from the six Astore Robot stores and Berni Vinyl in Japan, two boutiques in Italy, and occasional orders from Bloomingdales and small boutiques like Charivari and Suzanne Bartsch in New York. Though Vivienne had never craved riches, she was now approaching fifty years of age, and had tired of penury. She wanted not only recognition, but the financial security to pursue her work. It had been a long and difficult haul.

What particularly angered her was the manner in which she was treated by the fashion industry in Britain. 'Our Viv', as they disparagingly referred to her, was cast as a laughing stock rather than a talented designer. By contrast, on the Continent, in Japan and in some receptive quarters in America she was regarded as an important innovator and a celebrity. Romilly McAlpine, who had become a fan, deplored the way in which 'the British knock what is good. But,' she said, 'Karl Lagerfeld and Azzedine Alaïa have said to me at different stages that they both thought Vivienne Westwood is the most interesting designer in the world, and the only one they looked at.'

The British Fashion Council's prestigious Designer of the Year award, which was voted on by the leading members of the industry, seemed out of Vivienne's reach. It was especially galling to her that twice in a row, in 1987 and 1988, John Galliano received the award, given that she believed his work was so derivative of hers. His autumn/winter 1985 'Fallen Angels' collection, for example, included Hobo trousers held up with a single brace and misbuttoned shirts that were very reminiscent of Vivienne's designs in the early eighties. When Vivienne heard the announcement of Galliano's first award, she turned to the journalist Sally Brampton and 'launched into a tirade against him and how he had copied her'. The astute and experienced American photo-journalist Bill Cunningham agreed with her, but concluded, 'Vivienne is still wacky, whereas John is chic.'

That, in essence, was the reason why the largely conservative British fashion press overlooked Vivienne's contribution. In addition, the fashion establishment found it hard to forgive Vivienne's behaviour in the past: this was the woman who had challenged their traditions and ridiculed their monarch. Meanwhile, Vivienne smarted with resentment at being passed over.

In November 1989 Vivienne's gloom was partially relieved by a ray of light from New York. John Fairchild, the immensely influential publisher of *Women's Wear Daily*, published a book entitled *Chic Savages*, his account of the fashion world. In it he wrote:

> There are six designers today: Yves Saint Laurent, Giorgio Armani, Emanuel Ungaro, Karl Lagerfeld, Christian Lacroix and Vivienne Westwood – from them all fashion hangs from a golden thread . . . Of the six, British Vivienne Westwood is the designer's designer, watched by intellectual and far-out designers, including Jean-Paul Gaultier. She is copied by the *avant-garde* French and Italian designers, because she is like the Alice in Wonderland of fashion and her clothes are wonderfully mad – fantastic enough to be worn at the Mad Hatter's tea party. Yet,

copied as she is, Westwood struggles in her Worlds End shop in London, living from hand to mouth. What a pity she never did conclude a deal with Armani, who recognised her talent but couldn't manage the fantasy of it all. The last time I saw Vivienne she was dressed more like the Queen in Harris tweeds, but she still wore those high-laced pilgrim shoes.

Many readers were astonished by Fairchild's enthusiasm for Vivienne. Could he really be referring to that madwoman who made such unwearable clothes? The fashion journalist Suzy Menkes recalled: 'People were flabbergasted, but Americans are very literal, and have a high opinion of John Fairchild.' Would his imprimatur turn the tide?

Earlier that year Vivienne had been enticed back to teaching by Jean-Charles de Castelbajac, who recommended her as his successor as Professor of Fashion at the Vienna Academy of Applied Arts. She accepted the two-year post, which paid the handsome fee of £4,000 a month for three days' work. It was money she badly needed.

Vivienne had repeatedly voiced her disgust for the teaching methods in British art and fashion schools. She singled out Central St Martin's, which was at the vanguard of an experimental approach to design, as the worst culprit, for not working 'in a technical way . . . the only way you learn anything is through copying . . . good models'. In her opinion, the *laissez-faire* attitude which had prevailed since the 1960s had placed indulgent self-expression above learning the vital techniques of tailoring and dressmaking and a thorough understanding of the history of dress. As a result the students' work was, she felt, shoddy, ugly and unwearable.

When Vivienne took up her post at Vienna, and later in Berlin, she seized the opportunity to practise her more traditional teaching methods. Students were instructed to copy historic costumes and rustic dress in a disciplined and repetitive manner, sometimes spending months on a single piece. She was determined to impress upon them her conviction that every seam, fastening and stitch in a garment must have a reason, and to imbue in them her passion for the narrative in fashion – every garment should tell a story.

It is ironic that Vivienne, an entirely self-taught designer, should have chosen to impose the straitjacket of conventional techniques on her students. Her insistence on sound teaching based on learning from the masters of the craft stemmed from her background as a schoolteacher, her own acquired working methods and her frustration that she had not had a formal training in tailoring or dressmaking. Yet her own untutored amateurism was precisely the condition that had allowed her to invent in such an unbridled, unpredictable and, above all, fearless manner. If Vivienne had learned by rote how to set in a sleeve, hand-roll a hem or cut on the bias, would she ever have had the inclination, the innocence or the daring to explore and question every aspect of a garment's construction and, through exacting experimentation, to work out her own way of piecing it together?

Though many designers, including Gianfranco Ferre, had wanted the Vienna job, Jean-Charles de Castelbajac favoured Vivienne: 'I did not want to suggest a traditional designer to take over, but an iconoclast.' However, he now admits, 'I have regretted it ever since, because it was there that she met Andreas.'

Andreas Kronthaler, one of Vivienne's students, was the tall, handsome, twenty-five-year-old son of an Austrian blacksmith. His distinctive presence, enhanced by an artful flirtatiousness and the intensity of his darkly shadowed eyes, called to mind a laudanum-addicted nineteenth-century German romantic poet. Andreas was a seducer of men and women alike, though he preferred the former.

Vivienne was attracted not only by his physical charms, but by what she considered to be his exceptional artistic sensibility and talent. In a video made for her students in 1990, she says: 'I was slightly drunk last night, and I said something that might be true. The only thing that gives me an emotion thing, what I really care about, is genius, talent – extreme talent, anyway. I feel more upset for the genius of the past than people around me if they don't have intelligence ... I do relate to this in people. It is really quite a thrill for me to be here because it really exists in this school.' The 'genius' she was referring to was Andreas. She had fallen in love with him. Within weeks she had offered him work in her studio (it was the dream of many fashion students to work with Vivienne), and within months he was living with her at Nightingale Lane.

Vivienne believed Andreas was 'a man with civilisation', and that he knew more about art than she ever could. She was particularly impressed when, talking about the Second World War, it was the loss of great art, not human life, that reduced him to tears. After

Vivienne's confidence had been shattered by the failure of 'Pagan V', she sought solace in Andreas Kronthaler's arms. 'He got in that way,' says John Walford. 'Andreas worked on her, and got in.' The liaison was to have a dramatic effect on Vivienne's work as well as her private life. Once again, she had selected a mate who would steer the course of her work but who could not be depended upon to be sexually faithful to her, or to ease her sense of emotional anxiety.

9 THE WIFE OF BATH

1990–1993

Now of my fifth, last husband let me tell.
God never let his soul be sent to Hell!
And yet he was my worst, and many a blow
He struck me still can ache along my row
Of ribs, and until my dying day.
But in our bed he was so fresh and gay,
So coaxing, so persuasive . . . Heaven knows
Whenever he wanted it – my *belle chose* –
Though he had beaten me in every bone
He still could wheedle me to love, I own . . .
I gave my whole heart up, for him to hold.
He was, I think, some twenty winters old,
And I was forty then to tell the truth.
But still, I always had a coltish tooth . . .
I handed him the money, lands and all
That had ever been given me before;
this I repented later, more and more.'

Geoffrey Chaucer, *The Canterbury Tales*

It was not until influential figures in the fashion business abroad had acclaimed Vivienne's talent that she was appreciated in her own land. Besides John Fairchild, the most persuasive of these were Anna Piaggi of Italian Condé Nast, and the Paris-based designers Christian Lacroix, Karl Lagerfeld, Yves Saint Laurent, Jean-Paul Gaultier, Jean-Charles de Castelbajac and Azzedine Alaïa. Yet despite her belated recognition, she still could not secure significant wholesale orders or, more importantly, lucrative licensing deals to stabilise her company's finances. Her hand-to-mouth lifestyle continued, but John Walford believes she was eager to change it: 'She was really fed up with being broke, and once she had recognition and status she wanted something to come with it . . . she was definitely playing for money now.'

Vivienne's next three collections, 'Portrait', 'Cut & Slash' and 'Cut, Slash & Pull', were among her finest. Free from the distractions of a lover or her sons living at home, she spent considerable time and energy researching and preparing these shows, which included some of her purest and strongest designs. The clothes were a delightful fusion of historical research, flamboyant sexiness and vernacular items such as jeans and T-shirts, on which she printed images from old master paintings in the hope that they would inspire an appreciation of high culture.

Vivienne was not the first designer to have been stimulated by works of art. Cristobal Balenciaga, for example, consistently found inspiration in the devotional paintings of Zurbaran, the courtly portraits of Velázquez and the drama and colour of Goya. In the 1960s Yves Saint Laurent had printed images from modern masters such as Picasso, Cocteau and Mondrian on his clothes. Like Balenciaga and Saint Laurent, Vivienne was also inspired by the shape of past costumes. She had not yet fallen under the camp and melodramatic influence of Andreas Kronthaler and his homages to Thierry Mugler and Saint Laurent, so these clothes carried her distinctive signature.

'Portrait' (autumn/winter 1990–91) was named for the old masters from which Vivienne drew inspiration, and which were printed onto the various fabrics. It was critically and commercially, as she acknowledged, 'the turning point'. The clothes were strong and pleasing, and, being richly decorative rather than confrontationally didactic, they were readily appreciated by the fashionable mainstream. Many items which came to be popularly associated with her look were introduced in this small, well-edited collection: the corset printed with an Arcadian scene, the skin-tight stretch velvet dress decorated with a gold-foil rococo design (an expensive printing technique funded by her Viennese teaching salary), the platform court shoe called the 'elevated' (later a 'super-elevated' was introduced), huge pearl colliers and drop earrings, and fake furs printed with giant leopard spots. One of her enduring trademarks was distorted scale. She liked to design clothes, accessories and prints that were either exceptionally large or small, and this was a memorable feature of this collection.

'Portrait' was the first of a series of sumptuous collections which Vivienne introduced, with characteristic perversity, during one of the worst recessions since the 1930s. Most contemporary designers were timidly offering 'wearable' casuals, quiet classics or white garments, the last as a reaction to popular criticism that the built-in obsolescence of fashion was morally questionable and ecologically unsound. Vivienne on the other hand presented a series of boldly baroque collections. They were characterised by a richness, formality and attention-seeking drama which flew in the face of much current fashion. Modest, low-key design was anathema to her.

The inspirations for her baroque and rococo grandeur lay in the Wallace Collection at Hertford House in Manchester Square, London. Gary Ness had introduced her to the museum in 1979, and it had a lasting impact on her work. Its art collection was mainly accumulated by the 4th Marquis of Hertford between 1840 and 1870, and enhanced by his illegitimate son Sir Richard Wallace. What distinguishes it is not only that it is one of the finest collections of predominantly French taste and art in Britain, but that it is French art filtered through an English sensibility. The Wallace Collection introduced Vivienne to such eighteenth-century French artists as Boucher, Watteau and Fragonard, whose work often depicted classical trysts and sensuous delights. Just as she responded to advice given in the form of a parable, so she was attracted to paintings which told a story, particularly one of aristocratic hedonism or pagan lechery.

The collection also celebrates the painstakingly fine decorative detail of French *ancien régime* taste, exemplified in the brass and tortoiseshell inlays and intricate marquetry of André-Charles Boulle's furniture and the costume flourishes in Louise Elizabeth Vigée-Lebrun's portraits. Vivienne's decorative sensibilities were refined by her exposure to such works, and she developed a taste for ostentatious ornamentation which ran counter to the functional minimalism that prevailed in fashion and the decorative arts at the beginning of the nineties.

The historian David Cannadine has suggested that 'depression is the begetter of nostalgia, disenchantment the handmaiden of escapism', and perhaps Vivienne was drawn by the consolatory myth of better times, better places and better people suggested in eighteenth-century French art. 'Modernity is a fetish, a myth,' she insisted, convinced that 'the world can't improve, and the idea of perpetual progress is nonsense.' Despite her brash and upbeat exterior, there was a melancholy side to Vivienne. Not only was she frustrated by her own private and professional circumstances, but she was disaffected with the philistinism of her times.

While other designers revived post-war fashions inspired by mods, rockers, hippies and disco, Vivienne was virtually alone in sourcing her ideas from the distant and decorative past. She lifted images from the Wallace Collection to print onto her clothing. Corsets appeared with Boucher shepherds and shepherdesses lolling across the bodice. White Tana lawn blouses (originally shown in 'Time Machine') copied from Greuze's *A Lady* billowed under black velvet jackets inspired by Vigée-Lebrun's *Madame Perregaux*. Details from a Fragonard frieze were combined with the marquetry decorating the back of a Boulle mirror made for the Duchesse du Berry in 1713. Acanthus and vine leaves unfurled in golden foil down a series of skin-tight velvet tube dresses, bathing suits and a licensed range of hosiery and bodies for the high street retailer Sock Shop in 1992. Fake-fur stoles attached to elbow-length fingerless gloves were copied from Ingres' portrait of *Madame de Rivière* in the Louvre.

Indirectly, a broken record-player had prompted Vivienne to create the Boucher corset. While having tea at Gary Ness's flat she had noticed a dust-covered pile of long-playing records lying redundantly by her chair, as she had accidentally broken his record-player some months earlier. The sleeve on top of the pile showed Boucher's shepherdess and her lascivious companion, and Vivienne borrowed the image to use on her prototype. For the wedding dress at the end of the show she asked Gary to colour in the *putti* from Fragonard's *A Swarm of Cherubs*. He was infuriated when she provided him with a box of paints that looked as if they had been messed up by a child and a few paintbrushes worn to scruffy stubs. Although Vivienne intended to celebrate these images from fine art by photographically reproducing them onto clothes, in fact she unwittingly diminished the aura of the originals. They became vulgarised, commercialised and trite.

This was not the first time that Vivienne had printed famous images from art onto her clothing, and although she now declared 'There is no art in the twentieth century,' she had not thought so a decade earlier: for 'Savage' (spring/summer 1982), McLaren had suggested using prints of Matisse's cut-outs, Andy Warhol's *One Hundred Campbells Soup Cans* and Picasso's *Guernica* on her billowing togas. But Vivienne could discard a belief as promptly as she had adopted it, and it was precisely this mercurial side to her nature that made her so suited to the world of fashion, depending as it does on shifting enthusiasms. There were no eternal truths in Vivienne's design world, which is why she could so easily dismiss her previous work and disdained punk revivals.

The decorative theme of 'Portrait' was not only to be the grandeur of old master paintings, expressed in Vivienne's inimitable way by combining 'as many different fabrics as said luxury' – silks, satins, furs, velvets, tweeds, gold, pearls – as she possibly could into one outfit. She also added the photographic prints, 'because the fabrics were not enough to reproduce the luxuries listed in paintings'. She demanded that John Walford, her show producer, find 'a classy, snobby venue', refusing to subject her work to the British Fashion Council's large and impersonal catwalk, which she believed would not enable the audience to appreciate the details of her clothes. Walford came up with the perfect solution – a grand white stucco building on Pall Mall in central London which housed the Institute of Directors. Under crystal chandeliers, a gilded cupola and portraits of the royal family and eminent members of the British establishment, Vivienne staged her 'Portrait' collection.

Along with the 'snobby portraits', the show revisited Vivienne's classical Greek theme. It included a short, tightly-waisted jacket with a huge sheepskin collar, and was designed to look as though the wearer had slung a sheep over her shoulders. A trio of slender, bias-cut powder-blue dresses were Vivienne's favourites in the show, possibly because the pinched detail on the bodice and the bias cut showed off her technique inspired by Madeleine Vionnet, who had mastered bias cutting in the thirties and applied it to Grecian-style gowns. Largely unnoticed by the fashion press amid the splendour, they were prophetic of the fall in hemline that was to come the following year, and were closely interpreted by Galliano four years later. It was not the first or the last time that Galliano found inspiration in her work.

Gilding the glamour, Vivienne and Walford cast statuesque models who wore high platform shoes, to look, Vivienne explained, 'as though they were standing on pedestals and had just stepped out of a painting'. She hoped they would conjure up 'decadent concubines who could end up as duchesses'. The drunken, tarty models of her earlier shows were dropped, as Vivienne wished to communicate an idealised English upper class. Sarah Stockbridge, the Monroe-mimicking blonde, was paired with Susie Bick, a white-skinned, raven-haired Snow White, and apple-pie comeliness was provided by the American socialite-model Denise Lewis. Two Japanese models (one of whom financed her own trip just for the honour of appearing on a Westwood catwalk) were included, to help attract lucrative Asian custom. Vivienne again used older models such as Bertie Hope-Davis and Birgit, a handsome, grey-haired college administrator in her fifties whom she had met in Vienna, and also celebrated Stockbridge's forthcoming motherhood. Overnight, international catwalks were to feature voluptuous pregnant models and 'real people', a ploy taken up by designers in order to appear in sympathy with what the press dubbed the 'caring nineties'.

The corsets and elevated court shoes from 'Portrait' had a marked impact on young women. When Vivienne had initially introduced platforms in her 1985 'Mini Crini' collection the press had scoffed. Many of the under-thirties who came into the shop had only ever worn utilitarian trainers and sports clothes. High-heeled shoes and female fripperies were associated with their mothers' generation. Walking in these high heels, they said, was the first time they had felt like 'real' women. They were forced to move in a different way, and it amused them. Just as the corsets had given them the cleavage of a mature woman for the first time, so the shoes made them totter like starlets.

The press loved 'Portrait', and British *Vogue* featured it extensively. Sales began to increase in the wake of media exposure, and many influential designers visited Worlds End, including Jean-Paul Gaultier and Azzedine Alaïa, attracted by the shop's pantomime atmosphere and Vivienne's newsworthy originality. 'Portrait' also attracted a new type of customer, a more mature and sophisticated woman with considerable disposable income, such as the actress Sian Phillips, Lady Romilly McAlpine and Lady Charles Powell, wife of Mrs Thatcher's advisor. They relished what time and time again was described as the 'sensuality' and 'romance' of Vivienne's clothes. The tide had turned in her affairs.

In June 1990, Vivienne won foreign recognition when she was the first designer to be invited by the powerful Florence-based promoter of Italian fashion and textiles Pitti Immagine to exhibit on their catwalk. This was her first exclusively menswear show, and was entirely financed by Pitti Immagine and made by Marco Rivetti of Gruppo Finanziario Tessile, one of Italy's largest high-fashion manufacturers. Rivetti considered Vivienne 'without doubt the finest example of the *avant-garde* designer', and she hoped that his company would manufacture her line, but it did not happen. Sibilla della Gherardesca, head of public relations at Pitti Immagine, explains why the company chose Vivienne: 'In 1990 Rivetti was laying the groundwork for a profound transformation of Pitti Immagine. He wanted it to "change skin", and to look around the world in search of novelties. He wanted the Pitti shows to become an occasion for breaking from the old ways, for listening to different languages, for displaying international fashions. To achieve this, we had to bring all the designers, the important ones, back to Florence. We had to send a signal of change, but at the same time we had to present something with class, a real talent. We wanted to entertain, to surprise, and to show where fashion ideas are born. And then we wanted to go beyond Italy . . . That is why we invited Vivienne Westwood; she represented it all – and like no one else.'

The collection, shown at the Renaissance Villa Gamberaia, was called 'Cut & Slash', because the denim and knitted garments featured symmetrically arranged slashes which were cut or knitted into the fabrics. This was not a new trick. Not only had Vivienne used it during her punk period and in her 'Savage' collection (spring/summer 1982), but the technique dated from mid-sixteenth-century Germany, where the mercenary soldiers the Landsknecht paraded in magnificent clothes that had been slashed in battle, a style which reportedly prompted maidens to swoon and was consequently imitated in fashionable Renaissance courts.

Following research at the Victoria and Albert Museum and consultation with Avril Hart, curator of historical dress pre-1800, Vivienne copied the 1630s English version of the fashion. To flaunt their wealth, courtiers had pulled the expensive silk of their undergarments through the slashes in a display of contrasted texture and tone. Vivienne would have been amused to juxtapose this Renaissance style with the eighties habit of teenagers slashing their jeans to ape poverty, but frustratingly she was unable to perfect the technique for modern usage: the denim could not be machine-washed as the slashes joined up and the garment shredded. Other designers were to exploit this weakness and improve upon the technique. It is likely that another source of her inspiration for slashing was, once again, Derek Jarman's *Jubilee*, at one point in which the camera pans in closely on the hem of 'Queen Elizabeth's' gown, which is distinctly and crudely slashed in imitation of the Tudor fashion.

The show also evoked *belle époque* dandies such as Georges Duroy, of Guy de Maupassant's novel *Bel Ami*, and Charles Swann of Proust's *À la Recherche du Temps Perdu*, along with the real-life aesthete Robert de Montesquieu, immortalised as des Esseintes in Huysmans' *À Rebours*. From these real and imagined heroes and the characters painted by the fashionable society artist of that time, James Tissot, Vivienne borrowed the image of the well-dressed *boulevardier* in his black jacket and cream trousers, or cream linen jacket and dark trousers, attacking the modern convention of the matching suit. And in her practical way, she reasoned that her customers could buy two suits, one light and one dark, and interchange the jackets.

As she had done for women a few seasons earlier, Vivienne now challenged the wide-shouldered, two-piece suit that had prevailed in eighties menswear. She removed the padding and tightened the silhouette around the pectorals, explaining, 'This bloke bent down to have a look at my bike the other day and the muscles in his back looked brilliant under his suit jacket. I've always been attracted to male chauvinist men.'

The commercial items in 'Cut & Slash' included a range of slashed denim jeans and T-shirts, foppish white linen shirts and buff linen jackets. The catwalk highlight was an exceptionally pretty cerulean blue eighteenth-century-style cutaway frock-coat and hip-length waistcoat printed along the borders with voluptuous tea roses. Along with frock-coats, slashes and cravats, Vivienne revived another anachronism in this show, the codpiece. Bolder spirits loved it, and the glam-rock pop star Gary Glitter wore one with Puckish delight.

The 'Cut & Slash' show was well managed, featured top male models and culminated in a memorable finale – a sword duel and Scottish reel performed by the dancer Michael Clarke and his partner Steven Petronio. Pitti Immagine had offered to pay to fly in celebrities of Vivienne's choice for the show, but her staff were so disorganised – they tried to invite the Princess of Wales, Joan Collins and other Hollywood stars at the last minute – that few were persuaded to make the trip. Even on the plane to Italy, Vivienne was still casting around for a star-studded front row. By chance she was sitting next to an Italian-American architect called Peter Marangoni. Learning that he had a family home in Florence, she assumed he must know Gore Vidal, who had a house at Ravello on the Amalfi coast, and tried to strike a deal. If Marangoni introduced her to her literary hero, he could come to her show. The inelegant proposal came to nothing.

Vivienne was overheard at around this time asking with astonishing bluntness whether an acquaintance had John Paul Getty's address, or could effect an introduction to Miriam Rothschild of the banking family. Similarly, the journalist Lynn Barber was importuned for a list of celebrities' addresses. On being advised that Barber was busy and would return her call later, Vivienne retorted, 'Just fax me a list of the names and addresses. By 11 a.m.' It was 10.30 a.m., but Barber obliged. It was difficult to resist Vivienne's steamrollering.

The adept application of public relations and marketing skills is a prerequisite of success in high fashion, particularly since the 1980s. Top designers either hire the services of a public relations firm, at great expense, or employ an in-house professional. Vivienne, however, unceremoniously terminated her relationship with Jean Bennett and relied on young and inexperienced staff such as Yasmin Eslami, Ben's girlfriend, to take over this vital role. As a result, instead of being able to avail herself of the celebrity and fashion industry connections of an experienced public relations officer, she had to scramble around for them herself. It was a false economy, but an understandable one, bearing in mind her unorthodox, and frequently antagonistic, relationship with the media and her stretched budget.

The largely Italian audience at the Villa Gamberaia did, however, include some celebrities: the soon-to-be-disgraced Italian Foreign Minister Gianni de Michelis, and the actors Matt Dillon and Kim Basinger. The guests enjoyed the sheer theatrical fantasy of 'Cut & Slash', which must have been a welcome contrast to the usual Italian fashion show, epitomised at one extreme by Armani's austere androgyny and at the other by Versace's high-voltage extravaganzas.

The male models were decked out in peacock finery. The only woman in the show was Susie Bick, wearing a vast, floor-length slashed cotton 'circle dress', loosely based on the Greek chiton, which when gathered up with a belt resembled the dress in van Eyck's *The Arnolfini Marriage*. Valerie Mendes of the Victoria and Albert Museum, who acquired one for the collection, says that Vivienne 'knew what slashing can do. She manipulated to create pieces of sculpture that were swirling [once the belt was untied]. The colours were marvellous . . . some of the elements are quite mad, ridiculous, but it is inspired.' The dress was Andreas Kronthaler's first important collaboration with Vivienne. Priced high, at £250, it did not sell.

Gianni de Michelis, though, was so amused by Vivienne's romantic interpretation of menswear that he ordered some of her grey flannel suits to cover his ample girth. In July, in London for the G7 conference of leading industrial nations, he greeted the British Prime Minister John Major by opening his coat, pointing to the label and announcing, 'Your Vivienne Westwood!' De Michelis managed to slip away from affairs of state for lunch at Cecconi's restaurant in Mayfair with the Italian Ambassador to London, Count Giacomo Atolico, and an array of decorative 'assistants'. At one o'clock a pair of official black cars drew up outside the fashionable restaurant. The Foreign Minister and his entourage entered, eventually followed by a tottering Vivienne, who had chained her bicycle to a nearby lamp post. She wore a striped nightdress and ten-inch-high black patent super-elevated shoes. She removed her headscarf and took her seat, unaware that she had left a pink plastic roller in her orange-hennaed hair. When this was discreetly pointed out to her, rather than retiring quietly to the ladies' room, she struggled to untangle it, scattering pins over the table linen.

Unlike de Michelis, Vivienne was not content to discuss fashion. Instead she lectured the Foreign Minister and the Ambassador on the European Community and the follies of democracy. Diners at nearby tables were agog at this unlikely combination of people and their exchanges. During the lunch, de Michelis told a fellow guest: 'Vivienne Westwood . . . could easily be involved in fashion anywhere, so why not Paris? She is the most important fashion artist in the world and has continually influenced the top European designers.' In fact, Paris was exactly where she was heading.

Throughout the summer of 1990, the British entrepreneur Manny Silverman was deliberating between Vivienne and Marc Bohan, formerly at Dior, to take over as Designer-in-Chief at the house of the late royal couturier Sir Norman Hartnell. Hartnell's prestigious premises on Bruton Street in Mayfair could also house Vivienne's own label. Despite the outstanding quality of her portfolio, Silverman decided on Bohan, partly because the influential fashion PR Eleanor Lambert had advised him: 'If you sign Vivienne, you'll get column inches. If you sign Bohan, you'll get sales.' He concluded, 'You can't pay gas bills with column inches.' Nevertheless, lack of orders later forced Hartnell to close down.

Silverman and his partner Roy Dixon, a lawyer, had also been conducting negotiations with Vivienne and her son Joseph to invest in her label. Since she was widely copied, Silverman suggested, 'Who better to rip yourself off than yourself?' In return for investment in a diffusion range, Vivienne and Joseph agreed to allow the partners shares in the company. Silverman found Vivienne and Joe 'honest people to do business with', and was about to sign an agreement when Carlo D'Amario, who was willing only to grant him a licensing arrangement, stepped in and sabotaged the deal. 'Experience tells me,' Silverman says, 'that when Carlo becomes involved, what was possible, even probable, is no longer so.'

Vivienne's next show, 'Cut, Slash & Pull' (spring/summer 1991), was presented at the Institute of Directors in October, and echoed elements of the acclaimed menswear show. Tinkering with the outward symbols of male and female sexuality, she placed codpieces on the women. As she had done in 'Portrait', she dropped the hemline to the lower calf, at a time when the mini-skirt dominated fashion. Extending her old masters theme, she printed Bouchers onto swimsuits and introduced a surreal print of human hair photographed and enlarged virtually beyond recognition. This *trompe l'oeil* was reminiscent of the visual games that the patron of surrealist artists Edward James had commissioned for his Sussex home, West Dean, such as his wife Tilly Losch's bare footprint on the stair carpet.

At the end of the show, Vivienne stepped out onto the catwalk to rapturous applause, looking – but for the beer can in her hand – like a powdered, ringleted royal favourite from a seventeenth-century portrait by Sir Peter Lely. This double image of society aspirant-cum raunchy yeoman epitomised the contradictions in her personality. The press and buyers descended from the balustraded first-floor balcony to the hall below, where the designers Jasper Conran and Anthony Price and the artist Duggie Fields urged them to vote for Vivienne in the forthcoming Designer of the Year ballot. 'Someone has to *do* something,' Conran implored. 'The chances are it won't go to Vivienne – *again.* It's scandalous. She's our greatest designer; she's probably the world's greatest designer, and she hasn't even been recognised in her own country. The rest of the world is laughing at us because of it. What's the matter with the British? Do they *hate* genius?' But Bernadine Morris of the *New York Times* summed up the older generation's reaction to the collection: 'Well . . . interesting; but we're not as far out as you.'

Votes would be cast by an invited group of journalists, public relations officers and members of the fashion trade. Vivienne's colleagues and competitors – with the exception of a handful of designers and journalists like Sally Brampton and Brenda Polan – were reluctant to salute her achievements. This was partly because of her offensive former role as the queen of punk, but it was also due to incomprehension. Her peers could not understand her uncommercial, and at times unwearable and even ugly, clothes. Furthermore, the fact that she was self-taught rendered her, in some eyes, an amateur. This, together with her opinionated rantings and occasional downright rudeness, conspired to alienate her from others in the industry.

Vivienne had enjoyed a persistently abrasive relationship with the press. Mass-circulation papers such as the powerful *Mail on Sunday* ridiculed her as 'the bag lady', while Lynn Barber of the *Independent on Sunday* had accurately exposed her hubris and peculiar behaviour. Vivienne unabashedly stated in her interview with Barber that she was mystified that she had never received the Designer of the Year award: 'I honestly don't know why they do not hold me in the esteem that they *should* hold me.' Another journalist was told: 'My driving force is that I am unorthodox. My character is defined by that. I think it is a sign of great intelligence.' Such confident assertions were scorned in a country that preferred the famous to be – or at least affect to be – modest and self-deprecating.

Over recent years, however, a critical mass of younger journalists, who had grown up during the punk era and who appreciated Vivienne and McLaren's impact on popular culture, had reached positions of influence within the media, and at the annual televised gala in October 1990, hosted by her patron Jeff Banks, Vivienne received the award. Later she acknowledged John Fairchild's vital role in this overdue recognition: 'Mr Fairchild has been very important in constantly making it known to people in the fashion business what I originated. He sort of campaigned for me.' It was a tardy acknowledgement of her contribution to British fashion, made all the more insulting by the fact that some mediocre dressmakers who catered for the Sloane Ranger and court circles in Britain had received the award before her.

Gene Krell sympathised with Vivienne's bitterness: 'The British treated her unfairly. People knew she should have been Designer of the Year, and so she became representational of the hypocrisies of their culture. She was an *agent provocateur*. The British didn't quite understand the change she was trying to introduce. She was an anarchist with a certain sort of morality attached to it. She single-handedly created the British fashion industry where it hadn't existed since Carnaby Street. People came to London specifically to see Vivienne Westwood, otherwise they went straight to Paris. But she never received the accolades she deserved, and it affected her in the end, she was hurt by it. Paul Smith said that his award rightfully belonged to Vivienne and he refused to accept it. That was great.' (In fact Smith did not turn down his 1989 Designer of the Year award for that reason, but because he did not respect the prize or the process of selection.)

A welter of profiles appeared in the British press, and the hitherto sneering fourth estate immediately began to congratulate Vivienne, parroting the view that her recognition was long overdue, and that perhaps she was a 'genius' after all. But having waited so long for recognition from her peers, she felt no loyalty to them or her country, and publicly and privately upbraided them for their 'philistinism'. It was understandable, if unfortunate, that the more conservative and powerful elements in the British industry still viewed her with suspicion. Punk had been a calculated attack on their monarch and on the very idea of high fashion. It was equally understandable that people in the fashion trade abroad could applaud Vivienne: their national figureheads had not been lampooned. And so, spurred on by D'Amario and Gary Ness's correct assessment that both her acclaim and her sales would increase if she showed in Paris, she decided to abandon the London shows. Many of her compatriots criticised her, for a second time, for abandoning her homeland. But just as the international jewellery market was based in Geneva, financial services and old master paintings in London, and modern art in New York, so the fashion market was indisputably centred in Paris. If a designer could compete on the French catwalk, it was likely that he could sell his clothes internationally.

Meanwhile, Vivienne refurbished her second shop in London, which had opened in the autumn of 1988. Named simply 'Vivienne Westwood', its location, on Davies Street in the heart of affluent Mayfair, its surreal baroque decoration and its stock of handsome and wearable tweed and velvet suits were a definite statement of intent: she had moved up-market. She developed the instantly recognisable motif of human hair that she had used as a print in 'Cut, Slash & Pull', having it printed on the curtains and linoleum of her new 'couture' shop. The architect David Connors, who had contributed to the interior of Seditionaries, collaborated with her, and she invested a great deal of time in refining this flagship retail outlet which opened, after considerable delay, in December 1990. It was a striking and amusing showpiece to which, like Worlds End, many fans and some tourists came to marvel.

Vivienne's standing abroad was underscored in January 1991 when Hanae Mori's Fashion Foundation invited her for the second time to attend their Fashion Summit (previously known as the 'Best Five') and show 'Cut & Slash' in Tokyo. The Fashion Foundation had been established in the mid-eighties by the wealthy Mori and her son Akira as an annual showcase for the best fashion in the world. Once again, John Fairchild was working behind the scenes: he had recommended Vivienne to Mrs Mori. That year's other guests were France's Christian Lacroix, America's Isaac Mizrahi and Italy's Franco Moschino.

Hanae Mori possessed 'clout'. She was the first foreigner to be invited to join the CSHC, and was an early manufacturer of Western-style fashion in Japan. Mori provided first-class air tickets and hotel accommodation for each designer and one companion, but Vivienne insisted that both D'Amario and Usha Pohl, her German assistant, accompany her.

At Heathrow, Vivienne entered the first-class cabin wearing striped pyjamas, super-elevated shoes and a huge leopardskin-print coat. On take-off, she yanked a bottle of whisky from her luggage and offered it around to her astonished fellow passengers, many of whom hid behind their newspapers. From her first day in Japan, she behaved like an ill-mannered oaf, constantly complaining to her hosts and causing 'to-dos'. She demanded her own models, rather than those allocated to her, suspiciously comparing hers with those allotted to Lacroix. And despite the lavish hospitality, she demanded pocket money and free cigarettes, while complaining that she had received better treatment in New York.

In Japan, Vivienne was as famous as a pop star. Pursued by the media and propelled into what she called 'interview overdrive', she took the opportunity to climb onto her soapbox. No matter what question was asked, she lectured interviewers and television audiences, warning: 'We don't talk about the most important pollution of our times – not of the earth but pollution of our brain!' There followed an incomprehensible monologue of 'Gary-speak', delivered at breakneck speed while an interpreter scampered behind. During one interview she was asked, 'What is fashion?' A combination of exhaustion and boredom led her to answer with the first thought that came into her head: 'Fashion is about eventually being naked.' Though the Japanese were flummoxed, it was a succinct and inspired reply.

Vivienne appreciated her Japanese fans – they did not 'snigger' at her designs. 'I would like to thank Confucius, who influenced the Chinese and through them the Japanese, for his introduction of the cult of decorous behaviour. They are so polite, the Japanese. Whereas I've just come back from Italy and all the time, just because I've got these [Rocking Horse] boots on, people kept laughing and pointing. It's even worse in France, and of course in philistine Britain it's just dreadful.' Asked why she persisted in her crusade to wear the boots, she explained that she looked so good she was prepared to put up with the insults.

The highlight of the Tokyo visit was a dinner hosted by the Moris at their apartment. For a business associate to be invited to the home of a Japanese person is both a rarity and a great honour. The Moris indicated that they did not want D'Amario to attend and, as insurance, Victoria Fernandez, a founder member and public relations officer of the Foundation, was asked to escort Vivienne *alone*. However, when Vivienne entered the Mori apartment she noticed that the other designers had brought their colleagues. Beckoning Fernandez into the lavatory, she shouted and screamed her protest, indifferent to the scene she was creating. The next day, relations between Vivienne and her manager were visibly strained.

The final embarrassment occurred on the last day. Unable, or unwilling, to entertain her Japanese business associates and licensees at her own expense, Vivienne attempted to have them invited to the Moris' informal farewell dinner for their guests. When this request was denied, in a fit of pique she threatened not to attend. One fellow guest reported, 'Her behaviour was appalling. She has no sense of decorum and politeness.'

Despite her behaviour in Japan, it was during this visit that Vivienne struck up a friendship with the couturier Christian Lacroix. Expecting to meet 'an outrageous goddess', he recalled how he was 'both excited and frightened, because since my very beginning in fashion I not only admired her but I felt she had helped me in a way [as an inspiration].' He was struck by Vivienne's steely core, 'with this very tough way of following her mind'. Even if the Japanese audience was 'drowned with her ideas', he observed, she carried on proselytising. When he later discovered that her heart was set on creating couture in Paris, he recommended her to Patou, for whom he had designed his first couture collections. The board had by that time decided to drop the couture range, but it was yet another example of Vivienne's ability to rally support.

Vivienne would openly solicit help from any quarter. Valerie Mendes at the Victoria and Albert Museum would receive at least two calls a year requesting access to the archives. 'She's very directed,' Mendes recalled with characteristic diplomacy. 'She knows exactly what she wants to see . . . she's seen the eighteenth-century baroque and rococo silks with the heavy floral foliage repeats [copied for "Cut & Slash" and later printed on denim for the "Grand Hotel" collection] . . . and architectonic images. Actually the eighteenth century is what she's keen on, and of course the slashed costumes.'

Bunty King, the crisp and worldly publicity officer of the Wallace Collection, was bombarded with requests from Vivienne. She observed that while Vivienne zealously protested outside museums and on air that art and culture should be funded by patrons, she never paid a penny to the Wallace trustees for 'borrowing' their imagery. Nor did she even seek their permission. King complained in 1995, by which time Vivienne was making handsome profits from clothes decorated with Wallace imagery: 'So far we have had no money out of her at all. She has used the collection totally shamelessly and we have nothing. She has said it's her inspiration, but we've had no written publicity out of this . . . The one time we dug our heels in and said, "Right! No money – no publicity," she went and filmed at the Victoria and Albert Museum!' King was left in no doubt about Vivienne's ruthlessness. 'She cultivates this very charming manner, and you can see her looking through you, or sideways, and you know you're getting nowhere at all and she's not intending you to. She has obviously decided what *she* is going to do, and will not give an inch.'

King herself did not give an inch when a Swiss television station requested permission in 1994 to film a documentary about the inspiration Vivienne had drawn from the gallery. She agreed, provided a list of every member of the team was sent to her beforehand. At the last moment, three new names were added. One of them was Jeanette Charles, well known for her impersonations of the Queen.

King rushed to the front door just in time to see a large black Daimler drawing up outside. In the back sat a middle-aged woman dressed in a tweed crown, elbow-length white gloves and a fur. Digging in her heels, King cast the whole crew out, declaring that she would not have her Queen and country parodied in this hallowed building. The guards cheered as the pranksters fled.

The incident amused Vivienne, who loved mischief-making and 'to-dos'. She always thrived on the adrenaline rush of meeting a deadline at the last moment or causing a scene, and if she was asked to appear in front of an audience she would do her utmost to cause trouble. When, as chairman of the panel which decided the Designer of the Year, Vivienne announced the winner to a nationwide television audience, she declared that she disagreed with her fellow judges' decision. Similarly, when the nightclub hostess Gerlinde Kostiff asked her to be one of the judges for a dressing-up competition at her club Kinky Gerlinky, Vivienne orchestrated another 'to-do'. After the contestants had paraded before the audience, Vivienne held the stage and deliberated: 'Well, I quite like number thirty-seven, and I've written down number nineteen.' 'Pick one!' urged the compère. 'Well, I'd quite like to see them all again.' So they paraded once more, and Vivienne held the proceedings up for over half an hour, partly to annoy the crowd and partly to assert her authority. For the sake of peace, the organisers decided that the prize, a bottle of champagne, should be shared.

Vivienne could be ruthless and cavalier. When the Japanese cosmetics firm Shiseido saluted the milliner Stephen Jones with a retrospective and invited all the designers with whom he had collaborated to write a tribute for the catalogue, Vivienne wrote:

> When a lady wears a Stephen Jones hat she is an elegant lady wearing a hat. She would be greeted by, 'How lovely you are,' rather than, 'I like your hat.'

(Vivienne always referred to 'ladies', never the more politically correct 'women'.) Unsurprisingly, Jones was offended. But having worked on commissions for her over the years, he felt she consistently managed to 'pull out of you your best, because she demands it. She comes to you like an innocent child, and you feel you have to take care of her. But on the other hand you're aware that she has complete judgement and control.' By the early nineties Vivienne no longer collaborated with Jones, preferring to employ an in-house milliner called Prudence (despite several requests, her surname was never released by the company).

Not only did Vivienne disregard people's feelings, she also exploited their time and effort, taking the attitude that they were lucky to be working with her. Simon Smith, a young jewellery designer who had helped make the prototypes for the 'Harris Tweed' collection, was commissioned to make orchid brooches out of resin for the 'Grand Hotel' collection (spring/summer 1993). Vivienne accepted his prototype but, despite the considerable craftsmanship and expense he had invested, churlishly criticised the final versions and refused to reimburse him. Out of pocket by several hundred pounds, Smith sued Vivienne. She quietly settled out of court.

Gradually, Vivienne was acquiring the reputation of a pantomime dame for her unintentionally comic declarations on culture and society and for her outrageous clothes. Incapable of laughing at herself, she became an irresistible target for parody. How wise her 1981 statement now seemed: 'One of the reasons why I am not sure about giving interviews is that I don't want to put people off and make out there's some big heavy number about getting these clothes. They're colourful and they're exciting; I really would prefer the clothes to speak for themselves.' Unfortunately, she no longer heeded her own advice.

In 1990, appearances on ITV's *South Bank Show*, BBC Radio 4's *Opinions* and BBC television's *The Look* and *Newsnight* drew the British public's attention to her malapropisms, clumsy interview manner and unorthodox appearance. As if trying to remember her lines, she would curl up uncomfortably, close her eyes, thrash her arms about and struggle to communicate her message to the camera. Ignorant of whether a broadcast was live or recorded, she would halt halfway through a speech to ask, 'No, wait, can we start again?' When asked a question on Sky television by Selina Scott, she anxiously enquired, 'Shall I answer that now? Have we got time before the adverts?'

On the BBC's current affairs programme *Newsnight*, the usually acerbic interviewer Jeremy Paxman struggled gallantly to coax answers out of her, but she remained tongue-tied, her head cupped in her hands. She seemed confused by the topic – whether it was justifiable to spend £20,000 on a couture dress – and finally asked whether they could begin the interview again. It was live. Those in the studio speculated over whether she was nervous, drunk or on drugs. She was in fact merely exhausted and overwhelmed. A few days later, Derek Dunbar was searching round his neighbourhood for a lost cat and rang on a doorbell. By astonishing coincidence, it was Paxman's home. When Paxman discovered he was talking to an employee of Vivienne's, he asked, 'What was she on?' Dunbar's frank reply was, 'Nothing. Absolutely nothing, I'm afraid.'

Coming late to education, Vivienne recognised her weaknesses, admitting in public: 'my vocabulary is very bad, and I'll tell you why: I wasn't brought up in a family that used a lot of big words, and they're not terribly natural for me to use.' Such frankness helped endear her to the public, who loved mavericks, and she joined the ranks of British 'characters' such as the astrologer Patrick Moore and the romantic novelist Dame Barbara Cartland. People who had nothing to do with fashion began to recognise her in the street. While organising a photographic shoot, for example, in Chalk Farm, North London, Vivienne went into a shabby local pub frequented by the elderly and down-at-heel. The clientele queued for her autograph. At the Athenaeum, a sober London gentleman's club, a crowd of septuagenarian and octogenarian members – judges, archbishops, senior civil servants – were to be found huddled around the television engrossed in a Vivienne Westwood fashion show.

The press now queued to interview her, competing to capture her inimitable mannerisms and opinions. She still hated journalists, whom she typically held in contempt for spouting received opinions or dismissing her as 'wacky' (a word she loathed), and made a point of being difficult with them and late for appointments. Her public relations assistant, Karl Plewka, would point out to any journalist applying for an interview that his boss was 'quite an intellectual person, and she's using the interview really as a standpoint for what she wants to communicate ... it is her concern that she might be misrepresented in these ideas that mean so much to her, and I can understand really, because she doesn't talk on the same level as many people do, and so it's not always that easy to grasp immediately what she's saying maybe.' The media had a field day conveying this inarticulate portentousness.

To test the mettle of interviewers, she would turn the tables by asking them a question: 'So what can you tell me that's interesting?' 'Interesting about anything in particular?' replied one journalist.

'About ideas,' said Vivienne, 'that kinda thing . . .' If she believed a journalist was 'intelligent and educated' she would invite them to dine with her, typically at Khan's Indian restaurant near Gary Ness's West London flat, where she would ply them with red wine and tell them how clever she was. Once in her stride and fuelled by alcohol, she would tremble with the excitement of having so much to say and so many campaigns to wage. She regarded herself as a crusader, albeit an ill-equipped one, to whom the task had fallen to tell the truth: 'A lot of the time I don't know what I'm saying, but since no one else is saying them I feel I've got to. It's not politics, it's culture I'm interested in.'

In March 1990, Vivienne, heralded as 'Britain's most influential fashion designer . . . whose work baffles and outrages the general public,' was the subject of a documentary by ITV's prestigious *South Bank Show*. Although this was a significant milestone in her career – it was the first time the programme had featured a designer – Vivienne's foibles were much in evidence. While Sarah Stockbridge stood in front of an architectural folly modelling a Grecian-inspired outfit, the viewers were treated to Vivienne's thoughts on the ancients. But how could they fail to notice that the 'Greek Temple' was covered in scaffolding?

Gary Ness usually coached Vivienne before her media appearances, and it was patently clear when he had not. One of her best performances was recorded that September on the BBC Radio 4 programme *Opinions*, devised as a platform for people with views that questioned the status quo. Vivienne was an ideal subject. Initially, she wanted to criticise the shoddy manner in which, she believed, fashion was taught in British art schools, especially the prestigious Central St Martin's College of Art, whose alumni included John Galliano and later Alexander McQueen – 'I think St Martin's is dreadful,' she later declared. 'It should be nuked.' But with rare tact, realising that it would be better not to attack her own industry, she decided instead to tackle the issue of the rationalisation then taking place in British museums. 'The sacking of scientists is the equivalent of cutting down trees in the New Forest,' she exclaimed.

The producer Anna Robinson, who spent several days working with her on the programme, found Vivienne 'terribly intelligent – more intelligent than Gary – but clearly not educated. But she's not what you call logical.' When Robinson asked whether Lynn Barber's

Independent on Sunday profile, which 'made her out to be grasping and grabbing', had upset her, Vivienne seemed surprised, which led Robinson to conclude that she 'must have a hide like an antelope'. She was 'not a person who is interested in communicating . . . It does not enter her consideration whether she gets the message across. She is one of those intensely self-involved people who others think are crazy because they cannot modify their message to what other people expect . . . She's totally self-involved in her own creative project, and communication is a dirty word.' This solipsistic inwardness hampered not only Vivienne's ability to promote her collections, but also her personal relationships with lovers, family and staff.

Gary helped Vivienne write her script for *Opinions*. She opened the programme with the statement:

My ideas do not come from thin air, they come from
intellectual curiosity, from digging into the past, from
comparing one thing with another, and so you get
perspective and insight. And then you start putting
things together in a way that nobody ever did before,
even though the elements were there all the time.
This is the creative process and it comes from tradition
and technique. I want to talk to you about those bastions
of tradition – our museums, with their great
collections which are our heritage.

She went on to criticise Prime Minister Margaret Thatcher's market-driven, value-for-money overhaul of the civil service, which had led over the past two years to eight experts being made redundant from the Victoria and Albert Museum and sixty scientists from the Natural History Museum. 'When I heard this,' she declared, 'I put on my flesh-coloured tights, decorated with a green, mirrored fig leaf – Greek, you see, to make the point about civilisation – and I went to give my support to the scientists, who for the first time in history had come out on strike and were picketing the Natural History Museum.' Once again, as she had with punk, Vivienne utilised dress as a means of protest, though to most passers-by her outfit was such an oblique reference to 'culture' that it went over their heads. Unlike many British people involved in the arts, Vivienne professed an interest in the world of science and, if not bestriding the 'two cultures', she was at least alive to the value of both.

In disgust, Vivienne claimed, with some justification, that museums were little more than crowd-pleasers now: 'Disneyland taking over'. She debated on air with such illustrious names as Lord Morris, Chairman of the Museums and Galleries Commission; Sir David Attenborough, a trustee of the British Museum; Dr Peter Greenwood, Deputy Chief Scientific Officer of the Natural History Museum; and John Mallett, Keeper of Ceramics at the Victoria and Albert Museum. What impressed Anna Robinson most was her ability to 'draw out the consequences of an argument [with the interviewees]. If I had been doing it with another journalist they would never have gone so far. She drove me absolutely nuts . . . because she wouldn't accept the obvious . . . she just made the arguments more complicated than they needed to be, but I think it was justified in the end.' The broadcast was uncompromisingly opinionated, and some experts found Vivienne irrational and overbearing, but for her it was an opportunity to be in the company that she craved: the scholarly, the powerful and the 'posh'.

Just as Vivienne's return to the London catwalk in 1986 had been facilitated by the generous assistance of Jeff Banks, Jean Bennett, Keith Wainwright and John Walford, so her return to Paris was to be made possible by the designer Azzedine Alaïa. He invited her, free of charge, to show her autumn/winter collection, entitled 'Dressing Up', in March 1991 at his central Paris showroom. A London preview was shown at the Tall Orders restaurant in Soho. As so often, Vivienne's impetuous creativity resulted in last-minute changes. For example, just as a model was stepping out onto the London catwalk in a massive black tulle ballgown, Vivienne stopped her and said, 'I think we should rip and tear this'; the dress seemed too perfect and too predictable in her eyes.

Vivienne was on such a tight budget that she could not afford hotel bills, and so she travelled to Paris on the eve of the show, allowing no time for a rehearsal. Having freely consumed whisky on the journey, she arrived at Alaïa's studio too inebriated to greet him. Alaïa just left her asleep, slumped over a table. Realising that the budget for the show was minuscule, John Walford persuaded the floor supplier that, owing to a small unevenness of the boards, they should get a rebate. The show caused a stir in Paris, and many top designers, including Gaultier and Lacroix, attended.

Vivienne's Winterhalter-inspired black lace and white tulle ballgown. This image, published in the *New York Times Magazine* on 13 March 1994, led Barbra Streisand to order several made-to-measure Westwood outfits, with disastrous results.

Above: Linde Evangelista in the tartan silks, mohairs and tweeds mixed with Argyll knits from 'Anglomania', autumn/winter 1993-94.

Left: Evangelista models a grey flannel suit from 'On Liberty', autumn/winter 1994-95, featuring the bustle.

Right: Georgina Godley's bustle from her 'Lump & Bump' collection (spring/summer 1986) predated Vivienne's.

Above: Simonetta Gianfelici models the Brintons carpet crown, corset and 'criniscule', with Rocking Horse shoes.

Inset: Andreas, Vivienne and David Bailey working on the shoot for the Brintons Carpets advertising campaign, September

Andreas in the second Brintons campaign, January 1995. He and Vivienne designed *ancien régime* costumes to celebrate the

Above: Vivienne with her consistent champion, and one of fashion's most original stylists, Anna Piaggi of Italian *Vogue*, backstage at 'Vive la Coquotte', Paris, March 1995.

Above: Gore Vidal wants to talk fashion, Vivienne wants to talk literature. German *Vogue* dubbed it 'Snob Talk' at the Plaza Hotel in New York, summer 1994. Vivienne wears a gingham artist's smock and matching Brigitte Bardot headscarf from 'Salon', spring/summer 1992.

Above left: Fifty-three-year-old Jibby Beane, the Conduit Street shop assistant, overshadowed Vivienne with her star quality. Her Rocking Horse shoes rest on the hair-print linoleum of the Davies Street boutique.

Left: Vivienne and staff modelling corsets and promoting Gitanes, 1994.

Vivienne advocated a return to the male
peacock, but in Andreas's hands some felt
it became camp excess. 'MAN' collection,
spring/summer 1997.

Naomi Campbell falls off her ten-inch-
heeled, super-elevated lace-ups at the
author's feet in Paris, wearing
'Anglomania' tartan, autumn/winter
1993-94. The shoes are now a popular
exhibit in the Victoria and Albert
Museum, and have been used for British
Safety Council posters urging workers:
'For *Your* Job Wear Safety Shoes'.

Once again, inspiration for Karl Lagerfeld:
Vivienne's frayed wool suit from 'Vive la
Bagatelle', spring/summer 1997.

Keen to see an Yves Saint Laurent show, Vivienne instructed Yasmin to contact his press office at the eleventh hour for a ticket. Vivienne clearly did not understand French fashion protocol. A few hours later a courier was sent from Saint Laurent with a letter explaining that the front row of his show had already been allocated and, since a designer of Vivienne's status could not sit anywhere else, he, with regret, had to decline her request. She read this as a brush-off, but an enormous bouquet followed from Saint Laurent, and in each subsequent season she was given a front-row seat, on which she would occasionally sob in awe at the French couturier's skills. According to Pierre Bergé, Saint Laurent greatly respected Vivienne, believing: 'She is completely honest. It is not a question of bluff. And she works – really works.' Flowers also arrived from Lagerfeld and other leading designers. At last, Vivienne felt respected by her peers.

As its name implied, the new collection advocated dressing *up*, not down. It was a critique of the casual culture. The invitation, illustrated by Vivienne, depicted her favourite models, Susie Bick and Sarah Stockbridge, leaning over a dressing-up box selecting costumes. The show was a mix of historical and primitive styles, largely comprised of highlights from her previous shows which had not been seen in Paris. It included red 'Love' jackets, with black velvet revers which closed to form a heart shape, black velvet suits, fishnet and shark's tooth-print leggings, corduroy shooting skirts trimmed with a leather codpiece and a leather footprint patch on the bottom, the circle dress, 'Cut & Slash' black leather, the Boulle print (this time the gold foil was crushed to look like cracked old gold), 'Dangerous Liaisons' jackets (named after Choderlos de Laclos's recently filmed eighteenth-century epistolary novel, *Les Liaisons Dangereuses*) and traditional rubberised riding mackintoshes printed with Fragonard's *putti*. (Walking down Madison Avenue in one of these, Romilly McAlpine was stopped by more than half a dozen people who wanted to know where they could buy it.)

Another memorable piece from the collection was a high-necked, rib-tight, crocheted angora jumper with a built-in corset which was slashed across the poitrine to reveal the hemispheres of the breasts. The demurely Edwardian high neck stood in prim contrast to the peek-a-boo naughtiness of the slash, and the combination suggested a knowingness that was sexual dynamite.

'Dressing Up' was a critical triumph, and the French fashion establishment now took Vivienne to its heart. Afterwards she was asked by Jeff Banks, recording BBC television's *The Clothes Show*, how she had managed to get to Paris. She took the question literally, answering, 'Oh, we came in the van.'

The Westwood team now made twice-yearly trips to Paris in a hired electric-blue van bearing the legend 'Hedley's Humpers, Clapham'. It was usually driven by an old friend, Robert Pinnock, a tree surgeon and part-time handyman, and would be packed with the last-minute additions to the collection, together with Vivienne, colleagues such as D'Amario and Yasmin Eslami, Bertie Hope-Davis, Joe, Ben and Dora, and Dora's best friend, Madge. Enlivened by duty-free liquor and bouncing around like peas in a tin can – there were no seats in the back – the party bantered and caroused its way to Paris. Dora and Madge chatted up the boys, D'Amario sidled up to the girls, and Bertie Hope-Davis, in his urbane drawl, warned the horrified pair of elderly women that all they could expect to eat in France was horse meat.

During the visit to Paris in May 1991 for her interview with Daniel Piette of Dior, Vivienne also met Didier Ludot, the owner of a small boutique in the Jardin du Palais Royal which dealt in old couture. She spent a long time in the shop studying a black silk faille New Look suit by Manguin. The reason for her close scrutiny of the narrow-shouldered cut, the way the material was held in gentle pleats above the bust and the padded peplum which fanned out from beneath a handspan waist became apparent the following season, when a close interpretation of it was introduced in her 'Salon' collection (spring/summer 1992). It was initially called the 'Fifties' jacket, then renamed the 'Bettina' jacket by Andreas, after one of Dior's favourite models, Bettina Graziani. Vivienne had set her sights on the house of Dior, and was now inspired to reinterpret the founder's post-war designs.

Who could predict what would inspire her? 'Salon', shown in Alaïa's showroom, included printed denim separates which illustrated the show's title by being printed with a photograph, lifted from an interior design magazine, of a grand, gilded Victorian salon. Other denims featured the super-enlarged photographs of human hair or marshmallow-coloured *putti*. Vivienne explained, 'I'm trying to put a bit of culture into denim . . . because men with a taste for civilisation are the only ones we ladies want to court us.' At a fairground she and

Andreas had spotted a stallholder who, due to the hot weather, had cut his jeans at the knee, allowing the lower half of the trouser legs to slip down to his ankles. Vivienne thought this ingeniously practical, and showed jeans sliced across the knees and fastened back up with suspenders, like fisherman's waders. The sexual ambiguity of men wearing suspenders appealed to her.

The denims of 'Salon' were a perfect example of Vivienne's inability to commercialise a good idea. D'Amario insisted that they be manufactured in Italy, but the result was shoddy and expensive, retailing at £120 a pair. 'We lost the market,' Simon Barker said, 'because if you expected a young person to spend that money they should last for years. But they had bad flies, the pattern faded and they shrank. If you want them to keep their colour you have to have them dry-cleaned. That's ridiculous for that money.' Similarly, Vivienne dropped John Smedley at D'Amario's instigation and had her knitwear manufactured in Italy by Modello Tricot and Guyson, even though she loved to promote British manufacturers, and 'people really trusted the John Smedley quality'.

Just as she had earlier been captivated by the 'Care Bear', Vivienne was to put another soft toy to idiosyncratic use in 'Salon'. A young fan had left a gift for her at the Worlds End shop. Two matching rabbits had been drawn in felt tip on an old sheet, cut out, sewn together and stuffed with cotton wool. Vivienne was charmed, and had the rabbit copied exactly. The models were instructed to hug it as they walked down the catwalk.

The finale of 'Salon' featured the spectacular twinning of Susie Bick in the black floor-length tulle ballgown, and Sarah Stockbridge in a dusty white version. They both clutched red roses, and Stockbridge wore a gold chastity belt forged by Andreas's father, a blacksmith in the Tyrolean village of Fugen. Vivienne was memorably photographed by Lord Snowdon for British *Vogue* wearing the white version of the dress. Snowdon's lens penetrated beyond her upbeat brashness, poignantly capturing her pathos. It was a tender and subdued portrait, unlike most images of her.

Following 'Salon', Vivienne won the British Designer of the Year award for the second year running in October 1991. Yet there was still some prejudice against her in Britain, as was made clear when John Davis, Executive Director of the award's sponsor Lloyds Bank, opened the envelope containing the winner's name. In front of a large television audience, he announced, 'And the winner is ... Oh dear! Vivienne Westwood.'

Accompanied by the supermodel Linda Evangelista, Vivienne stepped up onto the stage wearing her Boulle dress and a huge coral necklace lent to her by Romilly McAlpine. She accepted the trophy with words from an Elvis Presley song: 'Don't ever kiss me once, kiss me twice, treat me nice.' Andreas may have been a Madonna fan, but Vivienne's fifties rock 'n' roll affections could not be shaken off.

A similarly insulting incident had occurred a few months earlier, when on 10 July she was made an Honorary Senior Fellow of the Royal College of Art. When Karl Lagerfeld arrived at the celebratory dinner, he received a standing ovation. No one stood for Vivienne. 'A few people did say I should mind,' she commented later, but she decided to brush it off as another example of the British lack of respect for their own designers.

Early in 1992 Vivienne was introduced to John Rowley, a fast-talking Liverpudlian who had worked in marketing for fourteen years with Colgate Pamolive, Playtex and the hosiery company Pretty Polly. Rowley, a burly, slickly-coiffed and -dressed salesman, came to Joseph Corré to propose a deal with the successful high street lingerie and hosiery retailer Sock Shop. He suggested that Vivienne should exploit her position as Designer of the Year and 'network herself into the high street' by designing a licensed range for them. At the time the entire Westwood business had a turnover of only £600,000 a year, supported by her two London shops and a few meagre wholesale customers in Japan, America and on the Continent.

The deal went through, and Vivienne printed the Boulle mirror design onto a range of see-through black bodies and leggings. She invited Rowley to become more involved in her business, to restructure it and to coach Joseph in marketing skills. 'Vivienne was very clever,' says Rowley. 'She saw me as a person who could hold Joseph's hand and act as a catalyst and take him through the ropes. He was the managing director.' Rowley agreed to take the job part-time, so that he could continue his other business interests.

A close friendship developed between Rowley and Joseph, the older man becoming something of a father figure to Vivienne's son. They shared a house in Pimlico, and Rowley came to admire Joseph for his willingness to work and his business acumen. But he also felt sorry for him: 'Joe never called her "Mum", always "Vivienne". It was strange, and they were so untactile. He never hugged his mother.'

It soon became clear to Rowley that the company was virtually on its knees – 'We didn't have a pot to piss in' – and that more licensing contracts were essential. Within months he had secured a deal with the Swiss fun watch company Swatch. They issued a limited edition (ten thousand) 'Orb' watch in July 1992, followed by a 'Putti' watch the following summer. (One young man repeatedly caught stealing from Vivienne's shop was summoned to her presence, lectured on 'the evils of the police state' and given an 'Orb' Swatch.) Vivienne's royalty was a mere 7.5 per cent, and she failed to capitalise on the introduction by offering a cheaper mass-market 'Westwood' Swatch.

Vivienne had outgrown the studio at Greenland Street, and Rowley's next move was to find new premises for the firm. They settled on a complex of old school buildings in Battersea, near her home. The company also changed its name from Casnell Ltd to 'Vivienne Westwood' reflecting the fact that Vivienne's status as a bankrupt had elapsed, and she was now able to act as a director of the company. 'It was a cosmetic change,' says Rowley. 'When we moved from Camden to Battersea we felt the company needed to have the Vivienne Westwood hallmark, especially as we were trying to attract potential sponsors and were dealing with foreign companies.' The new base, however, proved impractical. The staff were split up between various poky buildings, and had to brave the English weather when they crossed the schoolyard to see one another.

One of the most striking aspects of Vivienne's working practices, according to Rowley, was 'the loyalty she seemed to command. Ninety-eight per cent of the time she was able to get the best out of people because they were in awe of her, even intimidated by her, as if they were waiting for her to explode.' Most of the staff were young, foreign or, as Rowley dubbed them, 'lame dogs'. In this environment Vivienne, unchallenged and basking in the admiration of sycophants, could dominate, and be what she wanted to be.

Aware that Vivienne had failed to exploit the lucrative denim market, Rowley and Joseph came up with a business plan to develop three Westwood labels: the demi-couture Gold Label; the cheaper, ready-to-wear Red Label; and a new Blue Label for denim. This pragmatic solution allowed for the development of a 'cash cow', the Red Label, to subsidise the more exclusive, extreme and pure vision of Vivienne's designs, the Gold Label.

According to one colleague, it was Alberto Biani of Staff International who had the idea of creating the Red Label and of distinguishing between Vivienne's two lines. Biani 'thought that Vivienne's aesthetic was so extraordinary and was a thing you could not maintain every season and did not have to change every season. Instead he wanted to take her classics [such as the tartan suit or the Bettina jacket].' In addition, he would take lines that the Gold Label had featured a season before, simplify them, manufacture them in a less complicated cut and with cheaper fabrics, and incorporate them into the Red Label.

Derek Dunbar found an empty building in Mayfair's Conduit Street, facing the back entrance of Sotheby's, and opened it as a sales shop to offload the huge amounts of stock, going back to 'Time Machine', that the company had accumulated. The lease was later extended, and the shop began to sell Vivienne's menswear as well as sale items.

Since 'Harris Tweed', Vivienne had concentrated on the English craft of tailoring: 'It is such tiny, tiny adjustments that you make. You can make something look like Napoleon or a Danish fisherman, just by changing slightly the proportion of a double-breasted jacket, you know, and I recently did take the shoulderpads out of men's jackets. I have had to put them back because I couldn't sell them, but I myself love a man without all this padding on the shoulder . . . I had customers in my shop saying, "My neck is too long, and I can't wear this jacket," because they were looking at themselves differently. But I think it is just fantastic, this great big sort of shoulder in a sleeve. I think it changes your eye, and you do look vulnerable, but you do look also more sexual because, you know, your eye has got used to seeing something and it's not seeing the physical person inside.'

'Salon' was the first collection in which Andreas's grip tightened on her work. This was apparent in a surfeit of accessories (hats, gloves, bangles, etc.) which obscured the lines of Vivienne's tailoring and the strong silhouette. Whereas she had tended to favour a controlled colour palette and range of (largely British) fabrics, he introduced more lavish materials. 'On his own he'd only buy expensive fabric,' Vivienne says. He also contributed ugly, loose, brushed cotton separates ('unsaleable', according to Simon Barker, who was running Worlds End), clodhopping pastiches of Thierry Mugler's designs, such as tacky nurses' outfits in white leather, square-cut leather-crotch minis which barely covered the knickers, 'masturbation skirts' which were tucked under the crotch, and a corny – in Andreas's eyes shocking – gold vibrator which the models brandished with glee. He was leading Vivienne back to the adolescent bawdiness she had already explored with McLaren.

Vivienne's gentler sensibility was seen in her Madras cotton separates and gingham painters' smocks, based on the pattern for her Pirate shirt of 1980 and worn with velvet berets. Vivienne was now repeating favourite designs, and would wear elements of her latest collection with clothes she had designed with McLaren. She rarely wore another designer's work. While the smocks were being designed, an incident suggested to many in the studio the extent to which Vivienne had fallen under Andreas's spell. The prototype was decorated by him with smudged paint, in imitation of brushes wiped on an artist's smock. Vivienne asked one of her assistants to copy this effect on another smock, but when she inspected it she complained that it was nothing like Andreas's beautiful original. 'Do it again,' she instructed. Few in the studio could see any difference, so they decided to play a trick on her, and switched the smocks. Vivienne was duped. Clearly, her love was blind and Andreas's influence increased to the label's detriment. Nevertheless, the smocks (smudged only for the show, not for the stock) were successful, and Madonna ordered one to wear to the Oscar parties.

Dawn Robson-Bell of Locharron Tweeds, one of Vivienne's biggest suppliers of cloth, was taken aback by the extent to which Andreas began to influence the collections. 'His input is very, very strong. When her staff ring up they say, "Andreas would really like to see this or that."' Attending meetings at the Westwood studio, she noticed that it was Andreas who took the decisions, while Vivienne popped in and out, distracted by telephone calls.

One obvious impact made by Andreas from 1991, and encouraged by D'Amario, was Vivienne's use of supermodels, whom she had previously dismissed as 'two-dimensional'. D'Amario knew that employing them would ensure greater press coverage, as many editors would feature any garment on their front page as long as it was worn by a supermodel. But the company could not afford their fees. In London, models' fees for a fashion show started at £200, and in Paris at £500. Supermodels, however, could command astronomical fees, particularly after Gianni Versace had raised the odds by paying them as much as $10,000 a show. The public was astonished by these fees, without fully appreciating the commercial benefits of employing a supermodel. 'If you get the chance to dress them, they're worth every penny they earn,' John Walford insisted. 'The clothes sell right off their backs.' This was true, partly because of their fame and allure, and partly because the press would use a photograph of a supermodel whatever she was wearing.

Despite being unable to afford their fees, Vivienne managed to secure their services for virtually nothing, as they loved her clothes, appreciated that she was controversially newsworthy, and found the backstage antics at her shows amusing. In addition, Vivienne encouraged the stars to be themselves, and to add personality to her clothes. This was in marked contrast to designers like Helmut Lang, who wanted his models to assume a blank personality and proceed down the catwalk like automatons.

The supermodels agreed to work on Vivienne's shows in return for clothes, originally to the value of £200, later increased to £400. By the time of her 'Anglomania' collection (autumn/winter 1993–94), Christie Turlington, Naomi Campbell, Kate Moss, Linda Evangelista, Eva Herzegovina and Nadia Auerman were all modelling for her. An exception was Claudia Schiffer, who refused to cut her rates. The use of supermodels may have made commercial sense, but it detracted from Vivienne's distinctly English presentation, which had celebrated the 'girl next door' and the 'imperfect'.

Vivienne was extremely solicitous towards the supermodels, complimenting Linda Evangelista, for example, on her new hairstyle, or assuring Naomi Campbell that she had a special dress for her to wear in the show. Occasionally they would be paid in money rather than clothes, but Naomi Campbell was overheard saying that she could not be bothered to cash her £400 cheque, and that she would donate it to charity instead. The fact that Vivienne could secure these top models for so little showed her ability to inspire sympathy and support by self-consciously casting herself as a small, struggling artist, rather than a big fashion corporation, and also showed that the models liked to see themselves in her clothes. D'Amario exploited both of these elements to the hilt.

Since the 'Grand Hotel' collection in October 1992, the CSHC in Paris had ranked Vivienne as a Grade 1 designer, alongside the likes of Chanel, Versace and Valentino. This ranking was determined by the designer's sales, prestige and press attention. While Vivienne's sales were paltry in comparison to those of the other top designers, she scored highly on the other two categories. During the Paris shows only two Grade 1 designers were shown in a day, and they were placed advantageously on the timetable so that no other 'interesting' designer clashed with their allotted spot.

As Andreas's hold over Vivienne strengthened, he appointed Austrian and German staff to the studio, many of them from fashion schools in Vienna and later Berlin. At the same time, D'Amario was employing young Italians whom he could control. German and Italian became as common in the studio as English, to the extent that when in July 1997 the company placed an advertisement for staff in the *Daily Telegraph*, it was in Italian, and included a request that applicants should speak English. Gradually, the camaraderie of earlier years was replaced by a more hierarchical and less communicative atmosphere. Vivienne was now persuaded that the Germans knew more about tailoring than Savile Row, and she became increasingly fascinated by European culture, spending more and more time in Germany, Austria and Italy. She began to give Andreas greater freedom to influence the collections while the staff looked on in amazement. 'He's creepy, Andreas,' says one former employee. 'She does think he's talented. She adores him, and he's insinuated himself into everything and is taking over. He's getting everything out of it he can.' A fabric supplier who worked closely with the couple throughout 1993 declared, 'I do see Andreas having more influence, to the detriment of the collections . . . it's a pity.' A camp styling began to characterise the work, particularly the evening clothes. As Terry Doktor succinctly put it, 'It's drag queen, isn't it?' Staff such as Simon Barker and Leonie Edwards-Jones, who worked in the PR office, believe that 'Dressing Up' was 'the last true Vivienne collection'.

Whatever reservations some of Vivienne's long-standing employees may have had about him, Andreas worked hard and was dedicated to the development of the company. He virtually single-handedly oversaw the production of the Red Label, while Vivienne concentrated on the hand-finished Gold Label. Françoise Rust-Fourteau witnessed the tension between Vivienne and D'Amario when D'Amario attempted to wrest the manufacture of the clothes from Britain, and Vivienne's control, to Italy: 'At the beginning she was worried. She really wanted [production] to remain in Britain so she could keep her hands on surveying the quality of the clothes.' Despite the fact that British manufacturers' costs were higher, they were easier for Vivienne to oversee, and she considered their workmanship superior. In the end she and D'Amario compromised, with production of the Red Label, which brought in over 80 per cent of the company's turnover and the lion's share of the profits, moved to Italy. Staff International agreed to take on the production only on condition that the label be adapted to commercial and manufacturing realities, such as the use of simpler cuts and cheaper fabrics. Vivienne succeeded in keeping the more exclusive, though less profitable, Gold Label in Britain. 'It was her baby,' says Rust-Fourteau. 'That was the deal.'

Andreas played as hard as he worked, frequenting gay nightclubs and bars such as the infamous sado-masochist Fist in Brixton and the Market Tavern in Vauxhall. Typically he would go out on the town alone while Vivienne chose to remain at home reading. On many occasions he did not return to the flat at all. One evening, for example, he stayed at Simon Barker and Derek Dunbar's house in Brent, North London, and while taking a bath he summoned Dunbar and unsuccessfully attempted to seduce him. The following day Dunbar was sent a sinister Ektachrome showing an erect penis with a hand hovering over it holding a lit cigarette.

Vivienne told the press, 'I hate the division of labelling. I'm very against this "outing" of homosexuals. I think it's terrible. It doesn't matter if someone's homosexual or not. I can be attracted to homosexual men; they can be attracted to me. Things can change. This labelling just restricts the whole potential of everything. You're getting somewhere if you're somebody no one can put a label on.'

Few realised the extent of Andreas's hold on Vivienne until it was revealed in the *Sunday Mirror* in December 1993 that they had married in secret at the Wandsworth Register Office in South London on 14 May 1992. Ben and his girlfriend Yasmin were the only witnesses, and the secret was kept even from Dora. 'It was a complete shock to me, of course,' she commented later. 'I knew she was very impressed with him, so it was no surprise when he came to London. I knew they were good friends, but a shock to know they were married.' Vivienne publicly claimed that she had only married Andreas in order to allow him to remain in Britain, as Austria was not a member of the European Community. They had been subjected to standard Home Office interviews to prove they were really cohabiting, being required to describe their living quarters, down to the colour of the carpets and the number of cats in residence.

In love again, Vivienne, like Chaucer's Wife of Bath, was sexually infatuated with an ambitious man half her age, whom she described as 'so beautiful'. Indeed he was. Tall and athletically built, the foppish costume he affected did not diminish his masculine vitality. With an air of perpetual sexual suggestion, he flirted with both sexes, echoing and amplifying the lewd, Anglo-Saxon side of Vivienne's character. Perhaps she reasoned that if she was unable to hold the sexual attention of the man she loved, it would be emotionally easier to tolerate Andreas's infidelity with men rather than another woman. Yet Vivienne was unable to admit his bisexuality publicly. When the *Independent* newspaper carried a feature on men in kilts, illustrated by photographs of fashionable homosexuals such as Jean-Paul Gaultier, and including Andreas, she was furious at the implication that he was also gay. Marching into the studio brandishing the article, she insisted to her staff that it was a pack of lies. Some bowed their heads in embarrassed concentration on their work, others tittered in corners as their boss struggled to be believed in a room in which a number of the men had been sexually approached by her husband.

Notwithstanding Andreas's sexuality, Vivienne clearly felt motivated and creatively inspired by him; and creativity was, after all, her lifeblood. She needed a close companion to spar with over her designs, as in recent years she had been surrounded by adoring fans on whom it had become increasingly hard to rely. Like McLaren before him, Andreas dared to challenge her, and took her ideas in another direction.

'It's a brilliant marriage,' she gleefully assured the press. 'He's young, he informs me a lot about things, and he has a passion for art.' At the age of seven, she claimed, Andreas's father had taken him to the Rijksmuseum in Amsterdam, where he saw a Rembrandt portrait that had such an impact on him that he had painted a copy and sent it to his relatives. 'He was making fashion shows, paying to see his mother's clothes, glued to shop windows. Has done a lot of reading. Knows more about couture than I do. He'd soak himself in it. He's brilliant at draping,' she gushed. She had found a perfect design partnership: her tailoring and his draping skills.

Professional partnership was one thing, but marriage was another.

'Why did she marry a gay?' McLaren wondered. 'I don't think it was about love, but about domination ... Jean-Charles [de Castelbajac] and Lagerfeld haven't a good thing to say about Andreas, but with respect to Vivienne, she's not a very social being, and she needs to have a companion. Someone she can dominate. She's always been with gay guys after me – all those sycophants. Vivienne, being naïve, insecure and ... provincial, adores being praised by the gays because she thinks they're very hip.'

According to André Leon Talley of *Vanity Fair*, in her relationship with Andreas Vivienne found 'a cosiness and a sort of nomalcy. There they are, cycling together over Battersea Bridge with Alex the dog in the basket, and that normalcy is a good contrast to all the angst that she puts into her work.' Like her previous relationship with McLaren, and her platonic one with Gary Ness, Andreas has provided Vivienne with a creative companion. 'I would call it a Hollywood marriage,' says Talley. 'Andreas is something Vivienne must have dreamed of. He's incredibly handsome, so courteous ... She's a woman of fantasy, and her dream has come true. He's like a doll of a husband.' Andreas's manner towards Vivienne is always extremely respectful and courteous. He enjoys making gallant gestures, such as giving her an antique coral tiara and a diamond-spray brooch one Christmas. This must have been particularly flattering to Vivienne, who had confided to Talley 'how many lonely Christmases she had spent, sometimes just having Christmas dinner with a next-door neighbour, some really old guy'. In many ways Vivienne and Andreas's lifestyle together is so normal, suburban and married that Vivienne's life seems almost to have gone full circle. Talley concurs: 'She's very proper in a strange way.'

Françoise Rust-Fourteau who had worked in Paris for Hermès and Karl Lagerfeld, first met Vivienne in December 1992, and became her personal assistant. According to her, Vivienne regarded her young lover as 'the son she never had, because Joe is really Malcolm's son, and Ben never succeeded the way she wished'. Terry Doktor, who had known Vivienne since the seventies, thought that she'd 'missed the boat, sexually, and ... most men would not put up with her; they're afraid of her, she'd pop you one'. But he believed she still needed 'a man to lean on', and that perhaps Andreas fitted the bill. André Leon Talley, though, is convinced that there is a physical intimacy between the two. He recalls an incident when he was assisting

Karl Lagerfeld in taking a portrait photograph of the couple in Lagerfeld's Paris house. 'We were in no doubt that they were into intimacy. I mean, we almost felt we should look away and shouldn't be there.'

This dependency infuriated the possessive Gary Ness, who became as critical of Andreas as he was of D'Amario. Christine Harrison, who looked after the couture clients, remarks that 'Vivienne only seems to operate when she has a partner . . . She's always needed someone to bounce ideas off, and when she had no one – before Andreas – she nearly gave up designing.' In fact, though she may have been happier with Andreas around, from a creative point of view Vivienne's best work was done during two spells of great loneliness: after McLaren's departure, and again when she had ousted her sons from her flat and before Andreas arrived.

The couple became inseparable, dressing like twins in matching tartans – Vivienne even commissioned Locharron to create a tartan which was registered under the name 'MacAndreas'. Now Andreas's rather than Vivienne's favourite pin-ups began to appear in the collections: Marlene Dietrich, a German and gay icon, in her 'Always on Camera' collection (autumn/winter 1992–93), and Löden cloth, Nazi memorabilia, the paintings of Frans Hals, Hapsburg lace and the sprig prints that Europeans associate with traditional Liberty-print English children's wear were favoured.

'Always on Camera' was shown at Le Monde de l'Art in Paris in March 1992. Vivienne was now such a hot designer that brawls took place outside the venue as fans tried to gain entry – Joan Juliet Buck, Editor-in-Chief of French *Vogue*, says, 'Vivienne's shows here are huge events. I always get crushed and faint!' A typical Vivienne touch was the use of a print on some of the clothes of a 1930s Rolls-Royce, an image she had lifted from a book of old cars that Dunbar had found in the Oxfam charity shop next door to Worlds End. But Andreas's taste had permeated the collection, which included camp pectoral muscle pads placed under mohair jumpers, and lurex-threaded mohair mini dresses which were expensive to make and scratchy to wear. The show intended to parody the Hollywood interpretation of French *haute couture* of the thirties, when many leading couturiers, such as Coco Chanel, had been invited by the film studios to design for their leading ladies. This had usually been an unsuccessful alliance, as the subtlety of a fashion designer's work, normally visible only at close quarters, was lost on the silver screen. Cinema required the theatrical flamboyance of specialist designers such as Adrian, Norman Norell and Edith Head to satisfy its larger-than-life demands.

Not only did Vivienne's collections begin to change, so did her appearance. She lost weight, took considerably more care over her toilette (understandable for a woman in love), and her personal style shifted from quintessentially English to a camp harshness, inspired by Madonna, whom Andreas admired. The hennaed ringlets and scrubbed complexion were replaced by a peroxided short crop and pencil-arched eyebrows, recalling the Weimar Republic's bisexual nightclub prostitutes painted by George Grosz.

It was around this time that Lady Romilly McAlpine became a truly staunch supporter of Vivienne. Her position at the heart of the British establishment made her a noteworthy advertisement in influential circles for Vivienne's style. Whether she was attending the state opening of Parliament, tiara-ed and coiffed alongside robed peers, or dining with Margaret Thatcher at 10 Downing Street, she would be wearing the most glamorous Westwood outfit, plus the 'elevated' heels. (When the shoes were not in use, they became *objets d'art* displayed in her dining room.) Encouraged by her husband, she became a serious collector: 'Alistair loves Vivienne's really outrageous things,' she says. 'Like a wonderful cloak, striped in silk taffeta, which trails behind – the bigger the better, as far as he's concerned!'

Romilly McAlpine remembers that her first reaction on meeting Vivienne was that she 'could not understand this figure producing these clothes, and I had Malcolm McLaren in the back of my mind . . . she was so monosyllabic and so hesitant . . . Socially she's the most gauche person I've ever met.' Moving in Continental fashion circles, Romilly McAlpine was infuriated by the way the British knocked success. 'When the bustier came out [in spring 1992] it was so shocking and so innovative . . . Well, there's hardly a woman in London now who doesn't have a bustier,' she said, perhaps exaggerating slightly. Sometimes the reaction from society women to her clothes was 'positively aggressive'. They might approach to admire a dress, but on hearing it was by Vivienne they would respond, 'Oh, it's not possible. Only *you* could wear that!' But when Romilly McAlpine attended the launch party for Lady Thatcher's memoirs wearing a tartan suit with a bustle skirt, the former Prime Minister commented, 'Gosh, what a lovely outfit.' On being told who had designed it, she responded, 'Such a clever lady. I'm so glad she's British.' Few in the upper echelons of society saw it that way.

In the spring of 1992 the McAlpines became involved on Vivienne's behalf in unsuccessful negotiations to acquire the handsome Georgian building on Bruton Street, Mayfair, that had been occupied by Sir Norman Hartnell. Lack of sales under Marc Bohan, who had been appointed as Designer-in-Chief at Hartnell's in preference to the 'less commercial' Vivienne, had forced the house to close down. Lord McAlpine asked Derek Dunbar, who was assisting them, 'Vivienne hasn't got the OBE, has she?' Three months later, in June 1992, she was awarded the Order of the British Empire in the Queen's birthday honours list. To everyone's astonishment she had joined the ranks of the Great and the Good, and in doing so, she caused a new furore.

Vivienne had come a long way from the provincial outsider slinging abuse at the royal family. Many were amazed that she accepted the honour, assuming that she must have lost her campaigning zeal. 'I can understand why she accepted the OBE,' Romilly McAlpine says in her defence. 'Why shouldn't she? Vivienne dreams of glamorous occasions often enough. Why shouldn't she be allowed to participate in one?' With customary defiance, Vivienne issued a press release:

> Since being awarded the OBE, the question I have been asked is, 'Isn't it ironic that the establishment should award someone who attacks it? . . . it needs the people who attack it and the media is full of token rebels: nothing is more easy than to rally young people to rebel against the older generation because it's exactly what they want to do. It is not my desire that young or old should pander to this need . . . Since I realised all this some time ago I ceased to attack the idea of the establishment – I have ignored it: I am concerned with something more fundamental – the concept of civilisation itself . . . In that I have wished to avoid the automatic transition from rebel to victim it gives me great pleasure to receive the OBE.

In December 1992 Vivienne emerged from Buckingham Palace, having received her honour, to face a bank of photographers. She was looking suitably elegant in a Dior New Look-inspired grey flannel suit with a vast, midi-length circle skirt lined in champagne satin, a pillbox hat, gloves and super-elevated court shoes. Beaming with pride, she began her self-promotion: 'The Queen looked very nice when I received my OBE. Very comfortable. But she'd look great in this.' Asked why she had accepted the honour, she explained with a typically obscure 'Garyism': 'I am not a misanthropic recluse. I have to live in the world. Anyway, Socrates accepted a cup of poison because it was the consensus that he should.'

The photo-opportunity commenced, and to show off her full skirt, Vivienne began to twirl. 'Go on, Vivienne,' bayed the press pack, 'Faster, faster, lovey, keep twirling.' She obliged, basking in their attention. Meanwhile Ben, standing on the sidelines, was shouting, 'Mum, Mum, you haven't got your knickers on!' But she could not hear him above the jeers of the crowd. Vivienne was accustomed to going knickerless, as Mark Tarbard had noticed when doing fittings with her, and she did not realise how high her skirt had risen. The press got their lewd image, and journalists had a field day. With typical tabloid silliness, the papers feigned shock at the idea of a woman wearing no knickers. 'I thought, they're not going to publish that picture with her skirt up in the air,' Ben naïvely recalled. 'I was completely dismayed by them. They could have done the same story with a nice picture, instead [it was] detrimental. And she said, "You saw it. You should have dived on me." But I thought, they are never going to print it. My Mum's very open. She believes people won't be unfair. She won't be to them and they won't be to her. It's a case of her being very nice. A childish innocence, that's not lost. She believes people to be fair and decent.'

Although the press coverage the OBE incident attracted far exceeded anything Vivienne might have expected and although she did not, as has been alleged, deliberately expose herself to the cameras, she was impressed by the number of column inches her 'outrage' had produced. Interviewed by the *Mail on Sunday* on the day the pictures appeared, she was asked whether she was vain. 'No,' she replied. Then why, the journalist persisted, had she just spent over twenty minutes in the lavatory putting on her make-up? 'It was dark in there and I was having a sandwich,' Vivienne said, with characteristically startling frankness. Determined not to suffer penury again, she commented that the OBE was 'an offer you can't refuse – it's good for business'.

In early June 1992 Vivienne had been invited to a dinner at Kensington Palace attended by Princess Michael of Kent to celebrate the opening of 'The Costume Court', an exhibition of royal dress. Clearly planning a 'to-do', she wore a shaggy black wig, see-through lace Boulle dress and no underwear. It is hard to believe her claim that 'it's not really see-through – it was just penetrated by the flashlights. I did not go out deliberately to shock, but the dress felt better without any underwear.' Even before the cameras started flashing, fellow guests were left in no doubt that Vivienne knew exactly what she was doing. 'Of course she knew it was see-through,' says Simon Barker. 'She was always doing that kind of thing to get attention. It's a child wanting attention.'

Some of the attention Vivienne attracted was unwanted. Having met her on the BBC radio programme *Start the Week*, Craig Brown anonymously penned a spoof of her pretentious declarations on culture in the satirical magazine *Private Eye*. It began:

> I love books and not only that but I thoroughly enjoy them, and when I can find the time I especially like reading them all the way through, with or without pictures, the older the better. That Michael Proust was such a clever man, don't you think? What was it he said about temps? That's it – he said he was 'in search of temps perdu' which of course literally translated from the Italian means 'in search of lost temps'. Just imagine it, there he was, up to his neck in this great big book, that massive *oeuf*, as he would have called it, and the temps hadn't even bothered to show up. Poor lamb. I'm thinking of calling my next collection 'In the Footsteps of Michael Proust' in his honour, with all these beautiful girls dressed in the temp style, with little shorthand pads sewn into their noses, and fantastic six-inch platform heels shaped like typewriters. We need revolutions like that, because to my mind that's the only way that Britain will come to its senses and transform itself into a wholly cultural society along the lines suggested by Bernard Russell, the great philatelist.

Gary Ness was furious at what he saw as this attack on Vivienne's 'prestige', which he had been trying to raise by encouraging her to take an interest in art and literature. But Vivienne, thick-skinned as ever, dismissed it as unimportant.

'Grand Hotel' (spring/summer 1993), a homage to fifties tailoring with full-circle, lower-calf-length skirts and off-the-shoulder necklines, was shown at the hotel of that name in Paris. It was a poorly edited show, with many tacky outfits and no strong theme. Her summer collections had never tended to sell well, and Simon Barker says 'There were no real stunners or best-sellers in that collection.' Vivienne herself modelled in the show for the first time, playing the 'nanny' to Derek Dunbar's nephew, with Sarah Stockbridge as the 'mother'.

Before anyone appeared on the catwalk, a row broke out backstage. Vivienne had promised her shop assistant Jibby Beane that she could model. She was thrilled, and had begun to put on the clothes when Carlo D'Amario announced that only professional models would be used. A fight ensued in which most of Vivienne's associates, including Joseph and John Rowley, sided with D'Amario. Consequently, Vivienne naturally sided with Jibby, the underdog.

Then, just as the audience were sitting down, another argument broke out, this time in the front row. D'Amario was trying to get Lord and Lady McAlpine and their guest to surrender their seats to some store buyers. His insulting manner led to a row, in which Derek Dunbar defended the McAlpines. D'Amario tried to hit Dunbar, at which point the McAlpines' guest was so horrified that he got up and left. Partly as a result of the incident the McAlpines withdrew their active support from Vivienne's firm. They could not tolerate her business manager.

This was not an unusual reaction to D'Amario. His aggression was partly a result of his cocaine habit, which he did little to hide. On one occasion, Dunbar recalled, he arrived at the salesroom in Paris 'brushing white powder off his suit. It was all over his nose.' His state did not go unnoticed by the American buyers. Not only was D'Amario's behaviour losing Vivienne valuable associates, but some of his business practices were losing her profits. John Rowley remembers that D'Amario was manufacturing more garments than he reported back to Vivienne, and 'selling stuff in little boutiques along the Riviera. Derek [Dunbar] got the information, evidence, photographs, but she would not accept it . . . She's so crazy! Her judgement of people is the world's worst.'

So keen was Vivienne to remain in the public eye, a time-consuming occupation, and so ill-equipped was she to deal with the business as it mushroomed, that she gradually ceded all financial responsibilities to D'Amario. It was a calculated risk. Although she was constantly warned against him by her loyal associates Barker, Dunbar, Ness and Françoise Rust-Fourteau, she reasoned that since he was an adept businessman, he could keep the company afloat. As long as she was free simply to design and be a star, she would turn a blind eye to his activities.

Gradually D'Amario moved production of all the commercial Red Label and most of the accessories from Britain to Italy, underscoring his absolute financial control. The Red Label was manufactured by Staff International in the Veneto, while the couture Gold Label was largely made by outworkers and in small workshops around London. The former was significantly more profitable, and grew rapidly: when it was launched in 1993, Staff International produced four thousand units of clothing for its first season. By 1998 this figure had risen to forty thousand. D'Amario owned a significant share (estimates vary between 30 and 49 per cent) of the Italian arm of Vivienne's company, Vivienne Westwood SpA. Françoise Rust-Fourteau, a shrewd observer of proceedings and in a position to know, concluded that D'Amario had 'free rein'.

It could hardly have escaped Vivienne's notice that while D'Amario lived in splendour in Belgravia's Halkin Street, paying a rent of £1,400 a week and also owning villas in Tuscany and on Lake Como, she remained in her council flat. Yet he gave her enough money to keep her happy. When this was added to the £70,000 a year she was earning from her new teaching job as Professor of Fashion at Berlin's Hochschule, where she now worked three days a month, having moved from the Vienna Academy of Applied Arts, she felt rich. Compared to most of her fashion peers, Vivienne was far from materialistic. While Valentino collected yachts and art, and Lagerfeld amassed furniture and houses, she was contented as long as she had a £20 note in her pocket with which to buy a book or dinner. The company paid her travel expenses, the modest £200 a month rent to the local council and her domestic utilities bills.

Continuing to support Vivienne, Azzedine Alaïa invited her to present a twenty-year retrospective of her designs at the Bordeaux Museum of Contemporary Art in November 1992. Two hours before the show was due to begin, no clothes had arrived, but in her usual manner Vivienne remained remarkably cool. When the whole range of her work – from zip-scarred T-shirts and bondage trousers to bras worn outside dresses, corsets and nude-coloured leggings – was set before the packed audience of local worthies and students along with the press and fellow designers such as de Castelbajac, Jean Colonna, Christian Louboutin, Chantal Thomass and André Putman, it underscored her role as a pioneer in fashion. Writing in the *International Herald Tribune*, Suzy Menkes summed up Vivienne's design impact as 'first, but worst'. By this she meant that Vivienne regularly devised the imperfect prototype which was then perfected and commercially exploited by more professional designers.

Vivienne was not normally favourably disposed to lingering on her past work, particularly when it conjured up memories of McLaren. She had warned one interviewer not to talk to her 'about the old days . . . the way I used to think even ten years ago, is completely opposite to what I think today,' and it was surprising that she agreed to a retrospective. When punk was revived in 1993, principally by Gianni Versace, who charged astronomical prices for what had once been an anti-fashion, do-it-yourself street look, Vivienne was extremely irritated. Punk had been sanitised, robbed of all meaning, displaced from its context, and was now worn by fashion victims. Clothes without a message were meaningless decoration to her, and now that she was promoting a culturally informed notion of beauty, punk was irrelevant.

In February 1993 Roger Burton, the owner of Contemporary Wardrobe, which provided post-war outfits for films, held a retrospective of Vivienne and McLaren's 'couture' clothes from Let it Rock, Too Fast to Live Too Young to Die, SEX and Seditionaries, entitled 'Vive le Punk!' at his offices, an old horse hospital in Bloomsbury. He invited McLaren and Vivienne to come over on the eve of the opening and record a video of reminiscences about punk. McLaren, whom Vivienne had not seen for nearly a decade, agreed, but when Vivienne heard that he would be present, she declined. She had admitted to a journalist as recently as 1990 that thinking of McLaren still prompted her to 'ever so slightly begin to cry, but it doesn't break out properly. I used to cry so much when I was left by Malcolm – at least fifteen minutes every day – that I don't think I have many tears left.'

Despite her reluctance to attend, Burton persisted, telling her that this was her chance to 'put the record straight over who designed what' during that creative period. After many telephone calls, she finally turned up outside the horse hospital at ten in the evening.

Hovering at the doorway, she was too scared to enter, until finally she steeled herself and announced, 'I'll come in if I can have a double brandy.'

As she entered the room, McLaren was sitting in front of the camera boasting about his creative genius. After listening for a few minutes, Vivienne suddenly interjected, 'Malcolm, you didn't do that! I got that idea!' A battle ensued. 'I had so much respect for her,' Burton remembers. 'She really fought her corner, and it was clear that a lot of the ideas about punk had come from her, not him.'

The following night, Vivienne refused to come to the opening, at which McLaren basked in the glory. When Burton telephoned her to try to change her mind, she said, 'Roger, I won't come. It's all in the past.' She added, 'But I want to thank you for last night. I'm glad I came. I realise now that I don't love him any more.' Perhaps now that she had exorcised the ghost of McLaren from her heart, her pain would subside.

Vivienne's fame, or infamy, now began to attract licence deals. The most imaginative project came in the summer of 1993 when she was approached by the carpet company Brintons to collaborate on an advertising campaign. Brintons, among of the oldest carpet manufacturers in Britain – one might say the Harris Tweed of carpets – invited several advertising agencies to pitch for their first-ever advertising campaign. While most predictably suggested styling room sets, a small agency called Cowan, Kemsley & Taylor conceived the idea of dressing fashion models in clothes made from carpets.

The marketing logic behind this stunt was to appeal emotionally to the target market, relatively affluent and fashion-conscious women. As Mike Hardiman, Brintons' public relations and advertising manager, says, 'Fashion as a vehicle has enormous power over women.' The principal goal of the first campaign was to build brand recognition.

The advertising agency's Carena Mulholland realised that to have genuine fashion appeal, the campaign needed to commission an important British designer and a leading photographer. After Jasper Conran turned them down, the agency approached Vivienne, on the recommendation of Anna Harvey of British *Vogue*. 'Vivienne was unquestionably the one designer who would take up this challenge and would really enjoy it,' Harvey perceptively predicted. As soon as Vivienne saw Brintons' tartan 'Abbotsford' carpet, she loved the idea, adding with typical candour, 'I knew that if I didn't do it, someone else would, and they'd just make a mess of it.'

The selected photographer, David Bailey, was invited in to the agency to discuss his involvement. When he saw the first agency-made samples of the clothes he responded, with characteristic Bailey bluntness: 'Right, I get the idea. You make the clothes out of carpets. You stick 'em on a bird, right? And you want me to photograph them from a distance so we can see the whole outfit, but it still has to look like a carpet, right?'

'Yes, Mr Bailey, that's right,' the Brintons team replied.

'Well, whose fuckin' marvellous idea was this, then?'

'Mine, Mr Bailey,' Tim Johnson from the agency replied.

'Well, you're in the shit, aren't you, lad?'

Nevertheless, Bailey agreed to try 'the impossible'.

In October 1993 Vivienne visited the Brintons factory in Kidderminster. As she was notoriously bad at keeping appointments, the company took the precaution of sending a car to London to collect her. She was still one and a half hours late. Walking into the boardroom, she did not apologise, but bluntly asked, 'Does anyone have a cigarette?' Over lunch Mike Hardiman told her that this was the first advertising campaign Brintons had done in 210 years. 'Well, you don't want to go rushing into things, do you?' she replied. On her tour of the factory, Vivienne became fascinated by the looms and the whole process of constructing a carpet. Regardless of being dressed in a mini-kilt and Rocking Horse platform shoes, she insisted on getting down on all fours to peer under the looms in order to understand how they worked.

Using existing carpet stock, altered only by sanding down the backing, Vivienne and Andreas came up with a series of outfits, including mini crinis, crown, corset, super-elevated shoes. These were made up by a combination of carpet-fitters, who fused the major seams, and Iris, a German seamstress from Vivienne's workrooms, who painstakingly sewed together the thick, cumbersome wedges of carpet. Seven weeks later, the clothes were ready.

The campaign was launched with a series of glossy magazine advertisements on 6 October 1993. Within weeks, carpet retailers throughout Britain were reporting back to Brintons that women were coming into the stores and asking for 'the Vivienne Westwood carpets'. By November 1994 Brintons' market research figures showed that unprompted brand recognition of their name had increased from 4 to 13 per cent in a year. Hillary Clinton chose Brintons carpets to refurbish the living quarters in the White House. The campaign was a huge success both commercially and creatively, winning many advertising industry awards.

While Vivienne did not earn a huge fee from the collaboration, the press she gained was enormous. Hardiman calculated that the campaign netted £250,000 worth of free publicity in the form of editorials, reinforcing Vivienne's name in the public mind. In addition to her fee, Brintons carried out an extremely exacting special commission for Vivienne: a huge leopardskin-print carpet with a deep cream 'lace' border, which was laid in the ballroom of the Grand Hotel in Paris for her October 1993 show. The carpet was later lent to the film director Robert Altman for *Prêt-à-Porter*, his spoof on the fashion industry.

For the second campaign, launched on 2 January 1995, Michael Brinton, the chairman, decided that they should celebrate the year in which the company was founded, 1783, by making clothes from that period out of carpet. Since Vivienne and Gary Ness were already obsessed by the *ancien régime*, the idea instantly appealed to her. Bailey shot the campaign once again, adding grandeur to the already magnificent Gainsborough-style clothing. One of the carpets weighed ninety ounces a square yard, and the costumes were so heavy that the models, Saffron Burroughs and Simonetta Gianfelici, had to be lifted into position by two men, as they couldn't move under the crushing weight. Andreas modelled the man's outfit.

Dealing with Vivienne over these two complicated campaigns, Mike Hardiman found her 'down to earth, perceptive and discerning. She really knew about the textile business. We were impressed.' However, he did concede that she was 'not the easiest person to deal with'. Andreas, by contrast, was exemplary in his behaviour and got on famously with Bailey, who dubbed him 'the Austrian'.

In the late summer of 1993 Vivienne joined seven other former classmates (there had been thirty-five in her year), including Maureen Purcell, who came from South Africa for the event, Anne Shaw and Eileen Mellish, for a school reunion. They were due to dine at the George Hotel, in the centre of Glossop, where Vivienne was staying. She arrived, as usual, extremely late, and by the time they had stopped talking it was too late for dinner. They all went off for chip muffins, and rather than going back to her hotel bed Vivienne spent the night, as she had often done as a little girl, on the sofa in Celia Purcell's front room. John Rowley recalls that Vivienne had expected the reunion to be 'an awful experience', but that in the event she thoroughly enjoyed it, not least because 'she was treated like royalty and was the centre of attention'.

Not long afterwards Maureen Purcell died of emphysema at Oldham Royal Hospital. Vivienne came to visit her in her last days, prompting one of Maureen's relations to say, with faint praise, 'She's a kind person – underneath.' In her letter of condolence to Maureen's sister Marilyn, Vivienne wrote: 'Your sister used to be such a sexy little thing at school.'

Vivienne was now over fifty, and her burgeoning success meant she no longer needed to work for a living. Yet she continued to commit herself to the gruelling task of creating at least four collections a year. The furniture of Vivienne's mind had not changed over the decades. Material possessions were still of no interest to her; it was irrelevant whether or not she had money in the bank. What still drove her to work so hard was her abiding love of beauty and glamour. The creative process gave her great pleasure. Not only this, but fashion had provided her with a means of casting off her humble background – one reason why all her garments were plumed with culture, a culture she had only recently absorbed and which she greatly respected. But there were equally powerful emotional drives, central to her personality, that propelled her. They were, quite simply, the desire to prove to McLaren that she could succeed, and sibling rivalry.

Throughout their years as a design partnership, McLaren had always cast Vivienne as the assistant who complied with his authority. She felt he had undervalued her creativity and then abandoned her. The resulting pain and heartbreak had been the source of the exceptional energy that had driven her through those difficult years. And now she had proved to him that she was better than he could ever have imagined. He was so impressed by her success that he wanted to return to fashion – possibly, it was rumoured, in partnership with her.

Running alongside this powerful sense of anger was an older and deeper feeling of inadequacy. When Vivienne's sister Olga was born three years after her, she was so angry that she had wanted to 'dead her'. This jealousy did not subside with the years, but grew stronger.

To her mother's traditional way of thinking, it was Olga, not Vivienne, who had succeeded. Olga was, in her mother's eyes, 'proper'. She had a university degree, she practised a profession – psychology – and she had married and brought legitimate children into the world. Though Dora had come to Vivienne's rescue on many occasions during her precarious career in fashion, it was her younger daughter whom she held up for admiration. Sitting next to Dora once on a flight to Brazil, John Walford listened as she extolled the virtues of Olga: 'She didn't rate Vivienne's success. It was Olga she was proud of, and she made that quite clear.' In the twenty years that Simon Barker had known Vivienne, 'not once did she mention Olga. She didn't exist.' Olga, unlike her brother Gordon, was never invited to Vivienne's shows.

Vivienne shared many of her mother's traits: her energy, robustness and inclination to enjoy the company of young men. (Dora, now in her late seventies, had taken up with an eighteen-year-old motorbike despatch rider.) As mothers, both women displayed favouritism towards one of their children: Dora towards Olga, and Vivienne towards Joseph. One of Vivienne's former colleagues believes that Dora's attitude to Vivienne underwent a radical change once she had won critical acclaim and financial success: 'Now her mother is all over her like a rash. I thought that Dora only respected Vivienne's work when she started to make money from it. That's when it made sense to her. She used to be so critical of her, which is why Vivienne herself is so critical of everyone else.'

As Joseph matured it became clear to Derek Dunbar, who befriended him, that he was 'damaged, violent and more disturbed than Ben'. On one occasion the two young men were at the Wag Club in Soho when Joseph was caught by the bouncers making love to his girlfriend in the lavatory. When they tried to throw him out, he drunkenly refused and goaded them, 'as though wanting to be hurt'. He was beaten up, and staggered home alone, bleeding profusely. His injuries required stitches. Encountering Joseph at various nightclubs, McLaren gradually became aware of his son's heavy drinking bouts, and voiced his concern to Vivienne.

In the spring of 1993, Vivienne showed her 'Anglomania' collection at Le Cercle Republicain in Paris. Once again, fights broke out as people battled to get in. It was a handsome but over-styled show, thanks to Andreas's heavy hand. However, because the supermodels Christy Turlington, Naomi Campbell and Linda Evangelista modelled the clothes, the collection was widely featured in the American press, and Vivienne's sales picked up significantly there. Unfortunately, the show featured not only her top-quality Gold Label clothes, but also her Red Label and a range of tacky diffusion line handbags emblazoned with gilt logos. It is an axiom in the fashion business that it is unwise to feature one's main and diffusion lines together, as it confuses the clientele and debases the prestige of the main line.

The collection took its name from the frenzy for English dress that broke out in fashionable French circles in the 1780s, shortly before the Revolution. Young men discarded their formal frock-coats, lace, wigs and pomade in favour of English-style caped redingotes or greatcoats, relatively sober tailored suits, hats worn on their heads rather than carried foppishly under their arm, thick stockings and starched cravats. The look suggested revolutionary tendencies to some traditional eyes.

'Anglomania' became notorious when Naomi Campbell fell over on the catwalk while wearing a pair of ten-inch-high super-elevated shoes. The image appeared in newspapers around the world, and when the Victoria and Albert Museum placed a pair of the shoes in their foyer, the public flocked to see them. 'The shoes were a great publicity coup,' a member of the museum staff recalled. 'They were so popular that we had to put them in a case by the front door. The posters kept being stolen from the underground, and we sold hundreds of them in the shop.'

It was her very 'single-mindedness' – taking the line of greatest resistance – that had enabled Vivienne to succeed on her own terms. This quality had impressed Christian Lacroix: 'In such a world when everybody is struggling in such a fake way – just all for money, just for fame, or just for love – it's a treasure to be so faithful to one idea.' He admired her ability to design according to her own 'strict ideology' rather than the market's whims. 'I am weaker than her because the group [LVMH, for which he worked] is stronger than me, and sometimes you surrender. But . . . if you do a line for pleasing the way the people in the fashion world are thinking, you have to do it without guts. If you succeed it's a very pale success. If you fail, if you are wrong, it is terrible, because you are destroyed for fake reasons.' He saluted Vivienne for following her own path and eventually succeeding, but he concluded, 'in a way she will be marginal for ever. Sometimes I love to wish her the best, the success, but perhaps it's not right to wish her [that]. Perhaps we just have to wish her to just be beside [the mainstream] for ever without really being recognised as huge.' His words were prophetic, as he was to learn a year later.

Vivienne found solace in ideas, not money. She had not been religious since her early twenties, and she now fell under the delusion that intellectuals must be happier than lesser mortals, because they had found some elusive answer. This notion fuelled her intellectual quest at the expense of her fashion, a trade that she now denigrated, partly because it was *her* trade – she had done it – and partly because, particularly in Britain, it is regarded as an 'imbecile's trade', as Pierre Bergé, Yves Saint Laurent's manager and lover had stated. She insisted that 'fashion is not art because it's popular culture and has to sell to a certain amount . . . If it's popular, it's not culture.' Though this was a plausible stand against the creeping relativism that deems every creative effort an 'art', it also reflected her sense of frustration. She wanted to be seen as an artist, a figure of cultural importance. 'She's only doing fashion for one simple reason,' believes McLaren. 'She thinks she's making a major political contribution, and when she wakes up and realises, she'll find another way to make a political statement.' Despite her outward self-esteem, in her heart of hearts Vivienne regarded herself, and fashion, as second-rate. Now she was determined to throw herself into scholarly circles and improve herself.

With Gary Ness's assistance, she selected people with 'clout' and invited them to dinner at restaurants in Westbourne Grove. On one occasion they invited Professor David Starkey, a constitutional historian who regularly appeared in the media. Vivienne arrived late and, unaware that her guests were watching her through the window, chained her bicycle to the lamp post and methodically removed the red plastic 'Vivienne Westwood' shopping bag from her head, shook the rain off it and tied it onto the seat of her bike to keep it dry. Such practicality, no matter how uncool, was typical of her. (The image of Vivienne wearing the shopping bag on her head was captured by the Swedish photographer Inez van Lamsweerde, and from 1995 was printed on labels which were sewn into her Gold Label range, vain and self-deprecating at the same time.) Vivienne entered the restaurant and sat between Simon Barker and Ness. As Ness and Starkey began to spar intellectually, Vivienne turned dejectedly to Barker and asked, 'Do you understand what they're talking about?'

He shook his head.

'Neither do I,' she confessed.

Under Ness's tutelage, Vivienne had become convinced that 'the stagnation of society is a direct result of the isolation of intellectuals [i.e. Ness]'. Not only did Ness want to protect Vivienne from the 'pollution' of twentieth-century thought, but he hoped to mould her into 'a *grande dame*, an intellectual'. Through Ness, she became aware of the roles played by the salons of Lady Caroline Holland and Mmes de Staël, de Sévigné and d'Épinay in the seventeenth and eighteenth centuries. The original salons were power bases established by wealthy and well-connected women who, in their day, could not enter the political or commercial worlds. They provided a venue where writers, politicians, journalists and others could hear the latest gossip, exchange ideas, sharpen their wits and further their careers. Despite the domestic setting and the presence of beauties and socialites in order to promote an entertaining atmosphere, the salon was usually focused on a specific purpose: the advancement of a shared point of view, be it Jean-Jacques Rousseau's social philosophy, Whig politics or the royalist cause.

Fired by this example, Vivienne talked incessantly to the press and anyone else who would listen about opening a salon and launching a 'Foundation Against Philistines'. The salon would provide a platform for Ness's opinions, and a place to which she could invite those whom he and she deemed to be of sufficient intellectual and cultural worth, especially if they held 'heretical' views that challenged popular opinion. At first her ambitions were modest – her guests could meet for tea in a 'nice luxury café' – but gradually they became more inflated. She proposed publishing a magazine, and Ness's unfinished book attacking Anglo-American philistinism. Their salon would attract like-minded and hitherto isolated thinkers who would challenge the American cultural imperialism that had dominated European thought since the war.

Vivienne's ambition to become well-read having been frustrated, since she was a slow reader constantly distracted by the demands of fame, she hoped that a salon would provide her with instant culture, acting as her own private university where she could pick the brains of those with intellectual and social 'clout' and receive further useful introductions to the Great and the Good. Initially she calculated that she would require £50,000 to finance the salon, but this estimate quickly rose to £1 million. Vivienne naïvely believed that the money would be provided by others (Richard Branson was singled out as a possible benefactor), although by 1990 she had accepted that 'I'm not going to get it [the finance] until I get a certain amount myself, and I'm in a hobnob situation with other rich people.' She envisaged buying a building to house the salon and perhaps – holding out another carrot to her dependant – a flat for Ness. The salon was a fantasy that Vivienne propagated principally for the benefit of Ness, whose name she never mentioned in public: 'Of course, if my friend dies, I shan't bother.'

Lacking suitable premises or the funds to provide them, at first she used Lady Henrietta Bathurst's maisonette in Elm Park Road, Chelsea. Every month she, Ness and Henrietta hosted a *soirée* with a variety of acquaintances, including Jamie Sainsbury, art historian and gallery owner John Mitchell, journalist Emma Soames, textile historian Santina Levey, Barry Humphries, art dealer Alex Ossowski, television producer Helen Kirwan-Taylor and ceramics expert John Mallet. They met ostensibly to engage in enlightened and elevating conversation. 'When you have people talk about the quality of life today, they never talk about culture,' Vivienne protested. 'I don't believe in revolution or in change by political means. I think the only chance of making the world more worthwhile lies in cultural means. I believe in art for art's sake.' In fact she believed in art for *more* than art's sake, namely as an instrument of wider change.

Being socially clumsy, incapable of small talk and humourless, Vivienne was a poor hostess. When a joke was told, she would look away embarrassed, and wait for the laughter to stop. Her staff were so used to this that if a newcomer tried to amuse her with a joke they would watch the stranger's face, not Vivienne's, in order to relish his discomfiture. Vivienne was not light-hearted, and has no interest in fun: 'Every time I hear that word I cringe. "Fun"! I think it's disgusting; it's like running around. It's not my idea of pleasure. I'm more like Epicurus, I hope,' she declared.

The Elm Park Road salon disbanded after a few months, as the meetings became repetitive and attendance dwindled. Vivienne's personality was too abrasive to attract many prominent guests. She is not sympathetic, worldly or tolerant enough to foster a stimulating atmosphere for discourse, nor is she a good listener. And, unlike the successful salon hostesses, she does not possess the deep-seated confidence needed to allow her guests, rather than herself, to be the centre of attention. In the late twentieth century, when powerful women as well as men are free to operate in the public and commercial domain, Vivienne would have found it extremely difficult to welcome such women.

Early in 1993 Vivienne had met Jibby Beane, an ebullient bottle-blonde of the same age who had recently fled from a genteel marriage in suburbia. They found each other at the Designer and Decorators Exhibition in London, where Vivienne and Gary Ness had created a room-set based on an eighteenth-century French literary salon. While rearranging her hair in the ladies' room, Jibby Beane recognised her heroine. 'I had always wanted to have a conversation with her, and I thought, how wonderful, here's my chance!' She talked herself into a job working three days a week in Vivienne's shops. Jibby regarded her new work as a shop assistant as 'the biggest thrill of my life. Here I was, having had my children and seeing those clothes. I was like a child again. It was something just so exciting, and all my earnings went on her clothes.'

Vivienne had developed another crush. Jibby, a cartoon blonde, bore a remarkable resemblance to Sarah Stockbridge in her Monroe-esque looks and manner. Tall and voluptuous, she habitually wore a gash of vermilion across her lips, swags of pearls around her throat and the highest super-elevated courts. Like Vivienne, she had found a lover half her age, and was briefly projected as the mature embodiment of Vivienne's label. Her message was that life after fifty could be sexy and fun dressed in Westwood, and her sales technique was performance art delivered with arch, Noël Coward diction and peppered with 'Darling', 'simply wonderful', and even 'absolutely fabulous'. The media loved her, and customers at the Conduit Street shop would assume that the theatrical Jibby was Vivienne. Jibby loved the glory, and Vivienne became increasingly irritated by the attention her employee was receiving. In 1994, like Jordan before her, Jibby was sacked. Romilly McAlpine has observed, 'Vivienne's product is a star, but she hasn't got star qualities herself.' Vivienne affects a disregard for how she is perceived, but her press officer, Leonie Edwards-Jones, says, 'Vivienne's very concerned with how she's perceived. She likes being famous, while saying "Fuck fame." But she'll always give interviews, and she always appears at events.'

Vivienne was now one of the most famous designers in the world, but her attention was increasingly taken up with her intellectual pursuits and the communication of her unconventional views. The pressure to be a star, lecture the world on her cultural views and design several fashion collections a year was too taxing, and something had to give.

10 NON-STOP DISTRACTIONS

1994–1998

'Ninety-five per cent of my life is spent doing organisation or interviews. Only 5 per cent is design.'

Vivienne Westwood, 1993

'It's a question of non-stop distractions . . . People haven't got the time to think. They're just bombarded with the latest splurge which they can then declare are their opinions.'

Vivienne Westwood, 1995

In the mid-1980s Vivienne had ceded financial responsibility for her company to her manager and one-time lover Carlo D'Amario. Now, in the mid-1990s, she delegated much of the designing to her husband, Andreas Kronthaler. Though the clothes still bore the 'Vivienne Westwood' label, without Vivienne having consistently invested her inimitable originality in their conception and execution, they became mere pastiches of her own archive, and formulaic interpretations of the way she had put a modern spin on historical costume. Even loyal friends admitted their disappointment. Jean-Charles de Castelbajac considers: 'With Andreas her work is now not interesting. I went to the last show – so bad!' By 1996 Jeff Banks bluntly judged Vivienne to be 'part of the ordinariness and repetitiveness of fashion now'.

As well as ransacking Vivienne's backlist to reproduce bondage trousers, slogan T-shirts, pirate shirts, Miss Marple tweeds and Witches knitwear, Andreas indulged his own taste. Vivienne believed that under his influence the collections had become 'grand', when in fact they were just camp. Whether it was in the seedy, but no longer shocking, sexual dress rehashed from the two preceding decades, or *ancien régime* furbelows reminiscent of another Austrian, Marie-Antoinette, Andreas's signature was unmistakable. By January 1996, a few weeks before Vivienne's autumn/winter collection was unveiled in Paris, she had ceded so much control to him that when a close friend asked what it included she replied, 'I don't know, Andreas is doing it.'

Though Andreas's involvement in the collections was not revealed to the public, many insiders recognised it, and regretted the change in style. Leonie Edwards-Jones, who joined the company in 1993 from Chanel to work in the press office, observed in 1995: 'He's designed so much of the collections recently, and ... all that changes is the tartan ... Vivienne lets him get away with it because she's so busy. Carlo keeps dragging her off to Italy or she's too busy wanting to be an intellectual.' Mike Figgis, the British director who filmed Vivienne's 'On Liberty' show in 1994, unwittingly summed up Andreas's impact: 'The minute you put a man in that context they're obviously gay, and it changes the mix in an interesting way.'

Vivienne was guilty of what she consistently inveighed against – 'non-stop distractions'. For over a decade she had reproached the young for being distracted by commercially-driven popular culture. Now she submitted to the media's demands, making herself constantly available for self-promotion and punditry, even if the subject had little connection with her profession. Though she claimed (untruly) that she never watched television, and frequently professed her contempt for its superficiality, she began to make regular appearances on it, pronouncing on taste and education on chat shows, magazine shows and news programmes.

Vivienne relished the role of public personality. On 11 June 1994, having been briefed by Gary Ness, she lectured on fashion at the Cambridge University Union. In October she was the subject of an extended interview in the art magazine *Flash Art*, to coincide with exhibitions of her work at the Stedelijk Museum de Lakenhal and the Leiden Museum in Amsterdam. During the autumn she was also in discussion with the South Bank Centre and the British Council about the possibility of curating an exhibition of Fragonard's personal collection of prints, and in May 1995 the Institute of Contemporary Art chose her as the first winner of the Outstanding Achievement in Contemporary Culture award. These and other projects, including monthly duties at the Hochschule in Berlin, designing costumes for plays such as a German production of Brecht's *Threepenny Opera*, and trips to Brazil, the Tyrol, Sicily, Japan, New York, Sydney, Milan and Paris (the list is not exhaustive), distracted Vivienne from full-time designing.

During the autumn and spring of 1995–96, Vivienne virtually set aside design altogether to work with her brother Gordon Swire and his American wife Cynthia on a three-part television series entitled *Painted Ladies* for Channel 4's *Without Walls*. In it she explored the historical interplay between fashion and art, and delivered opinions – largely culled from the scholarly texts of costume historians Aileen Ribeiro of the Courtauld Institute and the American Anne Hollander – on the nature of elegance, the riches of historical costume and the manner in which she deployed them to elevate contemporary dress.

Interviewed on NBC's Superchannel in September 1995 by Selina Scott, whose sympathetic tones occasionally lulled a guest into revelation, Vivienne admitted, with a sigh, that being a fashion designer had become 'a job of work, almost a treadmill'. She wished to transcend fashion's limitations, as she saw them, and strive for greater intellectual standing. 'If I were to die only having worked on my fashion career,' she said, 'I wouldn't feel I'd achieved anything at all.'

At the beginning of 1995, while Carlo D'Amario was trying to capitalise on Vivienne's reputation as fashion's most important innovator to launch licensed ranges and her first perfume deal, she was publicly admitting that she delegated designing to her husband. 'Now Andreas is making many of the decisions for me. His decision might be a very different decision to what I might have made, but it's as good as I might have made. So he's taken the workload off me ... Andreas is fury to my serenity. My talent is cutting things very calmly with a spatial intelligence ... you watch Andreas working and you've never seen a more wild person with cloth. He's everybody's idea of what a designer is like, somebody terribly dramatic with everything. He's got a wonderful sense of drama.' But 'wild' was a euphemism for messy, and Andreas's 'drama' was camp. Her collections slid into a parody of Dior and Balenciaga's couture combined with the sort of costume usually associated with amateur dramatics.

The vernacular or 'street' element which McLaren had so successfully brought to the clothes he and Vivienne had designed together was eclipsed by Vivienne's cultural pretensions and Andreas's theatricality. She mistakenly thought that this was an improvement: 'My designs are becoming more grand in a very archetypal kind of way since being with Andreas.' Whereas in the past if, for example, she had designed a dress with a train, she intended the wearer to fling it over her shoulder in a modern gesture of practicality and defiance, now she was 'quite into the idea of people walking down the street and letting their train get as dirty as anything. I wouldn't have done that without Andreas. I was too practical, too female. What about the dry-cleaning bills? No more.' Now she became enraptured by the snippets of social history she picked up from her reading, such as seventeenth-century English aristocrats sending their linen to be laundered in France, or the Tudors selling a plot of land to pay for a lace collar. These were, to her mind, grand and laudable gestures, at once romantic and elegant.

For some time Vivienne had been hoping to appeal to the tastes of grown-up, affluent and elegant women. However, she failed to grasp that lightness and ease of upkeep were two of the most prized attributes of modern clothing to such women, and that these qualities were not necessarily inimical to beauty. Women were on the move, and true chic, even in the grandest circles, was being able to manage with hand luggage alone, even if one was passing a fortnight in a cosmopolitan capital with the attendant formal occasions. Issey Miyake's understanding of this was one of the reasons for his worldwide success in ready-to-wear, and even the most lavish couturiers were designing gossamer-light evening dresses, hand-painted rather than weighed down with beadwork. The new, technologically-improved textiles that provided warmth and water resistance without weight, and which could be rolled up in a small tote bag, shaken out and worn immediately, were ignored by Vivienne, who continued to favour heavy tweeds and high-maintenance duchess satins.

Vivienne's skill in the seventies and eighties had been seizing styles from the distant past – the pirate, the classical Greek, the French revolutionary – and dragging them into the twentieth century by fusing them with an icon of contemporary culture – a toy, a pop song, a pin-up from a 'skin' magazine. Even in the late eighties, she continued to work in this way. By the nineties, however, she was simply telescoping costume sources – placing an empire leg of mutton sleeve with a *belle époque* bustle – and copying them almost exactly.

If a journalist criticised her clothes for not being modern, she argued that since the fabrics used in the past were no longer available and she had devised new ways to create these looks, her clothes were, *ipso facto*, modern. It was a specious argument. At the same time that she was condemning her peers for ransacking the styles of the twentieth century in a lazy exercise in retro-chic, she was doing exactly the same with a more distant past. Timespan, not working method, was the only difference in their approach to design.

One of the most exciting qualities of Vivienne and McLaren's clothes, the rock 'n' roll roguishness that conferred modern stardom on the wearer, was now discarded by her. For years the big Italian and French houses had been eager to acquire and exploit the street credibility associated with British, and particularly Vivienne and McLaren's, fashion. 'The King's Road was the catwalk,' McLaren says. 'That's why the fashion people recognised us. The whole idea of the Italian thievery in fashion – the way those guys go down the Portobello and King's Roads or Camden Market on a pilgrimage to see us lot – we were the first people to bring street fashion onto the Paris catwalk. They poached our ideas and they just copied them.'

Once mainstream designers had, in Yves Saint Laurent's wake, brought the street and rock 'n' roll to ready-to-wear, it became less imitative of couture and more desirable to a larger buying public. It was typical of Vivienne to choose this moment to discard her mantle of modernity. Mainstream designers rushed to pick it up. Versace did his version of 'Seditionaries', Dolce & Gabbana did 'SEX', Gaultier did 'Buffalo', and in doing so profited from a partnership with the entertainment business. Rock and film stars began to associate themselves with fashion labels – Elton John and Sting wore Versace, Michelle Pfeiffer and Jodie Foster wore Armani, Madonna wore Dolce & Gabbana – in a promotional symbiosis communicated day and night across the globe by MTV.

Needing stars, the fashion and media industries systematically created them. In the early and mid-eighties they elevated designers, then, in the nineties, models. The myth-making had begun with British *Vogue*'s January 1990 cover of five models in white cotton singlets, which focused on the women rather than the clothes. But few rock or film stars selected Vivienne's clothes any more, and those who did were disappointed by her studio's lack of professionalism when they placed made-to-measure orders. Even long-standing fans such as Holly

Johnson of Frankie Goes to Hollywood said, 'I don't do Westwood any more. It's not Vivienne any more.' The magic had gone.

Andreas encouraged Vivienne to exploit her backlist. Although she had little interest in her past work, he was excited by her archive. He had not worn it the first time round, and wished to exploit it. It was not unusual for established designers to revive classics from their range: Yves Saint Laurent, for example, frequently included the pea jacket or the smoking suit in his collections. But as Vivienne's attentions were drawn to her other roles, Andreas and her studio tinkered with the ideas in her archives, and relied too heavily on them.

From 'Salon' onwards, the same articles of clothing appeared again and again in Vivienne's shows, only a change in the cloth registering the passing seasons. The waist-hugging 'Bettina', the double-breasted 'D.B.' and the courtly 'Dangerous Liaisons' jackets were recycled, along with rib-hugging blouses and overblown ballgowns. While Vivienne continued to control certain aspects of the collection – typically the first twenty outfits, that communicated its theme – students supervised by Andreas made up the rest of the hundred or more outfits, each of them designing one or two. Whereas most designers staged shows that lasted between twenty and forty-five minutes, Vivienne's dragged on for over an hour.

Vivienne tried to run her staff at arm's length. At any one time she employed five or so students, usually recruited in Vienna or Berlin. They would work in her studio for a few months, often without pay, until they either fell out with their increasingly difficult boss – always reverentially referred to as 'Madame' – or were forced to return home because they had no work papers. Immigration and Health and Safety officers frequently visited the Westwood studios to inspect conditions. By 1996 Vivienne employed five workers in pattern cutting, eight in sampling and five in design. Her creativity was becoming buried under gauche student outrageousness. There was no longer one single vision on the Westwood catwalk.

Andreas moved into the vacuum created by Vivienne's absence, and his ambition was plain to see. Dining in Paris one night with Andreas, Vivienne, Anna Piaggi of Italian Condé Nast and her companion Vernon Lambert, Vivienne's old friend Keith Wainwright heard Andreas boasting – out of his wife's earshot – that he was the true source of creativity in the studio.

'On Liberty' (autumn/winter 1994–95), shown at the Carrousel du

Louvre in Paris, exemplified Vivienne's preoccupation with historical costume and cod-philosophy. Just as conceptual art needed a manifesto in order for the viewer to understand the artist's message, so Vivienne's audience needed a lecture to enable them to read the meanings sewn into the clothes. In hand-outs placed on the seats, she drew their attention to the essay *On Liberty* by the nineteenth-century utilitarian thinker John Stuart Mill:

> Le Mieux est L'Ennemi du Bien . . . Liberty depends on encouraging minority views and the 'bien' must not be allowed to abolish the 'mieux'. As for fashion, couture must exit [sic] alongside mass production, just as socialites [sic] which nourish heretical coteries and slogans will not stagnate, but flourish.

In celebrating *haute couture*, Vivienne was not only defending the value of craft, but also of élitism. She seemed incapable of divorcing the two. Despite her claims that 'I always vote against the worst. I vote Labour,' her pontifications and demeanour became increasingly those of a Tory dressed up as a Whig. 'What one is rebelling against all the time is orthodoxy,' she insisted. 'The orthodoxy today is an ugly casualness which I believe is a tyranny imposed by Hollywood because no one's supposed to look better than anyone else. It's a tyranny of you're all supposed to look the same. It's against élitism. Whereas, in the past, everything that happened was the work of the *avant-garde* and they were always an élite, including a fashion élite; people who had the time and money to cultivate their appearance and who, by the way, had a contempt.'

'On Liberty' (the collection, not the essay) revealed not only something of the workings of Vivienne's mind but also the way in which Andreas had seized upon her ideas and exaggerated them to burlesque proportions. To Vivienne, fashion was a means of teaching, and she used it to convey both her anti-democratic sentiments and her appreciation of feminine voluptuousness. She knew that these preoccupations flew in the face of received opinion: the former angered liberals, the latter the fashion establishment.

With her inquisitive and undisciplined mind, Vivienne spliced together entirely unconnected ideas which she believed could coexist in an instructive synthesis. Having been told by Gary Ness that Socrates and John Stuart Mill had dismissed democracy as the rule of the lowest common denominator, it was a short step for her to conclude that democracy was flawed. Secondly, she learned that during the democratic age, which coincided with the age of plenty in the West, the masses had become well fed, even fat, and that it had become a sign of distinction and nobility to be slender. This emaciated silhouette was applauded by the fashion industry, not least because it was easier to hang clothes on a boyish skeleton than to shape them over a demandingly curvaceous female form. As a criticism of democracy and the modern ideal of the body, Vivienne padded out her models with huge, bustle-like pads on their bottoms, and dressed them up in arcane costume.

Initially, she had been unsure whether or not to introduce this radical new silhouette. If she had been working on her own, she would probably have created a subtler version, but Andreas found it so amusing that he encouraged her to exaggerate it. 'Men idealise women more than women do,' she insisted. 'It's men pushing just that little bit further. At first I was a little bit sceptical [about the padding] on a slim lady, but then I got really thrilled. The gorgeousness.'

Vivienne was particularly interested in nineteenth-century versions of the bustle, the 'tournure' (1870–75) and the 'strapontin' (1883–88). The bustle skirt was fitted with half hoops across the hips in order to accentuate the smallness of the waist and the arch of the back. The drapery was then hooked to the waist or formed by a second skirt. The protrusion had to be swung to one side if the wearer wished to sit down.

Vivienne's bustle consisted of a wire cage fastened onto girdle-like, high-waisted knickers which were worn under the skirt or dress. Racier customers simply wore the knickers on their own, without a skirt. The cages, based on the wire hemispheres used to hold flowers in position on gravestones, were forged by Andreas's blacksmith father in the Tyrol. Whenever a delivery arrived in Britain, despite a detailed carnet and extensive previous correspondence with HM Customs, a customs officer would telephone the Westwood offices demanding an explanation of these strange objects.

It is probable that two young British designers, Georgina Godley and Leigh Bowery, partly inspired the 'On Liberty' padded bottom. Though Vivienne denied ever copying – 'No, nothing from a designer today' – the exaggerated bottom had been incorporated into Godley and Bowery's creations in recent years, and Vivienne not only knew both the designers but had publicly admired their work. Godley's 'Lump & Bump' collection (spring/summer 1986) consisted of plain white Lycra dresses stretched over foam rubber exaggerations of feminine curves, such as the bottom and the belly. Unlike Vivienne, Godley was motivated by feminism. 'I was examining the female figure,' she explained. 'Azzedine Alaïa was a big influence at the time; with that American female who wanted to show off her worked body. But there was a strong masculinity to it which I found denigrating to modern woman, as though she was trying to have a man's body.' Godley's collection was an attempt to rekindle the love of the female form and its fecundity. Soon after Godley showed this collection, Vivienne was invited by Anna Piaggi's Italian magazine *Vanity* (March/April 1987) to select an outfit from a designer whom she admired. She chose a dress by Godley.

Leigh Bowery was an Australian performance artist who arrived in London in the early eighties and went to astonishing lengths to dress up. He became such a spectacle on the club scene that he turned his hobby into a profession, wearing his outlandish costumes to perform with his band, Minty (Chicago slang for lesbian). Two mutual friends connected Bowery to Vivienne. Richard Torry, who had inspired her tweed 'armour' jackets, was a member of Minty, and Michael Clark, the modern dancer who had modelled in Vivienne's 'Time Machine' and 'Cut & Slash' shows, commissioned Bowery to design costumes for his ballets.

Bowery delighted in physical exaggeration, parodying the excesses of the eighties in his massive costumes. His luminous catsuit was inflated to Michelin man proportions, his platform boots were elevated two feet from the ground, his jacket bristled with thousands of hair grips and his S&M mask was pimpled with a thousand beads. In 1986 his fashion tip was to 'emphasise the rear'. Like Godley, he was reacting against flat-bottomed androgens in tight-skirted working-woman suits. He devised a bottom-cage for Michael Clark, like a surgical prosthesis made from flesh-pink plastic and leather straps. It was a fetish object which drew attention to the dancer's enlarged haunches. Vivienne regularly attended both Bowery's and Clark's performances (she had developed a great love of ballet), and when her assistant Simon Barker sent her a birthday card in 1990 of Bowery dressed in a leather fetish mask illuminated with a lightbulb she commented, 'I think he's quite a talent. Ooh, I love that card so much, it's my favourite on my mantelpiece.'

Voluptuousness was not a new aesthetic for Vivienne. She had been working towards an exaggerated female form for some seasons with her cleavage-enhancing corsets and her high 'elevated' platforms which forced the wearer to jut out her (or, in some cases, his) bottom in order to balance. Typically, Vivienne marshalled a heavyweight intellectual justification for the style: 'They say that once the human animal stood on two legs it freed its hands and the brain developed . . . that upright posture is so beautiful. I think it's enhanced by high heels. These change a woman's posture and figure, making her bottom stand out in a sexy way and giving the possibility of playing around with that vertical dynamic.' In 1998 she was to say, 'I've become ever more obsessed with finding ways to reduce the ribcage area of a woman's anatomy.' This explains why many women complain that the fit of Vivienne's jackets and blouses is too restricted across the back and shoulders. She is striving for an optical illusion.

Few journalists and buyers were willing to accept Vivienne's anatomical exaggeration, despite her argument that 'It's a question of adjusting your eyes. It's only perverse because it's unexpected.' But Mike Figgis was 'amazed by how quickly I found the big bums beautiful'. Figgis had been introduced to Vivienne by his daughter Romney, who had been at school with Joseph. Vivienne wanted someone to make a film of 'On Liberty' for the record, and Joseph suggested Figgis. On meeting the director, Vivienne had no idea who he was – 'She has none of those contemporary references, and was fairly offhand and a bit superior,' he recalled. Nevertheless, he financed the film, encouraged by the fact that Vivienne seemed 'indifferent' to the project, and consequently gave him a free rein.

Figgis had many reasons for wishing to record Vivienne's work for posterity. Her bustles, corsets and accessories were so complicated and arcane that he wanted to capture the ritual 'from another century' of the two or three people dressing the models – 'It was like watching your mother get dressed, in an extreme way.' Secondly, since Vivienne's shows were constrained by their low budget, and she had a *laissez-faire* attitude to the preparations backstage, he was convinced that the chaotic improvisations would be 'an adventure'. Thirdly, since the clothes flouted politically correct feminism, he wanted to convey the sexuality they lent to the wearer and the manner in which they celebrated femininity. In a world dominated by male fashion designers who peddled their fantasies of how a woman should dress, Vivienne was an original. Figgis also approved of her use of 'imperfect or characterful' models: 'She's inviting them to be very strong about their bodies and sexuality, to feel good and powerful in her clothes – extravagant and flamboyant.' The clothes communicated a female sexual power and 'knowingness' which Figgis found, 'as a man, intimidating'. Despite the fact that Figgis's observation is certainly true, ironically much of 'On Liberty' was designed by Andreas rather than Vivienne.

It was exactly these signals on the part of the wearer – of being at the same time a serious sexual predator and playfully humorous – that he captured by dressing the actress Elisabeth Shue in Westwood clothes for her role as a whore in his 1996 Oscar-winning film *Leaving Las Vegas*. When the props team showed Figgis the bric-à-brac-filled apartment they had designed for Shue's character, Figgis complained that it was too tacky. But she's a hooker, they countered. 'Yes, but she's a hooker who wears Vivienne Westwood – so she's informed. She's not wearing Frederick's of Hollywood' (a mail order firm that sold raunchy lingerie). Figgis did not consider Vivienne's clothes 'in any way whorish'. They were empowering and worldly, and to instil these qualities in Shue and prepare her psychologically for the role, he asked her to walk along Sunset Boulevard dressed in a Westwood corset and a micro mini. She stopped the traffic.

Throughout the filming, Figgis found Vivienne unusually candid and undistracted from her purpose. When he showed her the finished film she did not offer an opinion other than, 'Ooh, we could use those tapes to show the Japanese buyers.' When he suggested that he make a long-term documentary of her career, she replied frankly, 'For my purposes my brother's doing a better job [he would make a record of her collections]. But thanks, anyway.'

Like the milliner Stephen Jones, Figgis was struck by Vivienne's 'talent to get people to work for her and put in 100 per cent by giving this sense of helplessness, which is not true. But she's not manipulating you. She's giving you the choice.' However, he was left in no doubt that 'The big plus with Vivienne is that everyone likes her and no one sees her as a threat.' This explained her popularity with other fashion designers, who were typically competitive, and sometimes downright bitchy, towards one another.

When *Leaving Las Vegas* was shortlisted for a number of Oscars, the slick public relations officers of top designers, including Armani and Versace, lobbied Figgis and his team to wear their clothes on the big night. Figgis preferred to promote a fellow Brit whose clothes appeared in the film, and when he was interviewed by journalists from *Vogue* or *Women's Wear Daily*, he made a point of mentioning Vivienne's name. However, though he had intended to wear a Westwood outfit to the Oscar ceremony, her offices failed to send one. A pair of cufflinks, one a penis and the other a vulva, that Vivienne had given Figgis were far too small to be noticed on screen. By Hollywood standards, her promotional efforts were a shambles.

Andreas's heavy hand distorted the presentation of 'On Liberty'. Rather than editing the collection tightly round Vivienne's new body shape, which was difficult to assimilate, it was over-accessorised and disfigured by a series of lewd catwalk pranks intended to attract the tabloid media. Kate Moss, the childlike British supermodel, tottered down the catwalk naked save for a bouquet that she clutched to her girlish breast, eliciting cries of 'Child prostitute!'; the Italian supermodel Carla Bruni threw open her fake fur coat to reveal that she was wearing nothing underneath except a matching G-string; Naomi Campbell stomped along wearing a flashing traffic cone on her head. Subtle humour was not Andreas's forte. The brouhaha over the nudity, combined with the press's rejection of the bustle as unwearable (with the notable exception of *Women's Wear Daily*), overshadowed an important element of the show: Vivienne's first collaboration with the London textile house and department store Liberty's (another reason for the collection's title).

The emporium was founded by Arthur Lasenby Liberty in 1875, and specialised in importing artefacts from the East and manufacturing fabrics inspired by the Orient and the late-nineteenth-century Aesthetic movement. Its fashion department had stocked Westwood since 1992, and in October 1993 Vivienne was invited by the enterprising young UK sales manager, Anthony Daley, to collaborate with Liberty of London Prints, the wholesale fabric subsidiary. Daley believed, like Tony Langford of John Smedley before him, that exposure to the creativity of a top fashion designer would jolt the long-established firm out of its complacency. Liberty's had enjoyed a long association with fashion designers such as Jean Muir and Yves Saint Laurent, and Daley wanted to extend this into a more active collaboration. He believed that over the past two years Vivienne had 'shed her punk image and was beginning to be taken seriously as a worldwide designer'.

Following Daley's initial approach, Vivienne and Andreas arrived late one Friday afternoon in October 1993 at Liberty's. Vivienne had hardly set foot through the door before informing Daley that she loathed the firm's policy of targeting the tourist gift market. Nevertheless, once they had spent some hours in the fabrics archive, it became clear that she was becoming excited – more so than Andreas; perhaps the reputation of the great fabric house eluded him. She quietly suggested that she return with Ness, who she felt would have an affinity with the collection, particularly as he was an admirer of Arthur Liberty's friend, the artist James McNeill Whistler.

Accompanied by Ness, Vivienne leafed through the archive until her eye was caught by a small book of silk floral prints in subtle colours from the thirties, the Lotus collection of sixties revival Art Nouveau prints and the peacock-feather 'Hera' print designed for the firm by Arthur Silver in 1887. Eventually she settled on a total of eight prints in thirty-nine colour permutations to use in her collection. Working alongside her during these weeks, Anthony Daley was astonished by her total visual recall. In the course of six hours' research during two visits to the archive she did not take one note, yet she showed 'a remarkable memory for the minutest detail of a design'.

Liberty financed the production costs. The printing was carried out in its print works in the south of France, which had originally been owned by the innovative pre-war fabric house Bianchini Ferrier. Vivienne insisted that the designs be printed not only on traditional flat textiles such as brushed cotton and silk georgette, but also on hairy Donegal tweed, thick-piled velvet, slippery PVC, needlecord and denim. The craftsmen rose to the challenge enthusiastically, despite the tight two-week deadline, thrilled to work with such a demanding and innovative designer.

The handsome range was to be exclusive to Vivienne Westwood until the end of 1995, and she paid a wholesale price for each metre of cloth used for her collection. However, she failed to exploit the archive effectively. While using the 'Hera' print on denim jeans was an example of her transmuting a cultural icon from the past and giving it contemporary relevance, as she had done with pirate wear in 1979, the prissy sprig-print blouses she also developed were neither original nor exciting.

Besides the big bottoms and Liberty prints, 'On Liberty' featured tight, hand-crocheted dresses and jumpers in hyacinth, steel-grey and lilac (which Vivienne insisted be described on stocklists as '*flieder*', the German for the colour, even though buyers were flummoxed). Scattered over the knitwear were three-dimensional crocheted nosegays. Vivienne was still unrivalled in her knitwear collections, and her own adeptness (like her mother, who helped crochet the prototypes) at knitting and crochet inspired 'ideas all the time'. She championed handicrafts, arguing that 'people are wrong to think they can be modern by using technology. Technology is a tyrant.' Yet while technology could impose limitations on the way in which a garment was constructed, this was not true of modern fibres and textiles, against which she maintained a Luddite prejudice.

'On Liberty' was shown during the season in which the American director Robert Altman was in Paris filming his disappointing satire on the fashion business, *Prêt-à-Porter*. Sophia Loren, Tracey Ullman, Kim Basinger, Marcello Mastroianni and other actors attended the collections, usurping front-row seats normally reserved for the fashion press. Some prestigious houses, such as Chanel, anticipating that the film would be critical of their trade or simply a fiasco, refused to cooperate. Vivienne, however, was less circumspect, flying to Paris to appear briefly with Andreas in a non-speaking cameo part.

One of the film's central characters, a camp fashion designer called Cort Romney and played by Richard E. Grant, was a male version of Vivienne – although it could be argued that the character more closely resembled Andreas, whose hand was now very evident in her collections. In his autobiography Grant recalls being fitted for the role by 'a very tired Austrian man with bad teeth' (Andreas). He was to wear a pink three-piece suit, a floor-length grey coat and twelve-inch-heeled, crotch-high black boots, and also sported eighteenth-century white make-up, a beauty spot and a kiss curl. Before the filming, Grant and Vivienne lunched together so that she could brief him on her character. Over two hours she covered 'everything from her relationship with Malcolm McLaren, how punk came to be, humorous quotations from Oscar Wilde, her sons, her theory of beauty, and her great passion to form a salon for artists and thinkers "like they had then", all punctuated with constant cigs, all of which might have ballooned pretentiously, were they not couched in her resolutely Northern "solid" sounds . . . Most of all, her passion for clothes and everything to do with them is as relentless as a heartbeat: the cut, The Cut, *The Cut*.'

Grant remembers Vivienne watching the filming, 'ubiquitous' in pearls, caramel beige sweater and matching trousers. 'She could have been a housewife,' he says, but for the twelve-inch tartan platforms. She flew to New York to attend *Prêt-à-Porter*'s first night, but later came to feel she had been unwise to appear in the film, and whenever she was asked about it she would reply brusquely, 'I don't want to talk about it.'

Now approaching fifty, Malcolm McLaren had begun to seek out his erstwhile lover's company. Vivienne was irritated by the way that, as she saw it, he was sucking up to her after she had found success, sending her congratulatory letters after each collection saying 'I'm proud of you.' 'I don't need him to be proud of me,' she said. 'He's a bit egotistical in that way, he doesn't like anything that he thinks belongs to him to sort of slip away.' Nevertheless, a rendezvous was arranged by Jean-Charles de Castelbajac in the Paris nightclub L'Arc after the 'On Liberty' show. Both D'Amario and Andreas, fearing that she might still love McLaren, felt threatened by the meeting, and attempted to break up the conversation. But de Castelbajac held them at bay while Vivienne and McLaren huddled in a corner and talked intimately for over an hour and a half.

McLaren suggested that Joseph should enrol in a university course, and claimed that he could get him into Trinity College, Dublin. To his dismay, despite all her public pronouncements that education was the key to civilisation, Vivienne dismissed the idea with the excuse that 'Joe doesn't like books.' She, unlike McLaren, knew her own children, and realised she could not force books on her unlettered son. McLaren recalled that 'all she really wanted to talk about was her own work and what a wonderful designer she was.' While her self-absorption may have angered him, was it any wonder that Vivienne, with all her insecurities, was desperate to prove to the lover who had jilted her that she had, at last and despite him, succeeded?

In recognition of the Liberty partnership, Vivienne presented 'On Liberty' for a second time in a catwalk show in the store itself. Dora, dressed in Nivea blue satin with matching eye-shadow, was seated in the front row alongside her friend Madge, Carlo D'Amario and other members of the Westwood team. Chatting with her customary thigh-slapping ebullience as she waited for the show to begin, she was unaware that her button-through skirt had become unfastened, revealing her underwear. When this was drawn to her attention she threw her head back with laughter and announced at the top of her voice, 'I haven't been up to anything in the back, you know.' Mother and daughter shared not only a taste for the bawdy but also a sexual jealousy of other women. Dora was often unnecessarily critical of them, whether she was harshly judging the supermodels or dismissing Ben's girlfriends as 'tarts'.

As Dora sat laughing in the front row, John Walford, who was producing the show, observed Andreas backstage 'tweaking all the models' breasts and licking them. It was too much, so the girls were complaining. Then he started kissing the barman from the caterers. He was really drunk.'

Leonie Edwards-Jones's first vision of Andreas when being interviewed for her job in the PR office was unforgettable. He stood before her in silver platform sandals, his toenails painted with matching metallic varnish. He told her that Yves Saint Laurent was the greatest couturier, and that he would happily live in a cardboard box if the maestro would make him a couture dress. 'Where would you keep it?' she asked, affecting a deadpan interest. 'Oh, with some boy or other,' came the reply.

Vivienne admitted that living with Andreas was 'a situation I could easily have done without. I was very happy living alone.' Alluding to his sexual peccadilloes, she said, 'We all nurse certain feelings of jealousy and possession about a partner, but I really don't care with Andreas, to the extent that I want him to be happy at all times; no matter what he wants, anything he wants, I won't mind.' On another occasion she told a daily newspaper: 'All I've ever wanted is for him to enjoy himself. If he didn't come home at night, I wouldn't care. I mean, sometimes he doesn't come home. I really don't mind. I'm not wanting anything from him. If he were to go away, which he won't . . . I've never been more secure about anybody in my life.'

Vivienne had cried herself dry over McLaren's philandering, and perhaps she now believed that she could not shackle another man. Her old friend Keith Wainwright watched the relationship develop with concern: 'She's never been good at choosing people . . . she has changed her political orientations, so perhaps he could change his sexual orientations one day. Let's hope.'

Colleagues speculated over her relationship with Andreas. Since she occasionally boasted about having had sex, they assumed it was not a regular feature of her married life. At one dinner, for example, she was sitting next to the shoe designer Manolo Blahnik, who was appalled to see her stealing food from other plates, 'like an animal'. When he asked her, 'So how are you these days, Vivienne?' she replied, 'Oh, I'm all right. I was fucked last night.' On another occasion, in 1994, she arrived at the studio with ripped and shredded stockings and told a colleague, 'I was taken on the bed by Andreas this morning. Don't you love this look?' Later in the day she was photographed by Juergen Teller in Battersea Park, still proudly parading the dishevelled *déshabille* of her sexual encounter. According to a close colleague, despite Andreas's active bisexuality, he and Vivienne did not practise 'safe sex'. They had been persuaded by the German punk singer Nina Hagen and her boyfriend Frank that AIDS was merely a psychosomatic illness, exaggerated by the media, and it suited them to subscribe to this comforting theory.

From the early nineties there was yet another distinct change in Vivienne's appearance. Formerly she had lived in turned-up 'Spot' jeans, a jumper given to her by Joseph decorated with an image of Jemima Puddleduck and Timberland boots, or alternatively a kilt, white socks, bare knees, and a twinset. But when Andreas stepped into her life, every day, even if she was just working in the studio, she made up her face, coiffed her hair and wore stockings – never tights – and a suit from the collection. Knee-socks and Rocking Horse shoes were discarded for his sake. Like a teenager in love, she determined to lose weight, sipping hot water rather than eating. She became so conscious of her weight that she could not help commenting on other women's bodies. When the pop singer Debbie Harry was trying on clothes in Davies Street, Vivienne remarked on how fat she had become, and on several occasions she contradicted customers in the shop by aggressively insisting that they were a size twelve, not ten.

On 3 April 1994 the tabloid *Sunday Mirror* announced: 'Fashion Queen Wants to be a Mum Again . . . at 52'. Claiming to have spotted Vivienne and Andreas on their way to Dr Severino Antonori's fertility clinic in Milan, the paper informed readers that Vivienne had been trying to get pregnant for the past few years, quoting a 'friend' who said: 'She is an intelligent woman and knows there are dangers with becoming pregnant at her age, but she has set her heart on the idea. She is very much in love with Andreas and they both want to have a baby.' Vivienne responded vaguely, 'I don't know where they got that from. They can write what they like. I don't care.' Two *Daily Mirror* journalists had followed her to Italy and trailed her for two days, which she passed in the company of her design assistant Murray Blewitt. Andreas was not present. Derek Dunbar, however, was not surprised by the article: 'Yes, I think the fertility treatment is true.' There was clearly a mole in her studio feeding the newspapers with gossip.

It is difficult to know whether Vivienne really did want a child by Andreas, but recalling her relationship with McLaren, perhaps she reasoned that a child would be an added bond between them. Deeply smitten as she was, medical orthodoxy on the inadvisibility of childbirth at her age would hardly impinge on her decision. Jean-Charles de Castelbajac observed, 'Vivienne is the one woman in the world I know who really needs to be loved, and she never has been. She is surrounded by sycophants. The only people who loved her were her sons.'

When not on the self-promotion bandwagon, Vivienne avoided socialising and headed for her bed, to read. Her pupil—teacher relationship with Ness continued, but a tug of war for her attention escalated, between him on the one side and Andreas and D'Amario on the other. Andreas, always wary of Ness's hold over Vivienne, was infuriated that the prints he had chosen with her on their initial visit to the Liberty archive were replaced by Ness's selection. D'Amario was suspicious of Ness's high-falutin' notions about 'prestige' and 'culture' – he was impressed by profits. And so Vivienne see-sawed between the two camps, knowingly playing them off against each other to maintain their attention and provoke Ness's persecution complex. He would chastise her with, 'Shut your cakehole, Hilda Ogden,' or 'You've been listening to brain-damaged morons again.' Only Ness could get away with speaking to her so sharply. He was appalled by Andreas's idea of calling the autumn/winter 1996–97 collection 'The Golden Shower' (a reference to the sexual practice of urinating over one's partner), and by D'Amario's plans to move the business lock, stock and barrel to Italy. But Vivienne was still bitter about the way in which she had been treated in Britain: 'Maybe I should leave now. England is so terribly puritan, and puritanism is rooted in envy.' A spokesman for the company quickly assured her public that she only intended to move her production, not her home, to Italy.

Ness remained at Vivienne's beck and call, and mutual friends witnessed how she manipulated him, one minute assuring him of his usefulness and defraying his medical costs (his health was failing due to years of alcohol and nicotine), the next abandoning him without calling for weeks. When, one hot summer, Françoise Rust-Fourteau bought Ness a small fridge, Vivienne was furious that her employee had usurped her own role, shouting, 'I don't see why you did that. It's not your matter. *I* take care of Gary, not you. If he needs something he asks *me*!'

Treating Ness as if he was a member of her staff, Vivienne would make last-minute demands on him, such as calling on the eve of a show and insisting, while the printers waited, that he devise a title for it, even though he had not even seen the clothes; or instructing him to research his idea for a *toile de Jouy* print based on seventeenth- and eighteenth-century French *cartes des tendres* (maps showing a topography of the emotions). By chance, at exactly the same time McLaren, who had returned to fashion, was toying with the idea of printing a 'map of feelings' on cloth for his 1995 collection, and was planning to line jackets with prints of antique three-dimensional maps of Paris. Vivienne, again coincidentally, had a similar map pinned on her noticeboard for inspiration. Clearly, the two still worked on the same wavelength, picking similar themes out of the blue.

Behind the scenes, Ness continued to act as Vivienne's ghost writer. When Editions Hazan in Paris invited her to write an epilogue to Marie Simon's study of nineteenth-century painting and fashion, *Fashion and Art*, Vivienne assigned Ness the task, went abroad and did not even bother to read 'her' text. All the while she held out the carrot to him that she would find him a new flat and install him in a 'salon'.

Weary and unwell, Ness was not only concerned about the 'fools' influencing his protégée, but also about her physical safety. On three occasions between 1994 and 1996 she arrived at his flat with a swollen face and a black eye. 'She's a victim, and maybe she likes it that way', says Françoise Rust-Fourteau. Vivienne's excuses sounded like a

battered wife's clichés – she had 'tripped own the stairs . . . fallen off
her bicycle . . . been to the dentist' – and did not prevent her friends
and colleagues from speculating about who was beating her up. John
Walford categorically dismissed the idea that D'Amario was to blame:
he used verbal, not physical, abuse to cow her. They were aware
that Vivienne's behaviour had in the past produced physically violent
reactions from McLaren, and they suspected her of provoking Andreas
too. Sometimes when she became frustrated by her inarticulacy she
would hit out, inviting retaliation.

Vivienne's marriage was under strain. By 22 October 1995, the
vigilant *Sunday Mirror*, which had chronicled the life and exploits of
the odd couple, their secret marriage and alleged fertility treatment,
reported that a trial separation had taken place, and that although
Vivienne and Andreas were cohabiting once again, 'friends' believed
it was only a matter of time before they separated for good. Though
the relationship occasionally exploded into rows – not surprisingly,
considering that two such creative and erratic characters shared a small
flat – the pair had become professionally and emotionally inseparable.
Vivienne was deeply in love, and Andreas was protective of his wife's
well-being.

By 1994, the couple spent more time designing in the flat than in
the studio. The eighteen-inch-high wooden mannequin that Vivienne
designed on was taken home, and she experimented there. The pressure
on her was eased by Andreas and others sharing the burden, and she
no longer spent ten- or twelve-hour days at work, preferring to read
or to walk their wire-haired fox terrier, Alexandra, on Clapham
Common or in Battersea Park. She periodically turned up at the studio,
sometimes two or three hours late for an appointment, to inspect
samples and instruct her staff. Andreas had taken over most of the
liaison with the Italian manufacturers of the Red Label, Staff
International, whom he visited at Noventa Vicentina once or twice a
month. He also took complete charge of the menswear collection.
Murray Blewitt handled the Japanese licences and designed the shoes
for the manufacturer Guido Pasquale (the partnership collapsed in
1996, and Amethyst Shoes in London replaced the Italian company),
and an Italian licensee, Braccialini, was given free rein to design the
bags and luggage. Murray Blewitt and Mark Spye became more and
more indispensable to Vivienne, who delegated design decisions to
them as well as to Andreas.

'MAN', Vivienne's menswear label, was launched in January 1996, and is principally Andreas's project. The clothes tend to be camp and theatrical depictions of men's costume: frock coats, breeches, spangled corsets. Lacking Vivienne's grounding influence, few of them are suitable for daily wear. Paul Smith guardedly comments of the label: 'It's incredibly specific. You either think it's fantastic or you just don't get it. Brave and directional, perhaps.'

As public interest in her behaviour and lifestyle grew, Vivienne's self-confidence turned to arrogance, and her once-provocative subversion to shrill self-regard. She lost touch with the sources that had inspired her in the past, such as the exhilarating London club culture. Her isolation became almost complete when a number of loyal staff members, who had once brought the outside world to her, handed in their notice, leaving her surrounded by sycophants who referred to her as 'Madame'. 'She's someone who definitely craves praise, and when she finds it she will hang on to it,' believes McLaren. The plain-speaking Rust-Fourteau says, 'She thinks very highly of herself. She makes you wait for an appointment and is always late. She likes the red carpet treatment.'

Where once Vivienne had been driven by her indignation about the injustices of the world, and had energetically challenged the status quo on behalf of youth, she now scorned the young, declaring, 'I don't have faith in young people any more. I don't waste time trying to communicate with them.' Instead, she wholeheartedly embraced Ness's defence of élitism, and demanded her place among the élite.

In 1993 D'Amario had moved to Britain full time, and friction started to build up between him and Joseph, who was nominally the company's managing director. Initially D'Amario moved into Joseph's flat in Pimlico, but the two were soon rowing bitterly. On one occasion D'Amario angrily declared that he was moving out, and Vivienne promptly offered to let him stay at her flat. Joseph and D'Amario refused to speak to each other for nearly a month.

The acrimony came to a head a few days before Christmas 1993. After several months' preparation and negotiation, Joseph and John Rowley, who had become increasingly involved in the business at Vivienne's request, had struck a lucrative licensing deal with the Japanese firm Itochu-Horizonti. Five days before Christmas they requested expenses to fly to Tokyo in order to finalise the agreement. D'Amario refused, insisting that if the Japanese were so keen, they could come to London. A major argument broke out in the office, which lasted from seven in the evening until one o'clock the following morning. According to Rowley, D'Amario dismissed the Japanese offer as 'a crap deal'. Rowley and Joseph tried to persuade Vivienne that D'Amario was only taking this negative view because it hadn't been set up by him, and in the course of the argument photographs were produced showing Vivienne's clothes being illicitly sold on the Riviera for D'Amario's profit. Finally, Rowley gave an ultimatum: 'Vivienne, it's him or me.' Vivienne turned on D'Amario, calling him a fool, then left to make a cup of tea. When she returned a few minutes later she delivered a monologue which ended with the words, 'I agree with everything Carlo says.' Rowley left the next day, telling Vivienne he found it impossible to work with D'Amario.

Joseph stayed on briefly, but as D'Amario's power grew he became increasingly frustrated. He did manage, on Rowley's urging, to conclude the Itochu-Horizonti deal, although D'Amario threw a tantrum in front of the Japanese at the final meeting, pleading with Vivienne not to sign. Soon afterwards Joseph resigned, officially to go to university in Dublin, as McLaren had planned, although he had little interest in further education. According to Rowley and McLaren, despite the fact that he had invested nearly a decade of work in his mother's company, he was forced to leave with no collateral in it. He and Vivienne did not speak for six months.

Why, despite entreaties from both her son and Rowley, who had been vital to the process which would see the company's annual turnover increase from £600,000 in 1993 to nearly £15 million by the beginning of 1995, did Vivienne side with D'Amario and allow both of them to resign? Manny Silverman, who had conducted business with her in the early nineties, found it incomprehensible: 'The enigma is, why is Carlo's hold on Vivienne so strong that she can betray her son in the business?' Vivienne felt perpetually indebted to D'Amario because he had saved her from bankruptcy, sheltered her in her darkest hour and put her business back on track in the mid-eighties. Without him, she believed, she would not have been able to continue to work in fashion. To some extent, this was a fair assessment of the situation. What other manager would have put up with her irrational behaviour, uncommercial designs and wilful disregard for the market over so many years? However, D'Amario had secured his pound of flesh, and was now an affluent man.

Vivienne's emotional and irrational decision was also influenced by her abiding sense of protection towards the underdog. As D'Amario was challenged by Joseph, Rowley and many other employees, including Dunbar and Barker, who consistently drew her attention to his financial improprieties, she felt compelled to stand by him, saying to Simon Barker, 'I hope you're wrong. I've got a history of being ripped off.' She was prepared to defend D'Amario partly out of her sense of obligation to him, and partly because she did not particularly care about company profits and her bank balance. She had enough to live on, and as long as D'Amario allowed her freedom to pursue her own designs, study culture and lecture the public, she was happy. Gene Krell, her friend of twenty years' standing, says, 'Look, she didn't have an alternative. You make choices, and anyway, over the business, she was not terribly concerned.'

Between 1993 and 1995 staff haemorrhaged from the firm. Two of Vivienne's most ardent supporters, Derek Dunbar and Simon Barker, who had worked alongside her since her return from Italy, left in spring 1994 and spring 1995 respectively, driven out by a combination of D'Amario's suspicion of their influence over Vivienne and their boredom with 'Andreas's collections', as they dubbed them. Neither found the environment at Westwood creative or happy any longer, and they could no longer tolerate watching Vivienne becoming cut off from her old friends by new courtiers. They believed that she had 'no conception of loyalty – none at all'. Dunbar, in a final attempt to break through Vivienne's carapace of self-esteem, warned her about the artful flatterers controlling her life, and about D'Amario's business practices. He demanded a decent redundancy payment, and threatened to report D'Amario to the Inland Revenue if he did not agree. D'Amario responded by reporting Dunbar himself, but after investigation his tax returns were found to be acceptable. Within a few months, however, the Inland Revenue were investigating Vivienne's activities. Other members of staff who left discovered that, contrary to the figures on their payslips, none of their tax or National Insurance contributions had been paid. In 1995 the company moved from the Battersea schoolhouse complex to a modern, charmless but functional three-storey building just south of the Thames in Elcho Street, still in Battersea. It consisted of a huge open-plan studio on the ground floor and boxlike little offices above.

With Joseph, Rowley, Barker and Dunbar all gone, Vivienne was left isolated. D'Amario boasted that in future he would only employ 'plain brains', simple and unquestioning staff who could not challenge his practices. On the rare occasions when Vivienne did query his actions, he would aggressively dismiss her concerns; Françoise Rust-Fourteau heard him shouting at her, 'I'm the one who runs the company. You just shut up and design.'

Rust-Fourteau – clearly not a 'plain brain' – was summarily dismissed by D'Amario in August 1994 with the insult, 'You're just a cow for producing children!' (she had three sons). At close quarters, as Vivienne's personal assistant, she had observed D'Amario's skilful manipulation of her: 'She is very clever, but she can also be very naïve, and he knows her very well and knows that she admires him. She thinks he's so intelligent, especially what he's done for the company. There is no way that you can change her mind on that. She doesn't want to open her eyes.'

D'Amario handled Vivienne with threats and flattery in equal measure. It was partly as a result of the latter that she began to become insufferably arrogant. Sally Brampton, a writer and journalist who had championed her long before she finally received public recognition in Britain, said at the end of 1995: 'The last time I saw her she was breathtakingly rude. In an incredulous voice, she said to me, "I hear you've written a novel." "Actually, I've written two," I replied. And she said, "Why did you bother to do that? Nothing decent's been written this century, it's just full of third-rate minds, you know." I kept my cool and just replied, "By your own admission, Vivienne, you've never read anything from this century, nothing except Huxley, so how could you know?"' It was a typical exchange.

After a fashion show in Berlin, a gushing German fan had compared Vivienne's work to Shakespeare's, and she liked to quote this suitably respectful appraisal. In 1996 she told a colleague that her latest collection was so good that 'it should be in a museum'. One curator who has dealt with Vivienne over the years found that her ego had swollen to such an extent that every encounter put her in mind of 'those Russian social-realist posters for propaganda: Mother Russia storming over her downtrodden people, who lie prostrate underneath her. She has one aim in mind – the grand picture – at everyone else's expense.'

Vivienne justified her behaviour by citing one of her idols, Bertrand Russell, who had written an essay on why the Americans and the British could not comprehend one another: whereas the British deplored bragging, the Americans were irritated by British self-effacement. Vivienne subscribed to the American point of view. Gene Krell says her behaviour is not arrogance but 'brutal honesty': 'Her feeling is that false humility was not a virtue. The fact that she had worked so hard and for so long before people recognised her talent – why should she have humility?' But 'brutal honesty' could be socially unacceptable. While dining in Paris with a curator from the Louvre, Vivienne was shown the work of his artist wife, who printed almost imperceptible images onto huge white canvases. 'There's nothing there. It's rubbish!' she announced, in front of the woman. Though the couple spoke fluent English, Vivienne kept turning to her other companions to provide a French translation, explaining, 'I don't speak French, you see, I speak Latin.'

Such incidents reveal Vivienne's continuing feelings of inadequacy and her desperate flight from ordinariness. 'Since my earliest youth I have not wanted to be stupid,' she says. 'I thought I was stupid, though. I thought that nobody around me had enough information to give me.' Aware that she had few social graces, she overcompensated by playing the oaf, but as a result she was becoming isolated: 'Today I do suffer from isolation. It's very very difficult to have a conversation with anybody. I'm not used to have [sic] to draw a diagram to explain every term I use so there's only a few people with whom I can have a conversation, by which I mean something to say. There are very few ideas around.'

Though from 1997 Vivienne was required to design six shows a year – two Gold Label, two Red Label and two menswear – she concentrated only on the Gold, leaving assistants and Andreas to design the other four collections. Her greatest joy was spending two or three days in her flat working on the introductory blurb that accompanied each show, like a student set an essay. 'It excites her more than design now,' Murray Blewitt says.

Vivienne had no sense of personal nostalgia, and was irritated by the punk revival of the mid-1990s, though she did appear on BBC television's survey of the movement for *Arena* in August 1995. She wanted no part of this nostalgia, even though she could have financially exploited it. By the time Gianni Versace and other mainstream designers were reinterpreting the look in kid-soft leathers for the Californian rich, with thousand-dollar price tags, it had become devoid of impact and as far removed from the social context that had produced punk as Marie-Antoinette dressed for her *ferme ornée* had been from a humble shepherdess.

Such was her disgust at the punk revival that when a curator at the Victoria and Albert approached her in 1994 to contribute to the museum's forthcoming 'Street Style' exhibition, she ridiculed the idea and refused to cooperate. She had come a long way from the woman who, bursting with pride, had informed anyone who would listen that the august museum had seen fit to collect her designs. Some weeks later, however, she arrived unannounced at the door of the V&A and asked to see the preparations for the show. Having been allowed in she 'feigned disinterest', and claimed that the real reason she had come to the museum that day was to see some eighteenth-century printed cottons. The curators were too busy working on the exhibits to assist her, but they were left in no doubt that she did not approve of the exhibition.

Original Westwood/McLaren designs were now much sought-after, particularly by costume museums, Japanese collectors and rock stars. Even Vivienne was collecting her past fashions, curated for her by Murray Blewitt. On 25 October 1994, to coincide with the Victoria and Albert's exhibition, the London auctioneers Christie's held their first Street Style sale. Pat Frost, Associate Director of the Textile Department, was surprised by the public response and the prices realised – a 'Destroy' muslin shirt was sold for £400. Not only did the Westwood/McLaren lots appeal to those who had worn the clothes at the time, but also to costume collectors who were attracted to fashions that were outrageous in their day, be they the turbans and lampshade dresses designed by Paul Poiret in the 1910s or the bondage trousers from SEX in the seventies. Fakes of Vivienne's work became abundant: her own company was copying some old pieces, such as bondage trousers, many of the original screens for the T-shirts which were not in the hands of the rival King's Road shop Boy had been mislaid, and there was no record of how many original T-shirts were made. Now, as well as buying up early Westwood/McLaren pieces for the archive, Vivienne was insistent that all Andreas's designs be meticulously kept.

D'Amario encouraged Vivienne's 'non-stop distractions'. Whenever she took to creativity with a vengeance, such as when she devised the 'Cut & Slash' series, it cost money. He could see that it was much more profitable simply to exploit the back catalogue and keep Vivienne diverted with her promotional and intellectual pursuits than to invest in research and development and complicate the running of the business. The company's profits were escalating as consumers began to understand Vivienne's work. Even the sartorially conservative Americans began to buy Westwood for the first time in some numbers from 1994. In March of that year the *Financial Times* reported that the company's annual turnover had reached over £3 million, and was increasing at a rate of 40 per cent a year. By 1998 it had climbed to over £20 million. Vivienne seemed to have attained the impossible: a manager who indulged her designs and lifestyle without making any commercial demands on her. 'With no backer and a small shop I had great freedom, and I found that however unusual a design was, someone would buy it as long as it was beautiful,' she said.

Many well-known British fashion designers have reached a turnover of a million pounds reasonably quickly, struggled slowly to peak at £1.8 or £2 million, then slowly fallen back again, unable to make the leap from a cottage industry to an established medium-sized company. By 1995 Vivienne had made that difficult transition. Commercially and creatively she was a designer of international importance. When the *Financial Times* asked a group of fashion professionals to rank a number of designers for creativity, long-term influence and commercial success, Vivienne came top in creativity and fourth in the overall ranking, just behind Armani, Gaultier and Miyake.

In October 1995 Suzy Menkes of the *International Herald Tribune* revealed the sell-through (the percentage of a range that finds a customer at full price in the stores) of the major fashion labels. Westwood's average was 36 per cent, and though this was well behind Armani's exceptional 81 per cent, it was above such fashionable names as Helmut Lang, Claude Montana, Karl Lagerfeld and Martin Margiela.

'On Liberty' sold reasonably well to buyers – often minus the exaggerated bum pads in America – and on 13 September the powerful New York department store Bergdorf Goodman, having committed to a substantial purchase of the collection, invited Vivienne to stage a catwalk show, her first in the United States ('Buffalo' and 'Mini Crini' had been shown informally in a nightclub). The clothes were displayed in its windows and in a specialist boutique within the store. Dawn Mello, Bergdorf Goodman's president, believed that Vivienne's designs were 'very wearable. If you look at the clothes the details are extraordinary. This is the first season we've had her, but I've always admired her direction. She's maybe the most important fashion leader we have today.' Nevertheless, it was late in the day for one of America's most powerful stores to begin stocking Westwood. Following advice from the Bergdorf Goodman sales staff, Vivienne sized up her clothes from the autumn/winter 1995–96 collection onwards: a British size fourteen became a twelve, and so on down the range. By the autumn of 1995 Saks Fifth Avenue was also selling her range aggressively in its Manhattan flagship store and throughout its American branches.

The Westwood company had become more commercially minded. In the same way that she responded to the American comment that her clothes were cut too small, so Vivienne listened to criticisms from another important customer, Joyce. This chain of fifty-eight fashion and lifestyle shops throughout Hong Kong, Taipei and Thailand, selling over two hundred labels, was owned by the entrepreneur Joyce Ma. Joyce had stocked Westwood since 1992, and Jimmin Lee, the chief buyer, had observed a 'phenomenal growth in Vivienne Westwood sales in that period'. Initially, Joyce focused on the Gold Label, which they saw as a 'really cutting edge designer' that Asian customers would be particularly excited by because it was so 'identifiable'. They were attracted to the characteristic qualities of Westwood design: the archly feminine cut, the fantasy, the interesting construction and the attention-seeking distinction which it lent to the wearer. And the most abiding quality was its ability to provoke an emotion in anyone who wore it. An Asian customer could believe that she was buying into the once great culture and lifestyle of the West. Paul Smith says, 'Vivienne's success in Japan has been an interesting one. It is really not based on the image of her fashion shows, but is to do with the accessories that bear the logo.' Indeed, the Gold Label was so distinctive and unusual that, according to Jimmin Lee, 'it requires a lot more selling than other designers' clothes'. Joyce's sell-through was between 35 and 50 per cent, which was respectable, but not outstanding.

By 1997, when Vivienne had decided to show her Red Label independently from the Gold, on the London rather than Paris catwalk, Lee predicted that the ready-to-wear label, particularly its range of trousers, knitwear, shirts and accessories, would be of greater interest to them. Soon it was indeed enjoying a much more profitable 70 per cent sell-through. Lee had observed a sea-change in the attitude of the Westwood company, instilled by D'Amario, in the previous year or so: 'It is much more receptive to feedback on weights of cloth, which were too heavy and seasonal before, and lengths and sizes.' It was a clear indication of D'Amario's determination to exploit the Westwood logo commercially.

D'Amario was in a constant promotional frenzy. '*Dai, Dai*! Promote Mama Inglese! Red carpet, for Vivienne. Dai!' he would scream at his staff. While Vivienne promoted, he collected licence contracts which Murray Blewitt designed – bags, shoes, umbrellas, all emblazoned with a pinchbeck orb. Vivienne distanced herself from the commercial business, assuring viewers of *The Look* in 1994 that she would not relentlessly package herself like Pierre Cardin (who put his name on goods ranging from sardines to skis), because she needed 'an intellectual framework' within which to operate. In March 1996 the Japanese licensee Hochu invested £20 million in Westwood, and in the late spring of 1997 a new five-storey Westwood shop was opened on Conduit Street in Mayfair. The company was clearly pitching for a more mainstream fashion appeal. The interior decoration of the shop was conservative, almost suburban in its commercial smartness. Gone were the days when Vivienne's new shops excited the same interest as an *avant-garde* art opening. Few celebrities turned up to the launch party.

Contrary to the public perception, Westwood stores which were opening outside London did not belong to the firm but were licensed under loose franchise arrangements. In November 1995 Vivienne's erstwhile financial manger John Rowley opened a licensed shop called Smith & Westwood (it stocked Paul Smith's designs as well as Vivienne's) in Manchester's Royal Arcade, fourteen miles from Vivienne's birthplace. The shop was destroyed by an IRA bomb in 1996. The following year another Westwood licensed store was opened in Leeds.

The Japanese were keen licensees. The master licensee was Itochu, who imported the clothes through a subsidiary called Horizonti, and controlled fourteen sub-licensees which manufactured a range of accessories. George Miyazaki of Astore Robot, who had been associated with Westwood since 'Harris Tweed' days, had six licensed Westwood shops in Japan, and Berni Vinyl still ran the tiny shop in her flat selling old and new Westwood collections.

Not only did Vivienne now have a less expensive ready-to-wear label, but she also put her name to a mail-order range for Littlewoods.

In January 1995 she launched a budget range (£28 a waistcoat, £58 a bustle skirt) in the French mail-order catalogue Trois Suisses. It seemed an appropriate moment to open her first Paris shop, so her press agent there, Sylvie Grumbach, was asked to find a prestigious site off the fashionable Boulevard Saint-Germain. Vivienne also intended to open a couture studio in Paris, and began laying plans with Sylvie Grumbach. In 1997 the Vivienne Westwood company leased a flat on the Left Bank, where Vivienne, Andreas and Gary Ness would stay when they were in Paris. As the company grew richer, Andreas had tried to persuade Vivienne to move out of Nightingale Lane and into the West End of London, but she refused.

Although the company was diversifying, Vivienne wanted to concentrate her own talents on a modest form of *haute couture*. By the 1980s, when couture was 'revived' by Karl Lagerfeld at Chanel and Christian Lacroix, it had only about five hundred full-paying clients in the world, and had been relegated to the function of a loss leader, exploited to sell scent, hosiery and other affordable accessories. Vivienne hoped to compete with the Paris ateliers, which were staffed by experienced professionals and which could surpass in technique and finish anything she and her young, inexperienced team could offer. She also hoped that a leading French couture house would invite her to become its design director.

Vivienne's public awareness in France was enhanced when she signed a contract with the French tobacco company Gitanes in 1994 to promote their cigarettes. She started tucking the distinctive blue packet into her cleavage (the veins of which she highlighted with blue eyeliner to give the appearance of a lactating mother), becoming so diligent in her promotion that when she appeared as a guest on Gay Byrne's *Late, Late Show* in Dublin she staunchly defended the right to smoke, waving the packet at the audience. Privately she admitted, 'I want the nicotine but I don't want the bother of the cough.' Further promotion of the Westwood label was secured through advertisement campaigns with Galaxy chocolate and Habitat.

One proven way for a design label to make large profits is to launch a successful scent. D'Amario duly began negotiating a deal with Catherine Disdet of Dragaco, but the liaison was marred by in-fighting, nepotism and inefficiency. One of the problems was that Vivienne did not have a single, consistent public image. Whereas the consumer could recall Karl Lagerfeld's fan and ponytail, or Jean-Paul

Gaultier's striped T-shirt and shorn head, Vivienne, chameleon-like, changed her appearance virtually every year. Aware that Vivienne had cajoled Gary Ness into investing much time and thought in the scent, Françoise Rust-Fourteau suggested that some of the proceeds be set aside as a 'pension' for him. D'Amario had other ideas. Jeopardising the negotiations with Disdet, he even proposed that his own, rather than Vivienne's, olfactory memories be encapsulated in the scent, to evoke his own upbringing. A fax entitled 'Memories of Carlo's Childhood' was sent to Disdet in the summer of 1996. It listed olive oil from his mother's kitchen, patchouli oil from his hippie trail, and the smell of the candles in his local church. In February 1997 Westwood announced the launch, planned for June 1998, of a designer scent with the German cosmetics company Lancaster, who also held fragrance licences for Jil Sander and Joop (the Joop beauty franchise had estimated wholesale global sales of over $130 million in 1996, while the volume of Jil Sander fragrances was about $90 million) in conjunction with Dragaco. 'Boudoir' was proposed as the scent's name.

Since Vivienne's flourishing business paid her household and travel expenses, and she rarely bought clothes, did not collect art or artefacts, and her children were self-sufficient, Vivienne had extremely modest financial outlays. Her handsome earnings were squirreled away, and instead of funding her literary salon herself, she continued to seek sponsorship for it. Andreas had more lavish expectations. Partly using the salon as an excuse, he urged Vivienne to move out of the Nightingale Lane flat, but she was reluctant: 'Actually, I don't much like change . . . now Andreas wants to move, and if I set up the salon, it will be essential to have somewhere large and central to entertain . . . but it would be difficult to move. I do love my home.' At heart, Vivienne was not a sophisticated city-dweller, preferring to live 'away from the smoke'.

Despite Vivienne's affluence, the flat remained undecorated and cluttered. It was hardly the home of an aesthete, but then, contrary to both her view of herself and that of many of her fans, she was *not* an aesthete. Although she professed a superior appreciation of beauty, she did not attempt to express her ideas in her own environment. Her aesthetics needed a stage on which to perform; the catwalk, not her home, was that stage. Even in her clothes design, whatever she might argue, she habitually subjugated aesthetics to didactics. Many of her outfits were overworked or littered with literary messages and invocations of costume history, flaunting research and artifice at the expense of visual harmony.

Having diligently explored the crafts of cutting and tailoring for more than two decades, she regarded herself as an accomplished tailor; but in fact her work remained unrefined, and many of her complicated and interesting constructions were awkwardly executed. She designed in three dimensions on her eighteen-inch-high mannequin, but effects that looked elegant in miniature could be clumsy when sized up: a three-millimetre dart would convert into a great gash across the breast. Unlike Jean Paul Gaultier, who also used tailoring – notably the jacket – as a base on which to inscribe his cultural affiliations, Vivienne did not have the advantage of *haute couture* training. In late 1994 a friend suggested that to alleviate this weakness she discuss the craft with one of Savile Row's most esteemed tailors, the Queen's couturier Sir Hardy Amies. Sir Hardy was intrigued at the prospect of meeting this infamous republican. In 1977, while he had been fitting the monarch into a pink crepe double georgette coat and dress on the occasion of her Silver Jubilee, Vivienne had been hand-printing cotton T-shirts inciting rebellion. He agreed to a meeting with the words, 'Love to, dear girl. Her tailoring's fucking awful!'

Escorted by D'Amario, Vivienne's arrival at her hostess's flat, an hour late, was unmistakable. As she negotiated the wrought-iron stairs in 'super-elevated' shoes, her cautious steps created a deafening clamour outside the front door. The variously-coloured tartans of her blouse, jacket and floor-length kilt jostled for attention, and her poitrine was pinned with an array of pinchbeck medals. Clutching her knees to her chest, staring into the middle distance to concentrate and without drawing breath, Vivienne proceeded to give her host a selective account of the history of mankind, culminating in her insistence that the twentieth century had no culture.

'What crap!' the octogenarian Sir Hardy replied.

'You can't talk to me like that!' Vivienne protested, and turned to a fellow guest to confide, 'Ooh, when I sit with these heels on my knees are higher than my thighs, and my legs really ache.' (A year later she admitted that she fixed wedges of tissue on the pressure points of the elevated shoes, and recommended that wearers eased the pain with rubber ballet toecaps or 'a couple of drinks'.) As the evening broke up, Sir Hardy suggested that Vivienne come for a weekend at his home in the country, so he could teach her 'a thing or two about tailoring'. Though she was tempted by the offer, distractions prevented Vivienne from taking it up. In 1998 she told an interviewer: 'I remember years ago Hardy Amies going on about how much difference a centimetre made to a cut. I thought, what an old fuddy duddy, but now I couldn't agree more.'

By the mid-1990s, Vivienne's themes had begun to shift from an English to a French sensibility, and from a post- to a pre-Revolutionary one. 'Because of the Protestant work ethic,' she informed an audience in Sydney, 'which is conformity and grim earnestness, elaborate fashions gradually became taboo in Anglo-Saxon countries. Meanwhile in France, clothing was considered one of the "arts", a living art. No doubt the French attitude to dressing is that dressing, like eating, since it has to be done, is best done in an artistic way.' English fashions since the late eighteenth century were traditionally simple, functional and tailored to suit a sporting lifestyle; as a result the tailored wool riding coat became the linchpin of both male and female dress. British society regarded this approach as 'intellectual' and essentially masculine. French fashions, by contrast, were elaborate and decorative, and were deemed 'feminine'. But according to the costume historian Aileen Ribeiro, the formality of French dress was cast aside by the Revolution, and 'a sense of unity of *toute ensemble* gave way to a new emphasis on the disparate elements of dress, a kind of deliberate disharmony'. In post-Revolutionary France the art of dress became a private, selfish pleasure rather than a public duty, and the democratic preference for uniformity of dress across the ages and classes and for most occasions discouraged overt displays of hierarchy and distinction, in favour of a livery of equality.

Inspired by the lavishness of the *ancien régime*, Vivienne applied her love of craft to decorative dress, be it three-dimensional crochet, lace veiling or embroidery. She had always relished craft which made her at odds with her time: since the sixties it had become marginalised, as ready-to-wear favoured unornamented, mass-produced simplicity. Only one other contemporary British designer, Jean Muir, consistently upheld the merits of craft and deplored the tolerance of mediocrity in ready-made clothes.

Despite Gary Ness's Francophile influence, Vivienne's designs retained an essentially English trait. With some notable exceptions, the English creative flair is expressed in words rather than in images. Even some of the country's most celebrated artists, including Blake and Hogarth, approached a canvas or sheet of paper as a literary or storytelling device rather than, primarily, a sensory image. It is hardly surprising that allegorical painters such as the Frenchman Nicholas Poussin or the Swiss translator-turned-illustrator Henry Fuseli were so favoured in Britain. Like their paintings, Vivienne's clothes could not, if they were to be fully appreciated, be separated from the narrative.

Vivienne abhorred modernism and its partner minimalism, which she dismissed as fear of committing a sartorial mistake on the part of the wearer, and laziness on the part of the designer: 'It is easy to make and sell – what is it but a tube with some spaghetti straps?' Instead, she shared Dior's love of nostalgic femininity constructed in a complicated manner: 'I just feel I'm carrying on that tradition.' While Dior took a stand after the war against the 'demoralising influences of our time', and wished to return to the idyll he associated with the memory of his mother, Vivienne believed that 'my work is important. It can stand as a criticism of the world in which we so miserably live.' Disenchanted with the present, and hankering for her notion of seventeenth- and eighteenth-century salons, she escaped in her imagination to these circles, and designed clothes that she believed conjured them up. Unfortunately, in their painted hyperbole and bawdiness, her clothes would more suitably have dressed racier contemporaries of the salons' aristocratic, educated women, who would never have been permitted into their august and select ranks.

In 1991 Vivienne signed a contract with the London publisher Thames & Hudson to write an autobiography. In the summer of 1995 she showed the first draft of Chapter One, on her childhood, to Gary Ness, in the hope that he would ghostwrite the book. She had a fortnight off in August, she said, and optimistically hoped that they could write the book together in that time. Nothing was produced, and Vivienne's editor at Thames & Hudson, Catherine Lamb, began to fear that they would never see a manuscript.

Instead, during 1997 Vivienne concentrated on a small-format illustrated monograph for the French publisher Assouline, published in Britain by Thames & Hudson and consisting mainly of colour photographs of highlights from her collections over the past twenty years. The selection is heavily weighted towards her later work with Andreas. Interestingly, in Gene Krell's short introduction, he refers – under Vivienne's instruction – to her friend and adviser 'Gary Bayle', a smokescreen to conceal Gary Ness's true identity. Vivienne continued, however, to harbour ambitions of being a writer, persuading herself that if she had not fallen into fashion, she would 'probably have written fiction'.

In the same year the German newspaper *Die Zeit* invited Vivienne to edit a complete issue of its colour supplement. She was free to choose the themes, conduct interviews, design the layouts and style the photographs. The magazine, published on 12 September 1997, included an interview with Vivienne by Peter Sager; a discussion on culture, art and French taste between Vivienne and her milliner Prudence (whose surname was not revealed); an article by Gene Krell on Vivienne's particular appeal to the Japanese; and fashion shoots featuring the celebrity sixties model Veruschka, who was exactly the same age as Vivienne, and a selection of young German women who wore Westwood clothes.

Regarding herself as an outsider, Vivienne constantly voiced her regret that, despite having 'a knack' for designing, she had not been properly trained. She relied heavily on the stream of cutters in her studio, such as the German woman Iris, whom she described as 'brilliant! Yves Saint Laurent, Chanel, anyone would agree that what she does is couture.' Vivienne shared the English reluctance to publicly admit to taking pains over her work, mistakenly believing that it would be more socially acceptable to put her success down to a combination of innate talent and luck. Privately, she admitted to a close friend: 'I've had such bad luck, the catalogue of bad luck I've had, my God! . . . I'm just telling *you* it's nothing to do with luck, but I can always pretend it is . . . I think it's quite clever to pretend you're lucky.'

Despite moments of self-doubt, Vivienne's ego continued to swell in line with her prestige and her bank balance. She might not be able to write, but she felt fully equipped to discuss literature with Gore Vidal. Having failed to make contact with him through Peter Marangoni in 1990, she did so eventually via German *Vogue*, whose editor arranged for the pair to have lunch together at the Plaza Hotel, New York, in the summer of 1994. The resultant article, published that October, was entitled 'Snob Talk', as Vivienne said she was 'convinced of the importance of snobbery'. She wore a long check dress and 'elevated' platforms, and her peroxided hair was cut aggressively short and covered with a cotton gingham Brigitte Bardot headscarf.

Vidal wanted to talk about fashion, but Vivienne opened with a meandering monologue taking in her thoughts on the isolation of the intellectual, Saint Dominic, Bosnia, the freedom of the press and ecological and cultural crises. She finally concluded, 'You once said that people don't read very much any more, but books are full of ideas. That's why I wanted to have this conversation with you.' Vidal attempted to bring the conversation round to fashion, but Vivienne protested, 'Oh, let's forget about fashion. I don't want to talk about that today.' She went on to discuss the craft of the writer: 'The artistic technique of a writer is in finding the right words, therefore I do not go to the effort of reading someone who has not gone to the trouble of finding the right words . . .' And so the ill-matched dialogue continued, finally collapsing into an exchange of 'Have you heard the one about . . .' jokes.

With similarly disjointed results, in August 1994 Vivienne was invited to appear on the Channel 4 series *The Vision Thing*, which was devised as a showcase for people – politicians, artists, scientists – with an idiosyncratic vision. The editors felt that Vivienne's views on clothes would make a fascinating programme, but she responded: 'People aren't interested. I want to talk about ideas.' Not only was she utterly insensitive to the editorial requirements of the programme, but she seemed determined to cause as much trouble as possible. She insisted that she be filmed in a grey suit that had been worn by the supermodel Christy Turlington. Charlotte More-Gordon, the programme's producer, had the impression that the fifty-three-year-old Vivienne wanted to prove that she could fit into the same size. When her taxi drew up outside her Davies Street shop, where the interview was to be filmed, she emerged backwards. The skirt was so tight that it was hitched up her thighs, and the slit gaped wide, 'revealing all her glory – wearing no knickers – and a bare bottom'.

Although Charlotte More-Gordon and the presenter, Sheena MacDonald, attempted to focus Vivienne's conversation on fashion, she veered off into a nervously executed and unintelligible speech 'in Gary's language' about 'what the Elizabethans meant by progress'. The footage was unusable, and the programme was never broadcast. Vivienne was furious at the way the interview had been conducted, complaining that 'they couldn't see the content in there. They're so brainwashed themselves that they couldn't even hear what I was saying. I know that people see me as an eccentric, and they wanted me to be outrageous, I'm sure. But I've come across this all my life, really. People know that I can give them something different, so they come to me asking for it. And then when I give them something different, they don't know what to do with it.' To her credit, Vivienne later asked for a copy of the recording, admitting that she found the process 'quite difficult, and it would be useful to see where I made mistakes'.

That summer French *Elle* booked the Wallace Collection for a photographic shoot to accompany a profile on Vivienne, whom it described as 'the Joan of Arc always ready to deliver the English from their inhibitions'. Throughout the shoot, the team was surrounded by vigilant guards. After five hours of delivering admonitions – 'Don't rest on that table . . . Please don't lean against that painting . . .' – they hardly noticed Andreas prancing naked round his wife. When the piece was published, the trustees of the collection were unfazed: 'We can survive the naked man, there are quite a lot of them round here [in gilt bronze or marble],' said Bunty King, the press officer. What did infuriate them was the fact that the model Susie Bick had leant on an eighteenth-century commode.

Vivienne's international profile was rising, and her clients now included Ringo Starr, Barbara Bach, Melanie Griffith and David Bowie's wife Iman. In May 1994 Barbra Streisand, who was performing in London, telephoned Simon Barker at the Worlds End shop. She had seen photographs of Vivienne's empire-line blouses and ballgowns in the *New York Times Magazine*, and wanted to order some outfits for her forthcoming American tour. The Westwood team was invited to call on her at her penthouse suite in the Dorchester. This was an important commission. Not only did Streisand intend to order a substantial number of couture clothes, but her patronage could open doors, particularly in Hollywood. Having extensively researched Streisand's taste in clothes – she liked solemn black or cream – and her body shape, Barker and Françoise Rust-Fourteau carefully briefed Andreas. They feared that he would 'come up with something completely daft', and repeat a previous fiasco when Naomi Campbell had hated the dress he designed for the launch party of her ghostwritten novel *Swan*.

On the day of the appointment Rust-Fourteau dressed in a smart black suit to highlight the more classic aspect of Vivienne's work, which she believed would appeal to Streisand's taste. Andreas, however, arrived in *putti*-printed jeans, while Vivienne chose fuchsia stockings,

Rocking Horse shoes, a tartan mini and a black jumper decorated with ornate golden arabesques – all under a tweed jacket. Having been screened once by the hotel staff in the foyer, and twice by Streisand's bodyguards, the trio entered the suite. Huge bouquets of long-stemmed white flowers and kilos of *potpourri* in bowls stood on every surface. Two assistants, dressed Streisand-like in black, with long, manicured nails and bobbed hair, greeted them with considerable gravity, and invited then to survey the star's wardrobe. Row upon row of black garments were hung with military precision over matching shoes, alongside equally numerous cream garments and their matching shoes. Françoise Rust-Fourteau glanced at Vivienne's attire, and sighed inwardly.

They waited in silence, lined up on a sofa. After some time a door opened, and their client entered dramatically. They were informed that Ms Streisand required a spectacular dress for an appearance before President Clinton, and another for an important concert in her home town, Los Angeles. She selected three outfits, all black, and three ballgowns, including one of *marron-glâcé*-coloured taffeta and one of empire-line white tulle veiled in black lace, for the presidential gala. The order amounted to £25,000 – 'As much as Bergdorf Goodman would order in an entire season,' Françoise Rust-Fourteau calculated.

A singer requires an unconstricted bodice, so it was vital that the Westwood team take the exact measurements of Streisand's chest. With great reluctance she allowed them to borrow one of her bespoke bras as a template, but they were instructed to come backstage after her Wembley show and return it: 'I really have to count on you, because it is very important to me,' she informed them, as if she had surrendered one of her most precious possessions to their safekeeping.

Streisand's two American galas were scheduled for July. The Westwood team missed the Washington deadline altogether, and sent the dress for the Los Angeles performance with five days to spare. It fitted so badly that she could not even close it. A junior in Vivienne's studio had been assigned the important job. Françoise Rust-Fourteau had to attempt to placate an understandably irate assistant at Streisand's office, and suggested that the dress be couriered back to London to be altered and couriered back, all at the company's expense. When D'Amario was informed of this, he at first pretended not to know who Streisand was, then, 'rudely referring to her race', said he did not give a damn and instructed the staff to courier some material to Los Angeles instead, so that Streisand's people could 'fix it themselves'.

The incident highlighted the chaotic and unprofessional workings of Vivienne's studio, particularly compared with the lengths to which other designers would go to secure the custom of internationally renowned performers. (Fortunately, when Kate Winslet, advised by Marion Hume, now editor of Australian *Vogue*, selected Westwood to wear to the Oscar ceremony in March 1996, the studio surpassed itself in style and service.) It was also revealing that Vivienne knew nothing about the inept handling of the Streisand order until some months later.

Vivienne had been one of the most sought-after tickets in Paris for many years, and her popularity reached a peak in October 1994 with the 'Erotic Zones' collection (which Andreas had wanted to call 'The Golden Shower'). The front row of the audience included half a dozen top designers, and various pop music celebrities such as Lenny Kravitz, Kylie Minogue and Vanessa Paradis. But by 1995 Vivienne's reputation for creative originality and contemporary relevance had begun to wane. Obsessed with too literal an interpretation of historical dress, her collections had become predictable, and it seemed that they contained nothing new. She had dropped the vital second ingredient of the creative collage taught to her by McLaren: the fusion of the romantically historic with the contemporary; high culture with popular culture.

Though she had developed the controversial padded silhouette for 'On Liberty' in 1994, she failed to develop or refine it. Instead she opted for a U-turn. 'Vive la Coquotte' (autumn/winter 1995–96), shown at the Grand Hotel in Paris, featured a conservative line and a minimum of accessories. Her interpretation of French couture drew heavily on the work of the Spanish-born Cristobal Balenciaga. Inspired by the court dress of Louis XV of France, he had experimented with the sack-back dress, with a panel of cloth that fell free from between the shoulderblades to the hem – the line had been captured in the paintings of Watteau, one of Vivienne's favourite artists. 'Vive la Coquotte' included a variety of knee-length versions of the line in gingham and a black-and-white print which looked as if a large paintbrush had been dipped in black paint and dragged over oyster-coloured raw silk.

Vivienne had a reason for her change of direction. Having taken the silhouette to its most exaggerated extreme, she now wanted to remove the padding and promote a more subtle and what she termed 'ladylike' line. Other excesses were stripped away. She abandoned the high shoes and lowered the hem to the knee. 'It's even more ordinary in a way now, but in order to get the message across you have to go to extremes and make this big statement, and then hopefully people will look at all the subtlety,' she said. But she had not allowed her public to explore and absorb the padded line, and the cut of the sack-back was not crisp enough, or the materials exciting enough, to make an impact. The show's presentation was also, by Vivienne's standards, restrained. She stripped the clothes of their usual accessories but in striving for subtlety she compromised her true signature – originality.

The rest of the collection was made up of clumsy shantung silk copies of 1950s paletot jackets and cocktail dresses. Vivienne also revived another trick, cutting mackintoshes out of highly decorative fabrics. But instead of enlarged cherubs she offered cornflower blue and puce *toiles de Jouy* that were so prosaic the clothes looked as if they had been made from old curtains. Gary Ness had not been given the encouragement or the funds to develop his *cartes de tendres* idea for a new *toile*, which would have distinguished it from the clichéd versions regularly featured in interior decoration magazines.

Clearly, Vivienne was no longer exploring all aspects of her collections, and the result was a series of half-heartedly executed ideas. Her distraction did not go unnoticed. Murray Blewitt often overheard D'Amario and Andreas haranguing her to come up with some new ideas. 'Look at her work now!' moaned D'Amario in 1996. 'When she had no money her work was the best ever. Now she's like a child in a sweet shop – too much choice and she doesn't know what to do.' She confused the shoe manufacturer Pasquale by sending six shoe lasts with five options for heel shapes and demanding them in twenty different materials in five different colours.

There was only so much that could be done with the back catalogue, and without Vivienne's full attention on her designs, Andreas could not sustain the label's reputation for innovation and surprise. The media now believed Vivienne's work had gone off the boil. The low point came with 'Storm in a Teacup' (autumn/winter 1996–97), which was entirely designed by Andreas, as Vivienne concentrated on preparing and filming the three-part *Painted Ladies* series.

It was particularly unfortunate that Vivienne should bring such a poor collection to the Paris catwalk in the spring of 1996. At that time Louis Vuitton Moët Hennessy, which owned the couture houses Dior, Givenchy and Lacroix, were considering candidates to replace Gianfranco Ferre as Design Director of Christian Dior. Vivienne's appetite for the job had been whetted by her trip to meet Daniel Piette at Dior in 1991 and, on hearing of Ferre's resignation, she set her sights on succeeding him.

The appointment was vital not only for the future of the vast luxury-goods conglomerate LVMH, but for the cultural prestige of France. Dior lay at the heart of French *haut bourgeois* culture. The wives of presidents, ministers, senior civil servants and members of high society were dressed with propriety – and a decorous nod to high fashion – by this great institution. European royals favoured it for public occasions. Dior was not just the world's most famous fashion label, but had been a national icon since the fifties. Dior was also big business: turnover in 1995 was almost thirty-one billion francs. That year Vivienne was invited by Louis Vuitton, a sister company of Dior within the LVMH group, to design a bag utilising leather printed with their traditional logo, the LV initials. She created a 'bum bag' which mimicked the bustle and enhanced what she called 'a naturally callipygous endowment'.

The first couture collection for the new appointee was scheduled to be shown in January 1997, the fiftieth anniversary of the founding of the house and the launch of Dior's famous New Look. To mark this anniversary the Metropolitan Museum of Art in New York added its own lustre to the name of the fashion house by staging a retrospective. Throughout the summer of 1996 Vivienne was on tenterhooks, and brazenly solicited Dior for the job. Jean-Paul Gaultier, Christian Lacroix and John Galliano were also mentioned by the media as possible candidates. Galliano, the Gibraltar-born British designer, had been a thorn in Vivienne's side for over a decade. Twenty years her junior, he had graduated in 1983 from Central St Martin's College of Art. His degree show, unmistakably influenced by Vivienne's 'Pirates' and 'Buffalo' collections, was immediately taken up by Browns, a reputation-making specialist fashion boutique in central London, and was an instant success. Galliano owed much to Vivienne's *modus operandi* of plundering historic costumes. Patrick Cox, the Canadian shoe designer who worked for both designers in the eighties, was frank in his assessment of Vivienne's influence on Galliano: 'I found it shocking when I worked for John that his work was so literally Vivienne's, and he got upset when Bill Cunningham wrote in *Details* a scathing review and said that John was pure Vivienne, right down to taking Vivienne's staff. John cried for days, but it was true.' Galliano's 'Anastasia' collection particularly riled Vivienne, as it seemed to her a pastiche of her work. She was convinced that the disc jockey Jeremy Healy, who had put the soundtrack to some of her collections, and who now did the same for Galliano, had divulged her methods to her younger rival. In Vivienne's mind Galliano was a mere copycat, and she had been infuriated when he was appointed Design Director of LVMH's other couture house, Givenchy.

While Galliano was indisputably influenced by Vivienne's approach to design – particularly her touch of weaving stories into her clothes – his technical execution was superior to hers. Though he did not challenge the accepted shape of dress in such a profound and groundbreaking way, his clothes were less radical and therefore more commercial. The essential difference between them was that when Vivienne inspected an original source, be it a bias-cut Vionnet gown from the 1930s or a pair of seventeenth-century breeches for her pirates, she explained that she 'spent years inside this research ... I am the only person who has ever used the original cut or slightly modified it, but other people who have been interested in doing the past have always used their own block and just sort of changed the details, but they have not got the essential dynamic of the cut – they superimposed the cut of the day'.

Galliano's strength was the importance he placed on skilled cut. Even in the mid-1980s, when he, like Vivienne, was operating in penury, he employed six extremely experienced pattern-cutters, while she had only one. Consequently there was a lightness of touch to his clothes, while Vivienne's hung heavy with effort. Tommy Roberts, the fashion retailer who had befriended Vivienne and McLaren in the late sixties, observes: 'It's been a hard graft for her, whereas Galliano is a natural. By taking the hard-work route she has made some interesting things, but I don't think she's a natural.' The late Ossie Clark concurred: 'I don't think she knows how to do it, I'm afraid. It looks spectacular, and the cloth is so expensive, but the models are so unsure of themselves on those shoes. They take their life in their hands when they walk, and the dresses rely on the girls' extreme height. You couldn't really use them on the average woman – she'd just look ridiculous.'

In July 1996, as the couture collections were being shown in Paris, speculation mounted on who would be named as Ferre's successor. Surely Bernard Arnault, the Chairman and Chief Executive Officer of LVMH, would make the announcement while the world's fashion press were gathered in the city. In the event no statement was made (probably so as to prolong the media coverage), but Vivienne's name continued to be bandied about as a likely candidate. Though the erstwhile Queen of Punk seemed to have little in common with France's leading couture house, in fact her design credentials, if not her personality, were appropriate. From a purely commercial point of view, couture was no longer anything more than a loss leader, sustained chiefly to attract free publicity to a brand name upon which a licensing empire could be expanded. Arnault, profoundly aware of this, was seeking a candidate who would attract maximum media interest, and there was no doubt about Vivienne's press appeal. Secondly, since 1991 Vivienne had been preoccupied with Christian Dior's body of work, and had systematically reinterpreted it and publicly acknowledged her indebtedness to his inspiration. 'Thank God, we've got Andreas', D'Amario commented, implying that should Vivienne be chosen for Dior, she could hand the reins of her eponymous label over to him entirely.

In August it was announced that John Galliano would take over at Dior, and that the twenty-seven-year-old Alexander McQueen, another alumnus of St Martin's, would replace him at Givenchy. 'I don't care and I'm not surprised,' Vivienne choked, trying to show a brave face, but in fact she felt publicly humiliated at having been superseded by a younger generation. One of her first reactions was to describe Galliano as 'the magician's nephew' and McQueen as 'the sorcerer's apprentice'. Her staff did not see her for a week, and when she returned she sacked several people. She became publicly foul-tempered, and in January 1997, when both Galliano and McQueen's first couture collections at their new houses were shown, she attacked them in the press for copying her.

Vivienne had longed to savour the fame, prestige and challenge attached to the role of Designer-in-Chief at Dior, which would have decisively given her the last laugh over her British detractors – and over Galliano, whom she regarded as a copycat. The job would neatly have dovetailed two of her ambitions. Firstly, it would unquestionably have made her a member of the heart of the chauvinistic French fashion establishment – and now that she had embraced French aesthetics, Paris would be a natural home for her. Secondly, she would have considerable funds to work with, and access to outstanding craftspeople. Dior in particular was a dream house for her, since she greatly admired its founder, and had spent much of the 1990s deriving inspiration from his cut and decorative details.

Perhaps, though, she did not fully appreciate how restricted she would have been in such a post. The managers of Dior expected collections that would thrill the press and cater to their constant demands for novelty. Bernard Arnault was more interested in column inches to sell branded goods than in *haute couture*. Vivienne was temperamentally unsuited to working under such conditions, and would certainly have balked at any attempts by the management to impose creative control on her. Nevertheless, her attention had recently been distracted from fashion design, and such a post would have provided a new impetus for her creative energies and concentration – at least for a time.

Vivienne failed to secure her dream job for three principal reasons. First, her creative originality had descended into a formulaic and virtually literal copying of past costume, and the conventional fashion world now considered she had little to do with high fashion. Even before the Dior appointment was announced, John Walford had said, 'We're coming to the end of the Westwood story. The most exciting period is over.' Secondly, many in the fashion world regarded Vivienne's arrogance as insufferable. Lucinda Chambers, fashion director of British *Vogue*, described her as 'just so prickly and difficult'. Most felt she would be a troublesome employee, incapable of adapting to the strictures of a large company like LVMH. As James Fallon says: 'Vivienne is not, in any sense of the word, malleable. She's extremely assertive. And her mood swings – from egomania to total lack of self-confidence – make her hard to deal with.' Thirdly, Vivienne was no longer highly newsworthy. While the American press (the most influential as far as Arnault was concerned) lauded Galliano and McQueen, they had become less gripped by Westwood, and Arnault required column inches to sell his licensed ranges.

In March 1997 Daniel Piette insisted that, despite the media speculation and Vivienne's clearly stated ambitions, she had never been seriously considered for the job. 'We had John Galliano in our stable, and it was easier for us to think about John for Dior ... Vivienne was already a company name, and ... it would probably have been a business or image confusion between her business and the Dior business. I think she's too big to work for anyone.' He added, 'It's very difficult to protect Dior from her own notoriety.'

Piette referred on several occasions to the youthfulness of Galliano and McQueen, and to Vivienne's age, and asked whether she had found a successor yet. Clearly he did not regard her as a long-term investment. He offered her some advice which revealed his opinion that she had had her day: 'I would recommend her to train a young designer to protect her style and attitude. She's a school of design and she's been a factor, definitely. You wonder when she's not there any more where her point of view will go.'

Manny Silverman, who had attempted to invest in Westwood in 1990, understood the business logic behind choosing Galliano and McQueen: 'If you are going to invest in a designer, really you are asking how much mileage does my investment have – not in years, but in public appeal. Those two boys, you could drive them for another decade. The commercial opportunity arrived five or ten years late for Vivienne.' For his part, Galliano readily acknowledges the importance of Vivienne's designs: 'Vivienne is constantly innovating, but her work during the punk and new romantic periods defined the era. It's impossible to think of the bands, the music and the spirit of both punk and the new romantics without Vivienne's work'.

It was unlikely now that Vivienne would ever be appointed to a French couture house, and to save face she publicly denied that she had ever wanted the Dior job, turning her attentions and energy to opening a small couture house of her own in Paris. Perhaps spurred on by the huge disappointment, she invested a great deal of research and effort into her autumn/winter 1997–98 collection 'Five Centuries Ago', inspired by the Tudor Portraits exhibition held at London's Tate Gallery a year earlier. Having exhausted her investigations into French eighteenth-century dress, Vivienne now stepped back further into history to seek inspiration in the costume of the Elizabethan court. But Tudor dress was court costume, not fashion. Without any injection of contemporary culture, Vivienne's efforts seemed heavy-handed, arch and irrelevant. Nevertheless, in October 1997 her status in France was officially recognised when she was awarded the Order of Arts and

Letters by the French government. The previous autumn she had accepted the accolade 'Fashion Legend' from the Fashion Group International of America, along with Jil Sander and Donatella Versace.

One of the many reasons Simon Barker had resigned in 1994 was that he was not given an advertising budget. Both D'Amario and Vivienne had regarded advertising as a waste of money, believing that clever manipulation of the press with amusing or shocking incidents would suffice. Look at the column inches they had secured with Vivienne's antics at Buckingham Palace, they said, or with Naomi Campbell falling off her shoes. But the editorial coverage given to a label in glossy magazines was now blatantly in proportion to the amount the designer spent on advertising. It was no coincidence that a cover picture given to a designer would invariably be accompanied by pages of advertising from that label. It was a straight *quid pro quo*. The green baize door that had once, so properly as far as readers were concerned, separated advertising and editorial departments on a magazine, had been kicked open in the eighties because of increased competition for advertising revenue. Now that Vivienne Westwood had a turnover of more than £20 million a year, the company could afford to invest in advertising, and for the first time in over two decades it launched a campaign.

On the recommendation of her longstanding supporter Anna Piaggi of Italian *Vogue*, Vivienne commissioned a young British illustrator, Richard Gray, to develop her concept. The brief he was given was to marry the imagery of Hans Holbein's sixteenth-century Tudor portraits, which had inspired the 'Five Centuries Ago' collection, with the accoutrements and atmosphere of sado-masochism. It is likely that many colourful anecdotes about Tudor life had been brought to her attention by the constitutional historian Dr David Starkey, who was working on a three-part television documentary on Henry VIII, and with whom she and Gary Ness regularly dined.

The advertising campaign consisted of ten photographic images: six for the Gold and Red Labels and four for the Japanese market (Gray had little to do with the latter, which are significantly weaker and less imaginative than the others). While Gray was delighted to be left 'entirely to my own devices' due to Vivienne's trust in his talent and her ability to tap into the young's creativity, she did however demand a narrative justification rather than historical accuracy for every accessory used in the images, whether it was a hi-tech modern crossbow or a marmoset on a chain. During the hours they spent working together, usually from six in the evening until late at night, Gray was struck by the strength of Vivienne's urge to teach. She seized every opportunity to recommend books to him, and showered him with historical anecdotes. Once Gray's immaculate and intricate drawings were completed, Vivienne commissioned the leading Italian photographer Gian Paolo Barbieri to interpret them. She herself posed convincingly as Elizabeth I, while Andreas became a royal favourite, possibly Robert Devereux, the Second Earl of Essex. Jerry Hall and a thirteen-year-old model also appeared.

In the summer of 1997, at the age of fifty-six, Vivienne became a grandmother when Joseph's girlfriend Serena Rees gave birth to a daughter. Vivienne insisted that she had the right to choose the name, and the child was called Cora Honeysuckle Corré.

At the beginning of 1998 Vivienne launched Anglomania, a mass-market diffusion line of unisex casual wear. Trawling through her archives, D'Amario had estimated that there were nearly ten thousand designs which could be copied and relaunched, to great commercial gain. With the clarion calls 'Rebellion!' 'Fantasy!' 'Romance!' and 'Glamour!' as the themes chosen to evoke the image of the new label, the company began to exploit Vivienne's past collections chronologically. A vaguely punk range started off the line for spring/summer 1998, followed by a pirate range for the following autumn/winter.

Every garment in the Anglomania range bears the logo of a raised pirate arm and cutlass, on buttons, zips, poppers, T-shirts and jeans, in order to distinguish them from the more expensive Gold and Red Labels, which feature the orb logo. When interviewed in February 1998 about her new label, Vivienne admitted, 'I'm going to have to start thinking about what people want. I've never had to do that. I've no idea what people want.' This was a marked contrast to her previous habit of disregarding who would wear her clothes and believing that if she felt something was beautiful, her fans would like it too.

The first Anglomania collection, for spring/summer 1998, was launched without a show but was brought to the public's attention with an advertising campaign, devised by Richard Gray in partnership with Vivienne, and styled by Anna Piaggi of Italian *Vogue*. Vivienne chose Géricault's epic nineteenth-century picture *The Raft of the Medusa* as her inspiration to communicate the adventure, excitement and drama of the clothes. Gian Paolo Barbieri shot the campaign using ten male and female models. Against a painted storm backdrop they precariously balanced on a raft constructed from reclaimed seventeenth-century wood and rope, while assistants armed with trays and buckets flung cold water over them and a huge sewage pipe directed a gale-force wind at them. The second, autumn/winter 1998–99 collection was promoted with a show in Milan in March 1998. The overt commercialism of the Anglomania range, and its dependence on past archives, suggested that Vivienne may finally have bowed to market forces.

Over more than two decades Vivienne has produced an astonishingly innovative body of work. Can she sustain that pace of innovation and renewal as she approaches her sixties? Jean-Charles de Castelbajac reasons, 'After twenty years, sometimes you throw your hands up [in surrender]. You want to stop fighting and start to be accepted.' Vivienne had tried so desperately to be accepted by the high-fashion élite of Paris, but despite the applause, her reputation as a leader and her tenacity, they had rejected her. De Castelbajac was not surprised: 'Artists should be fools in society, fools to the king. They should not try to be integrated and accepted in society.' Vivienne did not belong at the heart of French fashion. Manny Silverman stated the truth bluntly: 'When you have been an iconoclast, can you indulge in the luxury of being bitter? She wanted recognition by the establishment, and yet she went "Fuck you!" to the establishment.' The satirist was destined to remain an outsider.

Vivienne has never rid herself of McLaren's assertion that 'you should always remain a brat.' Nevertheless, by always having taken the line of greatest resistance, and rarely compromising her point of view, she has been the most important influence on fashion over the last twenty years, and her work has left its mark on every major designer. Because she could so intuitively recognise the future of fashion before anyone else, though her lead could take the form of exaggerated prototypes, at times vulgar and often badly executed, it was prophetic. She had a raw, unschooled, instinctive and passionate genius for design.

CONCLUSION

It is too soon to establish Vivienne Westwood's place in fashion history. One can, though, attempt to set her work in its historical context by asking how innovative it is, how much it is *her* creation, and what is the reach of her influence. Typically, she presented the least commercial and least well-executed version of each new look: 'first, but worst'. This does not, however, detract from her originality or her impact.

Vivienne has the mentality of a high-fashion designer rather than a commercial, ready-to-wear designer. As such her aim is to create fashion at its purest; to construct the most original and beautiful clothes possible for the female or male body. In many respects this form of fashion died in 1968, when Cristobal Balenciaga closed the doors of his salon, declaring the end of couture. Distinction had capitulated to equality. Couture's concern with individualism, élitism and drama did not sit well with the times. Haute couture is, as Pierre Bergé, the President of Yves Saint Laurent, says, 'an art of life, the high points of which were reached in the 1930s and again just after the war . . . people out there [in the street] don't care about couture any more, and they're right!' That manner of living died in the 1960s. There are no longer the occasions – the regular cycle of premières, grand opera openings, formal dinner and cocktail parties – nor the commitment to the lifestyle required to support and justify such a mode of dress.

Contemporary expressions of 'couture' bear little relation to real *haute couture*. They are simply spectacles performed to engage the media, loss leaders used by the marketing arms of luxury-goods conglomerates to sell branded hosiery, scent and gewgaws. Marc Bohan, former Designer-in-Chief at Christian Dior, admitted in 1983, 'Every couture dress I send out of my workrooms now loses money. I cannot charge what it really costs. That's why I need it to be worn by a certain type of woman, who will enhance the status and reputation of the house.' And that woman is merely a billboard for a brand name.

Instead of couture, women – even extremely fashionable and wealthy women – wanted clothes that were practical and affordable. Derided by feminists and egalitarians, compromised by mass manufacture and ignored by a less formal generation, couture by the late 1960s was regarded as an anachronism. 1968 was a watershed not only for politics, but also for fashion.

In the thirty years since then, fashion designers have explored three main options. Some, particularly the Americans, chose to practise democracy in dress, mainly through sportswear. Others toyed with high fashion's established canon in an ironic, post-modern exhibition of retro-chic. The third group, modernists like Issey Miyake, focused on the fabric of fashion by exploiting the technological advances in fibres and textiles.

The challenge to high-fashion designers since the 1960s has been to introduce innovation and beauty into the clothing of everyday life, to imbue ready-to-wear with a sense of the creative freedom, excitement and distinction of *haute couture*. Yves Saint Laurent has been the great exemplar of this. While his Rive Gauche ready-to-wear collections are designed specifically for the lifestyle and taste of a modern woman, he has lent them a touch of the magic that characterises his couture clothes. From 1960, when he showed his controversial 'Beat' collection for the house of Christian Dior, until the late 1970s, when he became burdened by fame, the demands of creativity and the abuse of alcohol and narcotics, Saint Laurent led fashion. Most women – even those only marginally touched by fashion – and many men have been influenced by his style. He made the trouser suit an acceptable piece of day wear for women, and the tailored jacket with a contrasting skirt or trousers a wearable option for both day and evening. Under his hand the smoking suit, requisitioned from the male, became one of the most seductive forms of evening dress for a woman. His taste and refinement made see-through shirts seem unshocking and chic. Elements of street, protest and proletarian wear – the pea jacket, the biker's jacket, leathers, the existentialist's black polo-neck, the fisherman's smock – were imbued with such propriety and style as to be acceptable to the most conservative. In a series of homages to his favourite artists – Picasso, Cocteau, Mondrian – Saint Laurent embraced the world of Left Bank artists and brought their aesthetics into mainstream fashion, which had traditionally been a Right Bank affair. He remains the unrivalled master of colour in dress.

At the same time his partner, Pierre Bergé, built up a remarkable fashion empire which made 'YSL' one of the most recognised logos in the world, and which is currently valued at over a billion dollars. And since the late 1980s Saint Laurent has re-emerged to build magnificently upon the fashion classics he introduced in those astonishingly creative years between 1958 and 1977.

In creative terms, Vivienne Westwood took up the story of fashion where Yves Saint Laurent left off, and in the last twenty years she has been its single most important innovator. Both designers played with the savage and the traditional, but where Saint Laurent Westernised and glamorised the costumes of ethnic peoples before placing them on the Paris catwalk, making them polite, and therefore saleable, rather than primitive, Vivienne left them raw. It was her deconstruction of dress, exemplified by her punk designs in the 1970s and her 'Buffalo', 'Hobo-Punkature' and 'Witches' collections of the early 1980s, that led the way for the Japanese deconstructionists Rei Kawakubo of Comme des Garçons and Yohji Yamamoto, and later the Belgians Ann Demeulemeester and Martin Margiela.

As well as Saint Laurent, a comparison can be made between Vivienne's work and that of Elsa Schiaparelli. Schiaparelli was the great pre-war fantasist, Vivienne the great post-war one. Both know, as Cocteau said of his friend and collaborator, 'how to go too far', and both, while creating some of the wittiest and most amusing clothes of the day, were utterly humourless women. The way in which Vivienne announced her political and cultural affiliations by scrawling or printing slogans onto her clothes recalled Schiaparelli embroidering and printing statements of her artistic allegiances – notably to surrealism – on hers.

Vivienne regularly plays with three themes: dissipation, poverty and deconstruction in dress. As a connoisseur of dissipation, she explores the contemporary moral vacuum and takes inspiration from the extreme forms of sexual and political dress: the accoutrements of the prostitute, the transvestite, the flamboyant homosexual, the political rebel and the outsider.

The principal contemporary taboo is no longer sex or political extremism, but violence, and Vivienne's preoccupation with it reflects a dark streak in her own personality. She taunts and titillates her public with violence. Initially she celebrated figures, such as the Cambridge Rapist, who represented the furthest extremity of violence.

Then she purveyed the image, which she considered erotic, of women whose appearance suggested that they had just been raped. Latterly, at a time when child molestation haunts the public imagination, she has toyed with the image of the underage girl dressed up with the sexual knowingness of a mature woman. If there is a consistent signature to Vivienne's clothing it is the tension between violence and romance: Dick Turpin, Rob Roy, the Pirate, the Apache, the molested schoolgirl, the rape victim in leggings and dishevelled shirt, the *ancien régime* courtesan hung with the trappings of a sado-masochist.

Vivienne Westwood has also promoted, in a more extreme manner than anyone had previously dared, the clothing of the poor as fashion. By inverting the hierarchy of fashion, she has built upon Coco Chanel's influence. Where Chanel between the wars set out to *épater les bourgeois* by dressing fashionable women in men's sports clothing and wool jersey, previously associated with hygienic underwear, Vivienne utilised *bricolage* in such an undisguised and unsanitised manner that the fashionable were persuaded to fasten cardigans made of dishcloth with buttons crafted from the metal lids of kitchen-scourer tins.

Innovators challenge orthodoxy. Chanel's clothes physically liberated a woman. Saint Laurent's gave her a sense of power. In the continuum of fashion history, Vivienne Westwood's work is a direct descendant of these two giants'. Once women's bodies had been freed, they needed the psychological reassurance to step out into the harsh public domain. Vivienne's clothes provide an ironic mask with which a woman can project many personae, and behind which she can hide her vulnerabilities and even her ordinariness.

The established traditions of tailoring and dressmaking are habitually questioned by Vivienne. Why should the neck of a garment be cut at the point equidistant from the shoulders? What would be the aesthetic effect if it were 'misplaced', to oblige an asymmetric contortion? Why should shoulders be padded or cut to rise to exactly the same height as one another? Why not tilt the shoulderline to create an arresting imbalance? Is it sexier for trousers to cling to the sensual muscle of the calf than to the buttocks? Isn't the shrug required to hitch a too-big shirt back onto a shoulder more provocative than an exact fit?

In pursuing these themes – often using 'poor' materials such as sackcloth, T-shirting, acrylics – Vivienne refused to adopt the shoddy standards of execution that became acceptable in ready-to-wear clothes in the 1960s. She aspires to the late Jean Muir's standards of excellence both in the quality of the – chiefly British – cloth she favours and in the construction of each garment. Despite this, it has been the execution of Vivienne's work that has consistently let her down. Her clothes often fail to reach the highest standards of fit and finish. The principal reason is that her designs are extremely complicated to manufacture, as she rejects any recognisable template or standard pattern. Consequently they need the attention of exacting and fastidious production managers, but she has not always had either the funds or the professionalism to employ them.

Today's narrative mood in fashion, exemplified by John Galliano's work, owes its origins entirely to Vivienne Westwood. Indeed, the whole stable of young British designers, many of them alumni of Central St Martin's College of Art, such as Galliano and Alexander McQueen, could be said to be, in some sense, her inheritors. From her they have learned how to conjure up romantic and nostalgic stories in their collections, whether Galliano's Afghan bankers and fallen angels or McQueen's Highland rape victims and Oriental streetwalkers. The difference between Vivienne's nostalgic fantasy and theirs is that hers is freighted with a message, ironic or critical of the status quo, whereas theirs is simply to be read on the surface, as a decorative device.

Vivienne has consistently rebelled against not only mainstream orthodoxy but also her own 'tradition'. This innate contrariness is a fundamental reason why her work has so often been fresh and unexpected. In 1979, when the fashionable on the streets of London, Berlin, New York and Paris, including the punks she had influenced, were mostly clad in black, she introduced colour and romance in the form of the pirate. Shockingly vibrant and escapist, it led fashion back from a bleak, monochrome landscape. In the mid-1980s, when those same fashionable streets were peopled by female yuppies in padded shoulders and abbreviated hemlines, Vivienne introduced the closely fitted, narrow-shouldered torso above a defiantly antiquated crinoline skirt, a silhouette that seemed vulnerable and pre-feminist by contemporary standards. In 'Pagan V' (spring/summer 1990) she rendered the hemline debate an irrelevance: the collection showed he tiniest miniskirts alongside ankle-length midis – the choice was yours.

In 1990 she offered a painterly sexuality that few women would resist: corseted handspan waists, ropes of pearls, fake furs, velvets and old-master images printed in gold onto cling-fit garments. The effect was reminiscent of the *scraffito* technique used in early Italian painting, whereby a panel was painted in gold, then a layer of paint was applied and scratched away, revealing the gold beneath. During the worldwide recession and ecological awareness of the early 1990s, other designers offered insipid comfortable sportswear as an apology for the built-in obsolescence and frivolity of their trade. With typical bloody-mindedness, Vivienne chose that time to reintroduce the unbridled Hollywood glamour associated with stars such as Dietrich and Garbo.

Three years later, the top designers followed her. They have always watched her and then copied her. And, as importantly, they have admitted it. It is not surprising that the most successful European designers – Yves Saint Laurent, Karl Lagerfeld, Christian Lacroix and Azzedine Alaïa, among others – consistently tie a label onto a gilt chair in the front row of their shows. It reads 'Mme Vivienne West-wood'. This is a public acknowledgement of their regard for Vivienne's creativity. The cynical might argue that they can afford such gestures: the cottage industry of Vivienne Westwood poses no commercial chal-lenge to their global empires, and her market reach is comparatively insignificant.

In 1994 I went to interview Emanuel Ungaro in Paris. I was wearing a tartan Westwood suit consisting of a Bettina jacket and an asym-metrically wrapped skirt with a long triangular panel which folded across the thighs and trailed to one side. As soon as I entered his *atelier*, Ungaro asked who had made 'this interesting skirt'. He bent down and for nearly a minute inspected its construction, then stood up and said, 'Hmm, she's interesting.' Rarely does a designer make a point of looking so carefully and undisguisedly at another designer's work in front of a journalist.

Vivienne is one of the great Emphatics of fashion. Like Schiaparelli and Diana Vreeland before her, she is extreme and uncompromising in her vision. These fashion Boudiccas share a loathing of the common-place. To their minds it is preferable to be extreme, even vulgar, rather than timid, conformist and dull.

Vivienne's body of work can be divided into two periods: pre- and post-1985. The division is not, as has sometimes been assumed, solely determined by her earlier preoccupation with street fashion and her subsequent dismissal of it, but depends to a greater extent on the influence of two extremely different men.

Initially she fell under the spell of the youth culture populist Malcolm McLaren. She herself has never been interested in the street: that is McLaren's taste and commercial preoccupation, and he exploited it in order to sell his pop music and clothing to the young. Even while she was designing punk clothes, Vivienne tried to introduce elements from high rather than popular culture gleaned from her research into historical and rural dress. Prompted by McLaren, she aligned herself with the growing body of those who attacked the British establishment.

The historically-preoccupied Gary Ness furnished Vivienne with the themes and messages that have marked her clothes since 1985. Though they have remained a medium through which she can voice her criticism of the status quo, she abandoned the celebration of the do-it-yourself ethic, aspiring instead to the highest expression of élitist clothing, *haute couture*. Under Ness's influence, her tastes and designs gradually moved from the proscribed to the prescribed, from the youthful – even childlike – to the grown-up, from the modern to the historical, and from an English to a French idiom. From 1985, for example, she stopped sending her models out onto runways to the pounding beat of pop music, preferring the high-culture associations of Tchaikovsky and Debussy.

Despite the fact that in many respects Vivienne Westwood has led fashion since the mid-1970s, she is not a modernist. The undecorated, hard-lined simplicity of the modernist movement is anathema to her. She hates its most obvious expression, minimalism, which she considers a timorous fear 'of committing an error of taste'. Vivienne's disdain for modernism is defensible. The very term is now a misnomer, having been applied to art in the 1910s, and to architecture, literature and clothing in the following decade. Cubism, the principles of the Bauhaus and the streamlined functionalism of Chanel and Patou's dress are now well over half a century old. The fashion industry has explored *ad nauseam* the ramifications of simplicity, from Chanel, through Halston, Zoran and Lang, to the ugly, tube-like high-street dresses hanging from T-shirt necklines or spaghetti straps – low-cost skimpiness masquerading as minimalist modernism. At heart, Vivienne is drawn to the decorative and the complex. Striving to stamp her clothing with a strong sense of the human hand at work, she crafts a garment, rather than submitting to the constraints of the machine-made and mass-produced. This has made her clothing extremely difficult to manufacture.

In one other respect, Vivienne has dragged her feet behind the vanguard of the new in the last decade. She has not embraced contemporary fabric technology, particularly modern synthetics which are light, warm and easy to maintain. She is a fashion Luddite who now favours traditional dressmaking techniques and textiles, preferring heavy tweeds, high-maintenance poplins or duchess satins and the paraphernalia – feathers, fans, gloves – of a bygone age. The nostalgia which has increasingly characterised her clothes since the late 1980s has understandably prejudiced many modern women, with the practical constraints of a busy life on the move, against her 'costumes'.

Since 1993, Vivienne having fallen under the influence of another man, Andreas Kronthaler, her style has ossified into an over-reverential pastiche of historical costumes. Disdaining twentieth-century culture, she claims that she 'prefers to have perspective. I don't care about keeping up with the times . . . I don't want to subscribe to the dogmas of the day which is that everyone is supposed to rush around looking for novelties.' No longer infused with her own idiosyncratic interpretation of modernity, her work has become too literal a recreation of historical dress. With each step back through time – from the nineteenth, to the eighteenth, and finally the sixteenth centuries – her clothes have lost immediacy, impact and contemporary relevance. It is possible that her greatest work is behind her. She has certainly fallen out of favour with fashion students, who until recently revered her, but now tend to dismiss her as a figure from the past. But it is a great deal to expect a designer to continue innovating year after year, and Vivienne has provided astonishingly original and iconoclastic clothes for nearly two decades.

The enduring appeal of Vivienne's clothes for many women is that they combine the promise of sexual self-determination with high romance and traditional femininity. Slatternly sexual dress is presented in a grand manner. You can dress like a hooker duchess or a royal courtesan. Her clothes combine fetish, freedom and romance, and suggest that perhaps you can have it all.

The contradictions in Vivienne's best clothes also reflect her personality. They are simultaneously sentimental and subversive, violent and romantic. Her work celebrates the rebelliousness of the 1960s and

1970s while emulating the *ancien régime*'s appreciation of handcrafted finicky details. Over the years, her love of couture and tailoring has led her to relinquish the loose-fitted in favour of the tightly girt. She restored fit to fashion in the 1990s.

Manny Silverman regards Vivienne as a 'flawed genius': 'Flawed in the sense that she has never been able to control her own destiny.' She has placed her fate in the hands of a series of men who have controlled her. Nevertheless, Silverman considers her 'one of the most important, if not the most important, figures as an influence on world fashion over the last twenty years. She has not left any major designer unscathed, because she is able to recognise the future before anyone else, albeit in an exaggerated way.'

Vivienne Westwood's impact is not restricted to the world of fashion. Particularly in conjunction with McLaren, her greatest influence has been a verbal and attitudinal one. The punk mentality fostered and popularised by the couple encouraged the young to question, to dismantle and, most importantly, to do it themselves as a challenge to the mass-produced. The anarchistic way in which Vivienne approaches design has allowed others to question orthodoxy, to think laterally, in whatever creative endeavour they are pursuing. Her kind of creativity can only evolve if the obvious is questioned, the adequate or efficient template is smashed and alternatives are proposed. Vivienne's whole body of work is characterised by this contrarian approach to design.

Vivienne Westwood is popularly cast as an eccentric; her marriage to a bisexual man half her age, her public pronouncements on culture and fashion, her unusual appearance and her daring designs make her an easy target for ridicule. Her compatriots like to feign amazement at this middle-aged woman who cycles around London in her strange clothes rather than driving a car or hailing a cab. Her renunciation of materialism despite her recent financial success is considered extra-ordinary, perhaps even a little heretical. The public marvel at the fact that, while other prominent fashion designers lead glamorous lifestyles, she refuses to move from her modest council flat. Her office at Elcho Street is carpeted with a garishly coloured, tartan-bordered rug stamped with a kitsch depiction of Boucher's Mademoiselle Murphy sprawled naked across a sofa. Though Vivienne might relish the high-culture associations that the image conjures up in her mind, the rug looks like a cheap tourist artefact.

Is it eccentric to choose to cycle around a city notorious for its frustrating traffic jams? For a busy woman who has neither the time nor the inclination to frequent a gym, isn't it a reasonably efficient way of keeping fit? Vivienne is not in fact an eccentric, but an iconoclast. Her contrariness is calculated. She assails cherished beliefs and, like many iconoclasts, she is puritanical. She disapproves of 'fun', whose pursuit she despises, and has no truck with those who are not dedicated to their work. She has little time or appetite for life outside her career, so it is understandable that she has found companionship within the fashion world, where bisexuality and homosexuality are commonplace. She seldom meets your average man. All three of her long-time lovers, Malcolm McLaren, Carlo D'Amario and Andreas Kronthaler, have worked with her. Not only do they inhabit the same profession, they also share an amoral outlook on life.

Her appearance is certainly unusual, not least when she test models her own latest designs. But unlike most designers, she invests her clothes with many complicated messages and images, thereby going some way to address Jung's criticism that the modern world suffers from 'an unparalleled impoverishment of symbolism'. To her mind 'fashion is the strongest form of communication there is . . . I do believe that appearances are everything.' It is this literal focus of her clothes that makes Vivienne Westwood a quintessentially English designer. The English have always been a more literary than a visual people.

Her renunciation of materialism is a result partly of habit and partly of choice. Her post-war childhood was, of necessity, parsimonious, and for over fifty years she has existed on a shoestring. She dismisses materialism as a tiresome, slavish adherence to American economic imperialism, and has always felt at odds with the 'American' way of life.

Above all, it is Vivienne's public pronouncements that have fuelled her reputation as an eccentric. She is not an adept communicator, yet she persists in trying to communicate relatively complicated ideas to her public. Because these ideas are only half-digested by her, then poorly and randomly communicated, she can come across sometimes as a ranting fool. Her conversation is punctuated by deep sighs, as if she is weary of trying to explain her point of view over and over again, to no avail. But are her messages really so eccentric? Few of them are either original or radical, most having been lifted from the works of thinkers such as Matthew Arnold, John Stuart Mill and Bertrand Russell. As a libertine, Vivienne rejects the restraints of moral law, particularly where sex is concerned. In the context of her times, is this such an unusual point of view? And despite her pronouncements on free sex, she is relatively monogamous, and naïvely romantic about the men in her life, no matter how badly they have treated her. As a single mother she has put career before parenthood, through a combination of necessity and choice. Is that such a radical departure from post-war conventions in the West?

Vivienne's blotting-paper mind is attracted to the contrary and the flagrantly unfashionable. She cannot resist advocating a manner of dress or a package of ideas that flies in the face of received opinion. As Gene Krell has observed over two decades, 'She has an unmitigated and undying devotion to continue to be a front-line freedom fighter.' She is almost calculating in her systematic preference for the unconventional. If a masculine, wide-shouldered, high-hemlined silhouette prevails, she will offer the converse. If the majority scorn sexual freedom, she will dress in a provocative manner and advocate promiscuity. She is an inveterate attention-seeker, and has been since she was a child.

To a certain extent, Vivienne's public image has been carefully constructed. As early as 1975, she remarked to Jordan that she admired McLaren's eccentricity, and intended to shed her boring provincialism and become eccentric too. Simon Barker, a friend and colleague for twenty years, watched the way in which she moulded herself into this image. Yet she now complains when the press misunderstand her and cast her as an oddity.

The irony of Vivienne's life is that while she dedicated most of her work to satirising and criticising the status quo, in later life she has longed to join the ranks of the establishment, yet has never been accepted. But as her old friend Jean-Charles de Castelbajac says, it is inappropriate for a character such as Vivienne to seek to belong. Her yearning to be appointed Designer-in-Chief at Christian Dior is a case in point. Though her taste and her interest in the archives of the house, combined with her original talent, would certainly have served the prestigious French label well, her failure can largely be put down to her awkward nature and, above all, her reputation. She is unbending, rebellious and opinionated, and tends to balk at corporate demands. Revealingly, when Daniel Piette explained why the LVMH group had appointed Galliano to Dior and McQueen to Givenchy, he dwelt on both men's youth and their compliant natures. Vivienne's age and her difficult nature clearly counted against her.

But perhaps her failure to secure the Dior job was actually a blessing in disguise. It seems unlikely that she could have tolerated working for a large corporation whose underlying and determining objective was to sell branded goods, rather than to promote *haute couture*. As Pierre Bergé puts it: 'Happily she did not get Dior. What has happened in couture is absolutely ridiculous. It's all rules and old world, and it isn't even interesting.'

Vivienne Westwood can be held up as an exception and an example. In the relatively conservative world of fashion, she has reached the top despite the fact that, unlike most successful designers, she is a woman, she only began designing in her mid-thirties and did not achieve commercial success until her mid-fifties, and she was brought up in a poorly educated, working-class background. Nevertheless, she is utterly free from self-doubt and has applied her passionate, romantic and creative nature to attaining her goal. That goal was not riches, nor a place in the pantheon of designers. She fell incidentally into fashion. What she craved, like a drug, was fame. By her own standards, therefore, she has been a success. But her impact and originality are undeniable, and her claim to a significant place in fashion history is larger than she could ever have anticipated.

'It is a lesson in life that anyone, from any walk of life, in any sphere, can take,' says Jeff Banks. 'That despite class, club, the right financial connections, if you have the commitment and desire to succeed, you can. That is Vivienne's story. In the face of monumental adversity, she sat down at the machine and sewed a shirt. That's a fairy tale.'

APPENDIX A

Vivienne Westwood: Chronology

8 April 1941 – Born Vivienne Isabel Swire, Glossop, Derbyshire
Autumn 1957 – Family move to Harrow, North London
21 July 1962 – Vivienne marries Derek John Westwood
3 September 1963 – First son, Benjamin Arthur Westwood, born
1965 – Meets Malcolm Edwards (aka McLaren)
30 November 1967 – Vivienne and McLaren's son, Joseph Ferdinand Corré, born
Autumn 1969 – Vivienne moves to Prestatyn, North Wales
Spring 1970 – Vivienne returns to London
November 1971 – Let it Rock opens at 430 King's Road
Spring 1973 – Too Fast to Live Too Young to Die opens
1974 – SEX opens; Vivienne dresses the New York Dolls
Autumn 1975 – Sex Pistols formed
November 1975 – Vivienne fined for 'exposing to public view an indecent exhibition'
December 1976 – Seditionaries opens
1977 – Vivienne meets Gary Ness
7 June 1977 – Vivienne and McLaren arrested after punk Jubilee boat incident
Spring 1980 – Worlds End opens
Spring 1981 – McLaren leaves Vivienne, their working partnership continues
Summer 1982 – Nostalgia of Mud opens
Spring 1983 – Vivienne meets Carlo D'Amario
Summer 1983 – Westwood/McLaren professional partnership ends; Vivienne moves to Italy
November 1983 – Vivienne becomes the first British designer to be invited to show at the 'Best Five' in Tokyo by Hanae Mori, with Calvin Klein, Claude Montana and Gianfranco Ferre
November 1984 – Vivienne's deal with Giorgio Armani announced

8 September 1985 – Vivienne's father, Gordon Swire, dies

Spring 1986 – Vivienne returns to live in England

July 1986 – Worlds End reopens

March 1987 – Westwood company sues Armani for breach of contract

Autumn 1988 – Davies Street shop opens

1989–1991 – Vivienne works as Professor of Fashion, Vienna Academy of Applied Art; meets Andreas Kronthaler

March 1990 – Vivienne becomes the first fashion designer to be featured on *The South Bank Show*

July 1990 – Vivienne becomes the first designer specially appointed to show at Pitti Immagine, Florence

September 1990 – Broadcast of *Opinions* programme, BBC Radio 4

December 1990 – Vivienne invited to show at the Fashion Summit, Tokyo, with Christian Lacroix, Franco Moschino and Isaac Mizrahi

October 1991 – Vivienne wins British Designer of the Year Award

1992 – Vivienne appointed Professor of Fashion at Berlin's Hochschüle

14 May 1992 – Vivienne marries Andreas Kronthaler

May 1992 – Vivienne awarded the OBE

July 1992 – Vivienne becomes the first fashion designer to create a watch for Swatch; appointed Honorary Senior Fellow of the Royal College of Art

October 1992 – Vivienne wins British Designer of the Year Award for the second time

November 1992 – Vivienne Westwood retrospective at Bordeaux Museum of Contemporary Art

1993 – Red Label launched

1994 – Vivienne invited by Littlewoods catalogue to contribute a mail-order range

May 1994 – Vivienne wins the first Institute of Contemporary Arts Award for Outstanding Contribution to Contemporary Culture

1995 – Vivienne Westwood offices move to Elcho Street, Battersea

January 1996 – 'Man' menswear label launched

Spring 1996 – Broadcast of Vivienne's three-part Channel 4 series *Painted Ladies*

1997 – Vivienne wins *Export Times* Award for outstanding export achievement

February 1998 – 'Anglomania' label launched

June 1998 – Vivienne's first scent scheduled to be launched with the German cosmetics company Lancaster

APPENDIX B

Vivienne Westwood's Collections

March 1981 – 'Pirates' (autumn/winter 1981–82)
October 1981 – 'Savage' (spring/summer 1982)
March 1982 – 'Buffalo' (autumn/winter 1982–83)
October 1982 – 'Hobo-Punkature' (spring/summer 1983)
March 1983 – 'Witches' (autumn/winter 1983–84)
October 1983 – 'Hypnos' (spring/summer 1984)
March 1984 – 'Clint Eastwood' (autumn/winter 1984–85)
October 1985 – 'Mini Crini' (spring/summer 1986)
March 1987 – 'Harris Tweed' (autumn/winter 1987–88)
October 1987 – 'Britain Must Go Pagan' ('Pagan I') (spring/summer
    1988)
March 1988 – 'Time Machine' (autumn/winter 1988–89)
October 1988 – 'Civilizade' (spring/summer 1989)
March 1989 – 'Voyage to Cythera' (autumn/winter 1989–90)
October 1989 – 'Pagan V' (spring/summer 1990)
March 1990 – 'Portrait' (autumn/winter 1990–91)
July 1990 – 'Cut & Slash' (menswear, spring/summer 1991)
October 1990 – 'Cut, Slash & Pull' (spring/summer 1991)
March 1991 – 'Dressing Up' (autumn/winter 1991–92)
October 1991 – 'Salon' (spring/summer 1992)
March 1992 – 'Always on Camera' (autumn/winter 1992–93)
October 1992 – 'Grand Hotel' (spring/summer 1993)
March 1993 – 'Anglomania' (autumn/winter 1993–94)
October 1993 – 'Café Society' (spring/summer 1994)
March 1994 – 'On Liberty' (autumn/winter 1994–95)
October 1994 – 'Erotic Zones' (spring/summer 1995)
March 1995 – 'Vive la Coquotte' (autumn/winter 1995–96)
October 1995 – 'Les Femmes' (spring/summer 1996)
January 1996 – 'MAN' (autumn/winter 1996–97)
March 1996 – 'Storm in a Teacup' (autumn/winter 1996–97)

July 1996 – 'MAN' (spring/summer 1997)

October 1996 – 'Vive la Bagatelle' (spring/summer 1997)

January 1997 – 'MAN' (autumn/winter 1997–98)

September 1997 – 'To Rosie' (Red Label, autumn/winter 1997–98)

March 1997 – 'Five Centuries Ago' (autumn/winter 1997–98)

July 1997 – 'MAN' (spring/summer 1998)

September 1997 – 'The English Girl Abroad' (Red Label, spring/summer 1998)

October 1997 – 'Tied to the Mast' (spring/summer 1998)

January 1998 – 'MAN' (autumn/winter 1998–99)

February 1998 – Red Label (autumn/winter 1998–99)

March 1998 – 'Dressed to Scale' (autumn/winter 1998–99)

REFERENCE NOTES

Chapter 1: The Girl from the Snake Pass

Author interviews with VW, 1991, 1994; Simon Barker, 1994;
  Reginald Barnsley, 1995; John Walford, 1996; Joyce Noton, 1995;
  Bob Noton, 1995; Malcolm McLaren, 1995; Eileen Mellish, 1995;
  Dora Swire, 1989, 1997; Jack Holden, 1995. Marion Hume inter-
  views with Ethel Mitchell, 1994; Dora Swire, 1994; Gordon Swire,
  1994
VW to Jim Shelley, *Blitz*, March 1988; to *Derbyshire Now!*, May 1994;
  to *Elle*, November 1995; to Yvonne Roberts, *Harper's & Queen*,
  October 1993; to Lynn Barber, *Independent on Sunday*, 18 February
  1990; to *Mirabella*, September 1987; to *Observer*, 22 January 1995;
  to *Today*, 18 October 1994; to Sarah Mower, British *Vogue*, 1986
Craig Bromberg, *The Wicked Ways of Malcolm McLaren*, Omnibus Press,
  London, 1991
Jack Holden, *A Very Special School: Glossop Grammar School, 1901–
  1965*
Aileen Ribeiro, *The Art of Dress: Fashion in England and France
  1750–1820*, Yale University Press, 1995
David Thomson, *England in the Twentieth Century*, Penguin, Harmonds-
  worth, 1965

Chapter 2: Meeting Malcolm

Author interviews with Caroline Baker, 1995; Simon Barker, 1994;
  Derek Dunbar, 1996; Jordan (Pamela Rooke), 1995; Malcolm
  McLaren, 1994, 1995, 1996; Helen Wellington-Lloyd, 1998.
  Marion Hume interview with Ben Westwood, 1994
VW to *Derbyshire Now!*, May 1994; to Lynn Barber, *Independent on Sun-
  day*, 18 February 1990; to *Sunday Times Magazine*, 6 September 1987

Craig Bromberg, *The Wicked Ways of Malcom McLaren*, Omnibus Press, London, 1991

Brenda Maddox, *A Married Man: A Life of D.H. Lawrence*, Sinclair-Stevenson, London, 1994

Jon Savage, *England's Dreaming*, Faber & Faber, London, 1991

Peter Silverton, *Observer*, 23 June 1996

Chapter 3: Prankster Retailing

Author interviews with VW, 1983; Simon Barker, 1994, 1997; Jean-Charles de Castelbajac, 1995; Derek Dunbar, 1995, 1996; William English, 1997; Bella Freud, 1997; Jonathan Gems, 1996; Lottie Hughes, 1995; Alan Jones, 1997; Jordan, 1995; Ben Kelly, 1995; Michael Kostiff, 1995; Gene Krell, 1995; Malcolm McLaren, 1995, 1996; Marco Pirroni, 1998; Tommy Roberts, 1995; John Rowley, 1997; Shirley Russell, 1998; Nils Stevenson, 1997; Helen Wellington-Lloyd, 1998; Peter York, 1995. Marion Hume interviews with Joseph Corré, 1994; Ben Westwood, 1993

Ash, 1980

VW to *Forum*, 1974; to *Women's Wear Daily*, 18 November 1992; video for Vienna fashion students, 1990

Clinton Heylin, *From the Velvets to the Voidoids: A Pre-Punk History for a Post-Punk World*, Penguin, New York, 1933

London Magazine, 1990

Legs McNeil and Gillian McCain, *Please Kill Me: The Uncensored Oral History of Punk*, Grove Press, New York, 1996

Jon Savage, *England's Dreaming*, Faber & Faber, London, 1991

Chapter 4: Cartwheeling to Casualty

Author interviews with VW, 1983, 1994; Sir Hardy Amies, 1993; Caroline Baker, 1995; Jeff Banks, 1996; Simon Barker, 1995, 1997; Robyn Beeche, 1997; James Birch, 1993; David Connors, 1995; Sebastian Conran, 1996; Paul Cook, 1997; Terry Doktor, 1995; Derek Dunbar, 1996; Duggie Fields, 1995; Bella Freud, 1997; David Huggins, 1995; David Ireland, 1995; Alan Jones, 1997; Stephen Jones, 1995; Jordan, 1995; Ben Kelly, 1995; Michael Kostiff, 1995;

Gene Krell, 1996; Andrew Logan, 1995; Malcolm McLaren, 1994, 1996; Suzy Menkes, 1996; Paul Mulvagh, 1994; Tony Parsons, 1997; Lorraine Piggott, 1995; Marco Pirroni, 1998; Dario Poloni, 1995; Philip Sallon, 1995; Jon Savage, *née* Sage, 1995; Jean-Louis Scherrer, 1983; George Slattery, 1995; Nils Stevenson, 1997; Keith Wainwright, 1995; Helen Wellington-Lloyd, 1998; Peter York, 1995. Marion Hume interviews with VW, 1994; Ben Westwood, 1994

VW to Catherine McDermott, *Blitz*, February 1986; to *Blitz*, 1987; to Catherine Bennett, *Guardian*, 27 June 1992; to Brenda Polan, ICA, 18 June 1993; to Sarah Mower, British *Vogue*, 1986; *A Passion for Fashion*, Carlton TV, 1997

Pierre Bourdieu, in Eric Hobsbawm, *The Age of Extremes: 1914-1991*, Michael Joseph, London, 1994

Caroline Coon, *Melody Maker*, 1975

Boy George, *Kaleidoscope*, BBC Radio 4, 1994

John Lydon, *No Irish, No Blacks, No Dogs*, Hodder & Stoughton, London, 1994

Colin MacInnes, *England, Half English*, McGibbon & Kee, London, 1961

Malcolm McLaren, 'Elements of Anti-Style', *New Yorker*, 22 September 1997

Malcolm McLaren to *The Times*, 23 August 1983; *Vanity Fair*, July 1996

Legs McNeil and Gillian McCain, *Please Kill Me: The Uncensored Oral History of Punk*, Grove Press, New York, 1996

Jon Savage, *England's Dreaming*, Faber & Faber, London, 1991

Search and Destroy, Vol. 3, 1978

Time Out, December 1977

Peter York, 'The Post-Punk Mortem', *Harper's & Queen*, September 1977

Chapter 5: World's End

Author interviews with VW, 1983; Caroline Baker, 1995; Simon Barker, 1994, 1995, 1996; Suzanne Bartsch, 1997; Robyn Beeche, 1997; Katie Braine, 1995; Roger Burton, 1997; Patrick Cox, 1996; Jean-Charles de Castelbajac, 1995; Joseph Ettedgui, 1997; John Galliano, 1998; Tony Glenville, 1995; David Ireland, 1995; Jordan,

1995, 1996, 1998; Michael Kostiff, 1995; Gene Krell, 1995, 1996; Christian Lacroix, 1995; Malcolm McLaren, 1995, 1996; Valerie Mendes, 1995; Lorraine Piggott, 1995; Philip Sallon, 1994; Mark Tarbard, 1997; Richard Torry, 1995; John Walford, 1996; Marysia Woroniecki, 1996. Marion Hume interview with Ben Westwood, 1994

VW to *Blitz*, May 1986; to *Evening Standard*, May 1983; to Jon Savage, *The Face*, January 1981; to Yvonne Roberts, *Harper's & Queen*, October 1993; to Brenda Polan, ICA, 18 June 1993; to Carolyn Franklin, *i-D*, 1986; to *Les Inrockuptibles*, 4–10 September 1996; to Georgina Howell, *The Times*, 23 August 1983; to *Sun*, 12 August 1981; to Liz Jobey, British *Vogue*, August 1987; to *Die Zeit*, 12 September 1997

Caroline Evans and Minna Thornton, *Women and Fashion: A New Look*, Quartet, London, 1989

Boy George, *Take it Like a Man*, Sidgwick & Jackson, London, 1995

Sunday Times Magazine, 3 May 1981

Joseph Corré to *Sunday Times Magazine*, 6 September 1987

Women's Wear Daily, 1 April 1980

Chapter 6: 'Without Italy, I Wouldn't Exist'

Author interviews with Simon Barker, 1997; Suzanne Bartsch, 1997; David Connors, 1995; Patrick Cox, 1996; James Fallon, 1997; Bella Freud, 1997; Dometilla Getty, 1997; Paola Igliori, 1997; David Ireland, 1995; Gene Krell, 1996; Malcolm McLaren, 1995, 1996; Lorraine Piggott, 1995; Philip Sallon, 1995; Nils Stevenson, 1997; Keith Wainwright, 1995; Peter York, 1996

VW to Catherine McDermott, *Blitz*, February 1986; to *i-D*, 1987; to British *Vogue*, August 1987 and May 1992; to Valerie Steele, *Women of Fashion*, May 1989; to *Women's Wear Daily*, 17 November 1983 and 18 November 1986

Malcolm McLaren to *Evening Standard*, 4 November 1983

Carlo D'Amario to *Independent on Sunday*, 2 November 1997

New York Times, 29 June 1986

Time, 9 May 1983

Giorgio Armani to *Women's Wear Daily*, 15 November 1984

Chapter 7: Rule Britannia!

Author interviews with Craig Alexander, 1995; Jeff Banks, 1996;
Simon Barker, 1995, 1997; Robyn Beeche, 1997; Terry Doktor,
1995; Derek Dunbar, 1996; Bella Freud, 1997; John Gustaffson,
1995; Robin Huggan, 1995; Stephen Jones, 1995; Gene Krell,
1996; Tony Langford, 1995; Harris MacKenzie, 1995; Ian
McKenzie, 1995; Malcolm McLaren, 1995; Philip Sallon, 1995;
Simon Smith, 1995; Keith Wainwright, 1995; John Walford, 1996.
Marion Hume interviews with VW, 1987; Karl Lagerfeld, 1994
VW to *Blitz*, February 1986; to Jim Shelley, *Blitz*, March 1988; to
Sally Brampton, *Elle*, September 1988; to Yvonne Roberts, *Harper's
& Queen*, October 1993; to Carolyn Franklin, *i-D*, 1986; to *i-D*,
August 1987; to Lynn Barber, *Independent on Sunday*, 18 February
1990; to Val Hennessy, *Mail on Sunday*, 1990; to *Mirabella*, November 1990; to *Sunday Times Magazine*, 6 September 1987; to James
Fallon, *Women's Wear Daily*, January 1985; to *Die Zeit*, 12 September
1997
Holly Johnson, *A Bone in my Flute*, Century, London, 1994

Chapter 8: Wear Your Brain on Your Sleeve

Author interviews with VW, 1990; Simon Barker, 1994, 1996, 1997;
Ann Barr, 1996; Sally Brampton, 1997; Patrick Cox, 1995; Jean-
Charles de Castelbajac, 1995; Bella Freud, 1997; Gene Krell, 1996;
Lady Romilly McAlpine, 1995; Malcolm McLaren, 1995, 1996;
Valerie Mendes, 1995; Suzy Menkes, 1995; Dawn Robson-Bell,
1995; Françoise Rust-Fourteau, 1994; Rupert Scott, 1994; Richard
Torry, 1995; Keith Wainwright, 1995; John Walford, 1996
VW to *Blitz*, 1987; to Brenda Polan, ICA, 18 June 1993; to Duncan
Fallowell, *Mirabella*, November 1990; to Ruby Wax; video for
Vienna fashion students, 1990
Sarah Stockbridge to *Blitz*, March 1988

Chapter 9: The Wife of Bath

Author interviews with VW, 1990, 1993; Simon Barker, 1994, 1995, 1996, 1997, 1998; Jibby Beane, 1995; Pierre Bergé, 1998; Joan Juliet Buck, 1998; Gianni de Michelis, 1990; Cathy Dingwall to Marion Hume, 1994; Derek Dunbar, 1996; Leonie Edwards-Jones, 1995; Richard Gray, 1997; Gillian Greenwood, 1995; Mike Hardiman, 1995; Christine Harrison, 1995; Stephen Jones, 1995; Bunty King, 1995; Michael Kostiff, 1995; Gene Krell, 1995; Christian Lacroix, 1996; Lady Romilly McAlpine, 1995; Malcolm McLaren, 1996; Peter Marangoni, 1994; Valerie Mendes, 1995, 1996; Bernadine Morris, 1990; Daniel Piette, 1997; Anna Robinson, 1995; Dawn Robson-Bell, 1995; John Rowley, 1997, 1998; Françoise Rust-Fourteau, 1995; Manny Silverman, 1997; André Leon Talley, 1998; Keith Wainwright, 1995; John Walford, 1996. Marion Hume interviews with Dora Swire, 1994; Ben Westwood, 1994

VW to *Daily Mail*, 13 June 1992; to Jon Savage, *The Face*, 1981; to Sally Brampton, *Elle* September 1988; to Catherine Bennett, *Guardian*, 27 June 1992; to Yvonne Roberts, *Harper's & Queen*, October 1993; to Tom O'Dwyer, *Helines*, 1991; to Brenda Polan, ICA, 18 June 1993; to Lynn Barber, *Independent on Sunday*, 18 February 1990; to *Independent on Sunday*, 5 January 1992; to *Mail on Sunday*, December 1993; to *Mirabella*, December 1990; to Sky TV, September 1995; to Megan Tressider, *Sunday Telegraph*, 21 June 1992; to *Women's Wear Daily*, 18 November 1992

David Cannadine, 'Brideshead Revered', *London Review of Books*, 31 March 1983

Karl Plewka to *Guardian*, 27 June 1992

Jasper Conran to Brenda Polan, *Independent*, October 1991

Suzy Menkes, *International Herald Tribune*, November 1992

Melvyn Bragg, *South Bank Show*, ITV, March 1990

Chapter 10: Non-Stop Distractions

Author interviews with VW, 1994; Jeff Banks, 1996; Simon Barker, 1994, 1996, 1997; Marc Bohan, 1984; Murray Blewitt, 1997; Lucinda Chambers, 1996; Ossie Clark, 1996; Patrick Cox, 1995; Anthony Daley, 1995; Countess Jehanne de Biolley, 1995; Jean-

Charles de Castelbajac, 1995; Amy de la Haye, 1998; Derek Dunbar, 1996; Leonie Edwards-Jones, 1994, 1995; James Fallon, 1997; Mike Figgis, 1997; John Galliano, 1998; Georgina Godley, 1997; Richard Gray, 1998; Anna Harvey, 1996; Gene Krell, 1996; Malcolm McLaren, 1995, 1996; Charlotte More-Gordon, 1995; Daniel Piette, 1997; Lorraine Piggott, 1994; Tommy Roberts, 1995; John Rowley, 1997; Françoise Rust-Fourteau, 1994, 1995; Manny Silverman, 1997; Paul Smith, 1998; Keith Wainwright, 1994; John Walford, 1996

VW to *Attitude*, March 1995; to *Derbyshire Now!*, May 1994; to *Financial Times*, 17 August 1996; to *Guardian*, 22 February 1997; to Yvonne Roberts, *Harper's & Queen*, October 1993; to Brenda Polan, ICA, 18 June 1993; to Selina Scott, NBC Superchannel, September 1995; to *New York Times*, 14 March 1998; to *OK* magazine, January 1995

Arena, spring/summer 1995

Daily Mail, March 1994

Elle, November 1995

Richard E. Grant, *With Nails*, Picador, London, 1996

Holly Johnson to Simon Barker, 1996

Alice Rawsthorn, *Yves Saint Laurent*, HarperCollins, London, 1996

Aileen Ribeiro, *The Art of Dress: Fashion in England and France 1750-1820*, Yale University Press, 1995

Nicci Gerrard, *Observer*, 22 January 1995

Sunday Times Magazine, 22 September 1996

The Times, 11 September 1993 and 15 October 1995

Today, 20 October 1995

Dawn Mello to *Women's Wear Daily*, 16 September 1994

Conclusion

Author interviews with Jeff Banks, 1996; Pierre Bergé, 1998; Marc Bohan, 1984; Jean-Charles de Castelbajac, 1995; Gene Krell, 1996; Manny Silverman, 1997

VW to Brenda Polan, ICA, 18 June 1993

ACKNOWLEDGEMENTS

Given the paucity of available diaries, letters or memoirs to refer to in researching this biography, I have been extremely dependent on the goodwill and cooperation of many people who have played a part in Vivienne Westwood's life: family, friends, colleagues, peers, rivals, customers, models, acolytes, supporters and detractors. Their conversations and interviews have made up a rich oral history. This has been the most fascinating aspect of researching this biography, and I am grateful to each one of them.

Some interviewees understandably wish to remain anonymous, but of the others I would like to mention: Craig Alexander, Caroline Baker, Jeff Banks, Reginald Barnsley, Ann Barr, Suzanne Bartsch, Jibby Beane, Robyn Beeche, Pierre Bergé, James Birch, Murray Blewitt, Pam Boland, Katie Braine, Sally Brampton, Michael Brinton, Craig Brown, Joan Juliet Buck, Roger Burton, Joan Bustein, Lucinda Chambers, Ossie Clark, Polly Clayden, John Connor, David Connors, Sebastian Conran, Paul Cook, Paul Cowan, Patrick Cox, Scott Crolla, Anthony Daley, Jehanne de Biolley, Jean-Charles de Castelbajac, Sibilla della Gherardesca, Terry Doktor, Allegra Donn, Simon Doonan, Tom Duggan, Derek Dunbar, Leonie Edwards-Jones, John Egan, William English, Joseph Ettedgui, James Fallon, Victoria Fernandez, Duggie Fields, Mike Figgis, Dan Franklin, Bella Freud, Pat Frost, John Galliano, Jonathan Gems, Dometilla Getty, Tony Glenville, Georgina Godley, Richard Gray, John Gustaffson, Ben Hanly, Christine Harrison, Avril Hart, Anna Harvey, Marion Hume, Michael Hardiman, Amy de la Haye, Jack Holden, David Huggins, Lottie Hughes, Marion Hume, Paola Igliori, David Ireland, Alan Jones, Stephen Jones, Jordan, Ben Kelly, Bunty King, Michael Kostiff, Gene Krell, Christian Lacroix, Tony Langford, Jimmin Lee, Andrew Logan, Celia Lyttelton, Lady Romilly McAlpine, Stella McCartney, Harris McKenzie, Ian McKenzie, Malcolm McLaren, Peter Marangoni, Eileen Mellish, Valerie Mendes, Suzy Menkes, Rossita Missoni, Charlotte More-Gordon, Paul Mulvagh, Joyce Noton, Robert Noton, Anna

Parkinson, Tony Parsons, Jeremy Paxman, Anna Piaggi, Daniel Piette, Lorraine Piggott, Marco Pirroni, Dario Poloni, Alice Rawsthorn, Tommy Roberts, Dawn Robson-Bell, John Rowley, Ken Russell, Shirley Russell, Françoise Rust-Fourteau, Philip Sallon, Robert Sandal, Jon Savage, Manny Silverman, Peter Silverton, George Slattery, Paul Smith, Simon Smith, Nils Stevenson, André Leon Talley, Mark Tarbard, Dawn Telford, David Thomas, Richard Torry, Emanual Ungaro, Berni Vinyl, Keith Wainwright, John Walford, Helen Wellington-Lloyd, Andrew Wilson, Marysia Woroniecki, Peter York.

Special thanks are due to Simon Barker, an original member of the Bromley Contingent of punks, who for twenty years worked and played alongside Vivienne, and whose first-hand familiarity with events and people, achivist's powers of retrieval and fair-minded judgements have been invaluable.

Two experienced practitioners of the biographer's craft, Brenda Maddox and Meredith Etherington-Smith, were generous in imparting their techniques and instilled an appropriate realism while providing encouragement.

Thanks are also due to Derren Gilhooley for fact-chasing, Robin Muir for help with photographs and Amanda Sykes for transcribing interview tapes.

Valerie Mendes of the Victoria and Albert Museum, Suzy Menkes of the *International Herald Tribune*, Professor David Cannadine, Director of the Institute of Historical Research, and Peter Norall kindly took the trouble to read the manuscript and to offer constructive advice.

Special thanks must go to my superb editors at HarperCollins, Richard Johnson and Robert Lacey, for their unstinting patience, understanding and professionalism. Juliet Davies was an excellent picture editor.

My agent, Mike Shaw of Curtis Brown, who placed me with such a good team, provided, as always, constant encouragement and wise advice.

Finally, I must thank my husband for his keen editorial eye and rigorous scepticism. His love and encouragement have considerably eased my task and were a constant support.

INDEX